LABOUR AND THE CHALLENGES OF GLOBALIZATION

Labour and the Challenges of Globalization

What Prospects for Transnational Solidarity?

Edited by Andreas Bieler, Ingemar Lindberg
and Devan Pillay

Pluto Press
London • Ann Arbor, MI

 UNIVERSITY OF KWAZULU-NATAL PRESS

First published 2008 by Pluto Press
345 Archway Road, London N6 5AA
and 839 Greene Street, Ann Arbor, MI 48106

www.plutobooks.com

Published in 2008 in South Africa by
University of KwaZulu-Natal Press
Private Bag X01, Scottsville 3209
South Africa
E-mail: books@ukzn.ac.za
Website: www.unznpress.co.za

British Library Cataloguing in Publication Data
A catalogue record for this book is available from the British Library

ISBN   978 0 7453 2757 0 (hardback)
ISBN   978 0 7453 2756 3 (Pluto Press paperback)
ISBN   978 1 86914 142 4 (University of KwaZulu-Natal Press paperback)

Library of Congress Cataloging in Publication Data applied for

10 9 8 7 6 5 4 3 2 1

Designed and produced for Pluto Press by
Curran Publishing Services, Norwich
Printed and bound in India

Contents

Figures

Tables

Acknowledgements

This project was initiated by Samir Amin and the World Forum for Alternatives (http://www.forumdesalternatives.org/?lang=EN). It is one of two related projects dealing with the issue of labour and globalization, while the other project covers peasant movements and their position in the global economy.

We are grateful to the Bank of Sweden Tercentenary Foundation, the Union of Swedish Transport Workers, the Union of Swedish Service and Communications Workers (Seko) as well as the Arenagroup of Sweden for financial support of a project group meeting in Stockholm in January 2006 as well as seminars arranged during the World Social Forum in Nairobi/Kenya in January 2007 in relation to this volume.

Earlier, extended versions of the chapters on South Korea, South Africa, India, Argentina, Japan, Canada, Sweden, Africa, Europe and trade union internationalism are published at http://www.nottingham.ac.uk/politics/gwcproject/Reports.php The original Spanish version of the chapter on Argentina is also available at the same location. The financial and technical support by the University of Nottingham/UK in establishing this website is acknowledged.

Finally, we want to thank Hannchen Koornhof for the copy editing of the chapters on Argentina, China and Japan as well as Fulya Memisoglu for her assistance in compiling the final manuscript and preparing the index.

Foreword: rebuilding the unity of the 'labour front'

Samir Amin

The linkage between the current scientific and technological revolution (with particular regard to its information technology dimension) and the socio-economic strategies implemented by the dominant forces (and particularly the most powerful segment of capital set up by transnational entities) have brought about far-reaching changes in the organization of labour and the working world.

The so-called 'Fordist' organization of production which marked a large part of the last century, which was based on the concentration of the big mechanized industries and access to markets seldom differentiated from mass consumption, had therefore specially structured the hierarchies of the working world (mass labour, supervisory staff and management) as well as the new social life in urban settings. This pattern of production had also created the conditions of procedures for collective negotiations (between unions and employers) at the base of the welfare state. The then-dominant forms of organization (socialist and communist parties and mass unions), like those concerning the organization of struggles (strike actions and negotiations, demonstrations and elections) produced in this framework turned out to be efficient and therefore credible and legitimate.

In the developed capitalist centres, the functioning of all these mechanisms guaranteed a high level of employment (almost 'full' employment and social security) and stable income distribution. The limitations of the system – ideologies and patriarchal or even male chauvinist practices, waste of natural resources and disregard for the environment – were criticized by women's movements and ecologists, who progressively raised popular awareness in this regard.

On the other hand, in the peripheries of the global system, this same model could at best be implemented only partially in the 'modernized-industrialized' niches immersed in an ocean lightly and especially inadequately integrated into the national set. The political formulas for managing such 'dualism' between the modern formal sector and the informal and peasant worlds generally implied an undemocratic 'control' and prohibition of direct expression among the dominated classes. The success of national populism, in which such management found expression, stemmed from the overtures it offered through social mobility upstream and the expansion of the new middle classes. Today, this page of history has turned.

The rapid dismantling and latent restructuring of the organization of the working world now dominate the scene. In the relatively privileged centres, this far-reaching change is manifested in the recurrence of mass unemployment, job flexibility, casualization of many employment opportunities, with the resultant resurgence of phenomena of 'poverty' (which inspires a language implying a reversion to the 19th-century 'charity') and proliferation of all kinds of inequalities, which in turn have a bearing on the democratic traditions in crisis. But simultaneously, this process ushers in the reconstruction of new forms of labour organization whose analysis in terms of 'networks' constitutes the most obvious expression, even if it is sometimes formulated in naïve terms out of inordinate optimism.

In the peripheries of the system the integration of peasant reserves into the sphere governed by the principles of neoliberalism, stagnation or decline of the modernized niches or even their expansion into formats dictated by job flexibility and insecurity, results in the gigantic growth of the 'informal' system with its deplorable social repercussions (such as metropolises of slums). This systemic crisis calls into question the forms of organization and struggles of the previous phase, which find expression in the crisis of parties (and of politics), union crises, and the fuzziness and fragmentation of movements.

Moreover, globalization imposes effects directed towards urban working classes in the centres and the peripheries as well as towards the agrarian masses in the latter. If they fail to take into account the interdependency of the conditions that affect one another, the actions taken by the working classes run the risk of being incoherent, and as a consequence inefficient.

THE NEW LABOUR QUESTION

The planet's urban population now represents about half of humanity, at least 3 billion individuals, with peasants making up the other half. In the contemporary stage of capitalist evolution, the dominant classes –formal owners of the principal means of production, and senior managers associated with bringing them into play – represent only a very minor fraction of the global population, even though the share they draw from their societies' available income is significant. To this we can add the middle classes in the old sense of the term: non-wage-earners, owners of small enterprises, and middle managers, who are not necessarily in decline. But the large mass of workers in the modern segments of production consists of wage-earners, who now make up more than four-fifths of the urban population of the developed centres.

This mass is divided into at least two categories, the border between which is both visible to the outside observer and truly lived in the consciousness of affected individuals. There are those whom we can label stabilized popular classes, in the sense that they are relatively secure in their employment, thanks among other things to professional qualifications which give them negotiating power with employers, and who are therefore often organized, at least in some countries, into powerful unions. In all cases this mass carries a political weight that reinforces its negotiating capacity. Others make up the precarious popular classes, which include workers weakened by their low capacity for negotiation (as a result of their low skill levels, their status as non-citizens, or their race or gender) as well as non-wage-earners (the formally unemployed and the poor with jobs in the informal sector). We can label this second category of the popular classes 'precarious', rather than 'non-integrated' or 'marginalized', because these workers are perfectly integrated into the systemic logic that commands the accumulation of capital.

From the available information for developed countries and certain Southern countries (from which we can extrapolate data) we can obtain the relative proportions that each of the above-defined categories represent in the planet's urban population. Although the centres account for only 18 per cent of the planet's population, since their population is 90 per cent urban, they are home to a third of the world's urban population.

If, as a whole, the popular classes account for three-quarters of the world's urban population, the subcategory of the precarious today represents 40 per cent of the popular classes in the centres and 80 per cent in the peripheries: that is, two-thirds of the popular classes on a world scale. In other words, the precarious popular classes represent half (at least) of the world's urban population, and far more than that in the peripheries.

A look at the composition of the urban popular classes a half-century ago, following the Second World War, shows that the proportions that characterize the structure of the popular classes were very different from what they have become. At the time, the

Table F1 Percentages of total world urban population

	Centres	Peripheries	World
Wealthy and middle classes	11	13	25
Popular classes	24	54	75
Stabilized	(13)	(11)	(25)
Precarious	(9)	(43)	(50)
Total	33	67	100
Population concerned (millions)	1,000	2,000	3,000

Note: percentages may not add up exactly due to rounding.
Source: own calculations.

third world's share did not exceed half of the global urban population (then on the order of a billion individuals) versus two-thirds
today. Megacities, like those that we know today in practically all
countries of the South, did not yet exist. There were only a few large
cities, notably in China, India and Latin America. In the centres, the
popular classes benefited, during the post-war period, from an
exceptional situation based on the historic compromise imposed on
capital by the working classes. This compromise permitted the stabilization of the majority of workers in forms of a work organization
known as the Fordist factory system. In the peripheries, the proportion of the precarious – which was, as always, larger than in the
centres – did not exceed half of the urban popular classes (versus
more than 70 per cent today). The other half still consisted, in part,
of stabilized wage earners in the forms of the new colonial economy,
of the modernized society, and in part of old forms of craft work.

THE OTHER SIDE OF THE CHALLENGE: THE NEW AGRARIAN QUESTION

Modern capitalist agriculture – encompassing both rich, large-scale
family farming and agribusiness corporations – is now engaged in a
massive attack on third-world peasant production. The green light
for this was given by the World Trade Organization (WTO). There
are many victims of this attack, mainly third world peasants, who
still make up half of humankind.

Capitalist agriculture governed by the principle of return on
capital, which is localized almost exclusively in North America,
Europe, Australia and the southern cone of Latin America, employs
only a few tens of millions of farmers who are no longer peasants.

Because of the degree of mechanization and the extensive size of the farms managed by one farmer, their productivity generally ranges between 2 and 4.5 million lb (1–2 million kg) of cereals per farmer. In sharp contrast, 3 billion farmers are engaged in peasant farming. Their farms can be grouped into two distinct sectors, with greatly different scales of production, economic and social characteristics, and levels of efficiency. One sector, able to benefit from the green revolution, obtained fertilizers, pesticides and improved seeds, and has some degree of mechanization. The productivity of these peasants ranges between 20,000 and 110,000 lb (10,000–50,000 kg) of cereals per year. However, the annual productivity of peasants excluded from new technologies is estimated to be around 2,000 lb (1,000 kg) of cereals per farmer.

Indeed, what would happen if agriculture and food production were treated as any other form of production submitted to the rules of competition in an open and deregulated market, as decided in principle by the WTO? Would such principles foster the acceleration of production? One can imagine that the food brought to market by today's 3 billion peasants, after they ensure their own subsistences, would instead be produced by 20 million new modern farmers. The conditions for the success of such an alternative would include the transfer of important pieces of good land to the new agriculturalists (and these lands would have to be taken out of the hands of present peasant societies), capital (to buy supplies and equipment), and access to the consumer markets. Such agriculturalists would indeed compete successfully with the billions of present peasants. But what would happen to those billions of people? Under the circumstances, agreeing to the general principle of competition for agricultural products and foodstuffs, as imposed by WTO, means accepting the elimination of billions of non-competitive producers within the short historic time of a few decades. What will become of these billions of humans beings, the majority of whom are already poor among the poor, who feed themselves with great difficulty? In 50 years' time industrial development, even with the fanciful hypothesis of a continued growth rate of 7 per cent annually, could not absorb even one-third of this reserve.

The major argument presented to legitimate the WTO's competition doctrine is that such development did happen in 19th and 20th-century Europe and the United States, where it produced a modern, wealthy, urban-industrial and post-industrial society with modern agriculture able to feed the nation and even export food. Why should not this pattern be repeated in the contemporary third-world countries? The argument fails to consider two major factors that make the reproduction of the pattern in third-world countries almost impossible. The first is that the European model developed throughout a century and a half along with labour-intensive industrial technologies. Modern technologies use far less labour, and the newcomers of the third world have to adopt them if their industrial exports are to be competitive in global markets. The second is that, during that long transition, Europe benefited from the massive migration of its surplus population to the Americas.

The contention that capitalism has indeed solved the agrarian question in its developed centres has always been accepted by large sections of the left, an example being Karl Kautsky's famous book *The Agrarian Question* (1899/1988) written before the First World War. Soviet ideology inherited that view, and on its basis undertook modernization through the Stalinist collectivization, with poor results. What was always overlooked was that capitalism, while it solved the question in its centres, did it through generating a gigantic agrarian question in the peripheries, which it can only solve through the genocide of half of humankind. Within the Marxist tradition only Maoism understood the magnitude of the challenge. Therefore, those who accused Maoism of a 'peasant deviation' show by this very criticism that they lack the analytical capacity to understand imperialist capitalism, which they reduce to an abstract discourse on capitalism in general.

Can we imagine other alternatives and have them widely debated? Alternatives in which peasant agriculture would be maintained throughout the visible future of the 21st century, but which simultaneously engage in a process of continuous technological and social progress? In this way, changes could happen at a rate that would allow a progressive transfer of peasants into non-rural and non-agricultural employment.

GLOBAL PAUPERIZATION AND THE DISEMPOWERMENT OF THE LABOURING CLASSES

The main social transformation that characterizes our time can be summarized in a single statistic: the proportion of the precarious popular classes rose from less than one-quarter to more than one-half of the global urban population, and this phenomenon of pauperization has reappeared on a significant scale in the developed centres themselves. This destabilized urban population has increased in a half-century from less than a quarter of a billion to more than a billion and a half individuals, registering a growth rate which surpasses those that characterize economic expansion, population growth, or the process of urbanization itself.

Modern pauperization is a phenomenon inseparable from polarization at a world scale: an inherent product of the expansion of real existing capitalism, which for this reason we must call imperialist by nature. Pauperization in the urban popular classes is closely linked to the developments that victimize third-world peasant societies. The submission of these societies to the demands of capitalist market expansion supports new forms of social polarization, which exclude a growing proportion of farmers from access to use of the land. These peasants who have been impoverished or become landless feed the migration to the shantytowns even more than does population growth. Yet all these phenomena are destined to get worse as long as liberal dogmas are not challenged, and no corrective policy within this liberal framework can check their spread. Pauperization calls into question both economic theory and the strategies of social struggles.

Conventional vulgar economic theory avoids the real questions that the expansion of capitalism poses. This is because it substitutes for an analysis of real existing capitalism a theory of an imaginary capitalism, conceived as a simple and continuous extension of exchange relations (the market), whereas the system functions and reproduces itself on the basis of capitalist production and exchange relations (not simple market relations). This substitution is easily coupled with the a priori notion, which neither history nor rational argument confirm, that the market is self-regulating and produces a social optimum. Poverty can then only be explained by causes decreed to be outside economic logic, such as population growth or policy errors. Its relation to the actual logic of capitalist accumulation is emptied of theoretical reflection. Yet this veritable liberal virus, which pollutes contemporary social thought and annihilates the capacity to understand the world, let alone transform it, has deeply penetrated the various lefts constituted since the Second World War. The movements currently engaged in social struggles for 'another world' and an alternative globalization will only be able to produce significant social advances if they get rid of this virus in order to construct an authentic theoretical debate. As long as they have not got rid of this virus, social movements, even the best intentioned, will remain locked in the shackles of conventional thought, and therefore prisoners of ineffective corrective propositions: those that are fed by the rhetoric concerning poverty reduction.

The analysis sketched above should contribute to opening this debate. This is because it re-establishes the pertinence of the link between capital accumulation on the one hand and the phenomenon of social pauperization on the other. One hundred and fifty years ago, Marx initiated an analysis of the mechanisms behind this link, which has hardly been pursued since then, and scarcely at all on a global scale.

THE RESPONSE: UNITY OF LABOUR, PEASANT-WORKER ALLIANCES, INTERNATIONALISM

The response to this challenge certainly holds consequences for the positive alternative policies that the popular movements could put forward as goals for their struggles. However, the success of these responses depends more on the effectiveness of their execution across the movements, which are the only ones capable of making the social forces favour the working classes, than on the intricate quality of the propositions. The challenge presents multiple aspects that complement one another. It calls upon the unions and the other working-class organizations on which falls the principal responsibility in the reconstruction of the united front which brings together the workers who are 'stabilized' and those who are not (such as the unemployed, the marginalized and those working in the informal sector) of the urbanized areas, in both the centres and the peripheries.

It calls upon the agrarian movements, the social and the political movements in the societies in the periphery which are confronted with the heavy responsibility not only to put in place policies for rural development, but also to draw up national macro policies that make the claims of the urban workers compatible with the demands of the rural world. It also calls upon all the concerned political forces to respond to the capital's globalized strategies through the reconstruction of an internationalism for the people.

This book analyses the 'urban challenge' through 13 studies of different cases and situations in the system's centres and peripheries. It starts to reply to the following questions:

- How should the challenge of the 'new labour question' be formulated in the specific concrete conditions of the country studied?
- How are the involved segments of the popular classes responding to these challenges: through passive adjustment or through struggles? Do these struggles obey some strategic

vision? Or are they simply day-to-day responses? What are the
lessons from the experiences of organized trade unionism? What
are the reasons for their eventual weakening in the present
conjuncture: lack of democracy, pressure on the labour market
from the growing mass of the unemployed, other reasons? Are
there some experiences of struggles of the informal workers?
What are the lessons that can be drawn from these experiences?
• What more effective alternative strategy could be suggested?

The complement to these studies regarding the other part of the
challenge (the struggle of peasants) makes up the object of another
of the World Forum for Alternatives' programmes. This programme
poses questions and puts forward several suggestions concerning the
goals of the struggle and alternative politics for the development of
agrarian societies.

Such a strategic set of targets involves complex policy mixes at
national, regional and global levels. At the national levels it implies
macro policies protecting peasant food production from the unequal
competition of modernized agriculturalists – local and international
agribusiness. This should help guarantee acceptable internal food
prices, disconnected from international market prices, which, additionally are biased by the agricultural subsidies of the wealthy
North. Such policy targets also question the patterns of industrial
and urban development, which should be based less on export-
oriented priorities (such as keeping wages low, which implies low
prices for food), and be more attentive to a socially balanced expansion of the internal market. Simultaneously, this involves an overall
pattern of policies to ensure national food sovereignty –an indispensable condition for a country to be an active member of the global
community, enjoying a necessary margin of autonomy and negotiating capacity. At regional and global levels it implies international
agreements and policies that move away from the doctrinaire liberal
principles ruling the WTO, and replace them with imaginative and
specific solutions for different areas, taking into consideration the
specific issues and concrete historical and social conditions.

Chapter 1
The future of the global working class: an introduction

Andreas Bieler, Ingemar Lindberg and Devan Pillay

The current phase of economic globalization[1] – expressed in the increasing transnational organization of production, the emergence of an integrated global financial market, the extensive informalization and deregulation of labour markets and the dominant ideology of neoliberal economics – has put the working class onto the defensive across the world. 'Working class' is here conceptualized in its broadest sense. It includes established, formal labour on secure contracts at the core of the labour market and non-established labour at the periphery of the labour market. The latter includes labour in the informal sector (for example street traders), 'semi-formal' workers within the formal sector on unstable temporary, part-time, casual or subcontracted types of contracts, as well as workers who occupy a grey area in between the informal and formal sectors, such as home workers who supply established firms.

The objective of this book is to analyse this situation and assess the possibilities for a revival of labour internationalism. In more detail, the aims of this volume are threefold. First, it is intended to provide a general overview of the situation of the working class around the world through a selection of countries in all the major regions. The division between formal and informal labour is of particular importance in this respect. Second, the responses of trade unions as well as other social movements, organizing the different fractions of labour in both the spheres of production and consumption, to the challenges of globalization are mapped out. This directly informs the third aim of this volume, the assessment of possible strategies forward for the various labour movements at different levels of policy making. Overall, the contributors to this book are driven by the normative purpose to study the possibilities of a revival of working-class internationalism based on transnational solidarity and its role in the resistance to neoliberal globalization.

This introductory chapter will:

- clarify our understanding of the main social phenomena we study and the concepts we use in doing so
- give some basic overall statistics to add to the picture from the country reports
- provide glimpses from the country reports of what our study is about.

THEORETICAL AND CONCEPTUAL STARTING POINTS

In the social sciences the global working class has been widely perceived to be on the retreat towards the end of the 20th century under the conditions of neoliberal restructuring of the global economy. Liberal international political economy (IPE) approaches have pointed to the structural changes related to globalization, and argued that the emergence of a globally integrated financial market and the increasingly transnational organization of production across borders have led to the emergence of new significant international actors. These include most importantly transnational corporations (TNCs), but also other actors such as international non-governmental organizations (INGOs), sometimes also called global social movements, and international trade union confederations. International organizations such as the IMF, World Trade Organization (WTO) and the World Bank too are argued to have increased in importance (e.g. Higgott et al., 2000).

Nevertheless, this assessment of the structural changes since the early 1970s overlooks the underlying power structure in the global economy. TNCs, INGOs and international trade unions are all treated as equally important actors in a pluralist understanding of policy making, which has been transferred from the national to the international level. The problem is that liberal IPE conceptualizes 'transnational actors as autonomous entities rather than as embedded in, and indeed constituted by, transnational structures' (van Apeldoorn, 2004: 148). The privileged position of transnational capital within the asymmetrical international power structure is overlooked, as is the crucial importance of the capitalist social relations of production. It is not understood that capital can only realize itself in the form of TNCs on a global scale to the extent that real production processes are created on this scale. Hence, 'capital is more geographically mobile than it was in the past because it now has more proletariats on which to land' (Coates, 2000: 255).

Beverly Silver (2003) captures the international power structure well in her broad historical and geographical analysis of worker movements since 1870. Through a close focus on the social relations of production and the inherent dynamic of capital's relentless search for higher profits, she is able to unravel the links between different instances of labour unrest in diverse geographical locations as well as different industries. Capitalism is characterized by an ongoing tension between alternating crises of profitability and crises of legitimacy (Silver, 2003: 20). During crises of legitimacy, an increasingly strong labour movement challenges the prerogatives of capital over the production process. In order to avoid the collapse of the system, capital responds through a compromise with organized labour. For example, in the post-world war Keynesian compromise (mainly in Northern Europe), workers accepted capital's continuing right to make decisions over investment and production organization based on the principle of private property in exchange for full employment and rising wages, which allowed workers to participate in the generation of increasing wealth. Mass production was closely related to mass consumption, backed up by bipartite or tripartite institutional systems, within which employers, trade unions and sometimes the state discussed the macroeconomic way forward. Yet 'the rapid growth of world trade and production in the 1950s and 1960s eventually sparked an overaccumulation crisis characterized by intense intercapitalist competition and a general squeeze on profits. It was in the context of this crisis [of profitability] that the postwar social compacts accommodating labor exploded' (Silver, 2003: 161). One way capital can respond to this crisis is through a spatial fix: mass production is transferred to other parts of the world with lower labour costs and less organized working classes, leading to the global structural changes referred to by Coates above. Second, a technological fix can help capital to lower production costs through the innovation of the production process, with the help of new technology partly replacing labour. A combination of spatial and technological fix has yet again an impact on the international division of labour, leading to a bifurcation of industrial relations. In developed countries:

> on the one hand, new innovations in organization and technology ... provide the basis for more consensual labor-capital-state social contracts, allowing legitimacy to be combined with profitability, albeit for a shrinking labour force. On the other hand, in poorer countries, where competitive advantage is based on a continuous drive to lower costs, profitability requirements lead to continuous crises of legitimacy.

> (Silver, 2003: 81)

Third, capital can overcome crises of overaccumulation through a product fix, in which it shifts investment from declining industrial sectors to new industrial sectors. Silver identifies the shift from the textile to the automobile industry as the new leading sector in the 20th century, and indicates that another shift is currently taking place to various areas of the service sector as new leading industries of the 21st century. Finally, and very similar to the product fix, capital engages in a financial fix, in which financial instruments become the focus of intensified investment and points of accumulation in their own right (Silver, 2003: 132–3).

Nevertheless, while Silver captures well the underlying power structure of capital restructuring at the global level, she overlooks important aspects which shape the organization and strategies of individual labour movements. Capitalism emerged in the 18th and 19th centuries in different ways and at a different pace in individual countries, developing different national trajectories. In other words, the historically specific national social relations of production and the state and its institutional set-up are under-conceptualized in Silver's account. She therefore first underestimates the possible division between national labour, engendered by domestic production sectors, and transnational labour, engendered by transnational production sectors. Her focus on leading industrial sectors makes her overlook other sectors which are often equally important for the formation of labour movements, such as currently the public sector in many Western European countries. Second, she overlooks the importance of national institutional set-ups. Forms of state, as neo-Gramscians would argue (see below), differ drastically from country to country, and offer different levels of protection to national labour. Positions on labour internationalism by trade unions are strongly affected by the possibilities or lack of possibilities to influence policy making at the national level (e.g. Bieler, 2006). Hence, we cannot do without this focus on different national institutional set-ups or forms of state.

We also need to remember that historically labour movements have mainly been formed at the national level, strongly influenced by the different paths of industrialization leading to different production structures as well as the different institutional formation of states in this process. While the British labour movement was initially characterized by a multitude of craft unions with little centralization (Edwards et al., 1998), strong, unitary and highly centralized unions emerged in Germany from early on due to the different process through which capitalist social relations of production were developed

(Jacobi et al., 1998). It is these different historical legacies which inform the structure of this book, with an emphasis on different national case studies. In short, for the purpose of this book, an approach needs to be developed which combines Silver's emphasis on the international dimension of trade union formation with a specific focus on the different domestic conditions within which national labour movements operate.

Historical institutionalist approaches and here especially the varieties of capitalism literature emphasize national institutional diversity. Kitschelt and colleagues, for example, understand globalization as external pressure on states. Then, they focus on how the various different national institutional set-ups mediate these pressures, ensuring a continuation of divergence of national models of capitalism (Kitschelt et al., 1999: 440–1). In short, the varieties of capitalism literature points out that there are different national institutional set-ups due to a historically specific development of capitalism, mediating globalization pressures in different ways.

Some argue that countries are likely to converge around two optimal solutions: either a coordinated market economy or a liberal market economy (e.g. Hall and Soskice, 2001); others speak of three models of capitalism: the market-led Anglo-American model, the negotiated/consensual model and the state-led model (e.g. Schmidt, 2002: 112–18). The main problem of this literature is, however, that it overlooks the social relations of production underpinning particular national models of capitalism (Coates, 2000: 176–7). Historical institutionalist approaches are therefore unable to explain why a particular set of institutions was established in the first place, as well as to assess change emanating from alterations in the production structure. Most importantly, the partial transnationalization of national production structures referred to above and its implications for states and national labour movements cannot be conceptualized.

In response, we offer here a neo-Gramscian perspective, which takes on board Silver's understanding of the geographical dimension of working class formation and combines it with a neo-Gramscian understanding of different national forms of state. In more detail, since Robert Cox's path-breaking work in the early 1980s (Cox, 1981 and 1983), a whole range of related yet different neo-Gramscian perspectives have been developed (Bieler and Morton, 2004a; Morton, 2007).

A neo-Gramscian perspective starts an analysis through an investigation of the social relations of production, where social forces are identified as core collective actors. The first division can be identified between capital, the owners of the means of production, and workers, who are 'free' to sell their labour power. Capital and labour, however, do not confront each other as two homogenous classes. Further divisions result from the transnationalization of production, as highlighted by Silver's point of capital's spatial fix, with national capital and labour being separate class fractions from transnational capital and labour (van Apeldoorn, 2002: 26–34; Bieler, 2006: 32–4). As far as the increasing marginalization of large parts of production are concerned, a further division can be identified between established labour with full-time employment and stable working conditions at the core of the labour market, often as employees of TNCs, on the one hand, and workers in the periphery of the labour market with unstable, temporary, part-time or casual working contracts on the other (Cox, 1981: 235). These potential divides between national and transnational, as well as formal and informal labour, already indicate some of the potential obstacles to transnational solidarity. They are discussed in the various chapters to this volume and will be engaged with in more detail in the conclusion.

In order to comprehend these potential divisions fully, a wider understanding of class struggle is important here. Van der Pijl argues that the crucial aspect of neoliberal capitalism as the latest stage of capitalist development is the extension of exploitation into the sphere of social reproduction through the (re-) introduction of the market into the public sector as well as an increasing exploitation of the environment. Resistance to this type of exploitation by social movements can be as much understood as class struggle as the resistance to exploitation in the workplace (van der Pijl, 1998: 46–8). This extended definition of class struggle allows us to conceptualize the possible cooperation of trade unions with new social movements, as well as the potential cooperation between formal and informal labour.

Furthermore, neo-Gramscian perspectives acknowledge the ideological component of globalization today. It is neoliberal restructuring, pushed by transnational capital as its hegemonic project, which drives the current phase of globalization (Rupert, 2000: 54). Neoliberal economics first gained credibility in the 1970s as the successful political economy critique of Keynesianism, and was implemented during the 1980s especially in the British and US forms of state, resulting in the deregulation and liberalization of domestic markets including labour markets, before it gained hegemonic status in the 1990s at the world order level of activity (Gamble, 2001). The fact that neoliberalism became dominant is, however, not due to some kind of inert quality. Rather, it was its material structure that pushed it to the fore, particularly the fact that it was pushed by the increasingly powerful transnational capitalist class fraction, supported by important forms of state such as the United States and Britain as well as international organizations such as the IMF and World Bank (and later the WTO).

In sum, neoliberalism is understood as the hegemonic project of an emerging transnational historical bloc with the transnational capitalist class as its leading class fraction (Robinson, 2004: 47–9; Sklair, 2001: 295), supported by its allies of small subcontracting and supplying firms, specialized service companies such as accountants and privileged workers (Gill, 1995: 400–1). It is further assisted by the global corporate media, spreading the neoliberal message, which holds this transnational historical bloc together (Robinson and Harris, 2000: 31). This discussion highlights, first, that neoliberal globalization is not simply some kind of external pressure, to which social forces like unions have to adjust. On the contrary, it is driven by clear agents, which can be opposed. Similarly, if it is understood that neoliberalism is part of a hegemonic project, then it also becomes clear that this ideology can be challenged.

Finally, in addition to the 'social relations of production' and 'world order' levels of activity, neo-Gramscians identify the 'forms of state' level. This concept is concerned with the relationship between civil society and the state, and is defined in terms of the apparatus of administration and of the historical bloc or class configuration that defines the raison d'état for that form (Cox, 1989: 41). States are, consequently, defined as a social relation, which confronts social forces as structures within and through which they operate. Specific state projects within a particular form of state are the result of class struggle. Thus, in a historical materialist understanding, 'the state is the institutionalization of class relations around a particular configuration of social production' (Robinson, 2001: 163). Transnational production implies that there are transnational class fractions. These do not, however, confront the state as an external actor, but are closely involved in the class struggle over the state project at the national level, and their interests may become internalized within the form of state in this process (Bieler and Morton, 2003: 485–9). In short, social class forces engendered by the changing social relations of production operate within and through different national forms of state, with the objective of having an impact on world order. How the different class forces operate, whether transnational solidarity can be established across the national and international divide, and the gap between formal and informal workers, are issues of open-ended class struggle.

The individual country studies of this book will, in their own, different ways, engage with these questions. Nevertheless, while it is important to study the domestic situation of labour movements, we must not neglect the transnational dimension. Hence, before providing a summary of the empirical insights of the various chapters, we first turn to a brief overview of the international situation of the global working class.

GLOBALIZATION, THE 'WORKING POOR' AND INEQUALITY

The impact of neoliberal globalization on the global working class is expressed through rising unemployment, the informalization (and degradation) of work and rising income inequality. The International Labour Organization (ILO), the only source of global labour statistics, publishes annual reports on employment trends. It uses three important standards of measurement, namely unemployment, which only includes those actively seeking work; an employment-to-population ratio, which measures employment in relation to all those of working age; and a relatively new measurement of the 'working poor', which is meant as a proxy, in the absence of actual global statistics, for what we refer to as 'informalized labour' – namely informal work within the informal sector (including for example street traders) and semi-formal work in the formal sector (including all forms of unstable work such as subcontracted, part-time, casual and temporary labour). There is, however, an increasing overlap between the informal and formal sectors, such as home-based work that directly supplies companies in the formal sector. It is thus not always easy to make clear distinctions between 'informal' and 'semi-formal' work (ILO, 2005; Chen, 2004).

Compounding this problem of measurement is the unreliability of data from many developing countries, particularly in Africa where informal labour is widespread, and official unemployment rates have little meaning, given the poor quality of most jobs, which pay under US$2 a day. The ILO adopts this 'upper' measure of poverty used by the World Bank despite criticism about its unreliability as a standard measure, as it does not sufficiently take into account what the poor consume as necessities, such as food. It is also too low to account for what is necessary to meet basic nutritional requirements in the United States. Further problematic is the weak informational base, considering that major countries such as China and India do not participate in the price surveys 'that provide the basis for constructing PPPs' on which 'equivalent' purchasing power is based' (Reddy, 2005: 172). Reddy suggests that the undercount of the extent of poverty can be as much as 30–40 per cent. For example, in contrast to the World Bank's 1998 figure of 1.21 billion people living under $1 per day in 1998 (24.3 per cent of the global population), Reddy and Thomas Pogge (cited in Kaplinsky, 2005: 36–7) calculate that the 1998 figure ought to be 1.64 billion (or 32.2 per cent of the global population).

Nevertheless, according to the ILO's January 2007 *Global Employment Trends Brief* (2007b), at the end of 2006 there were 2.9 billion people (aged 15 upwards) who worked, which is up by 1.6 per cent from the previous year, and by 16.6 per cent since 1996. GDP growth in 2006 stood at 5.2 per cent, and the world economy grew at an average of 4.1 per cent between 1996 and 2006. This confirms the view that neoliberal globalization is primarily a phenomenon of jobless growth. What little employment has been created has not kept up with population increases. Unemployment increased to 195.2 million people, an all-time high from just over 160 million people in 1996. In other words, the unemployment rate (those actively seeking work) stood at 6.3 per cent, which is up from approx 6 per cent in 1996. These figures do not, however, indicate the quality of jobs. Indeed, some jobs include begging or eking out a living at the margins of society. The ILO, on the basis of the dubious $2 a day measurement, calculates that the 'working poor' now stand at 47.4 per cent of total employment (apparently down from 54.8 per cent in 1996). In absolute numbers the working poor have risen to 1.37 billion people (up from 1.35 billion in 1996). In other words, even taking the flawed and conservative proxy figures derived from the World Bank, at least half of all those employed can be classified as the 'working poor' making a living in various forms of informalized labour. In regional terms, this translates to 87 per cent in South Asia, 86 per cent in Sub-Saharan Africa, 58 per cent in South-East Asia, 44 per cent in East Asia, 35 per cent in the Middle East and North Africa, and 31 per cent in Latin America and the Caribbean. The flawed measurement records only 11 per cent for Central and Eastern Europe (non-EU) and the Commonwealth of Independent States (CIS), and no working poor in the Developed Economies and the European Union.

Martha Chen and Joann Vanek have begun to develop a more accurate measurement of informal employment (ILO, 2002a). Despite insufficient data available (due to many national economies not yet capturing rates of informality), they use various indirect methods to measure the informal economy and informal employment, and paint the following picture for 1994/2000. In developing countries, informal employment comprises one half to three-quarters of total non-agricultural employment, ranging from 48 per cent in North Africa (of which 62 per cent is self-employment and 38 per cent wage employment) to 51 per cent in Latin America (60 per cent self-employment), 65 per cent in Asia (59 per cent self-employment) and 72 per cent in Sub-Saharan Africa (70 per cent self-employment). In developed countries non-standard or atypical work comprised 30 per cent of all employment in 15 European countries, and 25 per cent of total employment in the United States. While at this stage trends cannot be measured over time, this shows extremely high rates of informality throughout the world, much of which is extremely low-earning self-employment in the informal sector. High rates of growth and static or increased poverty indicate that a tiny few are reaping the benefits of the surplus produced. The United Nations Development Programme (UNDP)'s *Human Development Report 2005* records increased inequality both between the world's poorest countries and the rich countries, and within countries. For example, 'in 1990 the average American was 38 times richer than the average Tanzanian. Today, the average American is 61 times richer' (UNDP, 2005: 37). Using conservative estimates, the report shows that the income of the richest 500 individuals in the world exceeds that of the poorest 416 million people.

According to Milanovic as cited in Kaplinsky (2005), the Gini coefficient that measures inter-country inequality has risen dramatically since 1980, when neoliberal globalization began in earnest. The coefficient ranges from 0 (perfect equality) to 100 (complete inequality). Using a measure unweighted by population size,[2] global inequality rose steadily from 43 to 46 in 1980, and dramatically since then to almost 54 in 1999. By 2005, according to the UNDP 2005 report, inequality had risen to 67. The gap between the richest and poorest at a global level is greater than the worst income inequality at country level. For example, in Brazil the richest 10 per cent of the population is 94 times greater than the poorest 10 per cent, while at the global level it is 103 times greater. As the UNDP outlines, the massive inequalities between countries are mirrored within countries 'between rich people and poor people, men and women, rural and urban and different regions and groups' (UNDP, 2005: 55). Kaplinsky (2005) shows that out of 73 countries measured between the 1960s and 2000, 54 showed rising inequality, 12 were constant and only seven had declining inequality.[3] Most of the countries with rising inequality are the 'transitional' countries of Eastern Europe and developing countries, including China and India. It is correct that millions of workers have benefited from structural change in the latter two and achieved higher levels of living standards. Nevertheless, the vast majority of people in these countries have remained in an impoverished situation. Moreover, developed countries such as the United Kingdom, United States and Japan have also experienced rising inequality.

From the available global data, then, it is possible to construct a picture for the working class of increased effective unemployment, increased informalization of work (at least in absolute numbers) and increased inequality in a context of rising global economic growth and increased productivity. In other words, the general picture is increased power of capital over labour through a greater concentration of wealth in fewer hands.

A BRIEF OVERVIEW BASED ON COUNTRY REPORTS

Challenges – the situation of the working classes

A weakening of the position of labour in relation to capital and an increased informalization of work contracts can be summarized as the most important changes during the last 10 to 15 years in the situation of the working classes, as described in the country reports. We shall here provide glimpses from these reports, starting with the challenges and then the prevailing responses. Towards the end of the book we shall then sum up our own conclusions.

Democratic trade unionism was exploding by the late 1980s in **South Korea**, reports *Jennifer Jihye Chun*. However, an assault on the organizational power of workers grew during the 1990s, and the aftermath of the so-called IMF crisis led to the full-scale implementation of neoliberal governance in aspects of employment. Militant labour struggles were broken up by violent state intervention, including the use of riot police, teargas trucks, water canons and helicopters. From this South Korean experience Chun identifies a new type of repressive state, the neoliberal democratic state regime, replacing the old authoritarian developmental state regime with a new form of anti-unionism, designed to criminalize union militancy and weaken existing labour protections. The other major challenge to the Korean working class is the resegmentation of labour markets. In South Korea irregular (*bijunggyujik*) forms of employment now represents the dominant form of employment. The core zone represents 34 per cent of the total workforce and the peripheral zones together 58 per cent. Chun also highlights the gender characteristics of this segmentation, with a majority of male workers having regular types of employment and more than 70 per cent of women workers having irregular jobs. This segmentation of work is further aggravated through male-dominated unions which often even refuse to accept irregular workers as members.

South Africa with its background of apartheid has since the fall of the racist regime experienced a 'double transition' into political democracy and a globalized open economy, as *Devan Pillay* outlines in his contribution. Today, out of a potential work force of 20.1 million, close to 8 million, or nearly 39 per cent, are unemployed. Among those who have jobs, growing numbers are in the semi-formal or informal spheres. Only 33 per cent of the economically active population make up the core sector of the work force with a formal type of employment, while 15 per cent are counted as non-core (outsourced, temporary, part-time and domestic workers) and 52 per cent as periphery, consisting of the informal sector (inner periphery) and the unemployed (outer periphery). Social inequality has increased since 1994. Poverty has decreased slightly percentage-wise but the number of poor has increased from 20.2 to 21.9 million. Among those with jobs, the poorest 50 per cent received 12 per cent of total income, while the richest 5 per cent received 42 per cent. The challenges facing organized labour in South Africa, Pillay sums up, are increased informalization of labour, unemployment, persistent and extensive poverty and rising inequality.

In India, during the first phase of post-colonial rule, writes *Praveen Jha*, a small segment of the working classes, mainly in modern sector activities, managed to obtain recognition of some rights. The ascendancy of the neoliberal policy regime since the early 1990s, however, seems to throw out whatever progressive labour laws the country has had. Out of a total of 397 million working people in India in the year 2000, 369 million were in the unorganized sector. The proportion of the workforce without almost any protection was close to 93 per cent. Thus, the huge bulk of the labouring humanity in the Indian economy is extremely vulnerable.

China is undergoing a working class development, unprecedented in world history in terms of size, pace and economic significance. Out of 800 million people of working age, 500 million have rural residence status, and out of these 500 million at least 200 million make their living through non-farming jobs. Including family members there are about 180 million members of the 'migrant labour population' (15 per cent of the whole population of China). They have left their home villages for a non-agricultural job, staying mainly in the enormous industrial centres of the coastal area. In his analysis of China, *Wen Tiejun* emphasizes the creation of power blocs. In the late 1990s the process of reform and privatization of state-owned enterprises contributed further to the integration between power and capital and the creation of strong power blocs, with increasing influence on the entire system and the legal framework. Urban reforms were implemented via reassignment of lay-offs, reduction in the work force, increase in efficiency, protection of the interests of the investor and improvement of the capital yield. Educational and medical systems were almost marketized and converted into enterprises, charges were raised and public goods became means of gaining huge profits. Rising social inequalities are a major concern behind policy revisions following the 2002 Congress of the Communist Party.

Isabel Rauber, writing about **Argentina**, goes back to the second half of the 1970s when the country experienced super-structural adaptation to the neoliberal model through military dictatorships. Before neoliberalism Argentina had low levels of unemployment, poverty and marginalization. Its high level of wage-earning industrial workers were particularly important, and the labour movement played a significant role in a corporatist structure. Formal wage-earners now only make up 40 per cent of all workers, while the majority of workers are outside this sector and thereby outside traditional union organizing. Today, Rauber sums up, we see in Argentina a period of decline of traditional unionism, which historically was quite strong in Argentina with its connection to Peronism and its role as counterpart to the industrial bourgeoisie. But we also see new forms of organization growing up, to which we return below.

In **Brazil**, according to *Kjeld Jakobsen* and *Alexandre de Freitas Barbosa*, the labour market during the 1990s transformed itself into a mechanism for shutting out the workforce, expanding the industrial reserve army and reducing dramatically the share of labour in national income from 42 per cent to 36 per cent. New forms of social exclusion emerged, and informality, which had been contained in the industrialization period, spread to every sector and region, attacking especially the more 'developed' areas. Throughout the 1990s, unemployment has emerged as a mass phenomenon, leaping from 3 per cent to 10 per cent between 1989 and 2001, quadrupling the total number of idle workers, which rose to approximately 8 million by the end of the decade. Even the post-1999 recuperation of formal employment, though bringing a stabilization of employment and a drop in informality, has proved insufficient to overcome the heritage handed down by the 1990s. However, Brazil was one of the countries in Latin America where neoliberal policies were less easily internalized. This is shown by the retention of important state-owned companies, the national bourgeoisie's greater market and bargaining power, the expansion of social investments in the recent period, the inability of governments to pass radical reforms of the pension system and labour law, as well as the more critical stance the Lula administration has adopted in relation to the developed countries.

During the 1990s intense competition, in particular from Chinese manufacturing, led to wide-scale lay-offs in **Japan**, report *Wakana Shutô* and *Mac Urata*. Domestic costs were reduced by hiring more irregular employees. Unions in many cases were forced to accept mass dismissals, longer working hours and significant adjustment of retirement allowances. The percentage of workers on temporary contracts or working only part-time has gone up sharply from 21 per cent in 1995 to 33 per cent in 2005, the corresponding figures for women being as high as 39 and 53 per cent. The gap between regular and atypical workers in terms of wages, promotion and social benefits is considerably greater in Japan than for instance in Europe. The wage gap between the two has been widening every year since 1995. Only full-timers qualify for employee benefits and welfare programmes. Increasing groups of immigrant workers are not even employed as part-timers by the producing company but are provided by outside firms under conditions of extreme instability, often with high risks of unfair dismissals and industrial accidents.

The major change in employment in **Canada** over the past few decades has, according to *Geoff Bickerton* and *Jane Stinson*, not been the growth of the informal economy, as in many other countries. Starting in the 1980s attention focused on the erosion of the standard full-time, full-year employment relationship, as employers responded to competitive pressures and cut labour costs by cutting positions, hours and guarantees of work, and by lowering wages and benefits where possible. The 1990s were marked by increases in self-employment, homework, on-call work, part-time and temporary work. Women and racialized workers have been negatively affected most by the growth of precarious employment.

In West **Germany,** according to *Thorsten Schulten* and *Heiner Dribbusch*, after the Second World War a so-called 'German model' emerged on the basis of a national class compromise. It included the corporatist integration of trade unions, which gained a relatively strong influence in industrial relations and macro-economic policy making. The post-war class compromise was materially founded on an essentially export-led growth strategy. The reality of German capitalism today is characterized in many respects by the opposite: the dominant socio-economic features are comparatively weak economic growth, persistently high mass unemployment and rising social inequality. Growing parts of German capital have revoked the post-war class compromise. While capital itself is under increasing pressure to realize short-term profit targets, it refers the pressure to workers and demands a constant decrease in labour costs.

In **Sweden** too, in spite of a high rate of unionization and long periods of social-democratic governance, labour has, according to *Andreas Bieler* and *Ingemar Lindberg*, increasingly come under pressure over the last 30 years. The rate of marginalization has tripled since the 1960s and unemployment is up from 2 to 6 per cent. Transnationalization has intensified since the 1990s, as has the informalization of employment. Fifteen per cent of workers are now on temporary contracts, a 50 per cent increase from 1990. However, important elements of the earlier 'Swedish model', such as strong unions, nationwide collective agreements and large-scale social security protection are still in place, and yet Sweden is today classified by the OECD as one of the fastest growing economies in Europe.

Responses by organized labour and other social movements

In **South Korea** the refusal of unions representing regular workers to include irregular workers in their organizations has resulted in major clashes. These difficulties are largely attributed to the legacy of an authoritarian enterprise union system. Several struggles by groups of irregular workers, without support from the organizations of regular workers, have exposed a 'solidarity crisis', but also laid the basis for a broader-based movement of irregular workers with the Korean Confederation of Trade Unions (KCTU) Seoul Regional Centre as a hub. In the absence of support from KCTU headquarters, women worker activists have emerged as key support actors in the irregular workers' movement. Gradually a new set of organizations and social movements have emerged to respond to the issues of women workers and irregular workers; organizations which are often not recognized by employers, but which instead have to rely on public understandings of justice and fairness. Thus, somewhat paradoxically, global economic forces associated with the disintegration of trade union movements are also operating to revitalize their democratic character, *Jennifer Jihye Chun* concludes optimistically.

Rather than viewing frictions as splintering elements, the South Korean case highlights the importance of recognizing the possibilities and new directions that result from shifting lines of inclusion and exclusion under processes of globalization.

In **South Africa** the most viable organization of the working class remains COSATU, the Congress of South African Trade Unions. *Devan Pillay* reports that union density (as a percentage of all 'organizable' workers) is estimated to be around 34 per cent in 2005, down from a peak of 57 per cent in 1996. Declining sectors are metal, mining, clothing and textile industries, all sectors that are facing increased subcontracting and casualization of work. COSATU does not seem to have found a way to successfully recruit vulnerable workers, many of whom are women. Organization amongst informalized or flexible workers in the formal sector, Pillay continues, is not evident in any significant form, while organization within the informal sector is only sporadic and embryonic. SEWU, the Self-Employed Women's Union, is an interesting new initiative, organized along trade union lines and defining its members as workers, not as embryonic businesswomen. Its main function has been channelling the informal traders' demands for shelter, water, sanitation and later child care facilities to the city council. SEWU became defunct in 2004, but hopes to be revived soon. Clearly, a long road has to be travelled before innovative solutions are found to surmount the enormous obstacles to organizing informal workers in all their diverse forms, Pillay concludes. If COSATU is to continue its path of 'social movement unionism', it must face the challenge to take the struggle to where the most exploited workers are – the informal economy.

Indian unions have, according to *Praveen Jha*, been put in a 'defensive mode unlike never before since independence'. However, they have gradually begun to confront the anti-union challenges connected to neoliberal globalization. Much of their efforts and energies are devoted to broadening their work and base among (hitherto neglected) unorganized workers. Several major unions recount significant advances in this respect among street vendors, construction workers, rickshaw pullers, lorry drivers and others. One significant initiative is the New Trade Union Initiative (NTUI), an alliance of independent trade unions in India that arose in the mid-1990s and became formally constituted as a federation in 2006. NTUI today has a membership base of 500,000 workers in the formal sector and another 300,000 in the unorganized sector. Another important initiative is the Self

Employed Women's Association (SEWA), which was started in 1972 and is currently spread over six states in India – Madhya Pradesh, Uttar Pradesh, Delhi, Bihar, Kerala and Gujarat – with the aim of creating a trade union of women who earn a living through their own labour. At present, it has 61 cooperatives, 400 self-help groups and 4,000 saving groups.

In **China** the mainstream official unions, the only ones allowed by the regime, have traditionally been concerned mainly with social welfare, cultural affairs and aiding poorer families, reports *Wen Tiejun*. Through their awareness of the struggles for basic rights of the new working class (migrant rural labour) in the mid-1990s, the unions cautiously turned their attention to protecting the labour rights of those migrants, even though there were, and still are, many difficulties. A new contradiction has arisen among the working class. Workers for state-owned enterprises, who still form the core of mainstream official unions, dislike the fact that migrants, by adding to the competition within the labour market, tend to decrease the price of labour and reduce social welfare provisions.

In **Argentina** new patterns of organization have emerged. With formal wage-earners making up only 40 per cent of the total working class, and only a small part of the formal wage-earning class actually being members of a union, it has, according to *Isabel Rauber*, become impossible to rearticulate the political and organizational unity of the working class if the idea of traditional unionism is maintained. Traditional unions have been identified as monopolizers of the job market and protectors of the privileges of a minority of wage workers, creating an isolation of unions in relation to the non-unionized majority of the population. The Argentine Workers' Federation (CTA), which was formed in 1991, has based itself on an effort to build a new type of unionism, counterposing the market society with a society of humanistic production aiming at social reproduction, respect for differences, equality of rights and an environmental balance. On the organizational side CTA is based on direct membership, not necessarily through unions, and an effort to organize (and be organized by) all social actors that can unify the working class as a whole. Thus, Rauber concludes, union-led resistance has grown in Argentina, but this does not yet imply the maturation of an alternative project. Defensive resistance continues to be predominant.

As regards Lula's first government in **Brazil** (2003–06), it is worth underscoring that the new administration did not, according to *Kjeld Jakobsen* and *Alexandre de Freitas Barbosa*, represent a rupture of the existing economic model. In fact, it even reinforced it in some aspects. On the other hand, the privatizations programme was interrupted, priorities changed in the international negotiations arena and the BNDES (Brazil's development bank) started to focus more on investment in infrastructure and strategic economic sectors. Significant investment was made in social programmes, and credit lines for small rural farmers stepped up. Yet a programmatic alternative to neoliberalism was not put forward. At least partially, this is due to the incapacity of social movements, which shied away from adopting a clearer and more straightforward position in the internal confrontation of visions and power that characterize the Lula administration. They have failed so far to shift from a defensive strategy to another more critical and proactive position.

In **Japan** the dominant union RENGO has made the attainment of stronger legislation protecting part-time workers a top priority. Japanese unions have two plans for accommodating atypical workers: first, integration into a full-time employees' union, and second, reclassification of non-regular workers into regular workers, planning to take advantage of an anticipated labour shortage. On the whole, however, it would be difficult to say that Japan's labour movement has responded to the challenges caused by globalization, *Wakana Shuto* and *Mac Urata* point out. The inferior working conditions experienced by non-regular workers have been left to stand for quite some time. And the labour movement has not moved to organize the increasing number of foreign workers in the country, including illegal aliens, mostly on short-term and extremely unstable contracts. However, new forms of locally based community unions have started to appear in localities where many foreign workers live and work. While not recognized by employers, community unions are providing consultation services and support for workers facing dismissal or bankruptcy.

The effectiveness of the trade union movement in **Canada** in areas of collective bargaining, political lobbying and policy development has, according to *Geoff Bickerton* and *Jane Stinson*, been undermined, as members are fragmented into several unions which often compete more against each other than they cooperate with one another. Eight unions represent almost two-thirds of the total union membership, and four multi-sector mega-unions now represent more than half of the private sector union membership. There is a crucial need to extend the benefits of unionization to a broader group of workers. This is especially true for those in the Canadian labour market who are most exploited and disadvantaged, including women, racialized workers, young workers, disabled workers and aboriginal workers.

German unions have started to discuss and develop new political strategies which aim at a revitalization of the union movement. Two strategic approaches in particular are discussed within union circles, report *Heiner Dribbusch* and *Thorsten Schulten*. The first has a kind of 'back-to-the-roots' attitude and wants to concentrate union activities on the 'core businesses' of collective bargaining and workers' interest representation at company level. Its basic assumption is that unions will only overcome their crisis if they regain strength at company level. In contrast to that, the second approach wants to strengthen the union voice in the overall political arena by promoting social movement unionism and seeking new alliances with other social movements. Both approaches do not necessarily compete with each other but could form complementary parts of a comprehensive strategy, which aims at a restrengthening of both structural and associational power. This debate on strategies of union renewal is linked to a discussion on how to successfully organize transnational union action, and how to develop an internationalist answer beyond the neoliberal concepts of globalization and competitiveness. There are many in the German union movement who sympathize with the slogan 'another world is possible', but the discussion about alternatives is still very much open.

Swedish unions, still enjoying a strong position and a very high rate of organization, unsurprisingly have responded to globalization mainly by trying to uphold national collective agreements, labour law and welfare state arrangements as a weapon against increased risks of underbidding from 'the outside'. This dominant response, which *Andreas Bieler* and *Ingemar Lindberg* in their chapter label 'defend and restore', seeks mainly to pursue these traditional policies within national boundaries which, it is argued, have previously served Swedish workers well. An alternative response, labelled 'modernize and adapt' by the authors, argues that unions must accept new production patterns and new types of employment flexibility in order to meet increased global competition. This alternative response is predominantly being put forward by unions in the transnational sector and unions with mainly core workers. The authors also see certain, although still rather weak, signs of a more offensive response, which they tentatively label 'defend, modernize and strike back'.

In order to emphasize the link between national struggles and the international dimension of resistance, this book also contains a discussion of informal sector organizations and their relationship to unions in Africa, and a European regional perspective, as well as an analysis of different possible strategies by unions at the international level.

The question of responses from the side of **informal sector workers** is perhaps particularly relevant in **Africa**, where formal sector employment is generally very low. The situation in most African cities today could, according to *Ilda Lindell*, be described as a shrinking and 'aborted' formal economy and an extensive informal economy where the majority of people make a living. Africa and its cities are experiencing a new wave of informalization in the context of neoliberal restructuring. A new generation of people involved in informal kinds of work are increasingly asserting themselves as 'workers' – claiming the right to decent work, freedom from harassment and so on. While trade union membership declines, the number of informal workers continues to grow. Trade unions are often both disturbed by, and ill-equipped to deal with, these challenges. The informalization of work is giving rise to a variety of organizing initiatives, emerging both from within the informal economy and from the responses by trade unions. On the one hand, informal workers in a variety of contexts are increasingly organizing themselves to pursue their interests as workers, and are in some cases building organizations that are national in scope. On the other hand, trade unions are increasingly attempting to reach out into the informal economy and to bring into their ranks the vast number of informal workers. Lindell's chapter illustrates the highly varied nature of relations between trade unions and organizations of informal workers through an overview of how these relations are evolving in a number of African countries. It then takes a deeper look at the Mozambican case to discuss both the benefits and challenges involved in creating alliances across the formal–informal divide. The chapter concludes with developments in international organizing of informal workers, in which trade unions are also involved.

While many European countries find it increasingly difficult to uphold full employment, social partnership and extensive welfare state programmes at the national level, the **European Union** is frequently looked upon as the new, more appropriate level for upholding a kind of European social model in times of global restructuring. In their chapter on European integration, *Andreas Bieler* and *Thorsten Schulten* see an emerging contradiction between trade union support for European integration and the increasingly neoliberal character of EU policies designed to 'modernize' the European economy. As elements of an alternative 'social Europe' they would like to see a modern form of Euro-Keynesianism, a European minimum wage policy and a fundamental revision of the regulation of works councils in order to give worker representatives a real influence on transnational relocation and company investment strategies. They also discuss aspects of a European 'solidaristic wage policy' as a counter-model to the prevailing neoliberal concept of wages subordinated to the battle for competitiveness.

Does globalization mark the end of unionism as we have known it for 150 years, *Peter Waterman* asks in his report on **labour internationalism?** Or is it rather the end of the beginning? The challenges are perhaps greater than ever, but there is growing awareness that old recipes are inadequate and that new possibilities can be grasped. One possible response is raising the old notion of 'social partnership' with capital and state from the national to the global level. This seems to be the main thrust of the 'decent work' campaign by the International Trade Union Confederation (ITUC) during the 2007 World Social Forum (WSF) in Nairobi. The major areas of this union initiative are international labour standards, codes of conduct and corporate social responsibility policies. Global framework agreements between particular global union federations (GUFs) and multinational corporations are an important and possibly more active part of this strategy. The presence of the trade unions within the global justice and solidarity movement (GJ&SM) in general and the World Social Forum in particular implies the hypothetical possibility not only of adding maybe 150 to 200 million organized workers to the somewhat inchoate and changing constituency of the GJ&SM, but also of making 'work' as central to the WSF as trade, the environment/consumption and peace have been in the past. What the new movement does make hypothetically possible, Waterman argues, is the emancipation of the unions from two historical, and now archaic, notions of labour internationalism: one that suggested that labour was the privileged bearer of social emancipation and international solidarity, and another that conceived unions as junior partners of (sections of) national and international capital and (certain) inter-state institutions.

The following chapters will explore these themes in detail, before the conclusion assesses more broadly the possibilities for transnational solidarity.

NOTES

1   The authors recognize that 'globalization' is a highly contested, multi-faceted concept that cannot be reduced to its economic features, as is so often the case in popular discourse. It is also not only a phenomenon of the late 20th century onwards, but stretches back at least to the global expansion of capitalism, through colonial conquest, if not before. It is a highly contradictory phenomenon that contains both threats and opportunities for the working class. As a result, 'anti-globalization' has little meaning, when what we are really opposed to is neoliberal orthodox economics which dominates the most recent phase of economic globalization.

2   This reduces the distortion caused by China's size and dramatic growth rates since the 1980s (despite its own considerable rise in internal inequality).

3   This takes into account six countries that 'may have experienced rising inequality between 1998 and 2000' (Kaplinsky, 2005: 42).

Chapter 2

The contested politics of gender and irregular employment: revitalizing the South Korean democratic labour movement

Jennifer Jihye Chun

The reconfiguration of capitalist employment relations is a central feature of work in today's global economy. In place of regular, full-time employment under a single employer, a growing proportion of workers can be found in 'irregular' (*bijunggyujik*) forms of employment – that is, employment defined by structural ambiguity over what a 'worker' and an 'employer' is.[1] Nowhere is this more apparent than in South Korea, where irregular employment now represents the dominant form of employment, with more than 70 per cent of women between 1993 and 2003 employed as part-time workers, workers hired by temporary agencies (*pagyun*), workers hired under subcontracting companies, independent contractors, on-call workers, and day labourers among others. While insecure forms of irregular employment have been and continue to be a dominant pattern of employment for traditionally disadvantaged sectors of the workforce under historical capitalism, it is only since the so-called 'IMF crisis' in 1997–98 and the subsequent passage of flexible labour law revisions in South Korea that irregular employment has become synonymous with a systematic assault on labour. Today, the imposition of flexible forms of irregular employment is viewed as a key mechanism to downgrade wages and labour rights protection as well as break the power of militant trade unions.

To challenge the erosion of their living and working conditions in the post-IMF period, the Korean Confederation of Trade Unions (KCTU), the national centre of the democratic labour movement, has identified the 'abolition of irregular employment' (*bijonggyu chulpye*) as one of its major organizational priorities. Since the year 2000, the KCTU has waged mass rallies, petition campaigns, hunger strikes and joint solidarity actions with the more politically moderate, historically government-linked Federation of Korean

Trade Unions (FKTU) to condemn the assault on their wages and livelihoods under the guise of 'flexibility'. Despite these efforts, however, the KCTU-led labour movement's capacity to challenge the expansion of irregular employment and the repressive, cost-cutting practices associated with it is hampered by two key obstacles. First, the vast majority of KCTU affiliates represent male workers employed under regular, full-time employment in large enterprises, which is less than one-quarter of the entire workforce. Its narrowing constituency base has not only heightened tensions between KCTU's regularly employed union members and the irregularly employed workers who are perceived to 'threaten' their job security and wage standards, it has also plagued its ability to genuinely represent the workforce at large, especially the rapidly growing periphery of workers in lower-paid, more insecure and socially marginal forms of employment. Second, while its staunch opposition to authoritarian developmental state regimes in the past was a key feature in securing *de facto* labour rights and improving living and working conditions, the KCTU has been largely unable to expand democratic rights for workers in the post-authoritarian period. Ironically, since the installation of democratic state regimes in the 1990s, workers and trade unions face a rollback on formal labour rights and protections. This is largely a result, I argue, of the KCTU's inability to adapt its strategies and tactics to the anti-unionism of a new political regime – the neoliberal democratic state regime.

This paper reflects upon the challenges facing the South Korean democratic labour movement by investigating the shifting lines of inclusion and exclusion for labour under processes of globalization. In the first section I examine how 'the infiltration of market-driven truths and calculations into the domain of politics', or what Aihwa Ong (2006) calls 'neoliberal governmentality', is disciplining militant forms of unionism in both the workplace and the larger society. Whereas the mass mobilization of independent trade unions effectively undermined the legitimacy of repressive state regimes and employers under authoritarian industrialization, neoliberal democratic regimes in today's globalized economy are appealing to the logic of market competition and managerial authority to criminalize union militancy and weaken existing labour protections.

In the second section, I examine the deepening fault lines dividing the workforce on the criteria of employment status and gender. As more and more workers face the erosion of basic labour rights and meaningful forms of workplace leverage, unions are confronted with the need to adapt their strategies and priorities in line with the changing world of work. Although many scholars see such changes as the source of heightened fragmentation within the labour movement, in the third section I demonstrate how frictions along employment status and gender play a major role in developing new organizations and strategies that can organize the growing ranks of workers in the periphery, highlighting the contradictory and contingent dynamics of historical capitalism.

NEOLIBERAL DEMOCRATIC REGIMES: BREAKING MILITANT UNIONISM

Democratic trade unionism was exploding in South Korea by the late 1980s. Union membership levels skyrocketed, increasing from approximately 1 million to 1.9 million between 1987 and 1989. Real wage levels also rose, increasing by from 7.8 per cent in 1988 to 14.5 per cent in 1989. The state's foray into heavy manufacturing and its growing centrality in the national economy gave workers and unions the leverage they needed to undermine nearly three decades of state labour repression under export-oriented industrialization. Independent unions, which were imbued with a widespread sense of moral and political legitimacy, began dismantling government-controlled company unionism and establishing genuine representational organizations for workers. The militant democratic labour movement was poised to take full advantage of its newfound potential, expanding the scope of labour's influence into the governing structures of society. However, intensified pressures for South Korea to liberalize its markets and adopt the prescriptions of neoliberal globalization intervened in this historical moment of possibility. Instead, militant democratic unions faced renewed attempts by newly democratic state regimes to undermine their legit-imacy and reconfigure relations of power in line with the interests of a more aggressive and cost-cutting capital.

Although the assault on workers and trade unions is commonly highlighted to emphasize the downward pressures of globalized competition and capital mobility, it is crucial to provide historical and geographic specificity to this claim. In South Korea, the enhanced mobility of capital coupled with flexible economic restructuring poli-cies certainly weakened the basis of power for trade unions, especially in the case of labour-intensive manufacturing sectors, where plant closings and capital flight resulted in the failure of 80 per cent of trade unions in small and medium plants by 1990.[2] However, in more capital-intensive sectors where production was flourishing, the outright relocation of production to 'union-free' worksites was a much less feasible strategy. Beginning in 1989, *chaebols* (large conglomerates) in auto, steel, shipbuilding, electronics and public utilities started to dominate the national economy, contributing over 60 per cent of total domestic sales and two-thirds of total exports. Rather than jeopardize production in strategic sectors, large companies began granting union concessions in exchange for labour peace. Annual wage growth rates in firm-level collective bargaining agreements jumped from 6.8 per cent in 1986 to 17.5 per cent in 1989 (see Table 2 in Jeong, 2005: 44). Unions also secured stronger guarantees for lifetime employment, seniority-based promotions and welfare benefits, especially in *chaebol* enterprises that received financial assistance, support for technological development and protection from foreign competitors from the South Korean government.

To counter the increasing power of unions in large enterprises, employers went on the offensive. One of the biggest problems that employers had to contend with after 1987 was the transformed legal institutional climate regulating employer-employee relations. Before 1987, employers could count on coercive state intervention to intervene in labour disputes and strip workers of their *de jure* collective labour rights. However, Hagen Koo explains that during the 'Great workers' struggle' of 1987 and 1988, 'the state withdrew itself for the first time from the industrial arena and proclaimed a natural and hands-off policy toward labour relations'. Forced to deal with the strength of militant unionists head on, 'the capitalists began to take on that responsibility for themselves' (Koo, 2000: 235). In addition to aggressive strategies to reorganize wage payment schemes and automate production processes according to flexible managerial techniques, employers began advocating policy changes in existing labour law frameworks.[3] Although authoritarian state regimes in the past used the legal arena to suppress independent trade union activity, 'the laws were quite restrictive and protective of labour with regard to the issues of redundancy and layoffs'. Employers could not legally fire workers without cause, nor could they unilaterally downgrade wages and benefits to cut labour costs. To justify their demands for weakened labour rights, employers appealed to the increasingly hegemonic global discourse of 'flexibility'. They emphasized that the elimination of rigid rules and regulations in internal firm labour markets, especially in core sectors of the economy, was necessary for businesses to respond flexibly to the vicissitudes of a highly competitive global economy.

The burgeoning labour movement was somewhat successful in preventing employer-driven attacks, most notably the 1993 proposal for legalization of temporary agency work (*pagyun*), which reflected an authoritarian labour practice that was banned after 1987. Surprisingly, it was not until the installation of the first two civilian presidents in South Korea, both of whom had been well-known activists in the national struggle for democracy during the authoritarian period, that capital was able to institutionalize its demands for a weakened regulatory climate for labour. The first elected civilian president, Kim Young Sam, promoted the sweeping transformation of major institutions, from education to public administration to cultural attitudes, under the banner of *segyehwa* (translated as globalization). *Segyehwa* was aimed at dismantling the legacies of authoritarian dictatorships and catapulting South Korea into 'an advanced country active on the centre stage of world affairs in the 21st century'. South Korea's entry into the Organisation for Economic Cooperation and Development (OECD) was a key component of Kim's nationalist ambitions, and his administration established a Presidential Commission on Labour-Management Relations Reform to facilitate the process. From the standpoint of organized labour, the debates surrounding South Korea's entry into the OECD looked promising for abolishing repressive labour laws linked with authoritarian dictatorships. However, 'as the Commission's deliberations proceeded ... it was the voice of capital and the imperatives of global competition that increasingly held sway' (Koo, 2000: 238). Despite Kim Young Sam's promise to create a 'new industrial relations plan' in line with the protective labour standards of the International Labour Organization (ILO), he attempted to pass eleven new laws to weaken existing wage and employment protections during a secretly convened session of the National Assembly in December 1996.

The democratic labour movement responded by launching the first nationwide General Strike against the implementation of flexible labour law reforms.[4] Although the mass mobilization of both KCTU and FKTU unionists garnered unprecedented international solidarity, the consolidation of a neoliberal democratic regime under the next presidential administration further institutionalized the assault on workers and their collective organizations. In the context of a national emergency under the 'IMF crisis', President Kim Dae Jung passed two of the most significant laws that resulted in the erosion of labour rights once guaranteed under national labour law frameworks. Article 31 of the Labour Standards Act, 'Dismissals for managerial reasons', gave employers the right to lay off workers during periods of economic necessity, and the 'Temporary Agency

Law' allowed companies to hire temporary workers to reduce labour costs and strengthen firm competitiveness. Loan conditionalities attached to the US$57 million that the IMF lent to the South Korean government created the ideal conditions to implement neoliberal structural adjustment policies; however, 'the IMF had an enthusiastic partner in President-elect Kim Dae Jung who asserted that the full liberalization of South Korea's economy and society was both necessary and inevitable for resolving the national crisis and securing its future prosperity' (Crotty and Lee, 2005: 4).

The aftermath of the so-called IMF crisis signalled the full-scale implementation of neoliberal governance in all aspects of employment. Union consent was no longer required in managerial decisions such as hiring and firing and outsourcing. The passage of the Mass Dismissal Law also gave employers the green light to engage in arbitrary dismissals under the guise of 'necessary business restructuring'. The government was a major force behind mandatory lay-offs, ordering businesses to implement 30 per cent workforce reductions, regardless of the firm's economic condition. The state also cracked down on unionists who vehemently opposed mass dismissals, privatization and other components of the state's neoliberal restructuring programme. Militant labour struggles in sectors undergoing economic restructuring (*chaebol*-dominated heavy industries, state-controlled financial, banking and public utilities) were broken up by violent state intervention, including the use of riot police, teargas trucks, water cannons and helicopters to break up the Hyundai Motor Union's strike and the Mando Machinery union strike in 1998, both of which represented some of the first strike actions by protesting unionists against legalized mass dismissals in 1998.

In response to the climate of intensified employer abuse, the KCTU has attempted to re-escalate militant opposition to the deregulation of the labour market. However, the shift from authoritarian developmental regimes to neoliberal democratic regimes has significantly hampered the traditional source of worker power for the Korean democratic labour movement. Whereas militant unionism once exposed the contradiction between state repression and formal democracy, it is now considered a threat to national security and prosperity. Thus, even when democratic administrations invoke similar authoritarian labour practices to suppress militant unionism, such as violent police action against striking unionists, union militancy no longer exposes a contradiction between *de jure* and *de facto* state practices. Union compliance with flexible labour practices is viewed as a critical component of the nation's broader project of economic reform and recovery, especially in the context of the new regulatory climate for labour, which has legalized weakened labour rights protection.

The KCTU's repeated calls for international solidarity against increased police violence and government repression against striking unionists highlight the consequences of this new political climate for the democratic labour movement.[5] Almost every militant strike action by KCTU unionists has elicited police intervention by the state. Striking unionists also face severe punitive consequences such as imprisonment and onerous civil suits filed by employers for loss of profits and the provisional seize of property during strike actions.[6] A telling example of the hostile ideological climate plaguing militant unionists is captured by a quote from the mayor of Pohang the day the Pohang Regional Construction Union ended an 82-day strike against the POSCO corporation. In a 'letter to Pohang citizens', Mayor Park Seung-ho stated, 'The city of Pohang was dealt a crippling blow by the unprecedented strike that has drawn international attention [to] the headquarters of POSCO, which is the backbone industry of Korea. Let's join hands to get rid of [the] stigma as a strike-stricken city and to reinvent the city as a business-friendly place' (*Donga Ilbo* newspaper, 2006).

LABOUR MARKET RESEGMENTATION: GENDER AND THE EXPANSION OF IRREGULAR EMPLOYMENT

In addition to the intensified state of police repression under neoliberal democratic regimes, the KCTU-led democratic labour movement faces another major obstacle in the post-IMF era. Like workers across the world, Korean workers confront the resegmentation of labour markets in conjunction with neoliberal labour flexibility. Based on 2005 figures from the National Statistics Office, we see two major fault lines dividing core and peripheral workers by employment status and gender (see Figure 2.1). The core zone represents 34 per cent of the total workforce employed in regular, full-time employment workers, and male workers constitute 69 per cent of this total workforce. The peripheral zones represent 58 per cent of the total workforce employed in more unstable forms of irregular employment that are often outside the purview of basic rights and protections afforded to regularly employed workers. Female workers represent a higher proportion in both the first peripheral zone of temporary and daily workers (53 per cent) and the second peripheral zone of self-employed and unpaid family workers (47 per cent). While the unemployed population represents

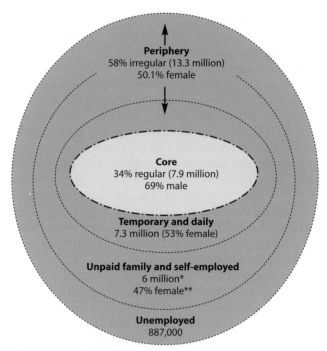

Economically active population: 22.85 million
Source; National Statistics Office, Republic of Korea, 2005 figures
*   Self-employed does not include employer category.
**   Gender ratio does not take into account the distinction between more
        conventional understandings of self-employment and informal work, which
        represent a predominantly female population.

Figure 2.1 Resegmentation of the Korean labour market[7]

a small proportion of the periphery, its relatively small size is attributed to the proliferation of workers in peripheral zones of irregular employment, as opposed to new jobs in the core.

Sharpened divisions along employment status and gender are reflected in the shifting boundaries of union membership. Not only did union membership drop to a historic low of 10.3 per cent in 2005, union membership represents a shrinking segment of the workforce at large: regular workers employed in the core zone of relatively privileged and protected employment (see Figure 2.2). If we look at union density in large enterprises (more than 299 employees), whose employees form the majority of the KCTU's membership, union membership increased from 60 per cent in 1989

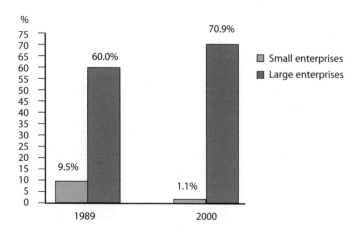

Figure 2.2 Union density, small versus large enterprises, South Korea, 1989 and 2000

to an all-time high of 70.9 per cent in 2000. In contrast, union density in small enterprises (with less than 100 employees) decreased from 9.5 per cent in 1989 to 1.1 per cent in 2000. These figures reveal more stark disparities when we consider the role of large and small enterprises in the labour market. In 2000, small enterprises hired 78.3 per cent of the workforce, in comparison with large enterprises which hired just 8.7 per cent. The increased unionization of workers in large enterprises has also taken place alongside the marked decline of stable, secure, full-time employment, which replicates the narrowing pattern of union membership. Of all wage and salary workers between 1989 and 2002, the proportion of regularly employed workers decreased from 54.76 per cent to 48.39 per cent, while the proportion of irregularly employed workers (temporary and daily workers) increased from 45.24 per cent to 34.45 per cent (see Figure 2.3).[8]

A closer look at the shifting gender composition of union membership over the past two decades highlights the significance of gender as another salient organizing principle of inclusion and exclusion for the labour movement. Unions overwhelmingly represent male workers, which has left female workers vulnerable to unfavourable wage bargains and insecure employment. In 1980, the height of female union membership, 347,751 women (36.68 per cent) belonged to unions while 600,383 men (63.32 per cent) belonged to unions. In 2003, this gap increased considerably, with

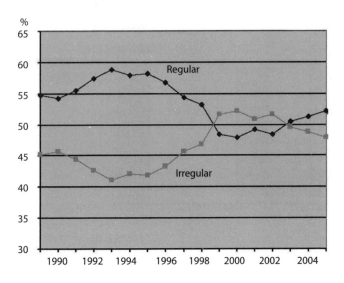

Figure 2.3 Employment status, South Korea, 1989–2005

322,619 women (21.07 per cent) versus 1,222,330 men (78.93 per cent) belonging to unions (see Figure 2.4).[9] While the increased gap between male and female union members since the late 1980s can largely be attributed to the decline of small and medium-sized manufacturing firms, male-dominated trade unions also neglected to address the disproportionate expansion of females in irregular employment. Despite the steady rise in the overall proportion of irregular workers from 1993 to 2005, particularly temporary employment which increased from 26.73 per cent to 33.29 per cent during this period, the proportion of male temporary employees decreased while female temporary employees increased (see Figure 2.5).

OVERCOMING EXCLUSIONARY UNIONISM: ORGANIZING THE PERIPHERY

The division between the core zone of regular employment and the adjacent peripheral zone of irregular employment is fraught with conflict and contestation. Although these tensions reflect deep divisions along employment status and gender, they also have catalyzed new efforts to overcome exclusionary forms of unionism for peripherally-employed groups of workers. These efforts represent two main categories: first, overcoming divisions between regular and

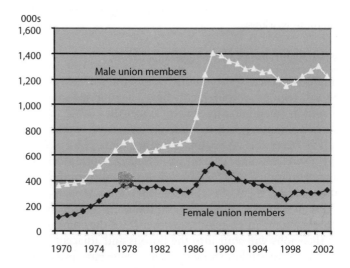

Figure 2.4 Union membership by gender, 1970–2003

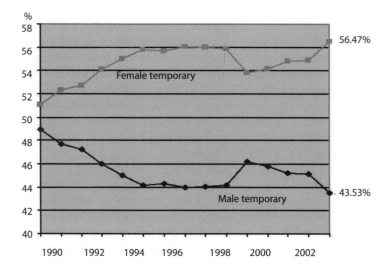

Figure 2.5 Temporary employment by gender, 1989–2003

irregular male workers, and second, overcoming divisions between male and female workers.

Divisions between regular and irregular workers

As I highlighted earlier, some unions representing workers in the core zone of regular employment have maintained and even increased union membership levels since the 1997 national economic crisis.[10] Although this relatively privileged sector of the workforce has been able to maintain higher than average market wages and exercise some degree of influence during collective bargaining negotiations, workers are not insulated from the hostile climate surrounding them. In addition to corporate bankruptcy, plant mergers, workforce reductions and the transfer of managerial rights to foreign companies, regular workers face the constant insecurity that their jobs will shift into the porous and adjacent zone of irregular work. Most studies show that employers have preferred to hire irregular over regular workers since the 1997 economic crisis as a way to reduce labour costs. Increasing wage disparities between regular and irregular workers indicate that employers can hire irregular workers at almost half the price of regular workers, emphasizing the cost advantage of hiring irregular workers. From 2000 to 2005, the wage rate of irregular workers as a proportion of that of regular workers declined from 53.7 per cent to 50.9 per cent. Hiring workers under short-term contracted employment, temporary agency employment, part-time employment and 'special employment' (tooksu goyong), a category similar to status as an independent contractor, allows employers to hire workers under virtually the same working conditions as regular employees (i.e. working hours, workplace supervision), except with no job security and little or no benefits such as paid overtime and paid sick and vacation leave.

The perceived threat of labour cost-cutting and job displacement has exacerbated tensions among KCTU's predominantly regularly employed membership and the growing workforce of irregularly employed workers. In their study of relations between regular and contract workers, Lee and Frenkel (2004) find that contract workers feel stigmatized and demoralized by the exclusionary behaviour and attitudes of regular workers, who exclude contract workers from social activities, blame them for taking jobs at such low pay and deny them resources and protections on the job. A study evaluating union attitudes by regular workers toward contingent or irregular workers, based on a 2002 survey conducted by the Korea Labour Institute (KLI), confirms these findings, high-lighting that the majority of union members and leaders are not willing to act in genuine solidarity with irregular workers, especially if supporting the latter brings about a loss of their own interests. While some union members and leaders indicated that they were willing to address some work-related grievances related to irregular workers, they are much less willing to allow irregular workers to join their organizations as equal members. The persistence of nega-tive attitudes of regular union members versus irregular workers is especially telling, given the strong tendency of employers to hire contingent workers in establishments where the rate of union membership is high and the influence of unions is strong. This finding supports the argument that employers tend to hire irregular workers to cut labour costs as well as weaken the constraints imposed by unions on managerial authority.

The refusal of unions representing regular workers to include irregular workers in their organizations has resulted in major clashes, both between irregular and regular workers in a single workplace and between unions representing regular workers and the leaders of industrial and national labour movement organizations. According to labour scholar Lee Byoung Hoon, these difficulties stem from the authoritarian and patrimonial legacies of the enter-prise union system, which undercut worker solidarity both across and within firms. The case of the Korea Telecom (KT) Contract Workers' Union illustrates the deepening 'solidarity crisis' dividing regularly employed workers from peripherally employed workers in the organized labour movement. From June to November 2000, 7,000 contract workers at KT were issued dismissal notices under a state-initiated effort to privatize public utilities and make its work-force more 'flexible'. KT had already shed 10,000 workers in 1998 through 'voluntary resignations', and the public sector shed 131,000 workers between 1998 and 2000, 11 per cent of the total public sector workforce.[11] Although contract workers were hired on an annual one-year basis, many had worked for the company for as long as ten years and stated that they endured low wages (less than half the average monthly wage of regular, full-time employees), 16-hour work days and the lack of benefits such as paid overtime and paid sick and vacation leave in hopes of securing regular, full-time employment at one of the country's most well-know public compa-nies.[12] According to one worker at the Daegu office, 'For six years, I worked harder than the regular employees, hoping to become one. So, the dismissal felt like a betrayal. Formal employment had been my hope, what I'd given my youth to achieve.'[13] The 'betrayal' by the company was intensified by the subsequent 'betrayal' by regularly employed union members, when the 10,000-member KT union went on strike on 18 December and declared victory against the company a mere three days later, leaving the dismissed contract workers to continue their fight alone.

For the next nine continuous months, contract workers escalated their struggle against KT, forming their own union and continuing their strike. According to union president, Hong Joon Pyo, the strike was a 'fight for their livelihoods', and unionists would not stop before they achieved victory (interview with author, 16 October 2001). The company, however, refused to negotiate with the union and only offered dismissed workers jobs in more insecure employment as independent contractors. Union leaders tried to intensify the stakes of the struggle by staging militant occupations that would draw attention to the desperation and seriousness of their plight: union leaders shaved their heads to symbolize the gravity of their plight, they stormed and occupied the central KT headquarters building, they climbed to the top of a major city bridge on a cold winter day, they camped out in front of the company headquarters in the middle of downtown Seoul. While the extreme militancy of their actions was pivotal in attracting the attention of the broader democratic labour movement to the plight of irregular workers, it also elicited increasing intervention by the state. The militant occupation of the KT company headquarters by 200 unionists ended with a violent crackdown by 600 riot police, and arrest warrants and prison sentences were subsequently issued for union leaders who had engaged in the 'illegal strike'. The KT Contract Workers' Union struggle also had become increasingly isolated from other unionists, particularly other KT workers and the majority of rank-and-file regular workers affiliated with the KCTU. Faced with increasing police repression, little solidarity from other unionists and no legal basis for their claims against the KT management, after 512 continuous days the Korea Telecom Contract Workers' Union ended their struggle with no resolution and dissolved their union.

The KT Contract Workers' Union struggle very publicly exposed the 'solidarity crisis' plaguing the KCTU-led democratic labour movement. One leading activist explained:

> The KT Contract Workers Union was significant politically. It was a fight against restructuring; it was the longest and most brutal of union struggles. Despite these difficulties, the union

members stayed devoted. Through the shear suffering their bodies endured, they awakened the rest of the labour movement to the severity of the issues facing non-standard workers.

(interview with author, 11 August 2003)

The KT Contract Workers' Union struggle, as well as an explosion of struggles by other irregular workers such as private home tutors, golf caddies, janitors, insurance salespersons, subcontracted workers at Halla Heavy Industries and Daewoo Carrier Corporation, and ready-mix concrete truck drivers among others, have laid the basis for an emerging and broader-based movement under the banner of irregular workers. While the KCTU leadership has formally embraced the issue, the thrust of the emerging irregular workers' movement consists of a mixture of rank-and-file leaders of irregular workers' unions, including those that folded after unsuccessful struggles, KCTU union activists that actively supported the struggles of irregular workers' unions, and labour activists that are linked to radical, left-wing labour organizations.

The KCTU Seoul Regional Centre is one hub of the irregular workers' movement. Because many existing unions refuse to allow irregular workers to join, irregular workers' unions began affiliating with regionally based union organizations such as the KCTU Seoul Regional Organization.[14] Since 1998 private home tutors, janitors and other building service workers, hotel workers and broadcast sector workers among others represent the diversifying array of workers that have affiliated with the Seoul Regional Centre by default. The Jaenung Education Corporation Private Home Tutors' Union is one of the KCTU Seoul Regional Centre's most dynamic members. In 1999 2,000 private home tutors formed a separate union for workers classified as 'specially employed workers' (*tooksu goyong*) and launched a series of strikes that secured a historic collective bargaining contract for these workers. Although their union has grown and they have maintained their influence at the bargaining table, they represent the exception, not the rule. Given that most irregular workers face an uphill legal battle for union recognition and possess little to no protection against employer retaliation for union activities, 'one out of every two new unions formed [by irregular workers] fails' (interview with author, 15 September 2001).

Alternative organizations such as Korean Solidarity against Precarious Work (KSPW) have also been established to support the irregular workers' movement. Before the KSPW was established in

2000, founding activists were key supporters of early struggles by irregular workers such as the 1999 struggle by dispatch workers at the KBS Broadcasting Company and the 2000 struggle by janitors at Seoul National University. The mass-based political orientation of left labour activists that founded the KSPW is a crucial element of their support of irregular workers. According to one left activist:

> Trade unions cannot become the kind of organization that just seeks to benefit their own members. Even if they are not members of their trade unions, in our society they have to fight for the issues that affect the entire working class. Concretely, if you think of it this way, what is an issue that affects the entire working class? It is the issue of non-standard workers. Even though they do not work at my workplace, they have no rights, they face much discrimination. We must work together to secure their rights. So, in my opinion, unions have to be the kind of organizations that can understand working class issues broadly.
> (interview with author, 11 August 2003)

As a solidarity organization, the KSPW focuses on worker education and training, research on irregular workers, policy advocacy and legal reform, and direct organizational support of union struggles by irregular workers. It has also played a key role in national campaigns to raise the minimum wage and broaden the focus of the labour movement to include non-union issues that affect the welfare of the working poor and the lives of the expanding periphery of irregular workers.

Divisions between men and women workers

The 1997–98 economic crisis also exacerbated discriminatory employer practices along gender lines. Because of the extreme wage differentials between male and female workers across every category of employment, women workers, who made up a small fraction of KCTU's membership and an even smaller fraction of the leadership, were consistently the target of irregular employment schemes.[15] In companies that were undergoing 'necessary workforce reductions', women workers were encouraged by company managers and union members alike to 'voluntarily' resign and accept re-employment as irregular workers at lower pay and with decreased job security. Although the media and the state emphasized the devastating effects of unemployment on men, particularly fathers, narratives by women workers revealed the disproportionate impact on women. Choi Sang

Rim, a former student activist who worked underground in the labour movement since the mid-1980s and later became the first president of the Korean Women's Trade Union, explained:

> The IMF regime provided a momentum for the change of Korean society as a whole. Without any social safety nets, the changes fell heavily on the society's margins, women. The trends on the informalization of women's work were also found in other countries' cases. However, when introduced, it was graduated or with social safety nets to reduce the total shocks. In the case of South Korea, however, the coercive situation called the IMF made the margins totally absorb the situation. Currently, the rate of non-standard women workers is over 73 per cent. This is nonsense.
>
> (Seo, 2004: 87)

The Korean Women Workers Associations United (KWWAU) attempted to publicize the discriminatory impact on women workers during mass rallies and marches by highlighting the 'women fired first' principle of economic restructuring. However, their efforts were largely ignored by the mass media, the state and unions. Any and all references urging unions to challenge discriminatory hiring and firing practices or address gender-specific grievances were also considered divisive and harmful to the broader unity of the labour movement. This included calls by the growing workforce of non-standard workers, both male and female, to challenge individual unions' role in fuelling the exploitation of non-standard workers. This was the case even in unions dominated by women members. At one union federation where I conducted participant observation between 1998 and 1999, the deputy director of the women workers' division consistently expressed disappointment that the union leadership viewed gender-related worker issues as subordinate and even detrimental to the more urgent struggle against structural adjustment.

In the absence of support by the KCTU and the broader labour movement, women worker activists have emerged as key support actors in the irregular workers' movement. Activists with the KWWAU, many of whom were linked to the women-led, *minjung*-based labour struggles in the 1970s and 1980s, repeatedly discussed the need to organize women outside the KCTU-led democratic labour movement during the 1990s. When the KWWA (Korean Women Workers Association) was first formed in 1987, leaders decided to establish an external support organization, rather than a mass-based popular organization, to allay the fears of male leaders that creating a women-only organization would divide the unity of the broader democratic labour movement. As the KWWA grew to include regional women workers' associations, it united under the umbrella of the KWWAU and engaged in worker education and training, research, policy and legal advocacy to address the intersecting dimensions of gender and labour. Although the women workers' movement identified their work as complementary and advantageous to the struggle for democratic unionism, the consequence of the KCTU-led labour movement's neglect and subordination of women's issues became all too clear. Despite the consolidation of the KCTU into a national centre and its capacity to mobilize hundreds of thousands of workers, rates of union membership among women workers dwindled to a mere 5 per cent and women were largely unprotected from intensified forms of employer abuse and discrimination.

The need to devise alternative organizational forms to strengthen the collective power of women workers sparked internal debate within the women workers' movement. As an NGO (non-governmental organization) not a union, the KWWAU was limited to individual-based advocacy and legal reform. Although grassroots-based counselling and advocacy were crucial for addressing the immediate needs of women workers, these strategies had done little to mitigate the wide-reaching and structural consequences of downgraded women's employment, especially in manufacturing-based regions. The KWWAU's international solidarity networks with organizations such as the Self-Employed Women's Association (SEWA) in India and the Women's Trade Union in Denmark convinced them of the benefits of establishing an autonomous women-only trade union. Internal conflict regarding the potential divisiveness of such actions on the broader labour movement kept these plans in the preparation phase; however, the onset of the IMF crisis in late 1997–98 changed the tenor of this debate. In 1999, the National Women's Trade Union (KWTU) was officially inaugurated as well as two other women's unions, the Seoul Women's Trade Union and the National Federation of Women's Trade Unions affiliated with the KCTU.

All three unions were formed as a 'definite and immediate reaction to the economic crisis and the neo-liberal restructuring which [had] thrown women workers out onto the streets and impoverished them' (PICIS, 2001). Women worker activists were also 'particularly motivated to install independent women's labour organizations separate from male-dominated labour unions and male-cantered labour organizations'. All three women's trade unions believed that existing unions – the vast majority of which were male-dominated in leadership and union priorities – were ill-equipped to protect the needs and concerns of the vast majority of women workers employed as non-standard workers. In many cases, unions themselves were responsible for the degraded employment of women workers. Unions also refused to adapt their organizational tactics and strategies to fit the lives and concerns of women workers, particularly married women workers. All three unions also recognized that organizing women workers required paying attention to gendered forms of discrimination and oppression in the workplace such as a the gender gap in wages, sexual harassment and violence, and the need for alternative union strategies to build the leadership of workers whose responsibilities were consumed by work inside and outside the home. According to KWTU president Choi Sang Lim, 'in order to organize women workers, we need a trade union model that takes into account the needs of women workers, such as maternity protection, juggling of work and family, and relationship-oriented interaction at work' (interview with author, 21 November 2002).

Although the predominantly male leadership of the KCTU largely resisted the formation of independent women's trade unions, women's trade unions, especially the KWTU, have demonstrated the success and necessity of their approach. One leader of the KWTU recalled:

> When they heard that KWWAU was forming a women's trade union, they criticized and scoffed, 'Maybe we should also make a men's trade union.' They did not acknowledge how much women are excluded within the labour movement and how much women are victims from restructuring policies that prioritize men. And actually, from what I remember, all the male unionists I knew opposed the creation of a separate women's trade union. They had absolutely no awareness around this issue. So, there was a lot of conflict and tension. Of course, now, they can't really say anything.
>
> (interview with author, 15 October 2003)

Because of its historical and organizational legacies, the KWTU has experienced the most effectiveness in terms of scale and scope. The

KWWAU's existing national infrastructure, which included branch offices in ten metropolitan regions (Seoul, Incheon, Pusan, Kwangju, Buchon, Ansan-Siheung, Masan-Changwon, Oksan, Chonju and Taegu) provided a ready-made infrastructure upon which to expand its union membership. In the first year, the union gained approximately 1,000 members and organized four local divisions – a union for golf game assistants at the 88 Country Club, cooks at Kyeongsang University, broadcast company media editors and part-time workers at Daewoo Heavy Industries. KWTU's emphasis on organizing women workers who are not covered by existing unions has also proved that some of the most vulnerable workers can, in fact, be organized. As most women in Korea are employed in the informal sector and under irregular contracts, they are often not covered by existing labour legislation or trade unions. However, during its first year, 80 per cent of the total members of the union represented non-standard workers and 70 per cent were married women in their 30s and 40s. These figures matched the current reality of women workers (64 per cent work in companies with less than five workers and over 70 per cent are non-standard). 'By actually expanding the labour movement and securing the constitutional right of workers to unite, the Korean Women's Trade Union is making significant strides in building a model of trade union organization for unorganized workers, which is a major task of the Korean labour movement' (Choi, 2000: 111). By 2005, the KWTU had grown to over 4,000 members and included members from a wide variety of sectors including the service, manufacturing and clerical sectors.[16]

CONCLUSION: THE FRICTION OF NEW DIRECTIONS

Contestation over major fault lines along employment status and gender has played a crucial role in revitalizing the broader labour movement. While I do not discount the very real and distinct ideological differences that distinguish the women workers' movement from militant factions of the democratic labour movement, frictions between regular and irregular workers as well as men and women have called attention to the exclusionary practices of the KCTU-led trade union movement and created pressures upon the leadership to renew its democratic commitment to represent the workforce at large. Left labour activists and women worker activists also provide a crucial source of support for irregular workers who are attempting to organize unions and secure collective bargaining agreements in the face of legal obstacles and employer hostility.

The forces fuelling the revitalization of the Korean labour movement reveal the significance of recognizing how global economic
forces associated with the disintegration of trade union movements
are also operating to revitalize their democratic character. In the
South Korean case, although the drive to implement neoliberal
labour flexibility has severely undermined the legitimacy and
leverage of union militancy – which is its historical source of power
– it has also exposed the uneven terrain upon which labour flexibility is carried out. While existing differences in the labour market
along gender and employment lines form the basis of an expanding
periphery of lower-paid, more insecure and socially marginal
workers, they also generate new frictions that are resulting in new
strategies and institutional forms to organize peripherally employed
workers. Thus, rather than view frictions as splintering sources of
unity and strength for the labour movement, the South Korean case
highlights the importance of recognizing the possibilities and new
directions that result from shifting lines of inclusion and exclusion
under processes of globalization.

NOTES

1   There are a myriad of terms to describe the array of insecure forms of
    non-standard employment, including 'casual', 'contingent' and 'tempo-
    rary'. For the purposes of this chapter, which address the issue of non-
    standard employment in South Korea, I shall use the term 'irregular' to
    refer to the Korean term *bi jong gyu jik*.
2   Rising real wages of workers in small and medium-sized labour-inten-
    sive manufacturing firms destabilized the low-cost advantage they
    gained from the 'cheap' labour force, and capital began fleeing en
    masse from South Korea's export-processing zones (see Kim, H.-M.,
    1997 and 1998; Kim, S.-K., 1996 and 1997).
3   Employers also introduced 'automation and rationalization technology
    to their workplaces' to reorganize production processes in line with
    flexible management schemes, and advocated new wage payment poli-
    cies that delinked job security and wage levels from internal labour
    markets (see Koo, 2000 and 2002).
4   KCTU responded by organizing the largest general strike in the nation's
    contemporary history. 400,000 workers from 528 different KCTU-
    affiliated unions participated in the one-month nationwide strike, and
    at its height, participation levels reached 1 million workers, which
    represented the first time that KCTU and FKTU went on strike
    together.
5   See calls for international solidarity on the KCTU website at
    http://kctu.org/; accessed 30 October 2006.
6   This tactic has led desperate unionists such as the branch president of

Hanjin Heavy Industries, Kim Joo-ik, to immolate himself in protest at the untenable fines that force workers as well as their friends and family into bankruptcy (KCTU, 2005).

7   This diagram is adapted from the model on the 'Flexible worlds of work' in Holdt and Webster (2006: 6). Like South Africa, where only 6.6 out of 20.3 million workers are employed as full-time workers, the core zone of relatively protected and privileged workers in South Korea also constitutes less than one-third of the economically active population. However, the size of the unemployed population is considerably smaller in South Korea, 979,000 versus 8.4 million in South Africa, making the irregular and peripheral zones a more significant and dynamic component of the flexible world of work.

8   Figures from National Statistics Office. Table: Employed persons by status of worker by gender.

9   Figures from National Statistics Office. Table: Labour unions and unionized members by gender.

10   In a study of five firms in the metal sector, the largest union grew from 34,829 members in 1997 to 37,625 members in 2001. The next two largest unions roughly maintained union membership levels over this five-year period, growing nominally from 11,413 to 11,494 and declining nominally from 20,936 to 20,859 (Jeong, 2005: 50).

11   Figures from 2002 report by the Korean Federation of Transportation, Public, and Social Service Union.

12   Contract workers mainly represented two groups of workers: 1) male workers that installed and repaired telephone and ADSL lines and 2) female workers that operated 114 telephone directory assistance.

13   J.W. Kim, six years, KT Daegu office. Quoted from Labour News Production feature documentary, *Friend or Foe*.

14   In the late 1980s, regional workers' centres represented the centre of radical organizing efforts by newly formed democratic unions (*minju nojo*) to overcome the constraints of enterprise unionism. As more local unions affiliated with industry-based national federations and more radical regional centres were suppressed by the state, regional centres mainly focused on addressing the grievances of non-union workers and other workers who 'slipped through the cracks' (interview with author, 1 October 2001).

15   If employers hire an irregular worker, they will pay only 52.6 per cent of the average monthly wage of a regular worker. If employers hire an irregular female worker, they will pay only 42.7 per cent of the average wage. This is the case in every employment category, where hiring female workers will reduce wage costs from between one-third and over two-thirds of what it costs to employ male workers.

16   For a more comprehensive analysis of specific cases of union organizing, see Chun (2005 and 2006).

Chapter 3

Globalization and the informalization of labour: the case of South Africa

Devan Pillay

INTRODUCTION

After a protracted struggle characterized by internal mobilization, armed activity and international pressure, South Africa finally achieved political democracy in 1994. This democracy in many ways reflects the balance of forces operating at the global level during the past two decades, where the neoliberal globalization of capital has placed the working class on the defensive. While the South African constitution is one of the most advanced and demo-cratic in the world, many of the rights enshrined in it cannot fully be exercised by vast layers of society who are either unemployed or part of the working poor.

This chapter examines the manner in which South Africa's 'double transition' to political democracy and a globalized, open economy (Webster and Adler, 1999) has affected the working class, broadly defined. While 'socialism' struggles to reassert itself on the national agenda, what options are available to one of the most well-organized labour movements in the developing world, led by the Congress of South African Trade Unions (COSATU), to stem the tide of informal-ization of labour, high unemployment, persistent poverty and growing social inequality that has characterized this transition?

THE TRANSITION TO DEMOCRACY IN SOUTH AFRICA

During the struggle against apartheid, two models of democracy competed for dominance within and outside the liberation move-ment. This included on the one hand a liberal, procedural form of representative democracy that facilitates elite rule and economic growth through private enterprise (Van Zyl Slabbert, 1992), and on the other hand a more radical, substantive model of participatory democracy that incorporates liberal freedoms, but also places emphasis on the equitable distribution of economic surplus through substantial state intervention (Habib, Pillay and Desai, 1998).[1]

During the height of the mobilization against apartheid in the late 1980s, the notion of 'people power' became widespread, as activists within the country dreamt of a new order where 'the people' in a deep sense would exercise power over their daily lives. These notions were in part inspired by an idealization of 'socialist' practice in 'actually existing' socialist countries, as well as revolutionary regimes such as the Sandinistas in Nicaragua, where the state was imagined to embody the will of the people, and supposedly acted in the interests of the entire population. They were, however, also inspired by the new discourse of civil society empowerment – particularly workers' power on the shop floor, street or neighbourhood committees in the townships, the rise of new social movements around the world and the rediscovered writings of Italian Marxist Antonio Gramsci, which provided theoretical tools within the Marxist tradition to challenge the statist Soviet Marxism that was dominant until the 1970s (Pillay, 1989 and 1996).

A key influence in the early 1970s, especially amongst intellectual activists in the re-emerging trade union movement, was Rick Turner's *The Eye of the Needle* (1972) – a radical democratic alternative to the vanguardist notions of 'democratic centralism' promoted by the Soviet-aligned South African Communist Party (SACP) in exile (SACP, 1962).

In its best sense, a vanguard party is meant to facilitate and coordinate a high degree of popular participation in public affairs (Gramsci, 1919/1980; Luxemburg, 1906/1925). This means combining centralism with maximum participation and decentralization, a practice that it arguably best approximated today by the Communist Party of India (Marxist)'s performance in Kerala, India (Heller, 1999; Williams, 2002).

The notion of vanguardism,[2] however, refers to the degenerative practice of Stalinist 'actually existing socialism', which subordinated all participatory initiatives to the iron rule of the party and/or its leader (Bienkowski, 1981). In this practice trade unions are mere transmission belts relaying instructions from party to workers. Democratic centralism, however, was not confined to Leninist parties, but was also practised by a range of other types of parties, including African nationalists such as the African National Congress (ANC), which had a close, interlocking alliance with the SACP. The conditions of exile imposed a centralist imperative on the illegal organizations which to some extent seeped into the post-1970s legal mass formations, to compete with more participatory styles of organization.

Because the liberation movements did not seize power as some had hoped (SACP, 1989), the socialist visions had to be tempered by the new reality of a negotiated settlement. By the early 1990s the competing notions of democracy and organization had for many activists crystallized into a conception of a strong, interventionist developmental state and a strong, self-activated civil society dominated by organizations representing the working class in its broadest sense (including the unemployed, students from working-class families and the rural poor) (Mayekiso, 1992; Friedman, 1992; Swilling, 1992; Ginsberg et al., 1995).

The stalemate between the liberation movements and the apartheid regime brought a negotiated settlement that has simultaneously transformed the sociopolitical landscape and preserved key features of the old order. Soon after the ANC came into office, it further entrenched procedural liberal democracy, albeit with some participatory features. The Keynesian proposals which were promoted by COSATU and the SACP were ignored by the ANC, with strong suspicions of International Monetary Fund (IMF) and World Bank influence in the background (Bond, 2005). By 1996 the government unilaterally adopted the Growth, Employment and Redistribution (Gear) macro-economic framework, which contained many classic neoliberal features, such as reduced fiscal deficit, inflation-targeting, tax reductions, privatization, trade liberalization and export-led growth (Marais, 2001).

Social democratic impulses were not entirely squashed in favour of neoliberalism, as the new state navigated choppy waters containing both currents (Hirsch, 2005). By 2004–05 the ANC began talking more explicitly about building a 'developmental state' (Southall, 2006), which culminated in the launch of government's Accelerated Shared Growth Initiative (Asgisa) in late 2005.

Many doubt whether the 'developmental state' discourse of government is being translated into meaningful practice, given the continued adherence to key neoliberal macro-economic principles, as well as a reluctance to forge deep state–society synergies that underpin a developmental state (Friedman, 2005). The constraints of global competition and the perceived need to attract foreign investment as a top priority have ensured a schizophrenic and incoherent policy environment.

While the capitalist class has retained its hegemonic position in society, this has not occurred without a struggle from below. Labour, while on the retreat in many ways, has claimed some success in forcing the limited shift of government away from its move overt flirtation with neoliberal orthodoxy since 1994, and remains a countervailing force of some significance. Nevertheless, in the context of capital restructuring globally and nationally, the labour movement in South Africa faces significant challenges.

THE REORGANIZATION OF LABOUR

The South African economy since 1994 has followed global trends of jobless growth due to labour-saving technology, increased unemployment, increased informalization of labour and increased social inequality. Given the unreliability of official statistics, the precise nature of this phenomenon is subject to much debate. The current view is that while there has been job growth since 1994, much of this has been of poor quality, and has not been nearly enough to absorb the large number of new entrants into the job market every year.

Official statistics shows an increase of jobs to 12.3 million in September 2005, which is an increase of 100,000 jobs since 2001, and of 2.8 million since 1994 (see Table 3.1). Nevertheless, although economic growth has not been entirely 'jobless growth', with over 5 million new entrants into the job market, the level of unemployment has increased during this period. According to Stats SA, the number of jobless, using a narrow definition that excludes those too discouraged to seek work, has increased from 16.9 per cent of the workforce (approximately 2 million people) in 1995 to 26.7 per cent (4.5 million people) in September 2005. Using an expanded definition, close to 8 million people (38.8 per cent) were jobless in 2005,

Table 3.1 Employment and unemployment in South Africa, 1995–2005

	1995	2000	2005
Employment (millions)	9.5	12.2	12.3
Unemployment: narrow definition (excluding discouraged work-seekers)	16.9%	25.8%	26.7%
Unemployment: broad definition (including discouraged work-seekers)	26.5%	35.9%	38.8%

Sources: Stats SA (2006), Altman (2005).

out of a potential labour force of close to 20.1 million (Stats SA, 2006). Since 2003 Stats SA has stopped using the expanded definition of unemployment, arguing that it is unreliable, and the official unemployment rate in September 2005 stood at 26.7 per cent (or 4.5 million people) (Stats SA, 2005).

South Africa has a total population of around 44 million people, with 29.7 million between the ages of 15 and 65 (an increase of 1.9 million since 2000). Of those, a little under 13 million of working age (between 15 and 65) are considered to be not economically active, including full-time scholars, full-time homemakers, the disabled or chronically ill and the retired.

As Table 3.2 shows, almost half of the employed are in the services and trade industries, with 40 per cent of trade workers (1.2 million) in the informal sector. Manufacturing is only the third largest employer with 1.7 million workers, although this is up from 1.5 million in 2000. This is followed by financial services, construction, agriculture and transport. The mining industry, once the dominant sector of the economy, occupies eighth place.

Between 2000 and 2005, there was a net increase of 403,000 jobs. However, because of a massive decline of 927,000 agricultural jobs during this period,[3] a clearer picture emerges if agriculture is excluded. Of the 1,326,000 non-agricultural jobs created, 896,000 were in the formal sector (a 12.6 per cent increase), and 430,000 were in the informal sector (an increase of 21.2 per cent). During 2004–05, of the 658,000 jobs created, 516,000 were in the informal sector (mainly trade and services). This indicates a growing trend towards the informalization of work.

By 'informal' Stats SA means small businesses that are not registered, and are 'run from homes, street pavements or other informal arrangements' (2005: xxiv). This includes self-employed workers, and dependent producers such as home workers. This does not include 'informal' wage labour within formal, registered businesses (but with no or unstable contracts), such as subcontracted, casual, temporary, seasonal and part-time labour. This wider definition of informal work constitutes a secondary labour market 'disproportionately constituted by women' (Lund and Skinner, 1999) and makes up more than the 3.7 million workers identified as 'informal' and 'domestic' in Table 3.2.[4]

In other words, while official statistics show that in September 2005, of the 12.3 million employed 8.6 million (70 per cent) are in the formal sector, it does not show that a rising proportionate of formal sector workers have become 'informalized'.

Table 3.2 Employment by industry in South Africa, September 2000 and September 2005 (in thousands)

	Formal 2000	Formal 2005	Informal 2000	Informal 2005	Domestic 2000	Domestic 2005	Total* 2000	Total* 2005
Services	1,880	1,972	359	423	930	859	3,169	3,260
Trade	1,440	1,805	982	1,204			2,422	3,024
Manufacturing	1,311	1,442	237	255			1,548	1,706
Finance	907	1,217	50	74			957	1,296
Construction	372	580	273	346			655	935
Agriculture	769	579	1,076	339			1,845	918
Transport	455	457	106	155			461	616
Mining	586	409	3	2			589	411
Utilities	91	98	1	2			92	100
Unspecified/Other	50	9	12	1			62	29
Total	**7,161**	**8,568**	**3,099**	**2,801**	**930**	**859**	**11,898**	**12,295**
Increase/decrease		+706		-307		-71		+403
		(+9.0%)		(-10%)		(-7.6%)		(+3.4%)
Total								
(excl agriculture)	**6,392**	**7,987**	**2,023**	**2,462**			**10,053**	**11,376**
Increase/decrease		+896		+430				+1,326
		(+12.6%)		(21.2%)				(+13.2%)

Sources: Stats SA (2005, 2006).
* 2000 totals own calculation; 2005 totals as they appear in Stats SA (totals do not add up perfectly).

Between 1995 and 2000 almost 200,000 jobs were lost in the public sector, following international trends towards downsizing and outsourcing (Naidoo, 2003). At least 20,000 of these have been in the telecommunications sector, where the parastatal Telkom was preparing itself for privatization. Major job losses since 1994 were recorded in the mining sector, especially gold mining, and manufacturing sectors such as clothing, leather and textiles. These sectors also experienced a rise in subcontracted and informalized labour (Bezuidenhout and Kenny, 2002; Mosoeta, 2001). Many former garment workers have been engaged as subcontracted home workers at similar levels of income, but without medical and pension benefits. The retail sector has also resorted to increased casualization of employment (Kenny, 2003). While there are as yet no figures available for the total impact of flexible labour in the different sectors, indications are that, in the retail sector, casual workers comprise at least 20 per cent of all employment. In construction, casual labour can be as high as 60–80 per cent. Some sectors, such as finance and the IT sector, also experience high levels of subcontracting, but at the high skills end of the employment ladder, where employees' bargaining power may make non-typical work preferable for them.

A study by the COSATU-aligned National Labour and Economic Development Institute (Naledi) shows high rates of atypical employment in the metal and engineering industry, one of the biggest manufacturing sectors. While atypical work constitutes only about 15 per cent of total employment in this industry, casual labour in one subsector has increased by 272 per cent between 1999 and 2002, temporary labour by 41 per cent and sub-contracted labour by 322 per cent (Naidoo, 2003).

As Theron and Godfrey (2000) argue, peripheral or atypical employment is on the rise, and there is a real danger that formal, stable employment will become the exception rather than the norm. This is especially so if the government gives in to increased demands by employers and opposition politicians for greater labour market flexibility, which means further entrenching what is already a *de facto* two-tier labour market, with a second tier of relatively unregulated, cheap employment.

Von Holdt and Webster (2005) characterize the reorganization of the labour force into three spheres of work, namely the core consisting of full-time workers with secure contracts, the non-core consisting of outsourced, temporary, part-time and domestic workers, and the periphery consisting of the informal sector (inner periphery) and the unemployed (outer periphery). Another way of dividing the workforce is by using the terms formal, semi-formal and informal, with the unemployed being a fourth category. Table 3.3 shows the proportion of workers in each category based on 2003 and 2004 figures compiled by Von Holdt and Webster (2005: 28).[5]

At present workers in the formal sector mostly have secure employment (6.6 million or 68–74 per cent of all formal sector workers). Insecure workers in the formal sector amount to 3.1 million, which includes 847,000 domestic workers. The informal sector comprises a further 2.2 million people, which means that workers with secure jobs comprise just over half of all employed workers.

THE PERSISTENCE OF POVERTY AND RISING INEQUALITY

A debate continues to rage about the extent to which poverty persists, and inequality has increased. Part of this relates to the lack

Table 3.3 South Africa's economically active population: formal, semi-formal and informal, 2003–04

	Millions	% of formal sector	% of employed	% of economically active
Formal	6.6	74 (68)*	55.4	32.5
Semi-formal includes domestic workers)	3.1	26 (32)*	26	15.2
Informal	2.2		18.5	10.8
Total employed	11.9		100	58.6
Unemployed	8.4			41.4
Total economically active	20.3			100

Adapted from: Von Holdt and Webster (2005: 28).
*Formal sector excluding domestic workers

of consistent statistics, and differing definitions of what constitutes 'poverty'.

Government claims that more recent statistics show that, despite persistently high unemployment, the poor have benefited from an increased social wage, in the form of improved access to housing, piped water and electricity, in addition to an increase in social grants from R10 billion in 1994 to R55 billion in 2005. Public works programmes have also provided 223,400 temporary jobs to the value of R838 million over five years. Government concedes that inequality is 'rather too high', but insists that poverty has declined from 18.5 million people in 2000 to 15.4 million in 2004 (*Sunday Independent*, 20 August 2006: 9).

COSATU, by contrast, insists that, after 12 years of democracy, poverty levels have not dropped, and social inequality is rising rapidly. COSATU's discussion document *Possibilities for Social Change* (2006c) surveys the latest research on poverty and inequality, and concludes that workers' share of the national income has declined, while profits have increased. In other words, even those with jobs have experienced declining real incomes. The South African Institute of Race Relations uses a poverty level of R3,000 per household, while former COSATU economist Neva Makgetla (*Business Day*, 2 June 2006), uses a lower poverty line (US$2 per person a day, or R1,500 per month). According to the

Labour Force Survey, 17 per cent of all workers earn less than R500 a month, a third less than R1,000 a month and about 60 per cent earn less than R2,500 a month (COSATU, 2006c: 2). These are what COSATU calls the working poor, and stands in contrast to the R56 million the CEO of national supermarket chain Shoprite-Checkers earned in 2005.

COSATU's discussion document puts poverty as whole at between 40 per cent and 50 per cent of the population, saying that 'poverty probably increased between 1996 and 2001, but declined marginally thereafter' (2006c: 2). This marginal decline can be attributed to increased social spending since 2000, particularly in the form of social grants. About 40 per cent of households now get child support, old age pensions and disability grants – but at a very low level.

Crime and HIV-AIDS have ravaged the population, with a dramatic increase in the number of deaths amongst young adults. In 1997, says the Secretariat Report, 'most adults in South Africa died when they were over 60. By 2000 most adults were dying in their 20s, 30s and 40s' (COSATU, 2006a: 127). This reflects a major social crisis facing the country.

Independent researchers confirm this picture of persistent poverty and rising inequality, despite some progress in service delivery. These include the 2004/05 South Africa Survey published by the liberal SA Institute of Race Relations (SAIRR), and a recent book edited by Haroon Bhorat and Ravi Kanbur (formerly of the World Bank), which concludes that despite 'widened access to assets and basic services for poor households', and declining rural poverty as a result of rural–urban migration, there is 'an increase in both absolute and relative income poverty', an 'increase in income inequality' and, despite some employment growth, increased unemployment rates due to a rapidly expanding labour force (2006: 33).

While white privilege has remained largely intact (notwithstanding a small rise in poverty amongst white people), affirmative action and black economic empowerment has allowed a few black people to rise up the socio-economic ladder. These include some formal workers, the main constituency of the trade union movement. A recent survey of COSATU members indicates that, by and large, they are satisfied with government performance. Where they are not satisfied, especially regarding service delivery at local level, they blame corrupt or inefficient local government, and not the national government (Pillay, 2006). This seems to accord with a shift in union membership, from unskilled and semi-skilled manufacturing and mining workers, which formed the core of COSATU in

1985, towards better educated workers, particularly from the public sector, who now dominate the federation (Buhlungu, 2006).

This raises the question, is the trade union movement, as COSATU claims, still mainly representative of the 'working poor', or is it increasingly becoming representative of a 'labour aristocracy' of formal, core workers representing less than a third of the labour force? Do they have an interest in organizing the semi-formal, informal and unemployed sections of the working class?

UNION RESPONSES TO THE CHALLENGES

The most viable organization of the working class remains COSATU. Born in 1985 after the re-emergence of union organization for black workers in the early 1970s, COSATU embodies two traditions of popular resistance: on the one hand, the dominant ANC/SACP tradition of non-racial 'revolutionary nationalism' or 'populism' that places emphasis on cross-class solidarity through 'the people', and on the other hand the 'workerist' tradition oriented primarily towards class solidarity against capitalist exploitation. While the former placed emphasis on the political struggle against apartheid during the 1980s, the latter was more concerned about building strong shop-floor-based organizations based on worker leadership.

By 1985 these distinctions began to blur, leading to the formation of the largest union federation in South African history, with approximately 500,000 members. This grew rapidly, through recruitment, new affiliations and mergers, to 1.8 million members in 2003. The largest unions were the National Union of Mineworkers (NUM) and the National Union of Metalworkers of SA (Numsa), leading representatives of the 'populist' and 'workerist' traditions respectively. While both these unions experienced declining membership during the 1990s, a major area of union growth has been the public sector, where union organization was effectively prohibited under apartheid. The largest public sector union is the National Education, Health and Allied Union (Nehawu).

Total union density[6] steadily increased from 15.4 per cent (702,000 workers) in 1979 to 27.6 per cent (1.4 million workers) in 1985. It reached a peak of 57 per cent (2.9 million workers) in 1992, before dipping and then rising to 57.5 per cent (over 3 million) in 1996. In 2006 union membership is estimated to be around 2.7 million workers, or 34 per cent of all 'organizable' workers.

While COSATU is clearly the dominant union federation, organizing around two-thirds of all union members, its membership has declined from a peak of 1.8 million in 2003 to 1.75 million in 2006.

Table 3.4 Union density and COSATU presence, 2005

Total employed (including informal sector and domestic work)	12.3 million	
Total employed in formal sector (including vulnerable or semi-formal workers but excluding domestic workers)	8.6 million	70% of total employed
Total employed in 'organizable' formal sector (i.e. excluding agricultural and domestic workers)	7.9 million	64% of total employed
Total unionized (approx)	2.7 million	22% of total employed
Union density (% of organized workers within 'organizable' formal sector)		34%
COSATU members		1.75 million
Percentage of all employed		14.2%
Percentage of 'organizable' formal sector workers		22%
Percentage of unionized workers		65%

Note: percentages have been rounded off.
Sources: Stats SA (2006); COSATU (2006a).

Other federations include the Federation of Unions of South Africa (Fedusa), organizing mainly white-collar workers, with a members of around 500,000. The National Council of Trade Unions (Nactu) claims of a membership of 350,000, but its real membership is probably a third of that. In 2003 a new federation grouping a range of unaffiliated unions, the Confederation of South African Workers' Unions (Consawu) was formed. These three federations are meant to merge to form a super union to rival COSATU, but this seems unlikely to materialize, given dissension in their ranks, partly over disputed membership figures. A third force within the union movement is Solidarity, a mainly white union with racist origins, but which is now trying to reinvent itself. These unions and a number of small unaffiliated unions organize the approximately 1 million non-COSATU union members.

With a union density of only 34 per cent, COSATU affiliates have an enormous challenge organizing the unorganized. This has been on the agenda of the federation, which launched a recruitment drive in 2005. However, only a few affiliates in the textiles, mining, police and prisons and chemical sectors have made some advances (COSATU, 2006b). The COSATU leadership has complained bitterly about the lack of commitment from affiliates to organize the unorganized and grow the federation's membership to its target of 4 million workers (COSATU, 2005).

The main areas of membership decline in recent years have occurred in the metal, mining and clothing and textile industries – sectors facing increased subcontracting and casualization of work. COSATU does not seem to have found a way to successfully recruit 'atypical' or vulnerable workers, many of whom are women. Continued male domination of the union leadership may be a factor, alongside serious financial, administrative and organizational challenges which have necessitated cutbacks in union activities. Another factor is a management strategy of bypassing the union through 'teamwork' strategies, or tempting union leaders with offers of promotion. Some unionists seem also concerned about the 'informalization' of their membership, and are thus reluctant to recruit within this sector (Naidoo, 2003; Horn, 2003).

COSATU rejects the allegation that it represents a new 'labour aristocracy' of core workers which for some explains its seeming reluctance to organize semi-formal and informal workers. Its general secretary Zwelinzima Vavi maintains that the bulk of all workers (71 per cent) are employed within the formal sector, in contrast to low-income countries where formal sector workers comprise a small minority of the population. He asserted in 2005:

> This situation means that the unemployed and economically inactive depend primarily on support from formal-sectors .... Most formal workers and even union members do not earn much above the poverty line. Some 40 per cent of union members earn under R2500 per month. Pay and benefits are worse for non-union members, who are found mostly in vulnerable sectors.
>
> (Vavi, 2005: 7)

In this context, Vavi argued that it would be 'suicidal' for the union movement to focus narrowly on formal workers only. It also stands to lose much if unemployment rises, which is why 'COSATU has since its inception tested its policy proposals against the impact on workers and the poor as a whole, rather than considering only its members' (Vavi, 2005: 8).

COSATU played a major role in the establishment of a new order that institutionalizes union participation in a wide range of tripartite and multi-partite bodies at national, provincial and industry levels, giving the union movement a powerful voice in the policy-making process. COSATU has had a major impact on key labour legislation that has given greater protection to permanent workers in the formal sector, although much remains to be done to ensure implementation. COSATU has established a parliamentary office which has given labour a voice in a range of legislative initiatives, and won the right to occupy 50 per cent of the trusteeship of all pension funds. However, this has sapped the energy of the labour movement, and the federation is currently undergoing an organizational renewal process to achieve greater strategic focus (COSATU, 2000, 2006a; Naidoo, 2003).

While COSATU's continued alliance with the ANC and SACP has arguably given it a degree of influence in the ruling ANC, it is very much a junior partner. This is most clearly revealed in the manner in which the government ignored it when it adopted the neoliberal Gear policy in 1996, and the way it has pursued the privatization of key parastatals and partial privatization of basic services such as water provision.

Nevertheless, concerted pressure by COSATU through the National Economic Development and Labour Council (NEDLAC) and other forums, buttressed by mass action, including two anti-privatization strikes in 2001 and 2002, has made government cautious about its privatization plans. While this influence in itself does not necessitate being in an alliance with the ruling party, a key reason for COSATU to remain in the Alliance is the fact that most of its members still support the ANC (Buhlungu, 2006). The conservative attitudes of its members could be altered with a different signal from the leadership, as McKinley argues.[7] However, this seems unlikely to happen in the immediate future as long as key COSATU leaders benefit from the Alliance, particularly as local councillors, and for some as beneficiaries of black economic empowerment (BEE) tenders at local and provincial level. Unionists are prime targets of consortia seeking to boost their BEE profile in order to win contracts.[8]

The 2006 COSATU congress reflected the tensions within COSATU around these issues. A number of resolutions reinvoked the ANC's 1955 Freedom Charter economic clause, downplayed by the ANC in recent years, which calls for the commanding heights of the economy to be nationalized. One resolution, sponsored by

Nehawu, went as far as calling for nationalization of key economic assets and workers' cooperatives as alternatives to BEE, whether 'broad-based' or not. The proposed resolution explicitly described current BEE policies as aiming to 'replace white monopoly capital with a non-racial monopoly capital over a number of years, thus entrenching ownership of wealth of the country in the hands of the few at the expense of the majority'.

The SA Municipal Workers Union (Samwu) and the SA Society of Bank Officials (Sasbo) supported the withdrawal of an alternative resolution emphasizing racial, as opposed to class, inequalities. This resolution, sponsored by the formerly left-wing Numsa and the SA Clothing and Textile Workers Union (Sactwu), both of whom have investment arms, called for the retention of a broad-based BEE strategy, but with more safeguards against workers' exploitation. A compromise was reached whereby a 2003 resolution on BEE would be amended to reflect these concerns, while the resolution on nationalization was adopted separately.

COSATU was clearly not in a position to abandon BEE completely. Indeed, many affiliates' investment companies are involved in BEE deals, as well as individual union leaders at various levels. This underlined the persistent schizophrenia over COSATU's socialist goals, and its compromises with capitalism. However, if BEE continues to enrich a few individuals, the drift towards more radical socio-economic proposals is likely to continue.

Although COSATU and the SACP are engaged in discussions about their future roles in the Alliance, given their strong critique of the government's 'neoliberal' policies (COSATU, 2006c; SACP, 2006), both realize that breaking away from the Alliance at this stage could mean a dramatic split within COSATU, and within individual affiliates, thus rolling back the tremendous gains in labour organization. Both organizations seem resigned to pinning their hopes on the next ANC leader.

The 2006 COSATU Congress was so distracted by the (temporary) dropping of corruption charges against ANC deputy president Jacob Zuma (the preferred candidate for ANC leader of many in COSATU and the SACP), that it only got through 30 out of 118 resolutions. Key resolutions, including those related to organizational matters, were deferred to the next Central Executive Committee (CEC). In addition, a worrying sign for some delegates was the fact that only a few top officials from most affiliates, particularly the president or general secretary, participated in the debates.

Worker participation, according to one former unionist,[9] seemed to be at its lowest level. Indeed, COSATU's own organizational renewal document points to increased bureaucratization and oligarchy within the federation (2006b).

These constraints have seen little done within COSATU affiliates to carry out the federation's resolution of building membership to 4 million by 2015. While membership had increased slightly by the 2006 Congress (merely catching up on lost ground over the past few years), little has been done to reach out to the more vulnerable sections of the workings class. COSATU affiliates remain largely located amongst permanent, core workers, many of whom earn well above the poverty line of R1,500 per month. Apart from the clothing and textile union, where the median wage is R536 per month, and the metalworkers, for whom it is R1,810 per month, the median wage in all other affiliates ranges from R2,400 to R9,000 per month (COSATU, 2006d: 9). Of course, the median represents the middle wage in each affiliate, and many fall well below that (as mentioned earlier, COSATU believes that up to 40 per cent of its members earn less than R2,500 per month). In other words, COSATU now represents a complex amalgam of the working poor and a rising class of workers that could be regarded as a 'labour aristocracy'. Other union federations are even more located amongst the higher-skilled, better-paid workers. The latter arguably now dominate the decision making of organized labour.

Those in atypical employment, including subcontracted, part-time and casualized labour, as well those in the informal sector and the unemployed, remain substantially out of the unions' orbit. In the context of rising unemployment and informalization of work, this failure will continue to weaken organized labour's ability to represent the broader working class.

As Vavi told the *Sunday Times* (24 September 2006) after the Congress: 'If we don't do organizational development and renewal … in each and every union … if we don't get better coordination and solidarity between permanent workers and casual workers and the unemployment, we are doomed.'

OTHER ORGANIZATIONAL RESPONSES

While organization amongst informalized or flexible workers in the formal sector is not evident in any significant form, revealing 'the limitations of industrial style unionism to deal with flexiworkers' (Webster, 2003), organization within the informal sector is sporadic and embryonic. A study of organizations amongst informal traders in 1999 revealed the existence of 13 located in Johannesburg, Durban, Cape Town, East London and Pretoria, with only four able to produce a constitution, and only one of these, the Self-Employed Women's Union (SEWU), which could be said to be controlled by its members (Lund and Skinner, 1999).

Most of these organizations had a few hundred members, with only six claiming more than 1,000 members. The largest claimed to be the African Council of Hawkers and Informal Business (ACHIB) with 100,000 members throughout the country, although this is disputed. While it did represent members in negotiations with local government, it had a loose male-led organizational structure with no constitution and little evidence of democratic participation. It often adopted reactionary positions against immigrant sellers in the streets, and has formed alliances with the Free Market Foundation. The Jabulani Trading Club claimed 6,000 members, and was closely linked to the traditionalist Inkatha Freedom Party. By 2004 this picture had not changed much (Devenish and Skinner, 2006).

SEWU, with 4,930 members located mainly in Durban but with broadening national reach, was until 2004 the most organized formation within the informal sector, focusing in particular on street traders and home-based workers. Formed in 1994 with the assistance of former COSATU trade unionist Pat Horn, SEWU was modelled on the highly successful Self Employed Women's Association (SEWA) in India (with over 600,000 members it is the largest registered trade union in that country). While SEWU had informal associations with COSATU, and was linked to the University of Natal and the transnational research and advocacy group Women in the Informal Economy: Globalizing and Organizing (WIEGO), it remained politically non-aligned, given the highly charged political environment in KwaZulu-Natal, with ongoing tensions between the ANC and IFP (Webster, 2003).

SEWU defined its members as workers and not embryonic businesswomen because 'they are dependent on their work in order to survive and do not have access to key productive resources'. They are organized along trade union lines with a paid-up membership and an elected, accountable leadership, focused specifically on women given the tendency of men to dominate organizations (Webster, 2003: 6).

SEWU's chief negotiating partner was the city council, with whom it has engaged in several skirmishes over the years. According to former general secretary Pat Horn, in 1995 street vendors won their demand for infrastructure such as shelter, access to water and clean toilets, and later negotiated for child care facilities. They also won a special market for muti traders, and have given members access to skills training (Webster, 2003). In addition, SEWU has played a prominent role in shifting national policy on informal labour, and used its international links to facilitate research on street trade, resulting in the Durban local authority turning to them for assistance with their own policy research (Grest, 2002). Unfortunately, SEWU disbanded in 2004 as a result of internal problems, but hope to re-emerge in a new form (possibly as a new formation within COSATU).

A range of new social movements exist within various communities around the country (Ballard, Habib and Valodia, 2006). These include groups with ANC members, but which are critical of government policy or inaction, such as the Landless Peoples Movement (LPM) fighting for faster land reform, the Treatment Action Campaign (TAC) fighting for faster access to AIDS drugs, and the Basic Income Grant Coalition, which wants government to establish a comprehensive welfare system to address increased poverty. Groups openly hostile to the ANC include the Anti-Privatisation Forum (APF), the Soweto Electricity Crisis Committee (SECC), the Durban Concerned Citizens Group and the Western Cape Anti-Evictions Group. These groups are led by a range of tiny left-wing forces, Trotskyist and non-aligned, that have been historically alienated from the 'Stalinist' SACP. Nevertheless, many have drawn on the support of former ANC members in townships facing electricity and water cutoffs, and intransigent local councillors who seem determined to follow a cost-recovery approach to basic services.

As Ballard and colleagues argue, in contrast to the view from the North which characterizes new social movements as being primarily engaged with identity-based struggles, the social movements in South Africa have shown that 'distributional issues are still central in South Africa. Indeed, a good proportion of the movements emerged as a response to the economic crisis and its manifestations, and they deliberately founded on effecting a redistribution of scarce resources in favour of marginalized communities' (2006: 409). They reached their peak in 2002 with a march of approximately 15,000 people against the UN World Summit on Sustainable Development in Johannesburg. Indeed, for a while new social movements seemed to put up a convincing argument that their consumption-based struggles were now poised to supersede production-focused struggles of the working class, as represented by the union movement. However, the inability of these movements to build durable organizations, in contrast to the union movement, has severely dampened this view. The ANC and SACP moved in to take up issues affecting working-class communities, thus stealing the thunder of these movements, who are now a shadow of their former selves. The one exception is the TAC, which remains a strong movement with good relations with COSATU.

It has become clear amongst the leading cadre within both the new social movements and the union movement that alliances across the production/consumption, formal/informal divides are essential to build a counter-hegemonic movement. The big question is how to make this a reality, given the severe political constraints at play.

CONCLUSION

SEWU, along with its sister organization SEWA in India, has challenged the traditional view still prevalent within the trade union movement that a trade union only exists within the context of an employee and an employer. Instead, argues Pat Horn:

> all trade unionists need to take the struggle back to where the most exploited workers are – the informal economy. They face the challenge of building working class alliances of workers in the formal and informal economies, which should include broad networking, as well as joint campaigns on the ground at a national level, and international solidarity.
>
> (Horn, 2003: 45)

This is the challenge facing organized labour, as it comes to terms with a changing economy and declining membership. While some within the labour movement are beginning to take this challenge seriously (Barchiesi and Bramble, 2003), a long road has to be travelled before innovative solutions are found to surmount the enormous obstacles to organizing informal workers in all their diverse forms. Part of the difficulty within the informal sector relates to a degree of ambiguity amongst informal workers: do they seek the formalization of their work, where they become small entrepreneurs, or do they want to become part of the broader movement of working people (Webster, 2003)?

Nevertheless, the future re-emergence and survival of groups like SEWU depend crucially on their ability to forge alliances with the established labour movement, inasmuch as the labour movement needs to fully recognize its need to embrace semi-formal and informal workers. The key is to recognize that no models exist in the developed world. This is primarily a developing-world phenomenon, and creative solutions have to be found within the developing world. Pat Horn (in Webster, 2003) suggests the following options:

- The scope of trade unions to be broadened to include informal workers.
- Existing union federations could form their own informal sector affiliates.
- A federation of informal sector organizations could be formed separately, and then form an alliance with existing federations.
- Union federations could simply work with informal sector organizations.

At the political level, the 2006 local elections underlined once again that, despite a lower voter turnout, there is no serious electoral challenge to the ANC. Individuals associated with the APF formed Operation Khanyisa to fight a few wards, and were roundly defeated. The ANC will maintain its dominance for a number of years, given its ability, honed in years of exile, to maintain unity within its ranks, despite increased unhappiness within the alliance. Nevertheless, while COSATU will remain in a political alliance with the ANC and SACP for the foreseeable future, it is likely to deepen its social alliances with organizations fighting particular issues, such as the TAC and the BIG (basic income grant) coalition. However, it will continue to distance itself from the groups to its left, like the APF, given the latter's hostility towards the Alliance. COSATU, along with the SACP, has decided that a change of leadership in the ANC at its 2007 Congress (leading to the 2009 national elections) is a key strategic objective. This has dismayed many on the left within and outside the alliance, who feel that the leadership of COSATU and the SACP have squandered an ideal opportunity, giving the social crisis, to galvanize the left into a genuine counter-hegemonic force.

Much depends on whether high unemployment, job insecurity, social inequality and poverty continue to persist, along with renewed privatization, deficient basic services to poor people, and conspicuous consumption by the old and new elite. The ANC is likely to continue with its two-track policy of increased integration into the global economy on the one hand, which includes tariff reductions, fiscal discipline and inflation targeting, while increasing public and social expenditure on the other, as long as revenue continues to grow. In this scenario, the centre will hold, and the Alliance will continue on its rocky path for a number of years to come.

The key to COSATU's influence, whether as part of the Alliance or outside it, remains its ability to organize and build solidarity

across the formal/informal, consumption/production and union/
social movement divides, such that it avoids becoming a labour aristocracy protecting the gains of its core membership. It remains
unclear whether COSATU has the foresight to overcome its various
constraints, and aggressively pursue this strategic objective.

NOTES

1 See Macpherson (1977) for a penetrating critique of western liberal
   democracy, Adler and Webster (1995) for a more extended review and
   critique of transition theory, particularly that of Przeworski (1991),
   and Le Roux (1996) for an overview of theories of the state in the
   context of South Africa's social transformation.
2 Vanguardism, where the revolutionary elite makes decisions on behalf
   of the working and other popular classes, derives from Russian leader
   Lenin's seminal work 'What Is to Be Done' (1902/1970).
3 Due to increased mechanization and displacement of farm labourers by
   white farmers fearful of new legislation securing rights of tenure for
   farmworkers, resulting in increased migration to big-city informal
   settlements.
4 Debbie Budlender puts the figure at 34 per cent in 2002 (*The Informal
   Economy: Statistical data research findings (Country case study: South
   Africa), 2002* cited in Horn, 2003).
5 These figures do not match the latest official figures cited earlier, which
   do not give a breakdown of semi-formal workers. Domestic workers
   are listed as a separate category in the official statistics, and straddle
   the formal/informal sector divide, given the small degree of protection
   they now enjoy under labour legislation, which allows for minimum
   wages to be stipulated. It also uses the expanded definition of unemployment, which includes discouraged work-seekers. Nevertheless, the
   broad trends remain the same.
6 The number of organized workers as a percentage of all 'organizable'
   workers during this period, i.e. excluding the public sector, the military
   and police, agriculture and domestic workers.
7 Interview with former SACP official and APF activist Dale McKinley,
   31 August 2004.
8 Discussion with Dinga Sikwebu, former NUMSA official, 31 May
   2006.
9 Discussion with author during the Congress.

Chapter 4

Globalization and labour in India: emerging challenges and responses

Praveen Jha

INTRODUCTION

The global economic order has been in a state of rapid flux for some time, with far-reaching implications for workers across the world. Various dimensions of the world of work have been overwhelmed by the forces of globalization, often in negative ways, and the socio-economic rights of ordinary citizens have eroded considerably (see the Introduction to this volume).

This chapter attempts to outline a perspective on some of the major challenges confronting workers in India in the current phase of neoliberal globalization. As is well known, the official declaration of the New Economic Policy in July 1991 is generally regarded as the transition from a state-led paradigm of economic transformation to a neoliberal policy regime, although some of the changes towards such a transition were clearly visible in the 1980s. It is not the objective of this paper to map India's journey from dirigisme. There are several accounts in the existing literature that the interested readers may find illuminating (e.g. Bagchi, 2004; Patnaik and Chandrasekhar, 1995; Chandrasekhar and Ghosh, 2002). This chapter charts the difficult situation trade unions face in India today. In the next section a brief overview of the Indian labour market is provided, before the following section outlines the trade union landscape. The conclusion illustrates the difficulties these unions face when confronted with neoliberal restructuring, but also points to examples of new ways of organizing, which provide at least some hope for the future.

THE INDIAN LABOUR MARKET IN HISTORICAL PERSPECTIVE

As is well known, India with a little over a billion people, that is approximately one-sixth of humanity, happens to be the world's second most populous country, and close to 70 per cent of its population currently live in rural areas. According to the standard data sources,[1] about 40 to 45 per cent of the population are categorized as workers, and the worker to population ratio has remained roughly constant since independence. The recorded data on participation of women in the workforce throughout this period has been consistently lower, by close to 20 percentage points, than that of men. The recent official estimates of worker to population ratio for females for the country as a whole are in the range of 25 to 30 per cent, with considerable variations across socio-economic categories, different states, and between urban and rural areas.

The other noteworthy feature is a very high dependence of the country's work force on the agricultural sector. Although the share of agriculture in India's GDP has come down to about a fifth, almost 60 per cent of the workforce, more than half of whom are wage-labourers, continue to depend on this sector. After agriculture, as a broad category, the unorganized/informal[2] non-agricultural sector happens to be the second most important employer, accounting for more than 40 per cent of the workforce and close to 40 per cent of the GDP. The so-called organized or formal sector, the most sought after in terms of remuneration and working conditions, employs less than 10 per cent of the country's workforce while producing about 40 per cent of the GDP. Of the total employment in the organized sector, almost 65 to 70 per cent is in the public sector (including public administration and defence services) and the rest in private corporate manufacturing, services and so on.

Clearly, unlike the expectations of much of the development discourses in the 1950s and 1960s, workforce transformation from agriculture to non-agriculture, in particular to organized modern activities, has been exceedingly slow in India's case, and it remains a major policy challenge. Furthermore, the share of the organized sector in total non-agriculture continues to be quite small, and even declining in recent years. According to information provided by the Ministry of Labour, total employment in the organized sector in 2004 was 26.3 million (17.9 million public and 8.4 million private), down from 28.1 million (19.4 million public and 8.7 million private) in 1999.

Further, there has been a large absolute decline in the number of enterprises that satisfy the minimum criterion to be classed as 'organized'. In 1998, out of a total 30.3 million enterprises, 0.8 million employed ten or more workers. By 2005, although the total number of enterprises had gone up to 42.1 million, the number of those employing ten or more had fallen sharply to 0.6 million. It is also worth noting that only 30 to 35 per cent of the organized sector employment is in the secondary sector, the remaining being almost entirely in the tertiary sector (except for a very small proportion in agricultural plantations). The recent increase in non-agricultural employment, almost about 40 million between 1999 and 2004, has been entirely in the unorganized sectors. Thus, India's labour market is constituted primarily by the unorganized sector, and the small organized segment is like an island in this vast fluid and floating mass of humanity.

For the huge majority of the unorganized workers, adequate and decent employment is a distant dream, as revealed by major indicators of well-being, generated by standard data sources. This sector is largely devoid of any social protection, and not surprisingly, is characterized by poverty on a very large scale. In a recent study for the International Labour Organization (ILO) by Sundaram and Tendulkar (2002), after netting out the unemployed, the number of working poor as on 1 January 1994 was estimated as 133.05 million, or close to 40 per cent of the workforce. One may do well to remember here that poverty in India's official methodology is conceived in the narrowest possible manner, that is, inadequate income to access enough food to generate a benchmark of calories. Close to half the workforce continues to be illiterate, not to speak of other aspects of human capital. Substantial sections of them are footloose, hunting and scrounging for work, often traversing long distances as short-term migrants.

National Sample Survey Organization (NSS) data provides information on the location of work, and it is quite revealing that in 2004–05 about 40 per cent of the urban and close to 60 per cent of the rural non-agricultural workers, as per the UPSS classification in the age group of 15–64 years, did not have a conventional designated place (such as a factory, office or any institution) of work. For female workers, at the all India level, this ratio was much higher, at 70 per cent, compared with 47 per cent for males. Approximately 6 and 8 per cent of rural and urban workers respectively reported 'street' as their location of work.

As is generally agreed, the masses in developing countries, including in India, can hardly afford to remain unemployed. Hence, work they must. If paid work is not available, some kind of self-employment has to be invented. Thus, it is hardly surprising that India's labour market has been characterized by the presence of a very substantial segment being self-employed. However, during much of the period since independence, the share of regular employment in total employment had been declining while that of casual employment had been going up. Hence, on the whole, the share of wage employment had shown a clear, albeit slow, rising trend. The most recent data for the year 2004–05 show that total wage employment has gone down compared with 1999–2000, and the proportion of self-employed has increased significantly.

According to the information pertaining to 2004–05, around half of the workforce in India do not have a direct employer and work for themselves. This is true not only for rural areas, where close to 60 per cent of the workers were self-employed, but also in the urban areas, where the proportion of self-employed was 45 and 48 per cent respectively for males and females. Even in the rural areas, of the total self-employed, almost 40 per cent were in non-agricultural activities. Only a miniscule proportion of the self-employed are at the higher end of skills and earnings whereas the overwhelming majority of them (quite like the wage-employed in casual contracts) work under extremely demanding conditions as they are typically engaged in low-productivity work that generates little remuneration. Nonetheless, in the absence of viable options, a majority of them are forced to be at it on a continuous basis. The 61st round of the NSS (pertaining to 2004–05) indicated that almost 92 per cent of males and 60 per cent of females among the self-employed persons in rural areas reportedly worked seven days a week. Comparable figures for urban areas were close to 95 and 62 per cent.

As should be evident from this brief profile of the structure of India's labour market, the world of work for the overwhelming majority of workers is quite precarious. Furthermore, in spite of a sustained high growth rate of GDP around 5 to 6 per cent per annum since the early 1980s, which in fact has received a further boost in recent years, the story on most of the labour market outcomes during the period of neoliberal economic reforms is quite depressing. For instance, during the 1990s, there was a startling deceleration in employment generation, particularly in the rural areas, but the most recent period for which data is available, between 1999–2000 and 2004–05, there has been a recovery in this respect. However, the reform period as a whole emerges in a much poorer light than the pre-reform decade.

As regards the variables relating to the quality of employment, it is an extremely dismal account, and the rate of growth of secure jobs has been close to zero, if not negative. In terms of returns to labour power, the story is nothing but scandalous, with massive slowing down of the growth of real wages almost all around. For instance, the average real non-agricultural wage rate, according to the NSS data, was almost stagnant between 1999–2000 and 2004–05. In one of most attractive employment options, namely, the organized manufacturing sector, the average real wages in the triennium ending 2003–04 were 11 per cent lower than real wages in the triennium ending 1995–96 (for details, see Ghosh and Chandrasekhar, 2007).

We shall have the occasion later to comment more on the adverse consequences of liberalization on India's labour market. The above remarks, however, are illustrative of the ravages of neoliberal globalization for the country's workers, and indicative of conjunctural difficulties, on top of a structural scenario sketched above, for the prospects of mobilization and collective actions by the working classes to improve their situation and to take the society on a progressive trajectory of transformation. A brief discussion of the trade union movement may be of some interest here to assess the prospects of workers' responses at the current juncture.

TRADE UNIONS IN INDIA: BETWEEN HIGH FRAGMENTATION AND LOW UNIONIZATION

The history of the trade union movement in India goes back to the colonial times, yet its spread and effective sphere of action have largely been confined to the small organized segment of the labour market. On the face of it, this should not come as a surprise, given the overall structure of the labour market and the huge difficulties in making organizational inroads into the informal sector. Nevertheless, this also reflects the obvious handicap/weakness (or whatever else one may call it) of the trade union movement, an issue that many of the unions on the left are acutely aware of and are trying to address nowadays.

Soon after Independence, the All India Trade Union Congress (AITUC), affiliated to the Communist Party of India, and the Indian National Trade Union Congress (INTUC), affiliated to the ruling Congress Party had become the prominent faces of the trade union movement in the country. The new-found glow of independence, a dirigiste regime of economic transformation, the ideas of social justice and welfare state as enshrined in the country's Constitution and the overall Nehruvian ethos of nation building provided a hospitable terrain for a state-led organized sector and the growth of unions in this sector.

As has often been noted, this was a period when public-sector white collar employment as well as public-sector unionism rose phenomenally (e.g. Bhattacherjee, 1999; Thakur, 2007). The number of unions rose from 4,623 in 1951 to 11,614 in 1962, and their membership also trebled during this period. It was a phase when the paternalistic state not only accommodated but appeared to be even encouraging unions, and state intervention in the overall framework for the functioning of unions was a visibly important feature. In several industrial sectors, wage boards were set up and in terms of the overall management of the industrial relations, tripartism (rather than collective bargaining and bipartism) became the norm in a context of centralized bargaining structures. However, beginning with the industrial deceleration and overall economic slowdown in the mid-1960s, the trade union movement started becoming more fragmented and fractious, inter and intra-union rivalries went on an upswing, and centralized bargaining and other industrial relations institutions started feeling the heat of dissent from below. With the division of the Communist Party of India (into the Communist Party of India (CPI) and Communist Party of India (Marxist) – CPI(M)), AITUC was also divided, and the faction aligned to CPI(M), known as the Centre of Indian Trade Unions (CITU) started gaining prominence, along with the Hind Mazdoor Sabha, from the mid-1960s. A number of other national-level unions, aligned with major political parties, started becoming visible in due course.

In general, along with an increase in the number of national unions, the trend towards a weakening of the power of such unions, and a proliferation of unaffiliated and 'independent' trade unions, became noticeable features from the 1970s. Increasingly, many of the new unions were plant-based, and thus the centralized wage bargaining industrial relations (IR) system, at least unofficially, started giving way to a decentralized IR system. Not surprisingly, the number of registered unions had increased substantially from less than 5,000 in the early 1950s to more than 55,000 by the early 1990s. However, during the same period, the average reported size of those that submitted returns decreased by about 20 per cent, and at the later date it was around 450 members per union. If we take into account the fact that the share of unions submitting returns (in the total number of unions) itself went down drastically over this period – from more than 50 per cent to just about 10 per cent – and that typically these were bigger unions than those not submitting returns, the decline in average size of unions would be much sharper.

On the whole, during the 1970s and 1980s, the trade union movement scenario appeared to be in a state of turmoil, and the
'paternalistic' state started withdrawing, if not in a *de jure* then at
least in a *de facto* sense, from the hallowed commitments frequently
mouthed in the Nehruvian era. Gradually, the stage was set for an
ambience conducive to the neoliberal reforms in the subsequent
years.

As mentioned earlier, the trade union movement in the country
has been confined mostly to the small island of the organized sector,
and the huge preponderance of the informal sector in the labour
market has remained largely untouched. This is, arguably, its biggest
weakness, and an obvious cause of poor union density. Furthermore,
even within the formal sector, India fares rather badly in the spread
of unions compared with other large developing countries.[3] We may
also note here that the data on membership of different unions itself
has been rather a tricky subject, and often there are significant variations depending on the source one uses. Nonetheless, the fact that
the union density in India is abysmally low is generally accepted.
Table 4.1 summarizes the information on the membership of major
central trade unions, operating in at least four states in India,
according to the record of the Central Government's Ministry of
Labour and Employment.

It is worth emphasizing here that membership numbers have
tended to be a contentious issue. The Labour Bureau of the Government of India, taking into account all the unions which submit
returns, puts the total membership at only 5.5 million in 2000,
which is way below the claimed membership for 1997, or even the
'verified' membership in 1989 shown in Table 4.1. The Ministry of
Labour and Employment is entrusted with the responsibility of veri-
fying membership claims advanced by different CTUOs (central
trade union organizations). Since 1989, this has not been done. In a
statement released by the Press Information Bureau on 16
November 2005, the bureau mentioned that 'the last general verifi-
cation of the Central Trade Union Organizations was done with the
date of reckoning as 31 December 1989. The results were declared
in December 1996 which said that the total membership of 12
CTUOs with 16,279 affiliated trade unions was 12,334,142.'

As should be evident from this table, the character of Indian
trade unionism is highly 'political', in the sense that the major
unions are aligned to major political parties, which often dictates the
course of their actions and thus becomes a barrier to build even
elementary working-class unity. Much of the energy of all the major

Table 4.1 Changes in the membership of central trade union organizations (CTUOs) from 1980 to 1997[4]

Union	Verified membership 1980 (million)	Verified membership 1989 (million)	Claimed membership 1997 (million)
INTUC	3.51	2.69	6.73
BMS	1.88	3.12	6.06
HMS	1.84	1.48	3.67
AITUC	1.06	0.94	3.62
CITU	1.03	1.78	2.86
UTUC(LS)	1.23	0.84	0.84
UTUC	0.61	0.58	0.58
NLO	0.41	0.14	0.14
TUCC	0.27	0.23	0.23
NFITU	0.53	0.53	0.53
Total	12.39	12.33	25.26

Source: Ministry of Labour, Government of India.
Acronyms stand for the following (parentheses indicate the political party to which the union is affiliated):
AITUC: All India Trade Union Congress (Communist Party of India)
BMS: Bharatiya Mazdoor Sangh (Bharatiya Janata Party)
CITU: Centre of Indian Trade Unions (Communist Party of India, Marxist)
HMS: Hind Mazdoor Sabha (Independent from Political Parties, broadly linked with different Socialist Parties)
INTUC: Indian National Trade Union Congress (Indian National Congress)
NFITU: National Front of Indian Trade Unions
NLO: National Labour Organisation
TUCC: Trade Unions Coordination Centre (All India Forward Block)
UTUC: United Trade Union Congress (Revolutionary Socialist Party)
UTUC (LS): United Trade Union Congress -Lenin Sarani (Socialist Unity Centre in India-SUCI)

union federations, such as INTUC, Bharatiya Mazdoor Sangh (Bharatiya Janata Party; BMS), AITUC and CITU, are spent on struggles for space in different branches of industry and trade. Unfortunately, in the process, there is rarely any attempt to coordinate on any single issue of importance. Moreover, fragmentation of trade unionism goes well beyond loyalties to political parties. As per the Labour Bureau's recent estimate, there were more than 66,000 unions in the country, of which approximately 10,000 were affiliated to ten major trade union federations, most of which are aligned to major political parties. Along with such a huge fragmentation, and in part as a consequence of it, obvious problems like inter-union rivalry on often trivial issues, uneconomic size, financial debility and dependence on outside leadership are order of the day for most of these unions.

As should be evident from the foregoing, economic developments since the early 1990s have hardly been conducive for strengthening the politics of labour. On account of the ongoing reforms many firms have closed down or downsized through voluntary retirement schemes (VRS), outsourcing, subcontracting and so on, and there have been dramatic declines in employment in the organized manufacturing industry (e.g. Nambiar, Mungher and Tades, 1999). The Report of the Second National Labour Commission (SNCL), released in June 2002, pointed out that particular industries like chemicals, tea, coffee and rubber plantations, household goods and toys have been massively affected by increasing imports, and large numbers of small-scale operations have been forced to pull their shutters down. Loss of jobs in the organized sector has obviously put further pressure on the unorganized sector, resulting in an increase in its share in the total workforce. Further, the developments in the agricultural sector during the reform period have been nothing short of a serious crisis, resulting in massive slowdowns in income and employment opportunities, adding to the burden of the urban informal sector.

All these have been documented and analysed carefully by several researchers working on the Indian economy, and it is recognized widely that the policies of de-reservation, liberalized imports, withdrawal of government from several important arenas and so on have contributed enormously to the growing economic disempowerment of labour in the organized as well as unorganized sector (e.g. Chandrasekhar and Ghosh, 2002; Utsa Patnaik, 2003; Prabhat Patnaik, 2003, 2005a, 2005b). An atmosphere of disappearing livelihoods and growing insecurity can hardly be considered appropriate for political empowerment of labour. Even in the public sector, as was noted by the SNCL, collective bargaining has been adversely affected, and the ground realities in the case of the private sector are much worse. Labour unions, not surprisingly, have clearly found it extremely difficult to check the barrage of policies and practices affecting workers negatively. Occasionally, they have even felt pressurized enough to provide tacit support to measures like VRS, to which, in principle, they have been opposed (Roychowdhury, 2004).

WHAT FUTURE FOR INDIAN TRADE UNIONS?

The labouring classes, in general, have hardly had any rights in India even after independence. The overwhelming proportion of workers have had to live and work under insecure and onerous conditions, and have largely remained excluded from the ambit of labour policy in the country. Nonetheless, a small segment of the working classes, employed mainly in a range of modern industrial activities, were successful in advancing recognition by the post-colonial state of some of their rights.[5] We may recall here that India's struggle for independence had drawn into its fold large sections of the country's peasantry as well as rural and urban workers. In fact, they formed the bedrock of one of most spectacular struggles for freedom from colonial rule anywhere in the world. The fantastic support from the masses was obviously based on an implicit social contract which was premised on not only getting rid of the colonial subjugation but also putting in place an egalitarian socio-economic order. As for the industrial workers, waves of strikes in the closing years of the colonial rule did influence the contours of labour policy. In fact the Industrial Disputes Act of 1947 was of great significance, and an explicit acknowledgement that the interests of labour cannot be allowed to be ridden roughshod by capital. True, such an acknowledgement, in the immediate context impacted only a tiny, although vocal and visible, section of the workers. Nonetheless, it was a matter of tremendous potential significance for the working classes in general. During the last two to three decades, as discussed in the Introduction, there have been relentless social, political, economic and technological changes, both globally and locally. Trade unions around the world are struggling to come to terms with these changes, many of which require a profound rethinking of their roles and practices.

In India, following the unfortunate defeat of the workers in the long-drawn-out Bombay textile strike in the early 1980s, employers mounted a concerted offensive against organized labour which has, in fact, become increasingly aggressive in the subsequent years. The system of industrial relations put into place during the first couple of decades after independence ran into trouble by the 1980s as managements resisted industry-wide collective bargaining and began insisting on firm-level negotiations. This was followed by first a gradual, and then a large-scale, restructuring of employment. It can be argued that after 1991, with increasing competitive pressure from product markets, deregulation was squeezing profits and forcing employers to reduce protection and remuneration for labour using a variety of strategies. From the early 1990s onwards they began to restructure through VRSs to induce large-scale exits from companies.

It may be appropriate to take the view that in the organized sector the industrial relations system broke down in the 1980s and was never put back on its feet in the years that followed. Managements were quite successful in grabbing the initiative in a decisive way after the union expansion of the 1960s and 1970s. The labour movement, even within the organized sector, entered the economic reforms era in a defensive mood and lacking any strategy for renewed growth. With the VRSs of the last few years, certain sectors of the union movement have seen major contraction, namely the so-called employees' unions which are tied to a particular plant or company. If the plant closes down, the union disappears unless it has members in other establishments. The downsizing of offices and factories has thus also been a downsizing of the more advanced and combative pockets of trade unionism in India. The ascendancy of the neoliberal policy regime since the early 1990s has only accelerated the assault on unions. The state seems determined to throw out of the window whatever progressive labour laws the country has had, so as to finally legitimize their violations and non-enforcement. The ultimate objective is none else but to disarm the working-class movement completely.

State and capital's concerted attacks on labour fit into a larger pattern where concerted effort is currently being made to roll back democracy, an unfortunate development noted by several scholars. For instance, as P. Patnaik argues, the feudal and semi-feudal elements have waged a relentless struggle for subverting democratic institutions from the very beginning of independence,. However, the significant development contributing to this rolling-back at the current conjuncture is neoliberal globalization. To quote P. Patnaik:

> The adoption of neo-liberal policies, symptomatic of the bourgeoisie's adopting a collaborationist role vis-à-vis imperialism and an explicitly hostile role vis-à-vis the people, in a clear reversal of the situation prevailing during the years of anti-colonial struggle and post-colonial 'national' development, necessitates even more urgently than before an attenuation of the democratic rights of the people. The interests of international finance capital being opposed to those of the people, the adoption of policies in favour of the former is incompatible with the continuation, with the same vigour as before, of the democratic interventions by the people. Hence attempts at an

attenuation of democracy, which have always been there, gather a new momentum.

(Patnaik, 2005b: 2–3)

In sum, the increase in the hostility of the organs of state towards labour is intimately and organically linked to the logic of globalization. The right to organize, right to collective bargaining, right to form trade unions, right to strike – all these are being scuttled at the workplace, with the indirect or direct support from the state, and the use of physical repression by the state apparatus to achieve such ends has tended to increase in recent years. A recent brutal assault on the retrenched young workers of Honda Motorcycle and Scooter India Private Ltd on 25 July 2005 at the headquarters of Gurgaon district (adjacent to the national capital) was one such incident that got wide media coverage for a couple of days. Even the mainstream media were completely appalled. As the *Indian Express* put it:

> Over [a] thousand workers were injured; that they had nothing to match the police's lathis; that they were lured into a closed compound to present a memorandum; that they were beaten up in an enclosed space until they lay prostrate on the ground and then some more of them were made to crawl while holding their ears and beaten on their backsides; that while many workers ended up in hospital, others simply 'disappeared'; that the Deputy Commissioner of the city joined in with a baton, and that the police had made advance preparations for teaching them this 'lesson' by requisitioning troops from Rewari, Rohtak and Faridabad.
>
> (*Indian Express*, 30 July 2005)

The spectacle of brutality was flashed from several television channels for a couple of days, and then all references to it disappeared as if nothing had happened. May be Gurgaon's proximity to Delhi resulted in the media taking note of the savage assault, which reminded many of the Jallianwala Bagh. There are several 'mini-Gurgaons' happening all over the country, almost in a systemic fashion now, without being taken note of.

One of the most eloquently hostile among the organs of the state towards the rights of workers has been the judiciary in recent times. A series of verdicts have been delivered by different courts, including the apex court, restricting the democratic space of the people (for a catalogue of the important ones, see Patnaik, 2005b). Among the most dramatic of these was the apex court judgment following the sacking of the officially reported figure of 170,000 employees by the Tamil Nadu state government headed by the then Chief Minister J. Jayalalitha in July 2003. The unofficial estimate of dismissal was over 400,000 employees, and even the official estimate was unprecedented during the post-independence era, breaking the earlier records of dismissals several times over. The case was taken to the Supreme Court on behalf of the employees, and the court complimented the state government for its decision. In its judgment, on 6 August 2003, the apex court held the strike as illegal and decreed that the government employees have no 'Fundamental, Statutory or Equitable/Moral' right to resort to strike, to the disbelief and dismay of even legal luminaries in the country. Thus, different organs of the state have been working in unison, and a pattern is firmly in place, aimed at destroying any organized initiatives from the working classes. The responses are often particularly vicious towards those opposed to globalization. Labour laws are seen by the organs of the state as thorns in the flesh of neoliberal economic policies, and thus attempts are afoot to obtain their annulment.

On the other hand, workers and their unions are engaged in a bitter struggle not to give up their ground. Major trade unions have repeatedly acknowledged in the recent years the importance of united action, the need to reach larger and larger segments of the unorganized sector workers as well as a variety of progressive social and political movements (where the focus is not so much on classes as on masses) and the importance of mobilizing women workers. In a series of conversations I had with some of the leading functionaries affiliated to different trade unions,[6] in September and October 2005, to get their sense of major challenges confronting the working-class movement at the current juncture and how to move forward, there was almost a unanimity in their understanding as regards the stance of the state. As one of them put it, and others reaffirmed: 'the state in post independence period has never been as viciously anti-labour as during the reform period since the early 1990s'. *De facto* dilution of every single labour law, massive job losses in the formal sector,[7] large-scale informalization of the formal sector,[8] were highlighted as major concerns by all of them. For a while, as Vardarajan of CITU put it, trade unions were almost numbed by these attacks and put in a 'defensive mode unlike never before since independence', but gradually 'they have begun to confront these challenges'. According to all our respondents, two most urgent tasks were, first, not to yield on any major changes in the existing labour laws (even though they largely pertain to the workers in the organized sector), as this would mean defeat and a 'beginning of the end'; and second, to rapidly broaden their work and base among (hitherto neglected) unorganized workers. All our respondents claimed that much of their efforts and energies at the current juncture were devoted to this task. Several of them recounted significant advances in this respect among street vendors, construction workers, rickshaw pullers, lorry drivers and others. Finally, for many of them, particularly the representatives of the left, the biggest challenge was to 'fight the scourge of economic liberalization'.

The conditions in the unorganized sector are hardly conducive to unionization: casual labour relations, a high degree of mobility, the unregulated and unprotected nature of work, absence of fixed working hours, small own-account, family-owned enterprises or micro enterprises, lack of support (most notably, institutional credit) from government institutions and so on obviously do not create an atmosphere to attract the attention of major trade unions in any significant way. However, in recent years, there have been some efforts, by both several party-affiliated and independent unions, to address this problem. One significant initiative in this direction is the New Trade Union Initiative (NTUI). This is an alliance of independent trade unions in India that arose in the mid-1990s and became formally constituted as a federation in 2006 (*India Together* 2006, http://www.indiatogether.org/2006/apr/eco-ntui.htm). With over 200 constituent independent unions under its umbrella, NTUI today has a membership base of 500,000 workers in the formal sector and another 300,000 in the unorganized sector.

We may also note that the inadequate attention to the gender issue has been another serious problem in the trade union movement. According to the major data sources, unionization among female workers is only a small fraction of that of male workers, and the traditional trade unions have shown greater apathy towards their unionization. In this regard, the Self Employed Women's Association (SEWA) (2007, http://www.sewa.org/) has done a commendable job which is worth mentioning. SEWA was started in 1972 by Ela Bhatt and is currently spread over six states in India – Madhya Pradesh, Uttar Pradesh, Delhi, Bihar, Kerala and Gujarat. It was founded with the aim of creating a trade union of women who earned a living through their own labour. At present, it has 61 cooperatives, 400 self-help groups, and 4,000 saving groups. The success of SEWA has resulted in its working principles being replicated by several organizations, including in other countries such as

South Africa, Yemen and Turkey. It is obvious that the trade union movement in India needs to address these and a whole range of other organizational issues with much greater vigour and commitment. In doing so, it needs to confront squarely the threats including the growing hostility of the state, inherent in the neoliberal macro-economic policy regime for the last couple of decades. Otherwise, it will be difficult to move forward.

ACKNOWLEDGEMENTS

The author is grateful to Himansu and Laxman Behera, research students at Jawaharlal Nehru University (JNU), and Bhupal Singh Bisht, also of JNU, for their valuable assistance with this paper. Part of the material for this paper was presented at the 47th annual conference of the Indian Society of Labour Economics, 15–17 December 2005, and was also published in the conference journal. An earlier version of this paper was presented at the meeting of the Global Working Class Project in Stockholm, 12–15 January 2006.

The author gratefully acknowledges inputs from all members of this project; in particular, suggestions from the editors of this volume, Andreas Bieler, Devan Pillay and Ingemar Lundberg, have been extremely helpful.

NOTES

1   The Population Census conducted every ten years, since 1871, and the periodic surveys conducted by the National Sample Survey Organisation (NSS) since 1949, are among the most important secondary data sources for the structural features relating to India's labour market. There is a substantial literature critically appraising their underlying methodologies and the information generated by these major data sources, which we need not go into here. However, a couple of points may be worth highlighting. First, workforce participation rates emerging from these sources are significant underestimates, particularly in terms of their coverage of the relatively vulnerable socio-economic groups, although NSS does better than the Population Census in this respect. Second, the underlying methodologies of these data systems are prone to over-estimating employment. Thus, the net result of both is a relatively rosier picture of the aggregate employment scenario.

2   As is well known, there are major conceptual and definitional problems in separating the 'informal' from the 'formal'. In India, the conventional basis of this distinction is the definition used in the Factories Act of 1948, according to which an establishment with 10 workers or more and using power, or an establishment with 20 workers or more without power, is defined as formal. An alternative conception of formal,

implied in the same Act, is based on the degree of regularity of employment. Thus those with regular contracts/salaries could be considered as belonging to the formal sector. Clearly, these two conceptions do not overlap in any neat fashion. We may also note that 'organized' and 'formal' are often used interchangeably. Finally, discussions on the subject often correlate the formal sector with a segment subject to a set of regulatory laws, and the informal as not being subject to the same. As it happens, in principle many such laws are applicable to the so-called informal sector, although these are never observed in practice. Thus, even if we adopt standard conventional routes, the distinction between formal and informal remains on slippery terrain.

3 Using the ILO *World Labour Report* data 1997–98, Bhattacherjee (1999) reports that 'union membership as a percentage of non-agricultural labour dropped from 6.6 per cent in 1985 to 5.5 per cent in 1995 (the corresponding figure in 1995 for Argentina was 23.4 per cent, Brazil 32.1 per cent and Mexico 31 per cent). Union membership as a percentage of formal sector workers in India declined from 26.5 per cent to 22.8 per cent between 1985 and 1995 (the corresponding figures in 1995 were: Argentina 65.6 per cent, Brazil 66 per cent, Mexico 72.9 per cent).'

4 Apart from the unions listed in this table, there are certain other organizations such as Hind Mazdoor Kisan Panchayat and the Indian Federation of Free Trade Unions, which have the status of central trade unions. There are also several organizations associated with regional political parties. The list provided above is therefore not comprehensive and consists of those organizations whose membership figures are available for the respective years.

5 The beginnings of labour regulations for a minority of workers have a long history, dating at least from the Workmen's Breach of Contract Act of 1859. Most of the important Acts applicable to the organized sector were enacted between 1926 and 1947, i.e. during the colonial period itself.

6 This included Rajendra Singh Chauhan, vice president, BMS; D. L. Sachadev and Amarjeet Kaur, secretaries, AITUC; and R. P. K. Murugesan, secretary, CITU, among several others.

7 According to Gurudas Dasgupta, general secretary, AITUC, 'nearly 10 million workers had been thrown out of their jobs and 600,000 units had closed down in the last few years'.

8 As R. P. K. Murugesan of INTUC put it quite pithily: 'permanent jobs are vanishing; casualization, contractualization, outsourcing, home based work etc. are becoming the norm. Earlier trade unions were often criticized for being confined to organized workers. However, globalization is making us now representatives of largely unorganized workers!'

Chapter 5

How China's migrant labourers are becoming the new proletariat

Wen Tiejun

PREFACE

It is well known that the idea of a division of interests between labour and capital, or the fact that this division of interests will lead to class struggle, is not Marx's discovery. This chapter has no intention of adding to theories which had been accepted by western economists even before Marxism was developed. In fact, the research in this chapter is based on empirical research and is a general discussion on the development of a new proletariat in China. It explores the background and characteristics of different periods during which urban and coastal China experienced an influx of rural labour. The chapter does not focus on ideological issues.

The last two or three decades of the 20th century saw the dramatic transference of manufacturing industries into developing and underdeveloped countries. This move was to the enormous economic benefit of first-world capitalist countries. Serious labour struggles take place following multinational industrial capital transfer and its related institutional translocation into developing countries. This was particularly true for China, and still is.

In 1992, when China adopted the policy of 'The New Socialist Market Economic System', 46 million migrant rural labourers initially appeared to be a large labour force, but this figure accounted for no more than 4 per cent of the total Chinese population of 1.17 billion.[1] Now, 14 years later, China is among the top industrial countries, with an annual growth in gross domestic product (GDP) of 9.5 per cent. Of today's 1.32 billion population, 800 million are in the working population age bracket, and about 500 million are classified as rural residents. Of these 500 million, at least 200 million make a living by doing non-agricultural jobs, and 120 million young people have left their home villages to become migrant labourers, and contributed to large profits for international and domestic industries. With the family members accompanying them, the 'migrant labour population' is about 180

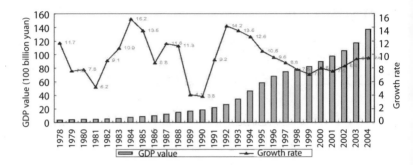

Figure 5.1 China's GDP growth trend

Source: *China Statistical Yearbook.*

million (in 2006), and accounts for about 15 per cent of China's total population.

By the year 2020, China's population in the group that are of working age will be 940 million. Most of the labour force is represented by migrant rural labourers. In a country where the ageing population outstrips the labour force as dramatically as China (see Figure 5.2), the burden on the working class becomes intolerable. There is constant (and accurate!) reference to China's apparently infinitely growing working-class phenomenon. This paper focuses on this phenomenon, but readers need to hold within that framework, the problems that accompany a society that has an ageing population – with the concomitant expenses and requirements – that is growing at a rate faster than the labour force.

This emerging, apparently infinitely growing working-class phenomenon is unprecedented, and requires some analysis.

BACKGROUND: 'MARKETIZATION' UNDER THE TYPICAL 'DUAL SYSTEM'

Three reasons for the 'new working class' in China: why peasants migrated to urban or coastal areas to find jobs in the 1990s

The first major reason is that the Chinese government relaxed the regulations governing the distribution of daily necessities. Peasant labourers began to migrate to urban and coastal areas in large numbers after 1992. Although there was some migration before in small numbers, peasants were kept in rural areas because of a policy that ruled that the distribution of food and daily necessities took

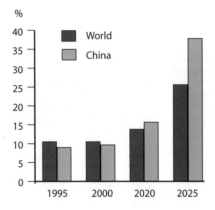

Figure 5.2 Strong labour resource until 2020: proportion of ageing population to labour force

place through a rigid system of ration coupons. Yet by the end of 1992, only a few counties in the north-west had not abolished the grain provision ration coupons. Once people were no longer compelled to use grain ration coupons, the major condition that prevented 46 million Chinese peasants from flooding to the cities to find a job fell away.

The second reason for the migration was that agricultural products did not sell well for three consecutive years in the early 1990s. The income gap between the urban and the rural population gradually became greater during the period of market-oriented economic reform.

In 1988 Deng Xiaoping, who was a real political leader in China, adopted a part of reformists' arguments and carried out market reform in the name of 'marketization of the price system', and what followed was high inflation (consumer price index (CPI) = 18.6 per cent). This pattern was also evident in other socialist countries that were in economic transition of institutions in the 1990s. This led to economic stagnation for three consecutive years in China after the 1989 political turmoil.

During that period, agricultural products sold poorly because of a decrease in consumption by urban residents; this in turn led to a decrease in peasants' income and rural consumption. Subsequently domestic demand decreased and foreign trade dependency started to increase in relative terms.

In the face of reduced income, costs for market-oriented education, medical services reform and well-modernized government taxes

Table 5.1 Contrast between the per capita income of urban and rural households in China, 1978–2005

Year	Annual per capita net income of rural households Absolute figure (yuan)	Index (previous year=100)	Annual per capita disposable income of urban households Absolute figure (yuan)	Index (previous year=100)	Ratio of urban and rural per capita income (rural resident=1)
1978	133.6		343.4		2.57
1979	160.2	119.2	405.0	115.7	2.53
1980	191.3	116.6	477.6	109.7	2.50
1981	223.4	115.4	500.4	102.2	2.24
1982	270.1	119.9	535.3	104.9	1.98
1983	309.8	114.2	564.6	103.9	1.82
1984	355.3	113.6	652.1	112.2	1.84
1985	397.6	107.8	739.1	101.1	1.86
1986	423.8	103.2	900.9	113.9	2.13
1987	462.6	105.2	1,002.1	102.2	2.17
1988	544.9	106.4	1,180.2	97.6	2.17
1989	601.5	98.4	1,373.9	100.1	2.28
1990	686.3	101.8	1,510.2	108.5	2.20
1991	708.6	102.0	1,700.6	107.1	2.40
1992	784.0	105.9	2,026.6	109.7	2.58
1993	921.6	103.2	2,577.4	109.5	2.80
1994	1,221.0	105.0	3,496.2	108.5	2.86
1995	1,577.7	105.3	4,283.0	104.9	2.71
1996	1,926.1	109.0	4,838.9	103.8	2.51
1997	2,090.1	104.6	5,160.3	103.4	2.47
1998	2,162.0	104.3	5,425.1	105.8	2.51
1999	2,210.3	103.8	5,854.0	109.3	2.65
2000	2,253.4	102.1	6,280.0	106.4	2.79
2001	2,366.4	104.2	6,859.6	108.5	2.90
2002	2,475.6	104.8	7,702.8	113.4	3.11
2003	2,622.2	104.3	8,472.2	109.0	3.23
2004	2,936.4	106.8	9,421.6	107.7	3.21
2005	3,254.9	106.2	10,493.0	109.6	3.22

Source: The contrast between per capita income of urban and rural households was calculated based on the data on p.108, *China Summary Statistics 2006* compiled by the State Statistics Bureau. The effect of price differentials between urban and rural areas has not been removed.

Notes:

Absolute figures in this table were calculated at 2006 prices while indices were calculated at comparable prices.

Disposable income of urban households = Total income of household – tax paid – individual's social security contributions.

Net income of rural households = Total income – household operating costs – tax paid – depreciation of fixed assets – contributions to relatives outside the village.

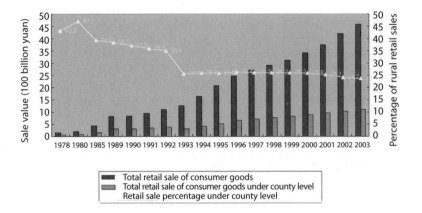

Figure 5.3 Total retail sale of consumer goods and its rural share in China, 1978–2003

Source: *China Rural Yearbook, 2004.*

did not decrease, but on the contrary continued to increase. Therefore, peasants had to find more lucrative working opportunities.

The third reason was that from 1980 to 1990, rural industrial development declined as a result of cyclical economic crises; this meant that the capacity of township and village enterprises (TVEs) to absorb non-agricultural peasant labour was greatly reduced. Before 1992, there were large numbers of non-agricultural peasant labourers, who had jobs in the villages or the vicinity of their villages – that is to say, they left the work on the land but did not leave their families. These new workers worked in local factories and not in the city, and this was the biggest difference from the urban migration of the 1990s. In 1984, when agricultural products did not sell well, peasants automatically adjusted to the economic situation by reducing grain cultivation by more than 70 million mu (1 hectare equals 15 mu), and at the same time increasing cash crops. Peasants could create or find jobs in buying and selling cash crops, and processing farm products. The activated rural economy led to an increase in cash income and expenditure. This created a golden growth period, which saw a massive rise of township and village enterprises – the result of an increased rural demand for low-quality consumption products.

It is worth emphasizing that in the middle of the 1980s, the

Chinese government had not relaxed the restrictions on consumption products such as grain and oil, and these were still distributed according to the government plan. At this time, the first batch of non-agricultural labourers found jobs in the rural areas: from 1984 to 1988, there were on average more than 17 million peasants gaining employment in the TVEs every year. The inflation crisis from 1988 to 1989 led to the stagnation of urban manufacturing from 1990 to 1991. Despite the crisis and stagnation, 12 million peasants still transferred to TVE jobs every year. Before the big urban migration of peasant labour in 1992, TVE industries had already absorbed about 130 million peasants.

Relatively speaking, this was a very effective and low-cost transfer of labour due to the lack of bureaucratic regulation and restrictions. In urban environments there were a variety of fees charged by government, admission standards demanded by industries, and social security fees required for enterprises to start up. This minimal cost transfer of peasants to non-agricultural jobs assisted the low-cost development of rural industrialization based on TVEs.[2] At that time, China had not copied western policies so radically. The government permitted TVEs to use farmland in the village for free; they also allowed 'rural-support funds' to be used before TVEs were taxed and subsidized village expenditure. Policies at that time were devised to meet China's needs. TVEs developed rapidly and created strong competition with urban areas in terms of raw materials and markets, causing considerable dissatisfaction within state-supported industrial sectors. This is referred to as state capital. The government began to adjust its policies to the disadvantage of TVE development. A nationwide rush for goods led to a run on credit applications from financial institutions. The government immediately adopted an austerity policy, affecting medium-sized and small enterprises, mostly TVEs, in a disastrous way. Without credit or financial support from banks, a difficult time ensued in the 1990s. The following Chinese saying summarizes it: when urban residents get a cold, it is peasants who take the pills.

The economic crisis precipitated by government measures to limit credit led to a decrease in the employment rate and a decline in cash income from TVEs, thus becoming the third reason for a large number of rural labourers to migrate to cities.

Urban reform and the two stages of urban migration

It is necessary to understand the cycle into which the economic crisis slid in the 1990s. China's CPI had reached 18.5 per cent in 1988; in some big cities such as Beijing the CPI exceeded 25 per cent, and in Guangdong province, it exceeded 30 per cent. This inflationary crisis led to the austerity policy of 1989. After 1990, which was the second year of depression, China began to experience a slow process from depression to recovery. The economic growth generated during that period was as a result of Deng's talks in his visit to the south of China in 1992. It must be made clear that it was not a result of the revival of the former manufacturing industry. Instead, Deng identified three high-risk areas in the economy for market reform: development zones and real estate, the market in financial securities (in about 1992), and the futures market (around 1993). In fact, after Deng's visit to the south, reinvestment in the traditional industries did not help the economy to an immediate prosperous rise. However, it was as a result of the focus on these three speculative areas that the economic crisis began to dissipate.

After Deng's visit to the south, the creation of more than 8,000 development zones all across the country led to major speculation in real estate. This in turn brought large-scale financial capital into ventures to pursue short-term profit. The speculation in real estates in 1992 resulted in bank credit extensions of 360 billion yuan over the following three years, and much of it became bad debt. This is one of the main reasons behind the 1995–97 macro readjustment policies, but at that time it was one of the reasons that motivated peasants to migrate to the cities in search of jobs. The declaration of development zones and real estate investments, as well as concentrated investment in energy, raw materials and setting up the infrastructure for industries, led to massive industrial expansion and a large increase in the import of machines and equipment. The severe decrease in national foreign exchange reserves called for drastic measures. The reform that was instituted in 1994 was to tie the foreign exchange rate to market levels. This induced a 57 per cent nominal devaluation of the domestic currency (RMB yuan) in one go. Although the economic heat after Deng's visit to the south was unhealthy, the accompanying tide of rural migration for urban jobs was a normal phenomenon. The launching of the development zones required, not general industrial workers, but a physically strong labour force, and the mainly male peasant migrant labourers could meet this demand.

The initial phase was the development of zones along the east coast creating a road, electricity and water supply infrastructure. This in turn led to an economic upsurge over the next three years. The number of rural migrant workers in the urban areas increased from 46 million in 1992 to around 60 million in 1994. Compared with the mid-1980s when industrialization caused a 130 million peasant migration within rural areas, the number of peasants involved in the urban migration in 1992–94 seemed small, yet the cost was high, and the Chinese government realized that 'economic overheating' was taking place.

The second phase had to do with Britain's return of Hong Kong to China in 1997. China had no intention of giving up any of its proposed sovereignty rights over Hong Kong, and the run-up to the handover resulted in the move of general manufacturing industries from Hong Kong into Guangdong province. At the same time, British colonial authorities orchestrated the substantial withdrawal of capital, personnel and projects from Hong Kong, in order to weaken Hong Kong's economy. China then adopted the 'political command of the state capital' policy, and organized 46 billion RMB yuan to be invested in Hong Kong within a short period. The vacuum caused by British withdrawal was filled.

Hong Kong real estate prices started to soar as a result of large investments from the mainland during this period, forcing a large number of Hong Kong's medium and small industrial enterprises onto the mainland. According to official figures from the Hong Kong government, around 1990, Hong Kong capital financed 20,000 enterprises in Guangdong province, employing over 2 million workers (Zhou, 2005: 50). After 1992, the influx of peasants from other provinces to Guangdong province was over 10 million per year. This figure rose to over 15 million after the turn of the century. Migrant workers of rural origin numbered over 20 million, if we include the number of peasants from Guangdong province working in the cities and in the Delta area (Zhou, 2005: 275). In the first half of the 1990s capital from Hong Kong or from overseas Chinese investors provided the finance for development zones along the south-east coastal areas where the infrastructure was ready. Despite the various problems arising in the process, there was indeed a real industrial capital transfer. Since production lines for toys, clothes and electronic appliances were introduced into the southern development zones, young female workers were in demand. As a result, the gender structure of the labour force changed after the mid-1990s. This changed the visage of labour relations, and industry had to deal with problems unique to female workers.

Generally in rural areas, men are the pillar of the family. Most male labourers would leave the cities and return to their rural homes after earning money. In addition, their consumption level would be relatively low. On the other hand, female labourers would tend to remain in urban areas. Because of the under-protection of women's rights under the rural land contracting system, women's property rights in rural areas and urban areas are very different. Without property constraints in rural areas, female labourers would be more likely to seek employment in cities. Urban demographics changed in terms of both the number of women who settled, and the youthful age group they represented. Problems started to arise of education, living conditions and medical services for the children that went with parents to the cities. Simultaneously, the ageing population and children left in rural areas presented a new set of difficulties. Most of the labourers in the 1992–93 urban migration were manual labourers, men of 30–40 years old. Not only young people, but also middle-aged labourers worked in the cities. These middle-aged labourers usually had families, so they would usually return to their rural home. However, with the establishment of the south-east coast manufacturing industries, the second wave of rural migrant labourers did not always return to their villages. After these two distinct migrations, there was no obvious distinction in the gender or age of rural people who entered the cities for a living, but what did change dramatically (with the second wave) were consumption patterns. Women and young people were more likely to accept urban consumption cultures. As a result, a change in the pattern of consumption and integration into urban culture among migrant labourers took place.

ANALYSIS

Labour and capital relations of recent times

The formation of power blocs governs the relation between labour and capital. Chinese urban reform was very limited before the mid-1990s. In the first half of the 1990s, a large proportion of the capital investment in real estate came from government officials or state capital, because these sectors had easy access to land that was monopolized by the government. Through government expropriation of land combined with government-controlled financial investment, the capital gains from state-owned real estate could be utilized to finance industrial development.

The data over 25 years show that economic growth caused rural land to 'shrink' because of construction, causing dispossessed rural landowners to migrate to the cities. This integration of power and

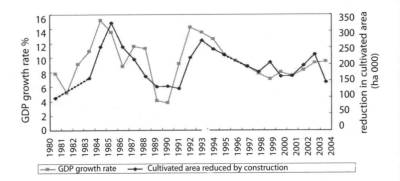

Figure 5.4 GDP growth compared with the reduction in the cultivated area as a result of construction in China, 1980–2004

Source: *China Statistics Yearbooks.*

capital gave rise to embryonic corporate capital in the late 1990s. State-owned enterprises were privatized and some privatized enterprises set up stock companies, which led to a major change: capital conglomerates started to appear in China.

In the 1980s, the first accumulation of capital was from the dual price policy, and whoever had the power to control the lower-price raw materials through the planning system immediately became rich. The second accumulation was from the speculation in real estate. With the formation of primitive capital accumulation, capital blocs quickly formed.

As advantaged groups appeared in the cities, inevitably disadvantaged groups ballooned. When the capital blocs and their representatives were strengthened, the structural framework this demanded – represented by corporate law – took effect. 'State-owned enterprises' quietly replaced 'people-owned enterprises' almost without a ripple, and the problem of low efficiency became the problem of workers. Reassignments, lay-offs, reduction in the work force, increases in efficiency, protection of the interests of investors and improvement of the capital yield were all part of the 'urban reforms' launched by the government at all levels. Capitalist enterprise grew, and with it the focus on individual advancement and accumulation of wealth. The entire economic system and legal framework were adjusted to this new mindset.

Meanwhile, mainstream intellectuals also made corresponding changes in their discourse. The main trend of the culture and the system became increasingly unfavourable to the labour force.

Analysis of changes in the urban labour groups

It is necessary to understand how the concept of the middle class in China has been redefined. In the period from the 1950s to the early 1990s, 'worker groups' in urban areas in publicly owned enterprises were in reality a kind of urban middle class, ensuring the stability of the country. Almost all the workers in publicly owned enterprises enjoyed social welfare from birth to death. Even though their income was not very high, they were regarded as having superior social status compared with 'peasants'. They were also the main body that controlled the ideological apparatuses in state politics. Therefore, they played a kind of middle-class role within the traditional system. Even Chairman Mao during the Cultural Revolution was constrained by his inability to mobilize the elite among them.

However, after the mid-1990s the relative status of the workers in state-owned enterprises declined dramatically with the reform of these enterprises and when the powerful capital blocs were formed. New urban policies were unfavourable to workers who used to benefit from the old system. Because of the big rush on goods caused by the failure of the price relaxation policy in 1988, financial institutions directly linked to the government finances faced a run on bank withdrawals. In order to avoid the loss of savings, the banks dramatically raised the interest rate on savings, but without increasing the lending rate. This caused a deficit amounting to around 46 billion RMB yuan in the financial year of 1988, which reverted into the state's deficit at the end of that year, namely of 50 billion yuan.

After that, this negative trend continued in central government finances. The deficit increased, as did bank overdrafts. Bank capital continued to drop, causing the worsening of the financial system. From 1989 to 1991, for three consecutive years there was a so-called 'triangular debt' (which is a vicious circle of non-servicing of debt), and bad debt grew. Hence, when it came to around 1993, bank capital was depleted, leaving an overdraft of 8.3 billion yuan. In short, the Chinese government had used up the public's savings. Since 1994, the central finance had to be maintained by the means of selling national savings bonds. The total amount of government bonds multiplied every year, reaching 5 billion, then 10 billion, then 20 billion, then 50 billion, then 100 billion, until it reached over 300 billion.

The fiscal crisis had an inevitable impact on basic social services such as education and medical care. The government introduced measures to ease their burden, and by the middle of the 1990s, educational and medical systems had been converted to government enterprises. The cost to consumers was raised significantly. These public enterprises became hugely profitable, changing the face of Chinese society dramatically. Urban problems such as lay-offs and unemployment became more serious, and poverty with its concomitant problems pervaded the urban environment.

China's trade unions in the era of reform

China is a typically dualistic society with a rural–urban divide. Historically, under the constraints of such structural contradictions, China's state-recognized trade unions have conducted their union work in cities only. In particular, from 1950 to 1980, when the state pursued intensive industrialization, workers were concentrated in the cities. This meant they had social security benefits such as pensions and medical benefits, and were given the status of 'masters of the country'. The urban proletariat, comprising 10 per cent of the population, had a much more privileged life than the peasantry, who formed the overwhelming majority of the labouring population. The government's 'scissors differentiation' policy extracted the surplus from agriculture on a large scale, and also deployed large amounts of surplus labour without compensation from the countryside through a collectivized system. Hence Liang Shuming, a famous intellectual in favour of Chinese democracy during the 1950s, had confronted Chairman Mao Zedong with the comment: 'Workers are placed up in the nine heavens, yet peasants are placed down on the nine earths.' During this period, Chinese trade unions, like the youth leagues and the women's associations, formed part of the 'mass organizations' of the Chinese Communist Party (CPC). Their role included campaigns to 'educate' workers in how to cultivate the spirit of loving their jobs, organizing recreational activities for workers, and offering assistance to workers or their families in difficulties.

After the reform of 1979, there was rapid business development on a large scale from the private sector and foreign investors. One increasingly important task for the trade unions was to defend the rights and interests of these workers. China therefore promulgated the Labour Law and the Trade Union Law. Chinese trade unions were no longer restricted to activities in state-owned enterprises, but were allowed by law to defend workers' rights in private and foreign enterprises. The workers in these enterprises had been in a position of absolute opposition with their employers; under the new legislation, employers had to enter into negotiations with trade unions and worker organizations.

It must be noted that the large-scale entry of foreign enterprises into China is not only because of the cheap labour that China offers. One important aspect is that China's economy is still undergoing monetization and capitalization. Foreign investors are keen to capitalize resources in developing countries, and China offers an abundance of such opportunities. Foreign capital will not stop its entry into China, nor will it relinquish the benefits from capitalizing resources. Thus, when China's trade unions insist on the recognition of the legal rights of workers, this does not constitute any substantial threat to foreign capital. Indeed, in recent years, multinational corporations (MNCs) such as Wal-Mart, which have refused to recognize trade unions in other countries, have been compelled to change their policy under pressure from Chinese trade unions. Furthermore, since relationships between capital and labour are an international issue, many multinational companies have introduced their own codes of practice and embarked on projects of social responsibility. These include the recognition of the legal rights of workers, and are to the benefit of Chinese trade unions.

In the late 1990s, the most urgent task for trade unions was to organize for the recognition of the rights of peasants who came to the cities for jobs. There are currently 120 million formerly rural workers working in the cities; they do not receive any regular trade union recognition or protection, and do not benefit from even the most basic pension or medical schemes. They have nowhere to air their grievances when they are exploited by supervisors or factory owners. It was only after 2002, when the 16th Congress of the Chinese ruling party was convened and the grand objective of 'comprehensive well-being' was proposed, that China's trade unions gradually took up the responsibility for defending the rights and interests of migrant rural labourers. However, the rights and interests of labourers in rural areas are not covered at all.

The role of the media

Most mainstream media discussed the conflict between rural workers migrating from the countryside and laid-off urban workers without discussing how the conflict arose and the background to it. Neither did they make mention of how the capital was accumulating in the country, how government funds were being used for private ventures, and how new interest groups were appearing. Not only did mainstream media neglect these issues, it also helped tycoons to rationalize and legitimize their wealth by presenting them in a positive light.

It is important to note (and acknowledge) that the alternative media and web voices played a significant role in highlighting these problems and issues. Then an unconditional 'amnesty' was introduced, absolving all past government corruption, and blood on the hands of entrepreneurs engaged in 'primitive' methods of capital accumulation. After that, it was a happy dance between the conglomerates, the press and the elite: a dance around money.

The issues outlined above explain the problems currently experienced by the urban labour force.

SOME PREDICTIONS

National constraints and related problems

At present, mainstream developmental strategy in China follows the mode of western modernization: privatization, market-driven development, liberalization and globalization. Although these tactics are logically interrelated, they are inconsistent with the state policies of building a well-off society on a comprehensive scale. This became starkly evident at the 16th National Congress of the Communist Party of China in 2002, and is seen constantly in the state's attempts to promote sustainable development.

China is a continent-sized country, but it does not have abundant resources. Although China is the most populated country in the world, resources are vastly inadequate. Moreover, there is the 'dual surplus' of labour and domestic capital, which adds to the same dual surplus in the globalized world. In recent years, people have rarely disputed the capital surplus. One of the classic signs is that the M2/GDP ratio[3] went above 180 per cent in 2002, while the US ratio is no more than 80 per cent. However, the number of labourers in China is over 800 million. It is impossible to reach full employment. The market economy cannot resolve the contradiction of the dual surplus, which leads to an unavoidable reliance on the expansion of industrial capital to increase employment opportunities. A serious shortage of jobs would have huge social consequences.

Three surpluses: long-term issues

First, like most countries that face the problem of surplus capital, China has to use the policy of promoting capital expansion through investment. The difference between Chinese policies and those of developed countries is that China needs to try to constantly increase employment opportunities in order to prevent social turmoil.

Second, because of the size of the rural labour force, labour prices decrease all the time. They might even decrease to below the level of simple reproduction of labour, and problems such as the lack of social services or ill payment of migrant labour become more marked than in other market economy countries.

Table 5.2 shows the structural composition of the per capita annual net income of rural households in the years 1990 to 2005. From this, it is clear that the ratio of wage income to rural household net income has risen in the last ten years, from 22.4 per cent in 1995 to 36.1 per cent in 2005. Wage income refers to the income from employment in urban enterprises or for individuals,[4] as well as employment in TVEs or in rural enterprises.[5] The income from working in urban areas was 398 yuan in 2004, comprising 40 per cent of that year's per capita wage income of 998 yuan (Chinese Academy of Social Sciences, 2007: 76). This is 13.6 per cent of the per capita annual net income of rural households in 2004.

Third, the premium on jobs makes it difficult to have labour organizations, labour ideologies and theories, or labour parties. So far there have been no labour movement or labour–management bargaining like those in the west. Thus, disregarding value judgments or subjective wishes of whatever nature, be that from the right, centre or left, a 'good market economic system' with some socialist characteristics of the Third Way promoted in Europe is very difficult to set up in China. Western-style democratic political reforms would also be difficult to implement because with an infinite labour supply, all of these ideal systems cannot be set up naturally and smoothly, unless one is willing to pay any price.

RESEARCHERS' FINDINGS

In 2002 Tan Shen, a researcher from the Institute of Sociology, Chinese Academy of Social Sciences, released a survey on 'corporate principles'. It found that in the context of globalization, even if some multinational corporations were to implement the old form of treatment of workers, local governments in China, whose role it is to attract foreign investment, do not support this idea. Entrepreneurs would lose their competitive edge, and workers themselves do not have the power to realize such basic human rights.

This survey mirrors present industrial relations in China. Industrial relations negotiations or social contracts according to normal market conditions in a western system are not feasible in China.

Table 5.2 Ratio of wage income to per capita net income of rural households in China, 1990–2005

Year	Per capita annual net income (yuan)	Per capita annual wage income		Per capita annual household production income		Per capita annual property income		Per capita annual transfer income	
		Absolute figure (yuan)	% of net income	Absolute figure (yuan)	% of net income	Absolute figure (yuan)	% of net income	Absolute figure (yuan)	% of net income
1990	686.3	138.8	20.2	518.6	75.6	29.0	4.2		
1995	1,577.7	353.7	22.4	1,125.8	71.4	41.0	2.6	57.3	3.6
2000	2,253.4	702.3	31.2	1,427.3	63.3	45.0	2.0	78.8	3.5
2002	2,475.6	840.2	33.9	1,486.5	60.0	50.7	2.0	98.2	4.0
2003	2,622.2	918.4	35.0	1,541.3	58.8	65.8	2.5	96.8	3.7
2004	2,936.4	998.5	34.0	1,745.8	59.5	76.6	2.6	115.5	3.9
2005	3,254.9	1,174.5	36.1	1,844.5	56.7	88.5	2.7	147.4	4.5

Source: *Summary of Chinese Statistics 2006* (in Chinese) compiled by the State Statistics Bureau, p.116; *China Statistics Yearbook 2004* (in Chinese), p.380.

It is also difficult to set up systems of legal recourse for workers. Therefore labour maltreatment and wage arrears are rife. Even if labourers resort to legal procedures and win law suits, implementation is very difficult. As a result, some workers climb onto high spots in construction sites to protest or commit suicide, or resort to personal revenge or group crimes that may resemble 'terrorism'. A large amount of domestic capital has been re-routed to North America, where the price of real estate in Chinese communities has risen. Social disorder as a result of exploitative labour conditions is a major reason why the rich are fearful.

If China were to simply copy the western development mode of modernization, these problems would never be resolved. Once the road of development is a one-way road toward a capitalist economy, there will be no U-turn. For the majority of the Chinese people, the only hope is that the CPC will realize its political promise of 'building a well-off society on a comprehensive scale' made at the 16th National Congress. Mao Zedong issued the following instruction to cadres to combat the unique problems of Chinese society: 'comrades must continue to be modest, prudent, humble and simple; comrades must continue to struggle with arduousness'; scientific development and the building of a harmonious society must be a priority. We can only promote policy revisions that correspond to Chinese needs; the blind copying of western models is inappropriate. Government officials and intellectuals must be willing to do practical, serious analysis, with the view to launching a movement of ideological liberation.

NOTES

1   Since this chapter is not for theoretical research, the data below are general figures.
2   The advantages of the low-cost labour transfer in rural areas have been neglected by many Chinese scholars coming back from abroad.
3   M2/GDP is an indicator of monetization. M2 means the total amount of currency in circulation.
4   This is defined in the *China Statistics Yearbook 2004*, p. 394.
5   Apart from TVEs and working in urban areas, some peasants obtain their wage income through non-agricultural work near their own villages, such as rural construction work. This labour force constitutes about 20 per cent of the total migrant labour force (Chinese Academy of Social Sciences, 2007: 70).

Chapter 6

The globalization of capital and its impact on the world of formal and informal work: challenges for and responses from Argentine unions

Isabel Rauber

The Argentine Workers Federation (Central de Trabajadores Argentinos, CTA) came into being in the midst of the establishment of a neoliberal economic model in Argentina. It was part of a search for alternatives by workers hit hard by the crumbling of the country's production sector, the downsizing of social welfare programmes run by the state, the repeal of progressive labour laws, and growing unemployment and destitution. The programme of action of the CTA included the recognition, affiliation and representation of all workers, employed and unemployed; direct affiliation, without having to belong to a specific industrial sector; and coordination with other social sectors for re-establishing workers' social power, the redefinition of production and work as the basis for nation building. Underlying the programme is the premise that political solutions should be linked to political unionism. Of course, unionism would allow for the organization of working-class members on a wide scale: from isolated and far-flung communities to migrant workers from other countries. By creating worker unity, it is hoped that it might be possible to build a movement strong enough to effect significant historical change. In this chapter, the next section will outline the challenges for the Argentine working class resulting from neoliberal globalization, before the various responses are discussed with a specific focus on the CTA.

THE IMPACT OF NEOLIBERAL GLOBALIZATION ON THE WORKING CLASS

From the second half of the 1970s, Argentina underwent a process of structural and super-structural adaptation to the neoliberal capitalist model. This process was imposed through violent military dictatorships, particularly, the one led by Videla in March 1976. The blood of thousands stained the 'magic' carpet of the triumph of capital in the 1980s in Argentina. The international socialist system was replaced with an era of globalization – a stage of re-colonization that began in the 1990s. Capital applied itself to reforming the organizational and structural functions of countries in the North and South, in line with the economic conditions that governed each. In the Latin-American region, Argentina had neoliberal economic conditions, and not surprisingly, a popular uprising that made international headlines took place in December 2001. The traits of the structural transformation of capital in Argentina can be summed up as follows: deindustrialization; stagnation; concentration of production and centralization of capital, and a resizing and redefinition of the industrial profile; reforms in the content and functions of the state and growing restrictions on its social responsibilities. Since the mid-1970s, manufacturing has had an increasingly smaller share in the overall gross domestic product (GDP) of the country. In 1975, industry represented approximately 30 per cent of the total GDP. By the late 1990s, that percentage was about 16 per cent. As Basualdo and Lozano affirm:

> The decrease in the relative influence of industry on global production and employment, as well as the accompanying expansion of services, is seen by some authors as an indicator of increased degree of modernization and/or development of an economy. Regarding such affirmations, it is asserted that 'developing countries' should be more focused on the creation and fostering of services than on primary and manufacturing activities. However, from an analysis of what happened in Argentina over the last few decades, important questions emerge regarding the validity of such affirmations, insofar as 'deindustrialization' – and its correlate: a greater aggregate gravitation of services – has been much more associated with the dismantling of production and the regressive restructuring of the sector that took place, and associated with that, with a bigger gap separating the Argentine economy from that of developed countries (relative stagnation), than with a greater level of development.
>
> (Basualdo and Lozano, 2000)

In the business sector, small and medium-sized businesses were greatly affected by the direction of economic policies, while a small group of oligopolistic businesses significantly intensified their participation in and control over various branches of industry. This situation – the way in which 'deindustrialization' impacted on large as well as small and medium-sized companies and workers – reflected the subordination of the state apparatus to the interests of the most concentrated sections of capital. The notable expansion of leading industries in the last quarter of the century was closely tied to the reinvestment of all profits, in accordance with state policy. The intention was to achieve industrial growth, the settling of foreign debt, influence on state purchasing policies, and the initiation of wealth-creation schemes (but schemes that would only benefit the already wealthy) to open up the economy.

From the National Economic Censuses, it emerges that between the mid-1970s and the early 1990s more than 15,000 productive units closed down. This meant an almost 25 per cent decrease in employment in the production sector. The dramatic fall in industrial employment in the early 1970s occurred at a time when the manufacturing sector had an employment/production elasticity of 0.65 (in other words, for each percentage point of production growth, employment increased by 0.65 per cent). This indicates that the concentration on local manufacturing (as opposed to imports) not only promoted an expansion of production itself, it also generated jobs. In the 1990s, that coefficient was about -3.7; that is, the reduction of a significant number of jobs.

THE INFORMALIZATION OF WORK IN THE FORMAL AND INFORMAL SECTORS: GROWING DETERIORATION OF WAGES AND THE LOSS OF EFFECTIVE WORKING-CLASS POWER

In the 1990s, the growth of the Argentine economy ran concurrently with a profound deterioration of the job market. In a context in which the global GDP expanded by an average annual rate of 4 per cent, significant increases were registered in the unemployment and underemployment rates (about 11 per cent and almost 8 per cent in the cumulative year, respectively). As a result almost 30 per cent of the economically active population was experiencing serious problems with employment by the turn of the century, when in the 1970s it was less than 14 per cent. As Basualdo and Lozano (2000) explain, in this period two clearly differentiated stages may be recognized. Between 1991 and 1994, the domestic economy grew by almost 23 per cent, while the unemployment rate doubled and the under-employment rate grew by a bit more than 30 per cent. Based on the crisis stemming from the

Table 6.1 GDP trend, the main indicators of the labour market,[1] the population living below the poverty line, and average wages, 1991–2000, Argentina

Year	GDP[2]	Rate of activity %	Employment rate %	Unemployment rate %	Under-employment rate %	Poor population[3] %	Destitute population[3] %	Real average wages[2]
1991	100.0	39.5	37.1	6.0	7.9	25.2	4.1	100.0
1992	114.6	40.2	37.4	7.0	8.1	18.6	3.3	104.0
1993	115.9	41.0	37.1	9.3	9.3	17.3	4.0	105.0
1994	122.7	40.8	35.8	12.2	10.4	17.6	3.4	103.5
1995	119.2	41.4	34.5	16.6	12.6	23.5	6.0	98.7
1996	125.8	41.9	34.6	17.3	13.6	27.3	7.2	98.0
1997	135.9	42.3	36.5	13.7	13.1	26.2	6.1	97.2
1998	141.2	42.1	36.9	12.4	13.6	25.1	6.1	95.0
1999	137.0	42.7	36.8	13.8	14.3	26.9	7.2	94.5
2000	139.0	42.7	36.5	14.7	14.6	29.5	7.8	92.7

Notes:

1 Corresponds to the annual October wave of the total of urban agglomerates revealed by INDEC's Permanent Census of Homes.

2 Baseline index 1991=100 per cent).

3 Information corresponding to the Greater Buenos Aires agglomerate (October wave of each year). For 2000, provisional.

Source: Institute of the CTA and IDEP based on information from the INDEC and FIDE.

so-called 'Tequila effect,'[1] a new stage opened, characterized by the following dynamic. When the economy grows, unemployment falls (although never to rates below 12 per cent) and under-employment rises, while when domestic activity contracts (as was the case with the recession that began in early 1998), unemploy-ment grows significantly, but under-employment remains unchanged.

Between 1970 and 1996, the economically active population – that is, the population able to work – grew by 56 per cent, but the number of unemployed grew by practically 470 per cent during these 26 years. This suggests that the unemployed population grew among all sectors of workers:

> the subsistence self-employed, those who try to survive individ-ually with a given activity in the economic process and are not connected with direct dependence, grew by about 80 per cent. That is, also over the average growth of the economically active population. What is also shown is that the number of family members who work without receiving remuneration – that is, those who work in a subsistence family unit as a means of support and don't even receive a salary – grew by 143 per cent, also well beyond the average growth of the economically active population. And it may be noted that the number of wage-earners over those 26 years grew by barely 18 per cent, very much below the average, and moreover, not even reaching 1 per cent annually.
>
> (Rauber, 1998: 50–1)

In relative terms, there was a constant decline in the number of formally employed workers. It is important to note that 'wage earner' refers to both formal wage earners and those wage earners who have neither welfare nor social coverage, are not registered, and receive their wages in cash so they are not registered for administra-tive or legal purposes. It must be considered that during this period the highest growth in the number of wage earners was among informal wage earners. The number of formal wage earners decreased to less than 18 per cent. Within this framework, formal wage earners constitute only 40 per cent of the total working class. It is this differentiation that creates the difficulties for a traditional union model to operate as a bargaining structure for the majority of workers. The organizing strategy of unions is focused exclusively on formal workers (see Rauber, 1998: 50–1).

Wages

These unprecedented levels of unemployment, as well as the growing precariousness of a considerable number of new jobs, have had negative repercussions on remuneration. The combination of a shortage of jobs and falling wages meant that producers could make higher profits while unemployment grew. According to figures from the CTA's Studies Institute, in 1975 wages amounted to 43 per cent of GDP, while currently that figure is no more than 20 per cent. Considering the 1990s as a whole, the population with an income below the poverty line grew by 7 per cent. This amounts to 75 per cent of the population. Between 1991 and 1999, the total income of the poorest 40 per cent of the country's largest urban agglomerate, Greater Buenos Aires, diminished by 10 per cent, and in the same period the income gap between the richest 10 per cent of the country's urban population and the poorest 10 per cent grew by almost 50 per cent. An increasing number of workers entered the labour market, which brought with it an increase in the labour supply; these newcomers to the labour market were desperate enough to undercut existing wages and to work under what had previously been considered unacceptable working conditions. This led to higher unemployment and a deterioration of job conditions for employed workers:

> Argentina before the mid-1970s was oriented in economic terms basically toward the domestic market. It had an economy with an industrial base, in which wages played a large, significant role within the whole of domestic demand. Wages were a central component in maintaining and expanding domestic demand, and rationality marked the strategy for agreements between union sectors and certain business sectors. ... This is what was broken in Argentine beginning in the mid-1970s.
>
> (Basualdo and Lozano, 2000)

By the late 1990s, average wages were almost 10 per cent lower than in the mid-1990s. Naturally, this persistent wage deterioration had an undisputable 'disciplining effect' on employed workers' behaviour. They were subject to unreasonable and inhumane working conditions, but accepted these in order to retain their jobs in a job market where there was an oversupply of labour.

RESPONSES BY UNIONS TO THESE CHALLENGES

The end of traditional (corporate) unionism

During the 1990s labour relations, the model of which was forged between 1950 and 1990, went into crisis. This model consisted of many labour regulations drafted by the state to ensure centralized negotiations. It meant there was state protection of business and the associated sectoral unions; negotiations were top-down; unions cooperated with business even though they were under pressure from their members; and unions operated away from the workplace, taking action only when they needed to obtain a collective agreement. Unions, instead of being class-based, belonged to the state, providing services to what was effectively an agreed state–union structure to benefit specific sectors. 'Today, the labour relations model tends toward more precarious employment; the decentralization of collective bargaining; flexibility; union decertification and privatization of unions' social projects' (Garza Toledo, 2001).

As Garza Toledo notes further:

> Corporatism was correlative to the social state, although not every social state implied corporatism. To this extent, corporatism came out of the attempt to reconcile economic growth with social peace, specifically labour peace, under the leadership of the state. As a result, labour relations were nationalized; state vigilance, institutionalization and coercion were placed at the service of labour governability, and relations between the state, unions and workers were greased with macro-, medium- and micro exchange systems. In underdeveloped countries, the exchange systems, in many aspects, had hereditary aspects.
>
> (Garza Toledo, 2001)

It is important to remember that before neoliberalism Argentina had low levels of unemployment, poverty and marginalization. It had high levels of wage earners, and industrial workers were particularly important. This was a workers' movement that was homogeneous and had an important structural presence. The level of organization and ability to influence through the structure of their unions, based on Peronism, permitted workers to fight for income levels substantially higher than those present in other Latin American countries. That produced the formation of a domestic market in which wage demand played a very important role. Today, the consumption profile indicates that about 23 per cent of consumer spending is done by wage earners. The rest is by high-income or middle-to-high income layers. This pattern of consumption also impacts on industry. In the past the domestic market determined which industries would be profitable. In addition, any increase in wages benefited certain business layers and the business owners of that sector. The type of union model that operated was that workers were organized within sectors, and workers and bosses were familiar with each other. Collective agreements[2] were bargained according to sectors or levels within sectors. In short, economic accumulation in Argentina was industrial accumulation. Stopping the industrial bargaining process meant stopping the accumulation process, and consequently, it created a power base for the workers. The power of the workers' movement was based on its ability to throw the accumulation process into crisis.

The relationship between the unions and employers in the industrial sectors needs to be seen against the backdrop of the relationship between industry and the powerful agricultural bourgeoisie. The considerable friction between these two sectors meant that a united and harmonious relationship between industrial capital and the workers movement was indispensable. This, of course, increased the power of the union movement. Unionism also had economic strength, because unions financed their activities not only with workers' contributions, but also through relatively lucrative social projects.[3] The tripod on which the union model of that period was built consisted then of sectoral unions, collective negotiations and social projects that increased financial power (Rauber, 1998: 47–50).

It is important to emphasize the strong political identity that workers embraced, Peronism. In reference to that, Víctor De Gennaro, general secretary of the CTA, explained: 'Peronism was the political unity that expressed and contained the working class. Union power was not only the structure, but the key identity: "Peron to power".'[4] The loss of power experienced by the union movement also had to do with representation, in the sense that traditional unions were constituted of formal wage workers, a sector that during the 1990s was hit very hard by neoliberalism. Not only were they no longer a majority, but the nature of shopfloor battles had changed to such an extent that the movement was no longer at the centre of social struggles. As Lozano says, 'for traditional unionism, the centre of organizing has always been formal wage-earners; therefore, while this today represents 40 per cent of all workers, it means that most of the working class is outside of the traditional union organizing' (quoted in Rauber, 1998: 51). Today it would be impossible to reconstitute the political/organizational unity of workers, first because of the above-mentioned reasons, but also largely because only a small minority of the formal wage-earning working class are currently union members. Harbouring traditional ideas of unionism is not only futile, but also places wave earners in opposition with non-unionized workers in the informal sector, and thus serves the needs of global capital.

In response to the crisis, corporate unions attempted at first to rebuild their old and obsolete alliance with the state, now under conditions of neoliberalism. They yielded their ability to control wages to the state so that the economic and labour policies favourable to neoliberalism could be established. The general result was – together with the important loss of labour victories, wage levels and living conditions – the loss of unions' status among workers. In any case, corporate-business unionism:

> became an obstacle to market flexibility and the work process ... because the neoliberal states reduced the space for union intervention in the design of economic, social and labour policies, in the party system, and in the institutions of workers' social reproduction; because collective contracts and labour laws became less protective of jobs, working conditions and wages. And finally, because the common sense recreated by neoliberalism identified the unions as monopolisers of the job market, protectors of the privileges of a minority of wage workers, the unionized. All of this led to isolation of the unions with respect to political parties, but above all in relation to the non-unionized majority of the population.
>
> (Garza Toledo, 2001)

The rapid establishment of neoliberalism signified, as Garza Toledo says:

> the decline of old union concepts and projects: for class agents, the collapse of the idea of state socialism; for the corporations, that of the authoritarian social state.... Nevertheless, neoliberalism, which has prostrated the unions, has not resolved basic contradictions and has developed others. One of the most important is the tension between the world of politics, with its representations of citizens, and that of work.
>
> (Garza Toledo, 2001)

In many Latin American countries, the unions – essential political actors in the fall of dictatorships and in the first stage of the not-yet neoliberal transition – became protagonists that have been dismantled, discredited and immersed in impotence and/or corruption. But that does not mean that they are going to disappear. From the perspective of workers who aspire to building their own alternative to the crisis and brutality imposed by neoliberalism, the challenge is to build a new type of unionism. The question that arises is: have options emerged in Latin America that are different from traditional unionism?

The CTA: a new strategy for organizing and representing workers

In 1991, in the town of Burzaco, right at the height of neoliberalism, what would soon become the Argentine Workers Federation (CTA) began to take shape. That was where workers' indignation consolidated in response to being sold out by the state, with the complicity of traditional corporate unionism, which had now become business unionism. Confidence sprouted in the idea that another country was possible, if workers took responsibility for building and developing it according to their interests and aspirations. Resistance to the handover of the country to the expansionist, imperialist voracity of capital, and in open opposition to corporate business unionism under the auspices of the General Labour Confederation (CGT), resulted in the decision of a group of unions to build a union organization capable of organizing and representing all workers, employed and unemployed. Among the group were the Association of State Employees (Asociación de Trabajadores del Estado, ATE) and the Confederation of Argentine Education Employees (Confederación de Trabajadores de la Educación de la República Argentina, CTERA).

The Burzaco developments and then the CTA laid the foundations for a new type of unionism, which later would be affirmed and would mature into the constitution of the CTA. In addition to reorganizing the employed and unemployed, a basic class alliance, the CTA set out to organize and coordinate with other social and political actors to build a new political and social order for Argentina. The CTA decided to design and construct a strategy that would enable it, first, to unify the working class as a whole, believing this to be the central force for any possible alternative to neoliberalism. Second, they recognized the need for a broad-based political movement that would include all those social organizations committed to end the imperial aims of global capital. Today, out of a total of 13 million workers in

Argentina, approximately 1.3 million are organized by the CTA, while the CGT has about 2.5 million members.

The foundation of the CTA

The CTA charted a line clearly different from traditional unionism. It strongly advocated political unionism, presaged by some experiences of the mid-20th century – like, for example, that of the CGT de Los Argentinos.[5] The new unionism strove to combine aspects of traditional unionism with the agenda of a national struggle. In other words, political unionism undertook to go beyond defending the sectoral interests of union members, and committed itself to reach out to other groups such as the unemployed, as well as social groups such as peasants and intellectuals, in order to overcome the social fragmentation of society. The goal is the formation of a broad-based organization representing all aspects of labour. Responsible citizens with an awareness of their interests and rights, who want to decide their own future, would make up the membership. It acknowledged both employed and jobless as workers, and by so doing, aimed to eliminate the potential for transnational employers to 'blackmail' workers into working under dire conditions, using the threat of unemployment:

> We understood at that moment, and today we reaffirm, that it wasn't enough to have unions, however decent they were in their conduct and however brave they showed themselves to be in defence of their comrades, if they did not break with the framework of corporatism by activity or by branch of activity, and if they didn't set themselves to working together with the unemployed who were beginning to organize themselves.
>
> (Micheli, 2004)

It should not be forgotten that neoliberalism has produced – along with a multitude of diverse groups of workers – intense individualism among employed workers, those who, in keeping with their workers' own strength, which is the embryo of the new historical subject in mercantilist logic, are identified as winners. Thus, for the CTA the rebuilding of the labour movement required coordination between employed workers and the unemployed.[6] The CGT, the union federation that advocated business unionism, did not, nor does it now, acknowledge the unemployed as members of the working class. It did not promote their organization, or support roadblocks when these were needed for the urgent defence of lives.

It remained, even in its most progressive aspects such as the Argentine Workers' Movement (MTA), within traditional unionism. Direct membership establishes this unity among workers in the CTA's constitution. It opens up the possibility for all workers, employed and unemployed, to be members of the federation, without necessarily having to belong to one of its unions.

This is a central, strategic proposal. The primary objective is to confront the structural fracturing of the world of work and recover the identity of the working class as workers. The concealment and distortion of the marginalization of the unemployed and their families has to be counteracted, and the CTA is turning its thought and action toward work. This is the central axis of the national problem, and consequently, also its solution. This assumes relationships with capital, with technology, with the markets, and as part of all this, the relationship between people: between the owners of capital and those who, in order to survive, sell them their labour power. The acknowledgement of the structural transformation of the world of work as the starting point for the transformation of the relationship of power between the main classes of Argentine society, and the effort to build and accumulate power for negotiating, challenging and 'creating a different sociopolitical project' by the workers, are the constituent elements of the CTA.

Rebuilding a popular movement

As Garza Toledo says, the challenge consists in:

> representing the actors in the plurality of their spaces of action: productive, political/electoral, reproductive, environmental, of gender, ethnicity, etc. The plurality of spaces also implies a plurality of friends and enemies, flexible, possible to reorganize in their alliances and conflicts. This leads to a reconsideration of the concepts of representation, legitimacy and democracy of workers' organizations that prevailed throughout almost the entire 20th century.
>
> (Garza Toledo, 2001)

The CTA anticipated that by [re]building a strong and unified working class capable of leading change first for the nation, but also for the continent, and finally encompassing a global labour force, transformation might become possible. Such a project would require that workers realize their own power through a raised consciousness, systematic organization and a sustained sense of unity. In

1999, referring to the CTA Congress held in Mar del Plata, its general secretary affirmed: 'It is the first consolidation of the CTA's identity. [Because] it is the first congress where discussion began on the strategy for power with our own strength starting with the workers.' This congress marked the beginning of a new era in South American politics: that of building a union federation. It meant going out to look for the millions of ordinary men and women who had to be won, to organize other sectors so that a collective movement capable of designing a new national and popular project could be created. These were the actions taken by the CTA during the period from 1999 to 2001. Big national marches, marches by the unemployed, roadblocks, encampments on roads and in fields spelled out the issues of unemployment and exclusion. The anti-neoliberal movement is not restricted to the capital of the country but is spreading. The building of a broad-based labour movement focuses on consolidation and on building from the bottom up.[7]

Union, political and cultural action have been developed in a multiplicity of spaces, forms of organization and representation. Each one of them is particular and at the same time collective. Representatives and the process of organization take place away from the workplace, which creates a freedom of expression and a diversity of action. It means a far higher profile and general awareness of the conglomerate that does not accept the 'virtues' of a neoliberal democracy ruled by the market. The aim has been to have a large number of progressive groupings to buy into the building of an alternative society. The purpose is, as the federation's builders say, to counterpoise the society of the market with the society of humanistic production so that social justice, equality of rights, solidarity, respect for differences and environmental equilibrium can be sustained. Barriers regarding the meaning and reach of politics and what is political have to be renegotiated, especially within the framework of a diverse group of participants, so that alternatives that encompass the demands and possibilities of the 21st century can be conceptualized. Union-led resistance has grown in Argentina, but that does not imply a mature alternative project. Defensive resistance continues to be predominant. The CTA aims to ensure that the labour movement can recover confidence that change is possible. Because there:

> still is great scepticism among people regarding many politicians, union leaders.... My concern is that with the excuse of not believing, they end up not believing in themselves. They end

up believing that it is not worth the trouble to show solidarity, to organize themselves, to be leaders, to fight for their freedom, for the rights that are theirs. This is our problem. Our problem is not convincing those who hold power that they have to modify and open the doors so that we can find our paths and figure out how to survive better .... Our challenge is to begin to convince our comrades that the only way to be able to change this situation and transform society is to believe again that it is possible, and to believe again that our only strength is in us. And with that perspective, it is the crisis that is worth confronting, because it is the crisis that can really resolve our peoples' problems.

(De Gennaro, 2001)

International integration, it is believed, must form part of the programme. The CTA works in conjunction with the region, mainly with the union organization of the Common Market of the Southern Cone of Latin America (MERCOSUR), and with workers' organizations and networks of the continent and the world:

We need better integration, greater communication for organizing not only unemployed workers, those in precarious conditions, but also for imagining new organizational forms. Today, a company has the ability to decide where it wants to go to exploit, because there are places where politicians offer the best conditions to exploit their people. They even compete to see who offers the best conditions, playing with the lives of our compatriots. We need regional and international organizations that are capable of restoring a different project, not just in our countries but also for the world.

(De Gennaro, 2001)

MAIN CURRENT CHALLENGES

After December 2001, and particularly after Kirchner's victory and his assumption of the presidency in May 2004, the process of building the federation confronted the obstacles that come with all social construction in politically receptive situations. 'When spaces are opened, our weaknesses and what we are lacking also show. It is a higher discussion.'[8] When something has emerged under the banner of opposition to neoliberalism, when some components of the neoliberal model are called into question by some government sectors, it is no longer enough to be the opposition. The ability to propose and build alternatives is fundamental. Proposals are not ideas, but, as Víctor De Gennaro says, relationships of forces. That is why, he states, 'it is no longer enough to be the opposition. Now you must have proposals and assume the responsibility of maintaining what you propose.'[9] This implies the ability to integrate the interests of the configuration of social forces, or perhaps, as a necessary previous step, the creation of such an ability. That is for the CTA, as for so many social actors of the continent, an urgent and central unresolved task.

The CTA's current challenges include the need to identify internal obstacles and contradictions, and seek to overcome them positively, empowering members to tackle problems and to believe in the possibility of labour victories. New political definitions determined by union actions will emerge as a new type of union federation operates within the confines of a market-driven economy in the current situation of the country, the region, the continent and the world. Transforming itself to transform while transforming would be, perhaps, the description that comes closest to the process of growth and constitution/self-constitution of the social actors that characterized the years of resistance, struggles and advances of the CTA. That process became at the same time an educational exercise in the formation of consciousness, organization, proposals, of power and although still in a fragmented way, of the project itself. The construction of a broad, plural and multi-sectoral social liberation force, together with the initiation of an alternative project that aims to transform the nature of the economy, sums up the greatest political, social and ethical challenges for the CTA at this point in time in the 21st century.

ACKNOWLEDGEMENT

The translation is by Rose Ana Dueñas.

NOTES

1   Informal name given to the impact of the 1994 Mexican economic crisis on the South American economy. The crisis occurred because of a sudden devaluation in the Mexican peso, which then caused other currencies in the region (the southern cone and Brazil) to fall. The falling peso was propped up by a US$50 billion loan granted by then-US President Bill Clinton.
2   In this case, reference is not being made to the formal legal question. It refers to the existence of a dynamic objective of economic functioning

that facilitates (politically) the worker–employer agreement by sector of activity, independently of the fact that such agreements may obtain legal recognition under the form of such agreement. These agreements depend on the prevailing institutional situation.

3   The social projects are directed by the union, but with operations and administration separate from the contributions of union members. They include medical centres, holiday camps, training schools and sports clubs. With the exception of state employees and educators, they were constituted with a percentage of contributions from workers' wages (between 3 and 5 per cent) and employer contributions (between 6 and 10 per cent). In collective agreements, clauses were also included regarding contributions to social projects. For example, a percentage of the first wage raise obtained through bargaining – for both union members and non-members – went to social projects. In addition, seven mixed institutes were created, including banking, insurance and national education, providing income in addition to the contributions mentioned above. However, the funds allocated to these projects were generally ill-used, and this often by the union leaders themselves.

Currently, shielding themselves behind these and other deficiencies, the social projects have been modified by decree. Employers' contributions have been reduced by more than 25 per cent with the argument that it is necessary to cut labour costs. This ignores the fact that contributions were made on the understanding that they constitute an indirect wage on the basis of workers' solidarity.

4   Comments by Víctor De Gennaro on this study. Buenos Aires, April 2006.

5   Name taken by a combative section of the CGT which, in 1968, separated from the bureaucratic leadership of the CGT, identified as the CGT Azopardo.

6   In a relentless struggle for their survival and their rights to work, health, education, housing and land, the unemployed became recognized social actors. Fighting for a place in society, they took to the streets to demand their rights. In their demonstrations with the greatest social impact, they have assumed '*piquetes*' – groups of people blocking the roads, streets or bridges – as a form of basic struggle. Hence, they are routinely identified as *piqueteros*. Some *piquetero* sectors joined the CTA through their affiliate organizations; for example the Federation for Land, Housing and Habitat (FTV) and the Territorial Liberation Movement (MTL). Others identify with and organize through the Class and Combative Current (CCC), or the Movement of Unemployed Workers (MTD), the 'Teresa Rodríguez' Movement, and the Territorial Liberation Movement, Barrios Risen Up, and others.

7   The concept 'from the bottom up' indicates that the orientation, proposal, construction or transformation is based on the roots of the problem or phenomenon under discussion. It indicates, thus, that at the

same time, those processes – understood to be radical – emerge from within the very phenomenon or process that they seek to transform.

8   Comments by Víctor De Gennaro on this study. Buenos Aires, April 2006.

9   Comments by Víctor De Gennaro on this study. Buenos Aires, April 2006.

Chapter 7

Neoliberal policies, labour market restructuring and social exclusion: Brazil's working-class response

Kjeld Jakobsen and Alexandre de Freitas Barbosa

This chapter first seeks to present the main social and economic characteristics of Brazil by the end of its industrialization process. Then we describe how Brazil entered a context of an increasingly globalized economy in a passive and submissive way, making use of the neoliberal policies recommended by the Washington Consensus. Third, we discuss the impact these policies had on the dynamics of the labour market. We argue that unemployment and informality have spread, and the country has experienced new forms of social exclusion. In the final part, we analyse how labour and social movements responded to this attempt at excluding society from the Brazilian economy.

BRAZIL FROM 1930 TO 1980: ECONOMIC DYNAMISM, INCOME CONCENTRATION AND THE ROLE OF THE LABOUR MOVEMENT

Throughout this period, which alternated between democratic and authoritarian regimes, economic policies were implemented – some more nationalist and others seeking to associate with imperialism – that instilled dynamism into the economy, building on domestic market growth and diversification.

Let us examine some broad indicators. Between 1930 and 1980, Brazil boasted economic growth rates of about 6 per cent a year on average. More importantly, the country shifted from an immense 'farm', in which 60 per cent of the workforce lived in the rural areas, to become an urban and industrial society. The industrial sector advanced in the more capital-intensive sectors, and by the late 1970s, the country had become the largest economy of the developing world. On the other hand, the adoption of an industrial copycat model rather than one driven by technological innovation held the country hostage to decisions taken by multinational companies, while the domestic market was restricted to the country's 'wealthiest' 30 per cent. That is, it encompassed at best the middle class and some strata of the factory working elite. Functional and personal income concentration increased dramatically. The country was not able during the industrialization period to set up a national financial system, becoming an easy prey to the international oscillations of the late 1970s.

The performance of the labour market, for the whole of the country, revealed some positive aspects. Formal salaried work grew more rapidly than the economically active population (EAP) (at 6.2 per cent and 2.6 per cent annual averages, respectively) between 1940 and 1980 (Pochmann, 1998). Throughout this long period, while the overall employment level grew in cumulative terms by some 186 per cent, occupation in the manufacturing sector expanded by 423 per cent, and even more rapidly in the case of governmental services, reaching 527 per cent (Barbosa, 2004).

As one of the outcomes of the industrialization process, Brazil was able to give birth to a national working class protected by labour legislation, even if such legislation did not benefit all segments. Meanwhile, the salaried middle class expanded, with technicians and professionals with a college degree and company and public sector managers gaining space, while the small bourgeoisie, at least in relative terms, lost ground. In 1980, over two-thirds of the Brazilian middle class was composed of salaried workers (Pochmann et al., 2006).

Still, and regardless of these indices indicative of the structuring of a relatively 'modern' labour market, Brazil would present distinctive features in relation to the pattern of employment prevalent in developed countries: high disparity between income levels, a high percentage of occupied workers in non-organized sectors and the lack of a universal system of social protection.

Concomitantly, we emphasize that of the country's total salaried workers – including both urban and rural areas – by the end of this expansive cycle, approximately one-third of them were still out of the reach of labour legislation. The country had failed to create a collective statute of labour; nor had it been able to create a salaried society as defined by Robert Castel (1999), with the country's landless rural workers (*bóias-frias*), small land holders and the big cities' mass of underemployed living in a permanent precarious state. If we add precarious self-employment in the city and in the countryside, domestic servants and excess workers, we reach the conclusion that these segments amounted to 35 per cent of the Brazilian workforce in 1981 (Santos, 2002).

It is worth noting that the government that seized power in 1930 and which modernized Brazilian capitalism under authoritarian inspiration took upon itself the task of regulating the functioning of trade unions, as well as introducing labour legislation. Apart from extending the rights achieved by some trade unions in the struggles of the 1920s, it also created a few new ones such as, for example, the minimum wage. Such rights were consolidated in a single piece of legislation in 1943 (Labour Laws Consolidation), yet benefited only urban workers with regular working contracts, while imposing a model of labour organization heavily controlled by the state. Collective bargaining agreements were scarce.

The only modifications this union model has undergone to date is that the new 1988 Brazilian Constitution eliminated the previously existing ideological restrictions against workers seeking to be elected to trade union boards, and the suppression of a provision that allowed the Ministry of Labour to intervene directly in the unions and even remove officials who had been legitimately elected by the workers. At the same time, collective agreements and conventions spread to various sectors.

Urbanization was another trend of the period. Between 1950 and 1980, the urban population had expanded at an annual pace of 4.4 per cent, leading to an urbanization rate of about 70 per cent in the country at the end of the period. The metropolises concentrated both the wealth and social exclusion. In that same year, 58 per cent of the poor were concentrated in urban and metropolitan areas (Rocha, 2004).

It is worth pointing out that in the 1960s, after the 1964 coup d'état, an important disruption took place. Brazil would continue growing in a dynamic way, and now internationalizing in commercial, productive and financial terms. However, the country would close the political arena for society's diverse sectors to express their interests in order to become an autocratic bourgeoisie (Fernandes, 1987), allied to oligarchic groups with the acquiescence of segments of the middle class, while the working majority would now be deprived of the benefits of increased growth and productivity. As a consequence the income concentration index soared: the gap between the average income of the wealthiest 10 per cent and the poorest 10 per cent rose from 21-fold to 47-fold between 1960 and 1980.

In this period, trade unions run by the left suffered direct intervention by the military regime, the majority of union leaders were removed from their positions, and many were imprisoned. At the time, the only organizing space was amidst the progressive sector of the Catholic Church. The period thereafter was of political dissension, culminating in the end of the military dictatorship and the indirect election of the first civilian president in 1985. A slow and negotiated process, without political disruptions, marked the transition period. However, despite the concerted transition, a strong social movement would simultaneously emerge, whose most vigorous expression was a series of strikes that broke out between 1978 and 1986 in high-technology sectors of the economy, and the rise of many leftist unionists to the boards of the most important unions.

This expansive process would be interrupted in the 1980s by the international crisis, which presented three facets: oil price hikes, falling commodity prices and rising US interest rates. To cushion that crisis, the Brazilian government signed agreements with the International Monetary Fund (IMF) which included raising domestic interest rates and the generation of trade surpluses. Increasing domestic public debt was the mechanism adopted to shoulder the cost of servicing foreign debt (Belluzzo and Almeida, 2002). Contrary to the conservative diagnosis, inflation levels did not yield, while gross domestic product (GDP) remained stagnant throughout the decade and urban unemployment levels rose.

Despite the re-democratization movement that led to the signing of the 1988 Constitution and the strengthening of social movements, the 1990s would be characterized by the introduction of a plan to stabilize price levels, which was to bring with it a drastic alteration of the role of the state and of the country's model of internationalization, based on a set of economic reforms geared toward deregulation and economic liberalization. As a result, an earthquake shook the Brazilian social structure.

ECONOMIC OPENING, PRIVATIZATION AND ATTRACTION OF FOREIGN INVESTMENTS: THE NEW FORMS OF DEPENDENCY

The 1990s may be considered a watershed in Brazilian economic history. Unlike the 1980s, an economic model of structural change was now pursued. In the vision of the architects of this new model, the Brazilian economy needed a shock of competitiveness to position itself in the global market and receive investment from the multinationals, a process which would raise growth and productivity rates, and naturally reduce unemployment, poverty and inequality. The state would kick-start reforms – privatization, social security and public administration – which would improve its efficiency, allowing for a fall in interest rates. To complete the package, labour legislation – regarded as rigid – would be made flexible in order to reduce production costs and informality. It was time to leave behind 'a past of inflationism, self-sufficiency and widespread nationalization', according to the view of one of the most famous Brazilian neoliberal economists (Franco, 1999). In this sense, the Real Plan – launched in 1994 – must be interpreted as much more than a mere stabilization plan. In fact it involved a strategy that at its inception combined fiscal adjustment, monetary reform and a dollar peg, with the real appreciating as foreign capital flowed in, eager for financial gains. The government raised interest rates, especially after the Mexican crisis of December 1994 and the instability it brought onto the financial markets.

From that moment onwards, the country experienced rising foreign deficits, which would exceed 4 per cent of GDP in 1998. Inflation stabilized at low levels, but economic growth slowed down and investments were postponed. New financial crises like the Asian crisis in 1997, and the Russian crisis in 1998, had a contagious effect on emerging markets. Interest rates rose significantly once again. In January 1999 Brazil devalued its currency, after having burned its reserves throughout 1998 to sustain an artificial parity with the dollar.

Due to an inflation increase, interest rates remained at high levels in the post-devaluation period, while an agreement was signed with the IMF, setting increasing primary surpluses to honour the rolling of the public debt. Yet this debt had grown precisely as a result of the high interest rates used to shore up that artificial parity. Thus, in macro-economic terms, because of the financial and trade liberalization – both initiated in the 1990s – Brazil was forced to attract capital to offset the current account deficit. Part of this capital took the path of easy gains in public debt bonds, and part was converted into foreign debt (some national companies had to turn away from the domestic market's forbidding interest rates) or turned to buying national and state-owned companies at prices below their market value.

Moreover, the competitive pressure on the internal market – fuelled by a contractionist monetary policy – prompted the closure of many companies, with a subsequent surge in the levels of unemployment, informality and outsourcing/subcontracting, as we shall see later on. In other words, the economic model did not work, or at least not in the way propounded by its advocates. The economy grew between 1994 and 2002 at an annual average of 2.3 per cent, slightly above the demographic growth, while investments stagnated as a percentage of GDP despite the robust inflow of capital generated by multinational companies. The sale of US$100 billion in public assets did not prevent foreign debt from skyrocketing from 30 to 60 per cent of GDP during this period. These factors weakened the role of the state in the coordination and implementation of investments.

Let us look at each of the following aspects separately: feeble economic growth and stagnation of investment as a percentage of GDP; volume and profile of foreign direct investment; the role and the impact of privatizations on some strategic sectors; and the internationalization model. As Figure 7.1 demonstrates, Brazil is a classic example of an economy subjected to 'stop and go'. The country only managed to grow above 4 per cent a year in the years of 1994, 2000 and 2004, characterized by a bonanza in the international market. With financial liberalization, in a context of fast movement of capital flows around the world, Brazil lost the autonomy of its monetary policy, leading to strong currency oscillations. Investment rates went up and down with the international changes, never exceeding 20 per cent of GDP.

As for foreign direct investment, we observe that it did not fulfil the dynamic role that neoliberal economists had assigned to it.

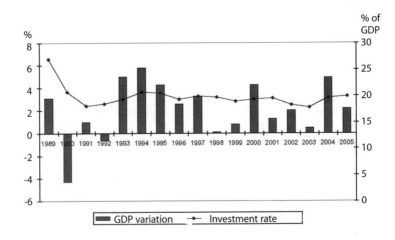

Figure 7.1 Investment rate (as percentage of GDP) and GDP/real variation in Brazil, 1989–2005

Source: IPEA.

Despite the increased productive internationalization of the Brazilian economy, the higher levels of foreign investment did not lead to a new stage of economic development in the country. This was largely because such investments targeted mainly the acquisition of national company assets (state-owned or private), and not the expansion of productive capacity. What is more, such investments were not coupled with policies designed to strengthen the country's productive chains, improve compliance with labour standards and price regulation/mediation mechanisms to prevent distortions, especially in the highly concentrated segments of the services industry. Indeed, what we perceive is that in the period comprising 1996 to 2000, when foreign direct investments boomed in Brazil, 80 per cent of this capital was directed to the services sector. Through the privatizations, the multinationals concentrated their investments on strategic services sectors, holding thereby an advantageous or quasi-monopolistic position in the market.

Not surprisingly, 70 per cent of the resources spent on privatizations (see Figure 7.2) concentrated on the energy, telecommunications and financial sectors. These sectors have a decisive impact on the population's purchasing power – high tariffs and interest rates – and on the capacity to define proposals for the universalization of access to services for the population.

It is worth noting though that the Brazilian case is exceptional

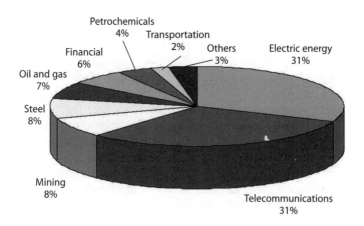

Figure 7.2 Distribution of privatizations in Brazil per sector of activity, 1991–2002

in that, unlike most of the other Latin-American countries, the federal public banks were not privatized and continue to play a strategic role in providing credit to small rural farmers and in the payment of income transfer programmes.

With regard to trade liberalization, the country started to focus more and more on the export of natural resource-intensive products, even though the devaluation contributed to an increase in trade surpluses in the industrial sector, quite often generated by multinational companies which, given the Brazilian economy's slow growth rate, had idle capacity.

In terms of tariff protections, we notice from 1990 onwards a radical transformation of the Brazilian trade policy, with non-tariff barriers being eliminated and a fierce reduction in the level and scope of tariff barriers taking place (WTO, 2004). The average import rate dropped from 44 per cent to 12.8 per cent between 1989 and 1994, which to some extent happened simultaneously with the Common Market of the Southern Cone of Latin America (MERCOSUR) tariff-elimination calendar. After the 1999 devaluation tariffs fell once again, flattening out at a 10.4 per cent level in 2004 (Pereira, 2005). From 1999 onwards, overall the liberalizing wave ebbs, despite a slight tariff reduction, and Brazil manages to retain a reasonably diversified industrial base. It is also worth pointing out that throughout the 1990s there was a considerable increase in the coefficient of penetration of imports in manufacturing industry, which leaped from 4.5 per cent to 13.4 per cent between 1990 and 2002. For most sectors, this coefficient dropped slightly between 2002 and 2004, which demonstrates the import substitution process that occurred in this period.

With regard to exports, influenced by the commodities boom the country succeeded in increasing more recently its trade surplus in the low and medium-technology mining and agriculture segments, but has become a net importer in the high-technology segments (IEDI, 2005). This trend may be even reinforced by the recent overvaluing of the currency. As a heritage of the neoliberal economic model, we are faced with an economy growing below its potential, in which the domestic market suffers competitive pressure from abroad, multinational companies occupy leading positions in strategic services sectors and refuse to be regulated, and the country remains vulnerable to the whims of the international financial market.

In conclusion, it was not taken into account that the potential benefits of the liberalization would depend on the national circumstances and on the gradualism of policy implementation (Stiglitz,

2002; Stiglitz and Charlton, 2005). Brazil undertook unilateral trade liberalization without demanding compensations from the developed countries. The capital market opened up suddenly, and the Brazilian currency was irresponsibly appreciated, with the country losing the opportunity to position itself actively in the context of globalization. When the local currency devalued and the domestic market regained some breath, the country once again fell for the fairy tale of seeking investment grade and exchange appreciation, fuelled by the commodities boom and the new short-term capital race toward emerging markets. The forms of dependence become more complex, restricted not only to the decisions made by multinationals or the export of more volatile goods in terms of prices, but dependent upon the submission to international financial capital, which establishes conditionalities for the internal economic policy, thus limiting the state's autonomy to set interest and exchange rates, and holding the state's investing capacity hostage to the international conjuncture.

The purpose of seeking the reconstruction of a national economic system that is minimally socially coherent and inclusive (Furtado, 1998) – with a foreign positioning driven by the assimilation of more value-added sectors – was frustrated, leading to a shrinking of the middle class and a *destructuring* of the working class. What actually happened was a counter-revolution orchestrated by capital in an attempt to defend itself from the alternatives that could have been set up by various segments of civil society, and especially organized labour, during its awakening in the 1980s.

INCREASED 'SOCIAL DEBT': UNEMPLOYMENT, INFORMALITY AND EXCLUSION

With the economic growth trends reversal and the trade and financial liberalization of the 1990s – coupled with stringent monetary policies and the privatizations programme – the labour market, which had modernized and generated ascending social mobility in the past, despite the high income concentration and the still pervasive informality, transformed itself into a mechanism for shutting out the workforce. As a consequence, the share of labour in national income fell from 42 per cent to 36 per cent. New forms of social exclusion emerged, and informality, which had been contained in the industrialization period, spread to every sector and region, attacking especially the more 'developed' regions and sectors.

Throughout the 1990s, unemployment emerged as a mass phenomenon, leaping from 3 per cent to 10 per cent between 1989 and 2001, quadrupling the total number of unemployed, which increased to approximately 8 million by the end of the decade. We point out that this figure refers only to open unemployment, measured as the total number of people offering their working capacity who do not have any form of monetary wages. When considering other forms of hidden unemployment, we observe that some metropolitan regions presented unemployment rates close to, or even higher than, 20 per cent (SEADE/DIEESE methodology[1]). Informal work in turn leaped from 49 per cent to 53 per cent of the total workers occupied throughout the decade. This indicator encompasses self-employed workers, or in family establishments without any monetary compensation, and those workers with no contract, who are wage earners, yet have no access to many of the rights guaranteed by the Brazilian labour law.

After the 1999 devaluation – the result of a small rise in the economy's growth rate and increasing exports – formal employment grew once again more than any other form of employment, but this however was insufficient to reduce unemployment levels (Figure 7.3).

During the 1990s, when analysing only urban Brazil, we perceive that the more dynamic jobs went to non-contract workers, followed

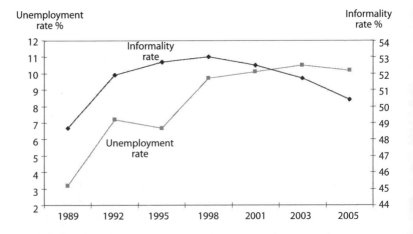

Figure 7.3 Brazil's unemployment rate (as a percentage of the economically active population) and informality rate (as a percentage of total occupied workers), 1989–2005

Source: PNAD/IBGE.

by household servants and self-employed workers. When we analyse the results per sector, we can verify that between 1990 and 1999, some 2 million jobs were eliminated in the manufacturing sector (a 20 per cent drop). With regard to the industrial job standard, there is a growing tendency toward precarious occupations, especially in the case of the metropolitan regions. The level of informality of the industrial employment in these regions jumped from 16.5 per cent to 29.3 per cent between 1991 and 1999 (Ramos, 2002).

With regard to agriculture, by using another database, the Demographic Census, with information for the years 1991 and 2000, we can verify a reduction of 3 million jobs in agricultural activities. This is a 26 per cent reduction in these jobs, concentrated on small rural farmers. According to the data in Table 7.1, more than 50 per cent of the jobs cut were subsistence jobs or non-remunerated jobs, usually linked to small rural production, most of which were done by peasants. Surely a significant part of these 1,250,000 workers expelled from small rural properties are engaged in the various social movements struggling for land throughout the country. It may be stressed that out of the 16 million existing jobs in farming and cattle production in 2002, representing 20 per cent of the country's occupied workers, around 60 per cent comprise small land owners and rural peasants, while 28 per cent are employed, directly or indirectly, by agribusiness, with only half of these workers being under the Brazilian labour code.

Table 7.1 Distribution of occupied workers and accumulated balance of employment in the agricultural sector per position occupied, Brazil, 1992 and 2002

Type of occupation	1992	%	2002	%	Balance 2002–1992	%
Permanent employee	2,917,606	15.7	2,353,825	14.6	(563,781)	23.1
Temporary employee	2,205,951	11.9	2,073,622	12.8	(132,329)	5.4
Self-employed	4,541,417	24.4	4,208,729	26.1	(332,688)	13.6
Employer	585,406	3.1	430,461	2.7	(154,945)	6.3
Non remunerated worker	5,123,681	27.6	3,976,055	24.6	(1,147,626)	46.9
Worker in production for own consumption	3,211,416	17.3	3,097,810	19.2	(113,606)	4.6
Total	18,585,477	100.0	16,140,502	100.0	(2,444,975)	100.0

Source: PNAD/IBGE.

The services industry, in turn, fulfilled the role of great demander of labour, generating formal and informal occupations and assimilating workers at the extremities of income and qualification. By the end of the period, the services and commerce sectors accounted for nearly 70 per cent of the jobs with working contracts, for 64.3 per cent of the non-contract jobs and for 52 per cent of the non-salaried jobs (Table 7.2). That is, while the manufacturing-sector jobs became more precarious, the services sector became more formal – which is due to the expansion of social services and low-skill services, but also to the process of outsourcing more modern activities. Not coincidentally, it is the sector with the worst individual income distribution compared with manufacturing industry and agriculture (Cardoso, 1999).

With regard to urban workers for the year 2000, according to Census data, less than half of the workers were under the Brazilian labour legislation. Yet more than 50 per cent of the total amount of urban workers were situated in the income range from the minimum wage to double it. If we add employees with no contract to the self-employed workers, these will total 17.3 million people in urban Brazil, against 15.6 million workers linked to the organized sector of the labour market.

Another way of analysing this socio-economic reality – in which the workers' structural excess appears as a characteristic trait, even prompting the expansion of the labour market's secondary segment, distinguished by labour illegality – is attempted in Figure 7.4. Here we perceive a factory working class –manual occupations with labour rights – that accounted for 28 per cent of the EAP in 2002, against a segment of informal workers with no college education, comprising 15 per cent of the EAP. In addition, there is a middle class comprising those occupations with college education workers, formal or informal, which represents 8.2 per cent of the job supply. Therefore, we come up to almost 42 million workers who have a position in society as workers, even if some of them earn low salaries and have no access to labour laws. Alternatively, when we put together the low-productivity, non-capitalist sector with the industrial reserve army – comprising, according to this methodology, jobless workers plus those informal workers who earn less than half a minimum wage – we reach a contingent of almost 41 million people.

That is, regardless of the angle of analysis, we can observe, on the one hand, the existence of a still structured labour market, albeit corroded by precarious conditions. And on the other, there is an

Table 7.2 Percentage of employment by sector in Brazil, 1989 and 2001

Type of occupation	1989			2001		
	Agriculture	Industry*	Services and commerce	Agriculture	Industry*	Services and commerce
Salaried jobs	13.1	29.4	57.5	9.0	23.4	67.6
With contract	4.8	38.1	57.1	3.6	26.8	69.6
No contract	25.2	16.6	58.2	16.7	19.0	64.3
Non-salaried	42.6	12.7	44.7	32.8	15.3	51.9

*Includes manufacturing, construction and public utilities.

Source: IBGE/PNAD.

Table 7.3 Occupational structure of urban workers in Brazil, 2000

	No.	**%**
Employee with working contract	15,625,318	46.5
Employee with no working contract	9,066,841	27.0
Self-employed	8,282,002	24.6
Apprentice or trainee/intern with no remuneration	187,244	0.6
Non remunerated helping household member	472,791	1.4
Total	**33,634,196**	**100.0**

Source: Census 2000, IBGE.

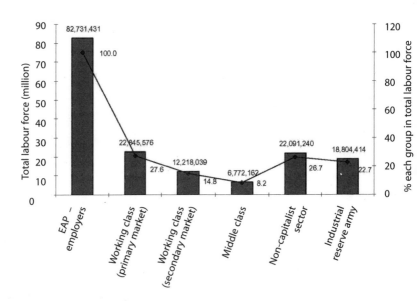

Figure 7.4 Distribution of Brazilian workforce according to share in labour market, 2002

Source: PNAD/IBGE. Own elaboration.

industrial reserve army that besieges the labour market (Lessa, 2005), and next to which grows a poorly structured core of non-capitalist activities, usually distinguished by their low income level and high occupational instability. Even in more modern metropolises like São Paulo, we observe that, rather than a free flow between

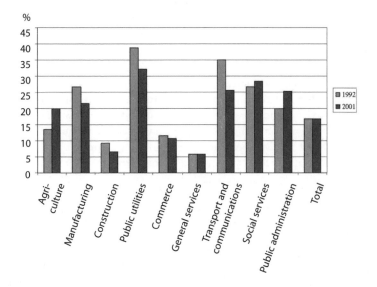

Figure 7.5 Unionization rate per sector of activity, Brazil, 1992 and 2001 (as a percentage of total workers)

Source: PNAD/IBGE.

unemployment and employment, two-thirds of the workers live in a grey zone, where workers are constantly in and out of a condition of unemployment, employment or inactivity (Guimarães, 2006).

Despite the rising precarious conditions of the labour market, the level of unionization in relation to the occupied workforce has remained stable at 16.7 per cent in the 1990s. This stability, however, hides remarkable cross-sector variations. In the manufacturing sector and in other industrial activities (public utility services), as well as in the transportation and communications segments, all of which were affected by a fall in employment, outsourcing/subcontracting and informality, unionization rates dropped dramatically.

In the agricultural sector, however, unionization expanded vigorously, as well as in social activities and public administration, due to the fact that the 1988 Constitution granted this right to public-sector workers. We can also observe that in service and commerce activities, in which employment expanded more rapidly, unionization rates do not exceed the 10 per cent level. At any rate, in a considerable share of the social segments that constituted the combative hard core of the working class until the 1980s, there was indeed an important decrease in unionization.

In sum, significant segments of the Brazilian working class experienced a regressive trend in terms of levels of income, access to labour law and union representation. The economic reforms, in this sense, transformed Brazil into an ever more advantageous space for the enlarged reproduction of capital, despite the low economic growth levels, making the country a champion of inequality. Even the post-1999 recovery of formal employment, though bringing a stabilization of unemployment and a soft drop in informality, has proved insufficient to overcome the heritage of the 1990s.

RESPONSES OF AND CHALLENGES TO THE WORKING CLASS AND THE SOCIAL MOVEMENTS

The social and political movement that stood up to face the neoliberalism of the 1990s had undergone a series of changes in the course of the three previous decades. In addition to the aforementioned rise of leftist activists to union boards in the early 1980s through electoral disputes, there was also the founding in 1983 of the first union confederation after the 1964 coup – the Workers Single Union (Central Única dos Trabalhadores, CUT).[2] Workers in agriculture obtained the right to organize unions in the early 1960s, but their National Confederation of Agriculture Workers (CONTAG) was created two months before the military coup and was soon under government intervention. Public employees, although they organized in non-union associations since the late 1970s, only had their unions recognized by the 1988 Constitution.

Both in the urban and rural areas, a strong and organized social movement arose. The urban popular movement organized in the outskirts of the cities in their struggle for the implementation of public policies like housing, health, transportation, sanitation, among others, plus gender policies, while the 'landless' movement laid its roots in the countryside, starting in 1986 and fighting for agrarian reform. This picture is completed by the return of many leftist militants from exile who, through the creation of non-governmental organizations (NGOs), brought new themes such as the environment and human rights to the political debate. With regard to party politics, on the progressive camp, we had the founding of the Brazilian Workers' Party (PT) in 1980, as well as that of other leftist parties soon after, like the Brazilian Socialist Party (PSB), and the legalization of the two existing communist parties. Yet, as the 1980s crisis deepened, including phases of higher unemployment, and as the new Constitution defined new rules for the political game, this entire movement's growth reached its peak and it began to become more defensive because of the adoption of neoliberal policies and their social impact in the country.

The first president to be elected directly by the people, Fernando Collor de Mello in 1989, defeated Lula, the candidate of the left, by a small margin. The fact that a leftist candidate had made it to the second round of the election, representing a political party with only nine years of existence, the PT, was surprising and demonstrated the progress the social movement had accomplished in the struggle for the re-democratization of the country. Collor's most immediate challenge was to reduce the high inflation rate, which had reached the figure of 100 per cent a month. He attempted to achieve that by means of an economic price and wage control plan, as well as interfering in the financial market. The plan flopped in a couple of months and inflation came back, though at lower levels. More importantly, the Collor administration would give the start to an ambitious denationalization programme, which was set off by selling the state-controlled steel and petrochemical sectors. The first company to be auctioned was steelmaking Companhia Siderúrgica Nacional (CSN), the biggest and the oldest of all. It had been chosen to be the first because it was a symbol of the country's developmentalist period, which, in the opinion of the mentors of the new government, had been supplanted. To keep CSN from being auctioned, demonstrators tried every means imaginable, including a siege of the Rio de Janeiro Stock Exchange. The auction came to be adjourned on a judicial decision, but the government managed to nullify the provisional ruling. From then on, the remaining privatizations in the steel industry encountered less resistance.

The labour movement tried to resist restructuring. Workers of the federal electricity sector went on strike for 30 days in June 1990 against the wage freeze, which in practice constituted a breach of the collective bargaining agreement in force. During the strike, there were moments when some regions had blackouts, but the movement was defeated and more than 200 workers, including many unionists, were fired. An important moment for one sector of the labour movement, the metalworkers, was the negotiation at the automotive sectorial chamber in 1992. In view of the crisis in this sector, tripartite negotiations resolved that the federal and state governments would reduce taxes and the auto companies grant job stability and wage increases, as well as price stability for a given period, which

increased the sector's production at the time and upheld the employment level until late 1994. There were attempts to extend this model
of negotiation to other sectors, such as petrochemicals and air transportation. This, however, failed because of the lack of interest of the
entrepreneurial sector in granting any concession, and the political
crisis which would soon after lead to the president's impeachment
on charges of corruption in the year 1992.

This political process that was set off by a denunciation by
Collor's own brother gained the streets, with CUT-affiliated unions
and the student movement playing a key role in organizing the
popular mobilization in support of the impeachment, which was to
be approved by Congress in that same year. Although the new
government headed by vice-president Itamar Franco granted an
amnesty to the electricity federal workers dismissed in June 1990,
and slowed down the privatization programme, it would proceed
with the implementation of the measures proposed by the Washington Consensus in an attempt to stabilize the economy and control
inflation, which had started to approach 20 per cent a month. The
adoption of the Real Plan, on July 1994, politically benefited the
then finance minister, Fernando Henrique Cardoso (FHC), who
launched his candidacy for president of the Republic for the October
1994 elections.

Candidate Lula was defeated for the second time. Perhaps there
was not much that could be done electorally in face of the recovery
of the purchasing power of low-income Brazilians with the end of
inflation. Yet the assessment of the leftist candidate's aides, also
shared by the CUT, was that the plan had electoral motivations, and
all the opposition started criticizing it emphatically. This assessment
proved simplistic and naive, for the government managed to back it
up for nearly four years. Some sectors of the left, especially from the
intelligentsia, judged that because of FHC's past – declaredly social
democrat, he had even been highly regarded as one of the creators
of the 'dependence theory' – he would head a progressive government. That was another mistake, for his administration adopted the
usual neoliberal premises from the beginning until the end. At once,
in addition to promoting the measures preached by the Washington
Consensus and reforming the Constitution's economic chapter to
liberalize certain areas of the economy which were still closed, such
as the exploration of the subsoil, he also carried out a bank reform
that cost some billion dollars to the public coffers in compensation
to banks for the financial losses brought about by lower inflation.

Once that had been settled, he unveiled an ambitious agenda for other reforms such as that of social security, as well as administrative, political and labour reforms. The most modest reform was the political one, for the only measure approved was the possibility of re-election for executive authorities, president, governors and mayors for one consecutive term, which FHC in fact devised to benefit himself. The administrative reform entailed chiefly the possibility of dismissing public employees in case of poor performance, something forbidden by the previous legislation. The civil servants stood up against it. They tried to call a strike against the amending of the law and refused to negotiate any alternative that included, for instance, the right to collective bargaining. This reform was also passed quickly. With the pension reform, the government intended, initially, to modify the regime from a defined benefit model to a capitalization one, as recommended by the IMF and the World Bank and adopted in Chile and Argentina. It was one of the most radical neoliberal proposals. However, it was concluded that its extremely high cost rendered it unfeasible for the Brazilian public coffers, so the solution was simply to reduce the benefits of the system in force.

The labour movement strategy, despite the internal tensions it aroused especially inside the CUT, was that of participating in the negotiations process set up by the government while simultaneously lobbying Congress. The law-making process was long, and changes were approved that implied the loss of some rights, but the essence of the public pension system was kept. If we compare the CUT mobilizations and its participation in the pension reform negotiations with the refusal by the public-sector unions to negotiate administrative reform, it becomes clear that, in spite of all, the strategy adopted in the case of the public pension reform was more effective.

With regard to the reform of the state, the FHC administration triggered two initiatives. One involved creating the so-called social organizations, a kind of NGO conceived to manage competitive, social services-related activities, which today manages public hospitals nationwide. The second was the beginning of the telecommunications, banking, electricity, mining, gas, and water privatization programmes.

The labour movement responded as well as it could, through strikes, injunctions and all types of mobilizations. The telecommunications sector and CVRD, a large mining company, were sold quickly. In the financial sector, which mainly comprised banks belonging to states, some banks were privatized, while others were transferred to the control of the federal government. The piped gas sector, in which only two companies operated, was also sold, while in the water and sanitation sector, which operates under a licence regime, only a few municipal companies were privatized because the legal status of these companies made it difficult to privatize them.

In the electricity sector, state-owned companies carried out most of the energy distribution, and almost all were sold, as well as two federal companies. The arguments used by the government to privatize these companies were reduced tariff prices, improved quality of the services, and attracting private investment to increase the offer of energy. In 2001, there was a longer drought and the volumes of water in the dams of the hydroelectric power plants went down dangerously, jeopardizing the energy supply in many parts of the country. Consumers realized then that they were paying more for a poor-quality service and that to top it all power would have to be rationed because the investments pledged had not been made. With that, there were no more political conditions for the government to carry on with privatizations of energy-generating federal companies. In the case of Petrobras, Brazil's biggest multinational company, it was excluded from the privatization programme from the beginning because that would surely have triggered enormous resistance from within the country's nationalist sectors across the political spectrum. However, the country lost its monopoly on oil exploration in Brazilian territory.

On the labour front, there was a speech in favour of the extinction of the corporative model that has regulated trade union organizations since the 1930s, with strong state interference, and that advocated a 'modernization' by downsizing the labour law. However, the modifications approved only provided for the adoption of flexible legislation, with the introduction of temporary job mechanisms, 'overtime hour banks' and the arbitration of small judicial claims. On the other hand, it is also true that many companies, taking advantage of the state's omission, increasingly made use of illegal and informal practices to hire workers. The difficulty of the Brazilian labour movement in dealing with informal workers must be acknowledged. There were several attempts, for instance, to organize street vendors through the traditional union structure. At the moment of the founding assembly of one of these unions, it was possible to gather almost 2,000 workers who, in addition to voting in favour of the founding of the new union, paid one monthly fee in advance. The next month, however, it was not possible to contact more than 20 of these workers, or 1 per cent, because vendors move their workplaces constantly. That is why it is necessary to look for another model and other causes to organize them.

As for the treatment given by the FHC administration to formal workers, it is worth recalling that when the oil workers went on strike in 1995 to demand the fulfilment of their collective bargaining agreement, the government resorted to the whole legal framework guaranteed by the old legislation to defeat the strike, in spite of all the reforming rhetoric. After a strike lasting more than one month and the dismissal of 75 unionists, additional exorbitant fines were imposed on unions.

In the rural areas, there was strong pressure for agrarian reform, which was never regarded as an important item on the FHC administration's agenda. FHC thought the issue had been dealt with in view of the productivity gains achieved by the booming agribusiness. Smallholdings were seen, by nature, as inefficient. Yet two workers' massacres that happened in Brazil's northern region, and which cost the lives of 31 people murdered by the police, put the subject high on the public opinion agenda and strengthened the mobilization capacity of the Landless Workers Movement (MST),[3] which had appeared in the south of Brazil in 1986. Today there are around half a dozen landless groups oriented by different political fractions or originated from different regional realities all fighting for settlements in rural areas. Nevertheless the MST is the strongest, and organizes around 300,000 people at present. The latter supported Lula's election and re-election albeit having been critical about certain governmental policies, in particular the pace of the agrarian reform and deals concerning the agribusiness sector. It has also been fighting for food security and against the application of transgenic seeds, positions not adopted by the government. The MST's leadership was quite tough in its criticism of Lula's rule during the Movement's national congress held in June 2007, but the rank and file applauded enthusiastically all the governmental representatives when they addressed the plenary. At any rate the MST has been one of the most outspoken Brazilian organizations against neoliberalism and imperialism at the moment, playing an important role in the attempt to organize poor and marginalized people in the countryside.

The CUT, the MST, several NGOs, the student movement and other urban groups, as well as many leftist parties, formed a social coalition that criticized and challenged the neoliberal policies. This movement was particularly successful during the campaign against the negotiation of the Free Trade Agreement of the Americas

(FTAA). With the Lula administration, such negotiations were ended through the presentation of a proposal refused by the United States. The only economic integration initiative supported by the Brazilian labour movement – although with some restrictions given its trade-based bias – was MERCOSUR. In labour's view, MERCOSUR had the potential to benefit the workers of the four countries by not only increasing intra-bloc trade, but also serving as a tool to revitalize the productive structure and as a strong political alternative to the American pressure for the FTAA, seeking as well to diversify its relations with other trade blocs and countries outside the region.

Since its affiliation with the International Confederation of Free Trade Unions (ICFTU) in 1992, the CUT in particular sought to play a leading political role in international union relations, electing for South-to-South relations and more direct union actions as more effective strategies to face globalization, multinational companies and multilateral agencies than the traditional and limited lobbying actions chosen by international labour organizations. In 2001, a huge Social Movements March to the capital of the country, Brasília, was organized to protest against FHC's neoliberal policies, which gathered approximately 100,000 demonstrators – a great accomplishment since Brasilia is hundreds of kilometres from Brazil's major urban centres.

When we assess the implementation, from the 1990s onwards, of neoliberal policies, we realize that Brazil, after all, was one of the countries in Latin America where they were less easily internalized. The keeping of important state-owned companies, the national bourgeoisie's greater market and bargaining power, the expansion of social investments in the recent period, the inability of the government to pass radical reforms in the pension system and labour law, besides the fact that the country took up, after the Lula administration, a more critical stance in relation to the developed countries, are marks of the Brazilian singularity. That does not mean that the neoliberal destructive avalanche was less powerful in Brazil, but simply that resisting it may be a less arduous endeavour here than in the rest of Latin America, in both political and economic terms. Anyway, in contrast with the new strength of neoliberalism – injecting into national collective life values like individualism and competition, at the expense of the ideals of solidarity – the social movement could not help but adopt a defensive strategy, except for a couple of important moments such as Collor's impeachment and the March of the Hundred Thousand to Brasília.

Also in 2001, in the city of Porto Alegre, the first World Social Forum (WSF) brought together militants from all over the world, sharing the same critical view of the current model of globalization. The number of participants – 30,000 – exceeded all expectations, though the figure would double the following year and it achieved almost 1000,000 participants in 2003. The WSF happens every year at the same time as the World Economic Forum, and has challenged the latter, sending out a clear and pedagogic message to the world's public opinion that the current globalization is exclusionary, aggressive and is concentrating more and more wealth in the hand of a few. It has contributed very much to gathering the international left and social movement in order to discuss initiatives to face neoliberalism and armed aggressions like the one of the United States against Iraq. Beyond the NGOs which were parts of the Brazilian Organization Committee of the WSF, CUT and MST also participated as representatives of the Social Movement. They share a view that social alliances and international actions are crucial to face the global conjuncture.

The Brazilian left – whose political representation in lawmaking bodies at the federal, state and local levels had been growing since the second half of the 1980s – won the 2002 elections with the Lula candidacy, an outcome that has contributed to new electoral victories of the left in other Latin American countries. As regards Lula's first government (2003–06), it is worth underscoring that the new administration did not represent a disruption of the economic model in force. On the contrary, the main strategy was to maintain the stability and confidence of the national market forces and international institutions. However, the privatization programme was interrupted and the BNDES (Brazil's development bank) started to focus more on investment in infrastructure and in strategic economic sectors. Significant investment was made in social programmes, and credit lines for small rural farmers were stepped up. Priorities also changed in the international negotiations arena, with the strengthening of South-to-South relations, the creation of coalitions like the G3 and the G20, as well as strong support to create a Community of South American Nations.

Yet a programmatic alternative to neoliberalism was not put forward. At least partially, that is because of the incapacity of the social movements, which shied away from adopting a clearer and more straightforward position in the internal confrontation of visions and power that characterize the Lula administration, albeit this government has been quite open to negotiation with the forces of society. That is, social movements in general failed to shift from a defensive strategy to another more critical and proactive position. Many representatives of the social and labour movements quickly changed their rhetoric, which may also be related to some extent to a process of cooptation orchestrated by the government.

Even though several changes engendered by the new government are worthy of merit, which indicates that Brazil today is capable of starting a new development model, it is ironic that this new project should depend more on political leadership linked to the government's machine, which still faces opposition from conservative national and international groups, and even from certain segments inside the government. We might say that, within the social movements, there exists today a divide between frontal opposition to the government and outright adherence, which makes it difficult for a less sectarian critical mass to emerge – coming from society's base – and push the incumbent government toward clearly putting behind it the legacies of neoliberalism.

NOTES

1 SEADE (Fundação Sistema Estadual de Análise de Dados) and DIEESE (Departamento Inter-Sindical de Estatística e Estudos Sócio-Econômicos) have developed a joint methodology to cover a total rate of unemployment, which considers both open and hidden unemployment.
2 http://www.cut.org.br; accessed 17 July 2007.
3 http://www.mst.org.br; accessed 17 July 2007.

Chapter 8

The impact of globalization on trade unions: the situation in Japan

Wakana Shutô and Mac Urata

INTRODUCTION

This chapter examines the impact of globalization on both the Japanese working class and the trade union movement. The first section gives an explanation of the specific characteristics of the conventional employment system of Japan. The Japanese employment system is known for its characteristic lifetime employment, seniority wage system and enterprise unions. Indeed, shortly after graduation from school, many young workers typically begin working for a company with which they will remain employed for the majority of their working lives. Stable employment coincided with an unemployment rate which held to just 2–3 per cent for the greater part of the post-war period (Table 8.1).

It has also been argued that the long-term growth of the Japanese economy has been in part sustained by companies that were willing to provide continuous job training to their employees, and until recently it has been assumed that long-term employment and the resultant high skills levels supported the sustained economic growth experienced in Japan until the late 1980s. Indeed, employee skills levels were also thought to be improved by seniority-based wages, characterized by wage increases being linked to worker age; trade unions, assured of one of their primary goals of employment security, did not regret their cooperation with management. Japan's trade unions (commonly known as enterprise unions, which are typified by their concession to the primacy of company profitability), took for granted the era's economic growth and stability, which made possible their cooperation with company managers. After the 1980s Japan experienced almost no strike action.

It is significant that in the conventional employment system in Japan, men and women adopt different types of employment. Lifetime employment and a seniority wage system are mainly available to male workers only. Many women are short-term, continuous-service employees, and their wage and skill levels have been held low as a

Table 8.1 Employment and unemployment in Japan (in 10,000s, per cent)

Year	Population	Population 15 years old and over (A)	Labour force Total (B)	Employed Total	Self-employed	Family workers	Employees (C)	Unemployed (C)	Labour force participation (B)/(A)	Ratio of unemployed in labour force (C)/(B)
1970	10,357	7,885	5,153	5,094	977	805	3,306	59	65.4	1.1
1975	11,158	8,443	5,323	5,223	939	628	3,646	100	63.0	1.9
1980	11,683	8,932	5,650	5,536	951	603	3,971	114	63.3	2.0
1985	12,078	9,465	5,963	5,807	916	559	4,313	156	63.0	2.6
1990	12,354	10,089	6,384	6,249	878	517	4,835	134	63.3	2.1
1995	12,520	10,510	6,666	6,457	784	397	5,263	210	63.4	3.2
2000	12,688	10,836	6,766	6,446	731	340	5,356	320	62.4	4.7
2003	12,758	10,962	6,666	6,316	660	296	5,335	350	60.8	5.3

Source: SB-MIAC (1970–2005).

result of being excluded from the levels of job training available to men. As a percentage of men's, wages for women in Japan are remarkably high compared with many industrialized nations, to the extent that female labour force participation rate still demonstrates the characteristic 'M' curve, but many women still leave the labour market upon marriage and childbirth. Many women in middle or advanced age are engaged in irregular employment, such as part-time work. Although men and women are generally segmented into corporate and domestic spheres, Japan has nevertheless attained an economically stable and relatively equal society within the family unit.

Today, the Japanese employment system is undergoing a significant transformation. During the 1990s, the long-term employment previously understood to be a pillar of the Japanese employment system was deeply shaken by the significant restructuring Japanese firms were forced to undergo in order to accommodate intensified international competition characteristic of the trend toward economic globalization. Moreover, the 'US styled global standard', based on neoliberal ideology and introduced to Japan during the 1990s, forced the government to ease labour regulations sharply. Under such circumstances, trade unions would generally represent the interests of their members and act to protect workers' incomes. However, the importance of unions had diminished considerably since the 1990s. By 2005, the percentage of workers belonging to unions had fallen to just 18.7 per cent (Figure 8.1). The number of union members continued to fall, bordering on 12,700,000 in 1994, and fell lower still, to 10,310,000 in 2004 – an average annual reduction of 2 per cent. An important reason is that the number of enterprise union members continues to decrease with the reduction in fulltime employees (Nakamura, 2005: 27–44).

This chapter focuses on the years from 1995 to 2005 in order to assess the impact of globalization and neoliberal policies on the status of labour, and will discuss the changing conditions for labour as well as the response to these changes by the labour movement.

INTENSIFIED GLOBAL COMPETITION AND CHANGES IN THE WORK ENVIRONMENT

The decline in working conditions

The Japanese economy can be characterized by a long upward growth trend lasting to the end of the 1980s followed by economic depression after the burst of the economic bubble in 1992. By the middle of the 1990s, intense competition from the rapidly expanding Chinese

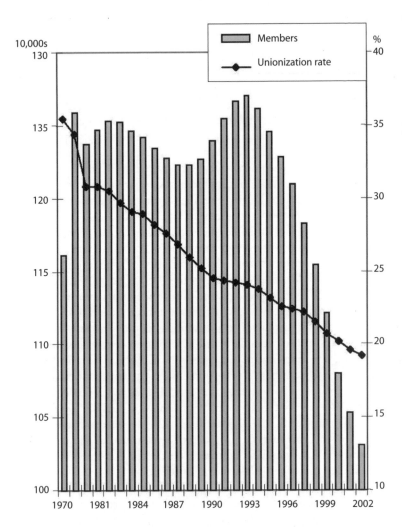

Figure 8.1 Number of union members and unionization rate, Japan, 1970–2002

Source: Japan Ministry of Health, Labour and Welfare (MHLW) (1970–2004).

manufacturing sector forced Japanese firms to further reduce expenditure through wide-scale retrenchments. As a result, the unemployment rate increased from 2.1 per cent in 1990 to 3.2 per cent in 1995, 4.7 per cent in 2000, and 5.4 per cent in 2002, an all-time high during the post-war period. Even corporations that had maintained their lifetime employment systems all through the 1990s were forced into wave after wave of retrenchments.

The manufacturing sector was most notably impacted by global competition. Setting the number of regular full-time employees (regular workers) in 1995 as a base of 100, the number of regular workers in manufacturing was by 2005 only 76.4; relative to 92.8 across all industries, the manufacturing sector bore the brunt of job decline. Most manufacturing concerns moved the base of their production to Asian countries such as China, where labour costs were significantly lower. Domestic labour costs were cut by reducing the rate of new workers and increasing the number of irregular employees.

Trade unions first sought to preserve employment, and second to maintain wages – not to increase them. Yet it is difficult to say whether they have achieved their aim. For example, although increased global competition forced Nissan (Nissan Motor Co. Ltd.) and Panasonic (Matsushita Electric Industrial Co. Ltd) to close their primary domestic production facilities, the representative unions agreed to mass dismissals and personnel restructuring as well as significant adjustments to retirement allowances. Although there has been some evidence that trade unions are able to effect controls of the rate of unemployment, recent empirical studies have shown this notion to be false (Tsuru, 2002).

Reductions in employees also led to a lengthening of working hours – workers now had to complete the regular workload with a reduced number of total workers on the job. Overtime hours for regular workers have increased by 1.3 times in the past decade (MHLW, 1995–2005). In many cases, unions have tolerated longer working hours because companies have paid overtime wages.

Increases in atypical workers

After the second half of the 1990s, companies have carefully controlled the total number of full-time employees and rapidly increased their hiring of non-full-time (atypical) employees. During, the past decade the number of full-time employees has declined by nearly 4.5 million while the number of atypical employees has increased by 5.9 million. The percentage of atypical workers increased from 20.9 per cent (39.1 per cent women) in 1995 to 32.6 per cent (52.5 per cent women) in 2005 (Figure 8.2). In the last ten years the rate of atypical employment has increased from one in five to one in three.

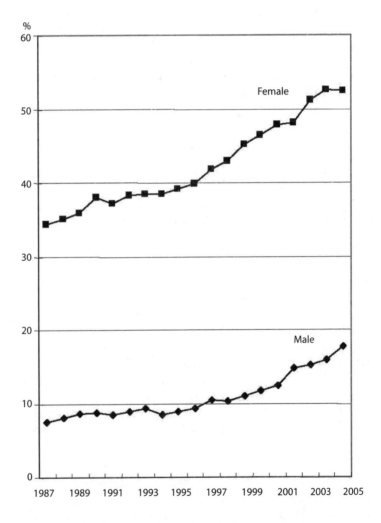

Figure 8.2 Ratio of non-regular workers in Japan, 1987–2005

Source: SB-MIAC (1987–2005).

Part-time workers

For the purpose of international comparison it is important to define 'atypical employment'. In this chapter, an employee is considered an 'atypical worker' if either employed for a contractually limited period of time or working less than full-time hours. The form of atypical work varies. For example, he/she might be a part-time office worker, for either a single or a few days per week; or an employee may be contracted for a specified project or period by a company; or temporary agency workers could be contracted through an employment agency, which dispatches suitably skilled workers to a company.[1]

In Japan, about 70 per cent of atypical workers are part-timers. However, the length of working hours is not the sole determinant of whether a worker is atypical – there can be significant differences in how the worker is classified in terms of overtime and job transfer status. While engaged in the same work as regular employees, 'part-time workers' (i.e. those who are not full-time) are about a third (MHLW, 2002a). Significantly, these employees are often called 'full-time part-timers'; however, even if working hours are comparable to full-time regular employees, the atypical employee is paid lower wages, has no opportunity for promotion and has no access to any employee benefits.

In comparison with the status of workers in Europe, the gap between regular full-time and atypical employees in Japan is large (Osawa and Houseman, 2003). Unlike Europe, there is no law in Japan requiring equal treatment. For example, a male part-timer makes 39.1 per cent of the hourly rate of his full-time counterpart. For women, the differential is 53.2 per cent (MHLW, 2002c). This gap has expanded every year after 1990. Needless to say, full-time and part-time employees may do different kinds of work, and the wage differential might be the result of this fact. However, according to a 2006 government investigation into cases where full-time employees and part-time workers are doing the same work, only 14.5 per cent of responding companies replied that they paid the same wages per hour: 12.8 per cent said they paid 90 per cent, 24.4 per cent 80 per cent, and 28.4 per cent only 70 per cent of full-time wages to their part-time employees (*Asahi Shimbun*, 20 February 2006: 3).

Similarly, in many cases only full-time workers qualify for employee welfare and benefits programmes. For example, the twice-yearly system of bonus payment comprises a significant portion of the salary for 79.3 per cent of full-time workers, but only 37.4 per cent of part-time workers, while only 7.3 per cent of part-time workers (compared with 66.1 per cent of full-time workers) qualify for their company's retirement plan (MHLW, 2003b). Furthermore, short-term employees are excluded from protection afforded under the Law Concerning the Welfare of Workers Who Take Care of Children or Other Family Members, including provisions for child care and family care leave. They are also excluded from social security and unemployment compensation. These exclusions and savings on social insurance premiums and welfare expenses provide an important incentive for employers to employ atypical workers.

Regular employees enjoy not only the advantages of full-time employment, but also a higher social status than atypical employees. Unions had tolerated the discriminatory treatment of atypical workers for a substantial period, but as various problems in the system of industrial relations emerged as the base number of atypical workers increased, unions have been forced to reassess their position.[2] The systemization of atypical employment became imperative when the full-time number of employees, who belonged to existing trade unions, decreased along with the ratio of organized workers. Considering that employers are unlikely to welcome union organization, there appears no alternative to worker's organization. The largest national trade unions, which dominate the national federation, RENGO, targeted the 'part-time problem' as early as 2000. Although the percentage of organized part-time workers was only 3 per cent in 2003, the rate is rising (MHLW, 1999–2003). Indeed, while the number of full-time employees belonging to unions has continued to decrease, the total number of part-time employees belonging to their representative union has increased on average 9.99 per cent per year for the past ten years (Nakamura, 2005: 10).

Unions have generally devised two plans for accommodating atypical workers.[3] First, non-full-time employees attempt integration into a full-time employees union, as typified by the AEON trade union (with 30,000 members, it is the largest trade union in the supermarket industry), which is planning to add 44,000 part-timers to its membership base. The AEON union has been working towards this goal since 2004, and expected to have in place the necessary bargaining agreement by the end of the summer of 2006. As a result, 80 per cent of part-timers are expected to have union representation. Similar plans have been proposed in the wholesale and retail industries which have many atypical employees.

The second trend is the increasing tendency towards the reclassification of non-full-time employees. Japan's post-war 'baby boom generation' is expected to begin retiring by the year 2007, and many anticipate a subsequent labour shortage. The manufacturing industry, including automobile manufacturers, has begun to move to reclassify their large non-regular workforce as regular workers.[4]

RENGO has called for a re-examination of the legal system and made the attainment of stronger legislation protecting part-time workers the primary goal of the labour movement today. Extant laws regulating part-time workers only specify the state of employment, but do not sufficiently regulate working conditions. RENGO's call for legislative revision requiring equal working conditions for full and part-time employees incorporates extending rights to long-term employees.

Youth employment

Although formerly atypical employment was the domain of middle to advanced-aged women, today the number of young people engaged in atypical employment is rapidly increasing. In 2006, the number of 15–34-year-olds engaged in atypical employment had increased by 32 per cent (MHLW, 2005). Previously in Japan, upon graduation it was common for young people to join a company immediately as a full-time regular employee, and work for that company for the rest of their working lives. However, during the second half of the 1990s the number of young people receiving tentative offers of employment upon graduation decreased rapidly, and many graduates have taken part-time or contract work in lieu of full-time employment. These young men and women have come to be called 'fûrîtâ' (freelance workers), and are a reflection of the more serious social problems in Japan today.[5] Many of them are employed by small-scale firms in the wholesale, retail and food service industries. Although 50 per cent are working the same number of hours as full-time employees, they are only making 60 to 70 per cent of the wages of full-time regular employees (Kosugi, 2004: 46).

The wage gap between full-time regular and atypical employees increases even more as the employees grow older. Many cannot even attain the minimum national living standard (welfare level). Many working poor are able to avoid poverty because they live with their parents. Because of the difficulties involved in living an independent life, the marriage rate of atypical employees, in comparison with full-time regular employees, is remarkably low. Moreover, there is a tendency to continue in a cycle of unstable employment. In Japan, once a young person has started the cycle of atypical employment, it

becomes very difficult to make the transition to regular employment. For this reason, the trend towards unstable employment is
spreading from the young to the middle-aged and the elderly.[6] It is
commonly claimed that changes in youth consciousness are the
causal factor for the significant shift in employment patterns in
Japan, but the more significant factor is fundamental changes in
employment practices. Since the 1990s, similar limitations on full-
time employment accompanied by an expansion of atypical
employment have emerged throughout the industrial world. Trade
unions in Japan have called on the government to improve working
conditions for young people, and the government has released a
radical new public policy for worker education, intended to reduce
the number of *fûrîtâ* by 80 per cent by 2010.

NEOLIBERALISM AND THE WITHDRAWAL OF WORKER PROTECTION

Working conditions have changed considerably over the past ten
years, partly as a result of intensified economic depression caused by
global competition, but partly also as a result of the global trend of
neoliberal deregulation of labour markets (Americanization). Of
course, the deregulation did not have an entirely negative influence
on workers. For example, the prohibition of the late-night shift
work and rules limiting holiday and overtime work for women were
abolished in 1998. Although these specific protections for women
were lost, the subsequent equal treatment under the law did advance
the status of women. This particular benefit notwithstanding, deregulation as a whole has had a significantly negative impact on the
status of the working class. To emphasize this point, the next section
will examine the laws regulating working hours.

Management of flexible working hours

In Japan at present, legislation sets the statutory working hours per
week at 40 (eight hours per day), and requires any overtime work to
be agreed upon by a worker representative or union. One consequence is that there is no clear or uniform legal regulation of
overtime work, which has led to long working hours becoming a
serious social problem.[7]
   Since the mid-1990s, deregulation of legislation working hours
has led to considerably longer hours for employees (white-collar
workers excluded), and this trend will likely foster even fewer
constraints for managers in regards to assigning working hours in

future. Thus far, even white-collar employees have experienced changes in the way their companies manage discretionary labour and *de facto* working-hour systems.[8] Unions had always opposed the introduction of the flexible work hour system on the grounds that it would result in longer working hours for no extra pay, and consequently cause real wages to fall. As a result, the introduction of flexible working hours was at the beginning strictly regulated. However, introductory requirements were eased in 2004.

Although only 4.5 per cent of companies had adopted flexible working hours by 1990, the number of companies that had successfully adopted flexible work hour policies had more than doubled to 9.8 per cent by 2004, and this number is expected to continue to rise (MHLW, 1970–2004). The discretionary spread in working hours also indicates that the criteria for the payment of wages have shifted from 'time' to 'result'. According to one government report, companies 'which in the past three years expanded the extent to which wages corresponded to achievements and result' reached 20 per cent, and companies which introduced performance-based wage systems continue to increase in number (MHLW, 1970–2004).

In the 1990s, the Japanese Federation of Economic Organizations (Nippon Keidanren), Japan's central organization for large businesses, strongly questioned the applicability of working hours, holiday and late-shift work rules for white-collar employees. The government echoed this concern, proposing in a January 2006 report the introduction of a new system which gives white-collar workers (and more importantly their employers) autonomy over the hours they work. It is expected that in the future white-collar workers will be exempted from legislation governing working hours.

The elasticity of employment forms

The 2004 Temporary Staff Services Law was revised in 2004, and recommended the separate categorization of atypical work. Until recently, the employment of temporary workers was restricted to short-term emergency situations in order to prevent substitution of regular employees with temporary workers; the employment period was limited to one year, with the provision that when the period of employment reaches one year there is the possibility of converting the position to a regular full-time one. However, the law was revised in 2004 to allow for a three-year extension.

Moreover, in the last ten years the types of industry to which temporary employees could be dispatched has also been expanded. Although only 16 types made use of agencies for the employment of temporary professionals and para-professionals workers such as interpreters and secretaries, the law was revised in 1996 to extend that number to 26. Liberalization took place in 1999, but a notable exception was the manufacturing industry. In order to prevent the destabilization of employment in the manufacturing industry, a key industry in Japan, the employment of temporary workers continued to be illegal. Nevertheless, further revisions to the law in 2004 removed that ban.

Employers have strongly urged further diversification of employment forms. In its 1995 publication, *The New Japanese Management of Time*, Nippon Keidanren proposed that workers should be divided into three categories:

- core jobs would continue to be regular full-time employment
- specialist personnel would be employed on fixed-term employment contracts
- all unskilled workers would be in a temporary category (Nippon Keidanren, 1995).

These new systems of personnel management are steadily being put into effect and are undermining the regulation of labour market in management's favour.

Establishment of a legal system for discrete industrial relations

Deregulation has produced flexible employment, wages and flexible working hours. In addition the number of people who are multi-skilled is on the rise, and it is becoming difficult to apply uniform criteria on any level. Diversification in employment has led to an increase in the number of workers who have had to negotiate their working conditions with employers. As the employment economy shifts from collective to individual industrial relations, the precariousness of employment for individuals becomes more pronounced. In 2004, the Japanese government began to consider new legislation on the basis of individual industrial relations.

The Labour Standards Law of 1946 defined only minimum criteria and left it to the representative trade union (the right to unionize was guaranteed under the 1947 Constitution) to negotiate the actual working conditions. The law, which specified the right and duties of employee and employer if a labour contract did not exist, relied on mediation in cases where the parties could not resolve their dispute on their own. While the number of unionized workers continues to rise, the number of individual worker disputes is on the rise, and labour leaders have petitioned the government for the establishment of a clear set of rules, which has not yet been forthcoming.

A case study: the effects of deregulation in the road transport industry

Koun Rokyo, the Japanese Council of Transport Workers' Unions, conducted a major survey on the working conditions of truck, bus and taxi drivers in 2005. The organization represents 18 national confederations of transport workers' unions, numbering more than 700,000 members. This was the first attempt by the Council to identify the effects of deregulation on a working environment; areas examined were safety, workers' fatigue and wages. The study traced changes in these areas from 1990 in trucking, 2000 in coaches and 2002 in buses and taxis. More than 10,000 road transport workers replied to the questionnaire through their respective trade unions.

In summary, the survey revealed that 'the competition that deregulation created has led to reduction in income, longer working hours and increased fatigue, thus putting safety of transport in jeopardy'. These findings bear closer scrutiny: 57 per cent of those surveyed replied that they had had an experience where they felt momentarily drowsy whilst driving on duty; 41 per cent said they were alarmed by their own driving when they realized that they were not paying adequate attention; nearly 40 per cent of taxi drivers said that they had had to take a break due to tiredness rather than drive to look for a passenger.

The vast majority of the taxi drivers said the time they spent behind the steering wheel had increased over the past five years. The same was true for 63.44 per cent of bus drivers and 41.98 per cent of truck drivers. More road accidents have been witnessed by 52.79 per cent of taxi and 45.16 per cent of bus drivers whereas only 16.75 per cent of truck drivers felt the same. As for earnings, 63.01 per cent of truck and 56.15 per cent of bus drivers said their income had declined after deregulation. Only 2.79 per cent of the taxi drivers did not agree that deregulation had had some negative effect on their earnings (or did not reply). It is unsurprising therefore, that 83.49 per cent did not wish to see their children become taxi drivers.

In Tokyo, a taxi driver aged 53.8 years with ten years of work experience would on average have earned 4,060,800 yen in 2005, according to a statistics released by Zenjiko Roren, the Japanese taxi unions' federation. That is a reduction of 148,700 yen from the previous year and 2,664,000 yen less than the average income of all workers in Tokyo.

Hiroaki Shibano had an annual earning of a little over 5,000,000 yen nine years ago when he joined the industry. Since then, due to deregulation, the number of taxis has increased while the number of customers has not. His annual income is now around 3,000,000 yen. Setsuo Shirai's monthly income is 100,000 yen after tax. He has been a taxi driver for 20 years. He now earns less than the starting salary of a college graduate. Conditions are much worse outside the capital and particularly in the rural areas. There are cases where the income is so low that the drivers can earn more by subscribing to welfare benefits.

Shibano and Shirai are amongst the 24 plaintiffs who filed a lawsuit against the '9.16 Notice' which came into effect on 16 September 2004.[9] They are demanding a symbolic financial compensation of 500,000 yen from the government. They argue that the 9.16 notice is illegal since it promotes unfair competition and the dumping of taxi fares. The notice was yet another push to deregulate the taxi industry further.

A bus driver employed by a large private firm in Yokohama wrote to the *Manichi Shinbun*, a major daily Japanese newspaper, about his conditions. His story was featured anonymously on 27 February 2006. The man is 41 years old with a wife and three children. He normally wakes up around 4.30 am and starts driving after 6 am. Then he is constantly behind the steering wheel. He has a 3–4-hour rest period in the afternoon but says it is not easy to relax in his depot as the place is so busy. Then back on his duty, he drives until midnight with almost no break. He has to wear adult disposable diapers because his schedule does not allow him to stop to relieve himself. At home, he may sleep for 3–4 hours. He takes 2–3 days of leave in a month. He served in the Marine Self-Defence Forces but says it is much tougher to be a bus driver. Recently, he felt dizzy on his way to work and could not walk. At hospital, he was diagnosed with autonomic ataxia and has been out of work for two weeks.

Historically, many regional commuter railways have had their own section to run bus services with the same accounting system. According to Shitetsu Soren which represents the majority of the Japanese public transport workers' unions, a large number of these companies are extending their bus operations into new areas. This is their response to the cut-throat competition created by deregulation. New entries to the bus market are reducing the fares substantially. The traditional operators are forced to refine their business and save every penny to meet the new challenges.

The bus industry had never been highly profitable to begin with. The burden and hardship, therefore, rest on workers. Where bus sections are divided, a 20–30 per cent reduction in wages is the norm. Bus workers who were transferred from the parent company may be financially better off than new recruits and continue to enjoy the status of full-time employees. That is a deal that their union negotiated with management. The survey conducted by Koun Rokyo confirms this trend: 51.62 per cent said their companies have separated the bus services and 92.84 per cent said there are atypical workers such as temporary staff at their workplaces.

An anonymous driver in Yokohama joined the company last year. He expected an annual income of about 4,000,000 yen. His senior colleagues who moved from the parent company earn 8,000,000 yen. The Ministry of Land, Infrastructure and Transport says that in 2004, there were 27 cases of bus drivers on duty being too ill to drive. Cardiac infarction and cerebral thrombosis were identified as conditions some of these workers were suffering. In at least one case, a driver lost his life as a result of sudden illness. Three years before, there were only four such cases, according to the Ministry.

Redefining the safety culture

It is not surprising that road accidents are on the increase under these circumstances. The Ministry accepts that the situation is serious. More than 700 people are killed in traffic accidents that were primarily caused by professional drivers. That is 1.4 times more than a decade ago. The Ministry also admits that deregulation had led to many new entries to the market, and that the safety measures that exist in the road transport industry need to be revised. The road transport workers' unions correctly argue that cost must not be the yardstick for measuring safety. Their view is shared with the other members of Koun Rokyo in the railway, aviation and maritime sectors.

The privatized Japanese railways saw its worst accident in 40 years when a commuter train jumped the tracks and smashed into an apartment in Amagasaki City on 25 April 2005. The 23-year-old driver from JR West Company was speeding, trying to make up for the loss of 90 seconds. He knew that he would be punished and humiliated by the managers if his train was late. As a result, 107 passengers died and some 500 were injured. The unions' call for 'safety before profit' enjoys the support of commuters and should form the basis for different stakeholders in the industry to take remedial action. A 'no-blame safety culture' becomes the point of emphasis when the industry is privatized. Instead of finding a culprit who caused an accident and blaming him, investigating the cause of the accident for the future prevention should be the priority of the company and the union. In debating these arguments, it is important to bear in mind that the vast majority of the Japanese unions are formed on an enterprise basis. Can they overcome this definition and formulate an industry-wide policy on safety and other related issues that may impact on profit?

INTERNATIONAL LABOUR MOVEMENT COOPERATION

Organizing the inflow of foreign workers

This section will introduce the issue of increased employment of foreign workers and the working conditions experienced by foreign workers.[10] In 2003, according to government estimates, approximately 800,000 foreign workers resided in Japan, including illegal aliens (legal resident workers are 570,000), and the number is increasing every year (MHLW, 2003a). It is said that immigration to Japan has been increasing since the second half of the 1980s (Yorimitsu, 2005: 46–7). During the 1980s, the Japanese economy had become exceedingly prosperous, and the subsequent demand for labour suited the growing economy. At that time, small and medium-sized businesses experienced an extreme labour shortage and managers began to use illegal foreign workers to alleviate the labour shortage.

Although the increased employment of illegal foreign workers was generally accepted in a very limited form, in 1989 the government, at the request of private industry, revised the Immigration Control and Refugee Recognition Act with the intention of stemming the tide. The revised law classified workers into technical workers and manual labourers, allowing the employment of the former while forbidding employment of the latter. However, the government simultaneously eased restrictions on immigration by people of Japanese descent (from first to third generation). The revised law did not restrict immigrants of Japanese descent from engaging in unskilled labour. Employers took advantage of the relaxed restrictions and the rate of immigration of foreigners of Japanese descent increased rapidly. In 2005, there were about 270,000 foreigners of Japanese descent registered as 'permanent residents', half of them from Brazil.[11]

Seventy per cent of foreign workers are employed by the automobile, electrical and electrical machinery industries. Half are employed by small and medium-sized companies, many with fewer than 100 employees, concentrated in local industrial cities outside Japan's major urban centres. In many cases, foreign workers are not directly employed by the company at which they work, but are supplied by outside agencies as temporary contract workers. This form of indirect employment is short-term and in most cases extremely unstable (Okubo, 2005; Yorimitsu, 2005). Moreover, many foreign workers (including illegal immigrant workers) do not qualify for protection from the Labour Standards Law, such as industrial accident compensation, unemployment and social security insurance. They are often subject to unfair dismissal and suffer from high rates of on-the-job accidents (Yorimitsu, 2005: 77–87, 93).

Until recently, Japanese trade unions have not taken any stance on the exploitation of immigrant workers. Since most workplaces where foreign workers are employed do not have union representation, it can hardly be said that foreign workers have been integrated into the labour movement. In cases where there are representative unions, unions have not been able to organize foreign workers since most unions are most involved in the interests of full-time, directly employed workers and not interested in those of foreign workers (Saka, 2001: 29). In fact, even national centres of the labour movement (RENGO) have not attempted to integrate new, foreign workers. The Japanese labour movement takes a cautious position on organizing manual workers and has focused on securing employment for Japanese workers; it is not currently proposing to organize foreign workers.

Yet foreign workers involved in the labour movement are not entirely unknown. The unions that are tackling the problem are neither enterprise nor industry-oriented, but locally based community unions. The membership of community unions is defined by the locality in which the member lives and works, not the type of business or industry in which he/she is employed. While still not a recognized union from the standpoint of the employer, community unions offer some support for workers facing dismissal or bankruptcy.[12] In communities with high populations of foreign workers, community unions have created some consultation opportunities.

International solidarity of the labour movement

Economic globalization presents a rationale for the internationalization of the labour movement. Economic globalization might be the force that precipitates international solidarity in the labour movement. Trade unions have generally fought for the interest of workers within a particular country, but the present situation prompts the creation of a global labour movement.

However, the prospects for international alliances do not appear favourable. According to interview research by JAW (Japan Automobile Workers' Union), in cases where Japanese companies do expand overseas, since unions tend to be enterprise-oriented, union leaders with the parent company have little relationship with the representative trade union for a subsidiary company. The JAW does not see the practicality of building international solidarity. It would be necessary for a labour movement to embrace all the laws and customs of the countries where businesses operated. In the case of Japanese automobile manufacturers, where the company has many overseas production facilities, it is rare for the Japan-based union to become involved in an overseas labour dispute. This is partly because there is a limit on the exchange of information between the Japan-based union and those representing overseas production workers. Today, the JAW is hardly progressing towards internationalization.

Not only is the internationalization of the Japanese labour movement behind schedule, it can be said that there is not even a schedule for internationalization. Criticism of the slow pace at which Japanese labour movement has moved to build international alliances is quite strong. In its quarterly magazine *Metal World*, the International Metal Workers Federation (IMWF) recently criticized Japanese multinational companies for cooperating with the labour movement at home while suppressing unions abroad (Malentacchi, 2005), pointing to not only Japanese companies in Asia, but also similar corporate activity in the United States.

Because it is home to many multinational companies, Japan is likely to play a pivotal role in the formation of an international labour movement. Although not yet organizing outside their representative companies, or beyond the borders of Japan, the trade unions of Japan are becoming a possible force for workers worldwide by building cooperation with labour movements in emerging Asian nations such as South Korea and China. Such a move will also be indispensable for the saving of jobs and improvement of working conditions in Japan.

Towards transnational bargaining?

Will this chapter then conclude without making proposals for building workers' international solidarity? By studying the history of the post-war trade union movement in Japan we may reach a different conclusion. Since 1955, unions in Japan have developed a unique system of negotiations with management over their wages and conditions through Shunto (the Spring Offensive). Each year, in the months of February to April, thousands of enterprise unions will enter their bargaining sessions with the management simultaneously. National union confederations would often coordinate these negotiations by setting an industrial benchmark on the wage hike. Confederations like Shitetsu Soren will ballot their members so that their unions can organize strike action if necessary. These confederations would also set their 'batting order' through the national labour centre so that the unions in the industries with better economic performance go first and gain as much ground as possible for the rest to follow.

Clearly the Shunto system was designed to overcome the weaknesses of enterprise unionism, where the employers will play such unions off the others through company-by-company bargaining. It is also true, unfortunately, that the significance of Shunto has changed in its 50 years of exercise, where the original confrontational attitude of the unions was substantially replaced with a more cooperation-oriented stance towards management since the Oil Shocks in the 1970s. Shunto is also under scrutiny today as the Japanese labour market is changing drastically.

Nevertheless, if there is anything that the Japanese trade union movement can offer, at least in theory, towards workers' global solidarity, one could suggest the original concept of the Spring Offensive. For example, if a multinational firm like Veolia Transport from France (formerly known as Connex) operates in more than 20 countries around the world, can the unions that represent Veolia Transport workers come together and set an international pattern bargaining system? Undoubtedly, unions' abilities for industrial action, including efficient work stoppage and its international coordination, would be crucial. Such practice would be far more radical than mere informational exchanges in a European Works Council or a conclusion of an International Framework Agreement.

The road transport workers and their unions in the ITF (International Transport Workers' Federation) have been experiencing some successful International Action Days under the slogan 'Fatigue Kills'. 'For five consecutive years across Europe (and elsewhere), bus and truck drivers have blocked border crossings and taken other action' (Wahl, 2002). In some countries, including the European Union states, new legislation was established to better regulate the industry. Potentially, such annual campaigns provide an opportunity to apply this bargaining concept.

CONCLUSION

The progression of globalization has drastically changed the form of working conditions in Japan, and this chapter has examined the ways in which Japan's trade unions have attempted to accommodate new trends. Over the past ten years, labour market fluidity and flexible labour management systems have radically altered the work environment.

It would be difficult to say that Japan's labour movement has responded to the challenges of changes in the workplace caused by globalization. There was little or no intervention from Japan's trade unions during the waves of dismissals that took place during the economic depression of the 1990s; the inferior working conditions experienced by non-full-time employees have not been addressed; and the labour movement has not attempted to organize the increasing number of foreign workers in Japan. Indeed, the prospects for the emergence of an international labour movement do not seem good.

However, Japan's trade unions have undergone gradual change. Although the number of full-time employees belonging to unions is decreasing, the number of part-time employees belonging to unions is on the rise. Recently, there has been a re-examination of the significant difference in treatment of full-time and part-time employees. Although enterprise unions have fallen behind, new labour activity by community unions organizing foreign workers can be noted. The hope for an effective labour movement is still alive in society. Recent research has found that about 70 per cent of unorganized workers consider a union necessary (Nakamura, 2005: 47–70). The necessity of a labour movement is being made clearer by the impact of globalization, and renewed union activism is likely to meet the hopes and needs of society.

DISCLAIMER AND ACKNOWLEDGEMENTS

The views expressed here are Mac Urata's own and do not necessarily reflect policies of the International Transport Workers' Federation (ITF). Both authors wish to thank Christopher Gerteis (Creighton University) for his assistance with the translation of this chapter.

NOTES

1   In addition, sub-groups of atypical workers are not included in these statistics. For example, contract company workers, who are employed full-time, but do not enjoy stable employment and may be discharged after the completion of their contract, are excluded. Workers who are transferred to another part of the same company or a subsidiary are also not considered. Given the types of employment not considered in the statistics, the actual ratio of atypical workers is likely to be higher.

2   Since only full-time employees are represented by the union, if the number of non-full-time employees comes to exceed the number of full-time employees it becomes impossible for a union to be representative in a labour–management consultation. Moreover, while the ratio of non-full-time employees is increasing, without any systematic inclusion of their numbers into the labour movement there is a corresponding acceleration in the rate of unorganized workers (Tokyo: MHLW).

3   However, it would be remiss to say that the movement as a whole has begun to address the issue. According to a national RENGO (Federation of Japanese trade unions) study from 2004, only 16.6 per cent of affiliated unions had developed a systematic strategy for attacking the 'part-timer issue'. While 52.5 per cent had said they were planning to, 16.9 per cent said they were not making any plans to develop a system for atypical workers (RENGO, 2004).

4   The trend is not necessarily the result union activities, but is more the result of supply-side adjustments in the labour force (Tokyo: MHLW).

5   Japan's 2.2 million *furîtâ* are generally 15–34 years of age. They are represented by high-school graduates, unmarried women, and those who are employed under circumstances other than full-time ((Tokyo: MHLW, 2005).

6   The proportion of individuals receiving welfare payments has increased drastically during the last ten years. According to government reports, the rate of those receiving welfare payments increased from 1995 to 2004 by 11.1 per cent. The reason is the increasing numbers of elderly, jobless persons, and those with unstable employment (Tokyo: MHLW).

7   On the other hand, strong union representation would enable considerable control over work hours under this system. One additional problem is 'overtime work without pay', which until the 1980s was one cause for the call to create legal criteria for the shortening of working hours; 'death from overwork' and 'suicide caused by overwork' were the slogans of the day. This problem is not yet resolved.

8   Actual time commitments are not negotiated, instead it is the system of managing working hours in the labour agreement.

9   Since December 1996, the ministry has been allowing more companies to start afresh in the industry, and has also been approving lower fares. The 9.16 notice was issued in line with this trend. It allows major corporate customers, who have contracts with taxi companies and pay

taxi fares in vouchers, to secure discounts of up to 30 per cent on fares. These voucher-paid taxi fares make up around 30 to 34 per cent of the drivers' fare revenue, and mean they will receive much less income than before.

10   There are both 'newcomers' and 'old timers' among foreign workers in Japan. During the Second World War, the Japanese government imported many Chinese and Koreans to do forced labour in Japan. Because of the split between North and South Korea, many were not repatriated at the end of the war and their descendents still live in Japan today. However, discussions on the recent phenomena of globalization have tended to focus on newcomers rather than these earlier populations.

11   The Japanese government is showing signs of converting to an open immigration policy. In 2005, the government announced tentative plans to abolish the requirement of being of Japanese descent (*Asahi Shinbun*, 31 May 2006: 2).

12   The membership of community unions does not tend to increase easily. When faced with wage cuts or dismissals, membership rises, but once these issues are resolved, many members leave the union.

Chapter 9

Challenges facing the Canadian labour movement in the context of globalization, unemployment and the casualization of labour

Geoff Bickerton and Jane Stinson

The Canadian labour movement faces several significant structural, organizational, and political challenges. Structural challenges arise from changes in the domestic economy, particularly due to greater international competition over the past few decades. These pose internal organizational questions and call for new political responses.

The intensification of international competitive pressure, encouraged by the Canada-USA Free Trade Agreement (CUFTA) and the North American Free Trade Agreement (NAFTA), has undermined the Canadian manufacturing and resource sectors, threatening jobs and reducing union power in sectors that were historically the economic and political strength of the Canadian labour movement. For several years the greatest job growth has been in the service sector, traditionally a non-union sector characterized by casual and part-time low paid employment.

Given the loss of members, several unions are restructuring into large, self-sufficient, multi-sector, mega-unions. Ironically, the concentration of unions has undermined labour's ability to approach organizing and collective bargaining from a strategic, sectoral perspective. It has also reduced the influence and power of central labour bodies. The perception of the labour movement as fragmented and weak encourages employers' demands for concessions.

The Canadian labour movement is currently stuck in terms of its broader political strategy. Most Canadian unions focus on debating tactics to elect the social democratic party, the New Democratic Party (NDP). Yet support for it continues to be weak among workers. The NDP does little to identify with or represent the unique needs of working-class people. Some unions have embraced community-based coalition politics, often to press for or against a particular issue (for a national child care programme or against private health care, for example) as a necessary part of their political action strategy. Other unions are redirecting support behind the Liberal Party (centrist and pro-capitalist) as a means of stopping the rise of the right-wing Conservative Party. The weakness of Canadian central labour bodies further inhibits the ability of the labour movement to discuss and debate the development of any united coherent strategy.

This chapter reviews the economic, social, political and ideological challenges facing the Canadian labour movement, and discusses the responses of unions and activists within the labour movement. This analysis focuses primarily on developments in the Canadian labour movement excluding the province of Quebec, in recognition of the distinct characteristics of Quebec society. However, we have included Quebec data in the overall discussion of Canadian data on union membership and density, and have provided a few examples of important organizing efforts in Quebec.

THE LABOUR MARKET CONTEXT

The 1990s were marked by significant job losses in traditionally strong sectors of the Canadian economy such as resource industries, manufacturing and public services. During this time public social spending was cut deeply, particularly in health, post-secondary education, social assistance payments, a range of social services and housing. Poverty deepened, as the rich got richer. Unemployment rose as did part-time, part-year and insecure employment. The sectoral, regional, gendered and racialized character of the Canadian labour market meant that some workers suffered more than others during this downturn. In recent years (2003 to 2006) there has been a reversal of this trend in the construction and resource sectors and some parts of the public sector (Cross, 2006). There was a rebound in the growth of full-time employment in that period. But more recently (May 2006 to May 2007) part-time employment grew faster than full-time employment (4.1 per cent part-time versus 1.2 per cent full-time) (CUPE, 2007: 3).

In some countries the loss of formal employment and growth in poverty would stimulate growth in an informal economy, but in Canada most of the population that works for money is employed in the formal economy. The informal economy is relatively weak in Canada compared with countries in Central and South America and Asia. This is partly indicated by the fact that neither Statistics

Canada nor any of the major Canadian economic think tanks provide current estimates of its value.

The informal economy is largely ignored and understated throughout most of Canada even though more attention should be paid to it, noting gender and regional concentrations. For example, in the absence of a national child care programme many women provide home-based child care arrangements that are not recognized as formal employment. Thousands more women are informally employed as domestic cleaners and also as 'escorts' or prostitutes. In the western province of British Columbia, informal economic activity in the cultivation, sale and export of marijuana ('BC bud') is considered to rival if not outstrip the formal forestry sector, the traditional backbone of the provincial economy.

Many workers who form part of an informal economy in other countries are in the formal labour force in Canada. This is because many of these workers are immigrants and come to Canada through formal immigration programmes for employment as migrant workers and domestic caregivers.

For example, many domestic workers in Canada are female and enter the country through the federal government's Live-in Caregiver Program. Some refer to it as a form of slavery because they must live in their employer's house and they can only work for that employer and only for a specified time. These conditions increase their vulnerability to sexual assault and can mean they are on-call 24 hours a day without overtime pay, facing threats of deportation to guarantee silence about exploitive working conditions (CRIAW, n.d.).

The erosion of stable, full-time, full-year work over the past decade has overshadowed developments in the informal economy in Canada. Full-time, year-round, ongoing employment with one employer providing benefits and other entitlements was the normative model of white, male employment in Canada, for decades following the Second World War. Starting in the 1980s attention focused on the erosion of this standard employment relationship, as employers responded to competitive pressures and cut labour costs by cutting positions, hours and guarantees of work, and by lowering wages and benefits where possible. The 1990s were marked by large increases in self-employment, homework, on-call work, part-time and temporary work (Cranford and Vosko, n.d.).

Women and racial-minority workers are most negatively affected by the growth of precarious employment in Canada. However, for many women and immigrant workers in small and decentralized workplaces in the service and competitive manufacturing sectors, the standard employment relationship never really applied (Cranford, Vosko and Zukewich, 2003).

THE STRUCTURE OF THE CANADIAN LABOUR MOVEMENT

It is difficult to generalize about the economy, politics, or culture in Canada given the vast size, geographic differences and the powers of provincial governments in the federal system. Canada is defined by very different realities that exist in its provinces and regions. The labour movement, divided along geographical and industry lines, incorporates many of the economic and political divisions of the country and is organized into national, provincial and local structures.

Nationally, 4.3 million workers, or approximately 32 per cent of the paid workforce, were covered by union agreements in 2007. Most unions, representing 3.1 million workers, are affiliated to the Canadian Labour Congress (CLC). The CLC includes 65 national unions and 40 international unions with headquarters in the United States. Now 71 per cent of all union members belong to Canadian-based unions, a sharp increase from the 1960s when international unions accounted for almost two-thirds of union membership in Canada. During recent years there has been a trend towards union mergers. The largest eight affiliated unions now represent 2.1 million members or 67 per cent of the total CLC membership (Bedard, 2005).

At the sub-national or provincial level, unions come together through provincial federations of labour. This is particularly important since provincial governments have jurisdiction over labour laws, employment standards, provincial economic development decisions and decisions about the organization and delivery of social programmes such as health care, education and a range of social services. At the municipal level, local unions are encouraged to come together in labour councils for mutual support and to plan common actions such as political action to influence local or municipal governments.

Union density

Although the rate of union membership in Canada is considerably higher than in the United States, it is low by historic standards. Overall union membership density in Canada dropped from almost 40 per cent in 1981 to 32 per cent in 1999, and has remained virtually constant since then. Almost all of the reduction in union density took place in the private sector, which declined from 29 per cent to 19 per cent of employees unionized. For the past 25 years the rate of unionization in the public sector has remained constant at about 75 per cent. This underscores the significance of the unionized public sector for Canadian union density (Morissette, Schellenberg and Johnson, 2005).

Canadian unions have had difficulty organizing in smaller workplaces. Whereas 53 per cent of employees in workplaces with over 500 employees are organized, only 15 per cent of employees in workplaces of 20 workers or fewer are covered by union agreements (Akyeampong, 2006).

Over the past 25 years, the gender composition of the Canadian labour movement has changed dramatically. In 1968, 38 per cent of male workers were unionized compared with 16 per cent of females. Today the gender split is even, at 32 per cent of both male and female workers covered by union agreements (Statistics Canada, 2006b). This is partly due to the rising labour force participation of women in heavily unionized sectors of the economy, particularly public services. It is also partly due to the loss of male employment in unionized sectors of the economy such as manufacturing and resource industries (mining, wood and paper, fishing, etc.). Currently, women comprise 49 per cent of the paid workforce and 50 per cent of the total union membership.

Although the unionization rate of workers of colour and aboriginal workers is growing, it remains below the national average with 21 per cent of workers of colour and 31 per cent of aboriginal workers being unionized. Union membership among workers with disabilities reflects the national average at 32 per cent; however it should be noted that representation of aboriginal people and working-age persons with disabilities in the paid workforce is well below average.

A considerable decline in the unionization of younger workers is another dramatic change in the composition of the Canadian labour movement. During the period 1981 to 1999 the proportion of unionized workers under the age of 35 years dropped by almost 50 per cent, and today fewer than 20 per cent of these workers are organized compared with 34 per cent of workers 45 years of age or older (Bedard, 2005). This loss of union coverage for young workers is largely explained by changes in employment patterns for youth. Most youth are employed in the growing private service sector where there are few unions (Morissette et al., 2005).

Significant geographical and sectoral differences exist in the level of unionization in Canada. Alberta and New Brunswick are the two least organized provinces, with unionization rates of 24 per cent and 28 per cent respectively. This can be compared with 41 per cent in Quebec and 38 per cent in Newfoundland and Labrador (Bedard, 2005).

Likewise there are significant sectoral and occupational differences. Only 13 per cent of retail sales workers are organized compared with 40 per cent of workers in construction. Only 13 per cent of part-time workers in the private sector are organized compared with 69 per cent of part-time workers in the public sector (Akyeampong, 2006).

Understanding the decline in union density 1981–99

Several factors contributed to the loss of union density in Canada between 1984 and 1999. Deindustrialization related to neoliberal globalization, deregulation, privatization, public -sector cutbacks, the growth of the private service sector and casualization of employment have all played a role to different degrees.

Deindustrialization caused the share of employment in manufacturing to decline from 16.9 per cent in 1984 to 12.8 per cent in 2006. This was the result of economic recession, outsourcing of non-core operations on the part of large manufacturers and the restructuring of several industries that followed the signing of NAFTA in 1993. There was also a reduction in the relative employment of other highly unionized sectors such as utilities, transportation and forestry. During this same period the proportion of total jobs included in the highly unionized public sector decreased from 26.1 per cent to 22.2 per cent because of cutbacks and contracting out. At the same time that employment in the traditionally highly unionized sectors diminished, there was a considerable growth of jobs in the largely non-union service sector (Jackson and Schetagne, 2003).

The reduction of employment in highly unionized sectors is only one part of the story. In many industries, this period was characterized by greater competition from non-union entrants within sectors. This accounts for the reduction in union density in the manufacturing sector, which dropped from 46 per cent to 35 per cent between 1989 and 1998. The decline in union density resulting from non-union entrants was also especially acute in the forestry and mining sectors, where the density dropped from 46 per cent to 26 per cent. Federal deregulation of the transportation, trucking and telecom sectors contributed to expanded employment levels in non-union competitors and reduced employment levels in unionized companies. The auto sector witnessed the growth of non-union parts plants and the Japanese auto companies establishing large non-union production facilities (Morissette et al., 2005).

The increase in new industry entrants coincided with an increase in the proportion of smaller firms employing fewer than 500 workers. There is a consistent pattern of lower union density rates in smaller enterprises in Canada.

Many employers responded to the pressure of greater economic competition from neoliberal globalization by increasing their use of part-time and temporary workers to reduce labour costs and gain greater flexibility in employment levels. During the period 1989 to 1999 the proportion of temporary and part-time employment increased from 21 per cent to 26 per cent of total employees (Cranford et al., 2003).This also contributed to the loss in union density, as the rate of unionization among part-time and temporary workers is considerably less than that of full-time workers.

Barely holding our own, 1999–2006

From 1999 to the present the Canadian union movement has maintained the same level of union density in the workforce over-all. But while the overall decline in density has been arrested, the decline of union density within the private sector and within traditional blue-collar industries continues to worsen.

Maintaining the overall level of union density is only partly due to new organizing efforts. Despite considerable increases in the organizing budgets of many affiliates, the organization rate (number of workers covered by certifications granted each year divided by the total number of non-union workers) has been declining slightly since the 1970s. In recent years the organization rate has hovered at 0.73 per cent, with about 70,000 workers covered under new union certifications annually (Jackson, 2006). This reflects a slight reduction of organizing success from the previous two decades.

Between 1999 and 2006 the level of union density varied considerably between regions and industries. Union density increased in Quebec, Prince Edward Island, Manitoba, Saskatchewan and New Brunswick, and declined in the other five provinces. The level of unionization also increased in small workplaces with fewer than 20 employees, among part-time workers, retail sales clerks, nurses, and workers in child care, education, healthcare, public administration and construction. These increases offset losses in union density that occurred in manufacturing, mining, forestry, transportation, finance, food services, culture and recreation, and large private-sector enterprises employing more than 500 workers.

THE ADVANTAGES AND CHALLENGES OF ORGANIZING

The economic benefits of being a union member in Canada are well documented. On average unionized workers receive wages that are 25 per cent higher than their non-union counterparts. While the gap between men and women workers remains very significant in the overall society, the gap within union operations has diminished significantly. Overall the annual earnings of women workers are only 72 per cent of those of men, but unionized female workers in full-time occupations receive wages that are 92.5 per cent of those of their male counterparts. Workers of colour and younger workers also benefit from higher wages as a result of unionization (Akyeampong, 2006).

Despite the advantages of unions there are many significant obstacles to organizing one and successfully negotiating a first contract. In recent years several provinces have introduced legislation requiring employee votes as a condition of certification. This allows employers time to intimidate workers with threats of layoffs or closures.

Wal-Mart and the banks: case studies in Canadian organizing

The experience of the labour movement with Wal-Mart, the giant American retailer, and the banking sector, illustrates some of the challenge facing unions in Canada.

As Canada's largest retailer Wal-Mart controls about 40 per cent of the Canadian discount and department-store retail market. In 1997 the United Steelworkers of America successfully organized the first Wal-Mart store in Windsor, Ontario. The union was unable to negotiate a first contract and eventually decertified as a result of Wal-Mart's ongoing campaign of coercion and intimidation. Since then there have been numerous successful efforts by the United Food and Commercial Workers (UFCW) to convince the majority of employees in individual Wal-Mart stores to sign union cards. Yet as we write in August 2006 there is still no certified unionized Wal-Mart location in Canada.

Wal-Mart has used intimidation and threats of store closures to thwart union organizing drives. When scare tactics failed and workers have voted for union recognition, Wal-Mart has closed the store. In September 2005, the Quebec Labour Relations Board ruled that Wal-Mart's decision to close and lay off workers was not made for economic reasons but was rather an illegal dismissal of workers for engaging in union activity. Even though Wal-Mart was found guilty, it was not stopped from closing the store. While Wal-Mart's campaign of intimidation has not stopped workers from signing union cards, the company continues to resist unionization.

The Wal-Mart campaign illustrates many of the difficulties unions face in organizing large multinational companies. Labour laws prohibiting intimidation are proving ineffective. Labour legislation that requires certification of individual workplaces favours large powerful employers who can create endless delays in negotiations, engineer de-certification votes through their hiring practices and close their operations if necessary to remain union-free.

The Canadian labour movement faced very similar challenges when it unsuccessfully attempted to organize bank workers in the late 1970s. Canada's banking system is very centralized, with a few large national banks dominating the sector with hundreds of branches across the country. The bank organizing campaign was funded by a special financial levy on CLC-affiliated unions and was coordinated by the CLC itself. It involved experienced organizers from many affiliated unions and was a major campaign of the labour movement for several years. Several branches of national banks were successfully organized but the unions were never able to attain a sufficient rate of union density to exert influence over the banks.

Collective bargaining agreements for individual bank branches were eventually negotiated with several major banks. However these agreements did not provide sufficient gains to inspire workers to undertake the risks associated with organization campaigns. Over time, many of these workplaces decertified from the union (Warskett, 2004).

In Canada organizing new workers is seen as the responsibility of individual unions. The British Columbia Federation of Labour sponsors an Organizing Institute that trains organizers and encourages cooperation between unions and outreach to community organizations. Some local labour councils conduct public awareness campaigns and attempt to coordinate organizing activities of affiliates. However this type of involvement by labour central organizations is the exception rather than the rule.

Even when it comes to organizing Wal-Mart, which is seen as a major initiative for the entire labour movement, there is little involvement in this as a collective struggle. Although the 2005

CLC convention called upon the CLC to strike a committee of affiliates to assist UFCW in organizing these workers, this committee had not met as of August 2006. It is doubtful that any single union will be able to make enormous headway against the banks or companies such as Wal-Mart by using the traditional means of organizing separately individual workplaces.

Serious consideration must be given to combining the collective strength of the labour movement and community allies behind regional or community organizing campaigns.

The end of union jurisdiction and implications of mega-unions

In Canada the union movement has experienced both a reduction in overall union density and a reduction in specific union density in several industries, since so many different unions are now organizing in the same sectors of the economy. The result is that even in industries where overall union density may be high, the effectiveness of the trade union movement in areas of collective bargaining, political lobbying and policy development has been undermined, as members are fragmented into several unions that often compete against each other more than they cooperate with one another.

The loss of union members in the traditional union strongholds of manufacturing and primary industries has led several unions to look to other sectors as organizing targets. And they have been successful. As a result of organizing, raiding and mergers the Canadian labour movement has been restructured so that eight unions represent almost two-thirds of the total union membership. Four multi-sector mega-unions now represent more than half of the private-sector union membership. Today workers in automotive assembly and parts plants are a minority in the Canadian Autoworkers Union (CAW). Fishers, hotel, healthcare, airline, rail and retail workers now comprise a large majority of the union's membership. The situation of the United Steelworkers of America (USWA) is similar. USWA members employed in the steel industry and mining, the union's traditional jurisdictions, now comprise approximately 25 per cent of the union's 260,000 members. USWA members can now be found in almost every sector of the economy, including offices, security services, hospitals, banks, universities, hotels, transportation, bakeries and communications.

The development of these multi-sector unions poses a significant challenge to the structure of the CLC, which was based on the principle of one union within each sector. The Canadian labour movement was built on the concept of 'industrial' unionism where unions represented all of the workers in a particular industry regardless of craft or political affiliation. There was a consensus that workers were better served by organizing into single unions that could dominate specific industries. Achieving significant density within one sector or industry would enable unions to engage in pattern bargaining, and develop the specialized knowledge necessary to provide good service to the membership.

The result of the breakdown in union jurisdiction is that workers in the same industry, and even in the same facilities, are often divided into several unions in which they represent only a small fraction of the overall membership. General healthcare workers are divided up between three or four unions (not including registered nurses or technicians who have their own unions) in most provinces. For example, in Ontario, depending on the hospital, nursing assistants are represented by the Canadian Union of Public Employees (CUPE), the Ontario Public Service Employees Union (OPSEU), Service Employees International Union (SEIU) and CAW. Nursing home workers are represented by one of these unions or USWA. Almost every major union represents small numbers of casino, child care and bank workers. Almost every major union is organizing call-centre workers. In recent years retail workers have merged with autoworkers, woodworkers with steelworkers, and paper workers and chemical workers have merged with one of the communications unions.

There is not only stiff competition to organize new workers outside of traditional union jurisdiction, but several unions have engaged in very high-profile union raiding. During the past five years both the CAW and the International Woodworkers of America (IWA) have been found guilty of raiding already unionized nursing home and hospital workers. The Teamsters Union has been found guilty of raiding already organized casino workers.

In addition to raiding situations, unions often are forced to compete with each other to win government-supervised certification votes conducted as a result of employers restructuring in a manner that combines members from different unions into the same bargaining unit.

Employers benefit from these divisions within the labour force when different unions represent workers in the same facility, company or industry. In March 2005 there was a very public display of the problems associated with multi-union representation in the same company when Bombardier canvassed both the CAW, which represented workers in the Toronto facility, and the Machinists' Union, representing workers in Montreal, to see which would offer concessions in exchange for location of the final assembly of a new passenger airplane with 2,500 jobs. The Machinists' Union offered a wage freeze and other major concessions. The autoworkers, having previously agreed to a 2003 contract which included a wage freeze and changes in work rules that cost the local plant 360 jobs, refused to consider further concessions. The production was located in Montreal.

CHALLENGES FOR THE CANADIAN LABOUR CONGRESS

The emergence of multi-sector, mega-unions also presents challenges to existing labour central organizations such as the CLC and provincial labour federations. Large, multi-sector unions such as the CAW, USWA, CUPE and the National Union of Public and General Employees (NUPGE), fulfil many of the functions that are traditionally associated with central labour organizations. They have their own departments specializing in organizing, research, health and safety, education, human rights, legal and communications. Some unions, such as the CAW, have their own international departments. These new mega-unions are capable of developing and implementing policies independent of any actions undertaken by other unions or central labour bodies.

While the new mega-unions have been expanding membership and introducing new departments and areas of specialization, the responsibilities and services of the CLC have been restructured to focus less on services and more on policy development. Over the past 25 years the CLC has eliminated its collective bargaining and organizing departments and scaled down its educational services. The absence of the CLC in the areas of collective bargaining and organizing effectively remove it from playing a role in the central struggles of the labour movement.

Increasingly it is the provincial federations of labour that provide leadership in terms of organizing workplace and community actions to support affiliates or pressurize governments. In the 1990s the Ontario Federation of Labour organized a series of one-day general strikes in opposition to anti-worker measures being undertaken by the provincial government. In October 2005, the British Columbia Federation of Labour organized regional general strikes in two areas of the province to support a province-wide illegal strike of primary and secondary school teachers. At the national level the major affiliated unions have been content to relegate the CLC to the areas of political lobbying and policy formation. It has been 13 years since the CLC was authorized to organize a major national demonstration and 30 years since the CLC organized a national general strike.

The situation in Canada is not as precarious as in the United States where several major affiliates have left the AFL-CIO in favour of the 'Change to Win' federation. However many of the same tensions that led to the rift in the United States exist in Canada. Buzz Hargrove, president of the CAW, expressed the situation well when he stated, 'At this point in history the CLC is being fundamentally challenged to prove its relevance and justify its existence as anything more than a cosy anti-raiding club for union leaders' (Hargrove, 2000).

Local labour councils

The Canadian labour movement is often weak at the community level where it actually requires the greatest strength. Currently every major urban centre has a local labour council responsible for implementing activities and campaigns determined by the CLC, promoting labour's political agenda at the local level, and organizing strike support for affiliates when required.

Some local labour councils, such as the Toronto and York Region Labour Council, do play a leadership role in their metropolitan centre, undertaking many campaigns to improve conditions for workers. However many other labour councils are undermined by voluntary affiliation and very low financial contributions The CLC constitution that requires affiliates to join labour councils is not enforced. Many unions have little involvement, and some have established their own parallel local structures that compete for resources. The financial structures within the labour movement are heavily weighted to the provincial and national levels at the expense of the community organizations, reflecting a past era when the CLC provided more direct services to affiliates. For example the dues for a worker based in the city of Ottawa are $0.35 per month to the Ottawa and District Labour Council, $0.63 to the Ontario Federation of Labour and $0.70 to the CLC. This is in addition to the dues paid to the parent union. Very little of the dues collected nationally or provincially is rebated back to the local labour councils. The net effect is that the local organizations that are the most important and relevant to the membership suffer from a chronic shortage of finances and resources.

Structural review necessary

The existing structures of the Canadian labour movement were created when most unions were small and required centralized structures to provide services such as collective bargaining, organizing, education and policy development. This is no longer the case. The decline in jurisdictional boundaries and the proliferation of multi-sector unions prohibit effective collective bargaining strategies, discourage broader-based or sectoral bargaining, inhibit effective political action strategies and stop the development of effective organizing strategies.

There needs to be a full discussion about the changing structure of the Canadian labour movement and the impact of these changes on our ability to meet the challenges posed by the internationalization of production and the political move to the right. We need to examine the functions and financing of our central labour bodies. This debate needs to occur at the local level where labour councils are starved for resources, and also within the larger affiliates that dominate the CLC.

The attack on public-sector union rights

Responding to the attack on public-sector union rights is another fundamental challenge for the Canadian trade union movement. The public sector is the most highly organized sector in Canada. Taming the power of public-sector unions and trying to reduce public-sector labour costs has been a major goal of federal and provincial governments' industrial relations strategies for the past three decades.

Under Canadian law, public-sector workers have the right to organize and negotiate collective agreements. Most public-sector workers also have the right to strike provided they follow a prescribed series of actions that usually include the participation of some form of third-party mediation and usually require an advance notice of strike action.

Since the late 1970s Canadian governments have taken various measures to attack the rights of public-sector workers and the power of public-sector unions. These attacks have included privatization of services and public-sector enterprises, deregulation, and direct legislative denials of union rights. Since 1982, 170 separate pieces of legislation have been passed that restricted, suspended or denied collective bargaining rights for workers (Fudge and Brewin, 2005).

The three major types of restrictions imposed on public-sector unions have been generalized wages restraint programmes, back to work legislation, and ad hoc legislation imposing the terms of collective agreement provisions. Frequently the latter have involved the removal of previously negotiated protections and the imposition of wage rates.

Rationales used to justify attacks on public-sector unions have included the need to reduce and eliminate public-sector deficits and debt, and also the need to reduce public-sector expenditures to permit greater harmonization of taxation policy with the United States, and to address the negative impact that wage-driven price inflation was having on the internationally competitive position of Canada's export industries.

The trade union movement in Canada has been unable to force governments to uphold public-sector union rights. Canadian unions have repeatedly submitted complaints to the International Labour Organization (ILO). Indeed since 1982 Canadian unions have filed more complaints with the ILO's Freedom of Association Committee than the national labour movements from any other of the ILO's 177 member states. The Canadian media has largely ignored the many ILO decisions against the federal and provincial governments and simply repeats the government's pledges to promote ILO standards (Adams, 2006).

Despite the widespread attacks on public-sector unions there has never been a coordinated campaign, involving major public-sector unions and labour central bodies, to explain the importance of union rights for public-sector unions and demand unfettered public-sector union rights.

Need for a unified political strategy

The Canadian labour movement also requires a comprehensive political strategy to address the numerous challenges it faces with respect to free trade, organizing, privatization, contracting out, deregulation and the denial of collective bargaining rights.

The Canadian labour movement, including the CLC, has been very active in the political struggles against globalization and the corporate agenda. At the 2005 CLC convention the affiliated unions agreed to organize in coalition with progressive organizations in Canada to 'work for the ultimate abolition of free-trade agreements (including NAFTA and the WTO) replacing them with ... more democratic and transparent trading agreements'.

However, while the union movement has developed a critical opposition to neoliberal globalization it has not engaged in any serious examination of the potential alternatives to capitalism. Several individual unions have developed education programmes that analyse the inherently anti-worker basis of the capitalist system, and some try to imagine alternatives to the status quo. However none of the unions has articulated a socialist alternative. Perhaps this is more appropriately the role of a political party, but trade union research and education could play a greater role in stimulating discussion and imaging of alternatives.

Indeed, in English Canada, the discussion of political alternatives in the trade union movement is largely limited to a debate around electoral strategies and coalition work. Some unions officially support and are institutionally linked to Canada's social democratic party, the New Democratic Party (NDP). Others have no official linkage but provide various types of support to the NDP at election time. Several unions distribute information to members as to the various positions of all of the major parties and leave it to them to draw their own conclusions. Some unions support individual candidates from a range of parties including the Liberal Party.

In Canada the traditional socialist and communist parties have largely declined, and currently have no prospect for electing members of parliament either federally or provincially. Currently there is no union in English Canada that supports any party to the left of the NDP, officially or on an unofficial basis. Most major unions work with and support a broad range of social justice organizations and coalitions. These groups play a crucial role in opposing various aspects of the corporate agenda. However they rarely articulate a clear alternative based on socialist principles.

The dominance of right-wing pro-business political parties poses an enormous threat to the trade union movement and social justice. In the short term the labour movement must develop an electoral strategy that will result in the election of pro-labour governments. Over the long term, labour must also work internally and with others to develop a consensus around alternatives to capitalism, which are necessary to create a world based on economic and social justice and to form a political party that will make this possible.

CONCLUSION

The labour movement in Canada faces significant challenges if it is to continue to make significant improvements to workers' wages, conditions of work and quality of life. Despite some slippage, it has been possible to maintain a significant level of unionization and a union advantage of higher wages, benefits and workplace rights for union members over the past 25 years. There is a crucial need however to extend these benefits to a broader group of workers. This is especially true for those in the Canadian labour market who are most exploited and disadvantaged, including women, racial-minority workers, young workers, disabled workers and aboriginal workers.

This relative success to date of the Canadian labour movement is due to the active involvement and militant actions taken by union members at key moments such as during the negotiation of collective agreements and in mounting political protests through demonstrations, community-based coalition campaigns and general strikes (even though the latter have tended to be one-day events organized on a community or regional basis).

However these achievements are being challenged by greater economic competition from private companies intent on taking over and profiting from the construction and delivery of public infrastructure and services, and from the forces of globalization, especially the increasing ability to outsource an ever-increasing range of work to low-wage countries.

The Canadian labour movement needs collectively to develop coordinated strategies to address the problems concerning organizing, political action and collective bargaining rights. It must also seriously examine its own institutional structures to promote greater working-class power within society, at the bargaining table and in the political area. In addition to waging defensive strategies to protect established gains, the Canadian labour movement must also develop an analysis and programme of real alternatives to neoliberalism.

DISCLAIMER

The authors express their own views in this chapter, which do not necessarily reflect their unions' policies.

Chapter 10

German trade unions between neoliberal restructuring, social partnership and internationalism

Heiner Dribbusch and Thorsten Schulten

INTRODUCTION

Until the 1990s German capitalism was widely regarded as a 'distinct kind of capitalist economy, governed by nationally social institutions that made for high international competitiveness for high wages and, at the same time, low inequality of income and living standards' (Streeck, 1997: 33). After the Second World War the (west) 'German model' emerged on the basis of a national class compromise which included the corporatist integration of trade unions. The latter gained relatively strong political influence via comparatively far-reaching co-determination rights at company level, the development of a comprehensive collective bargaining system at sectoral level and the overall enhancement of corporatist welfare state institutions (cf. Müller-Jentsch and Weitbrecht, 2003). Ideologically legitimized by the concept of 'social partnership' (*Sozialpartnerschaft*), the post-war class compromise was materially founded on an essentially export-led growth strategy which was able to provide both high profits and steadily increasing wages. Since the system allowed for a continuous improvement of living standards for a large majority of people it also gained broad political support among the working class.

In comparison with the old German model the reality of German capitalism today is characterized in many respects by the opposite. The dominant socio-economic features are comparatively weak economic growth, persistently high mass unemployment and rising social inequality. The class compromise came under pressure when the economic environment changed following the end of the Bretton Woods system. Growth in German capital has led to the revocation of the post-war class compromise and a call for a neoliberal restructuring of German capitalism. First attempts towards more fundamental changes to the German model date back to the

1980s, when the conservative-liberal government started to promote the liberalization and privatization of the economy and the deregulation of the labour market, including cuts in social benefits and a certain relaxation of employees' protection rights. Until the late 1990s, however, the neoliberal policies in Germany had been relatively moderate, so that the basic institutions of the German welfare and labour market regime remained relatively stable. Following 16 years of conservative-liberal governments it was ironically a red-Green coalition government led by the German Social Democratic Party (SPD) which pushed for fundamental changes in social and labour market policy.

The transformation of German capitalism since the 1990s has been widely regarded as an adaptation to the 'needs' of globalization. We shall therefore first briefly address the myth, reality and impact of globalization. Second, we look at the changes in employment patterns and the development of union organization and their impact on employee's bargaining power. Finally we present and discuss unions' responses to these challenges.

THE MYTH, REALITY AND IMPACT OF GLOBALIZATION

The concept of globalization is often used in a rather vague way, and includes many different aspects and developments. Its main purpose, however, is the idea that capitalism has entered a qualitatively new stage which differs fundamentally from the old postwar period of capitalism. Although globalization is the result of a deliberate worldwide shift towards neoliberal policies, since the 1980s, it has widely been regarded as a secular and irreversible development which diminishes fundamentally the possibilities for political intervention:

> Market-modifying and market-correcting political intervention in the economy, including publicly associational self-regulation, can take place only within nation states, because it is only here that the public power necessary for the purpose can be mobilized. Economic globalisation, therefore, erodes the conditions for such intervention and ... leaves only de-politicised, privatised and market-driven forms of economic order.
>
> (Streeck, 1997: 53)

Globalization is not only an ideological construction devised by neoliberal politicians but also a reality which mirrors the structural changes in the organization and governance of capital. There are two dimensions that are of growing importance here. One is the meaning of the globalized financial markets and the immense influence of transnational investment funds which promote a shareholder-value orientation in the governance of capital, and determine steadily increasing profit margins. The other is the development of transnational production networks which on the basis of modern information and communication technologies make it much easier to shift certain activities from one location to another. The result is a continuous enforcement of competition between and within transnational corporations (TNCs). Companies are under increasing pressure to realize short-term profit targets, and they pass on this pressure to workers by demanding continuous reductions of labour costs. Governments enter into a competition of lowering corporate taxes and social security contributions in order to retain and attract investments. All this has an important impact on labour relations in the private and public sectors and affects workers' bargaining power.

The German economy – a winner

In Germany the prevailing debate on globalization has focused primarily on the issue of competitiveness. According to the neoliberal mainstream, the traditional German welfare and labour market regime no longer fits into a globalized economy, since the labour costs and taxes it implies are too high and undermine the competitive position of the German economy. Comparatively weak economic performance and high unemployment since the mid-1990s have been used as arguments that 'under the conditions of globalization' fundamental 'structural changes' to the German labour market and welfare state institutions are required, in order to diminish the financial burden for capital. Demands have included the limitation and even the repeal of the statutory protection against dismissal, the restriction of employees' consultation and co-determination rights, the decentralization or even individualization of wage setting, the privatization of social security and a substantial reduction of corporate taxes.

However, considering Germany's international economic relations and its trade surplus this neoliberal perspective on globalization has to be contested. The German economy is more a winner than a loser in the globalization process. An export-led growth strategy with a significant trade surplus has always been one of the basic features of the post-war western German economy. Since the mid-1990s, this trade surplus has grown tremendously (Figure 10.1).

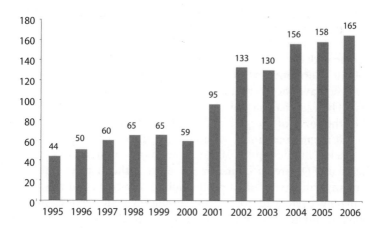

Figure 10.1 Germany's trade surplus 1995–2006 (in € billion)

Source: Statistisches Bundesamt, Fachserie 7.

The development of international trade relations, however, is only one dimension of the globalization process. Another one is the cross-border transfer of capital. Since the 1980s the foreign direct investment (FDI) of German companies has always been much higher than the investment of foreign companies in Germany (Deutsche Bundesbank, 2006). Between 1990 and 2004 the number of employees working in German companies abroad nearly doubled from 2.3 million to 4.6 million, while employment by foreign companies in Germany grew by only 25 per cent, from 1.8 million to 2.2 million during the same period. Regular company surveys on behalf of the German chambers of commerce have shown that the share of German investments abroad will continue to increase in the future (DIHK, 2006).

Globalization and employment

Related to the discourse on competitiveness, the German debate on globalization also focuses very much on relocations. The sharp increase of German FDI in the 1990s became widely regarded as an 'emigration' of capital from less profitable production possibilities in Germany. Against the background of some prominent cases of actual relocations, which attracted widespread attention from the media, the public notion of globalization is that German capital is switching more and more of its activities abroad mainly because German taxes and labour costs are too high.

The increasing internationalization of German capital has become widely used as an argument that globalization is threatening jobs in Germany. More detailed analyses of Germany's FDI, however, have shown that its employment effects are far from being clear. The vast majority of German FDI is not about relocations but takes the form of mergers and acquisitions, where German capital buys foreign companies without any direct employment effects (Deutsche Bundesbank, 2006). The more indirect or mid-term effects of FDI are of course much more difficult to evaluate. If a company shifts parts of its production to low-cost countries this can ultimately even lead to a positive employment record, since the company might improve its overall competitiveness with positive repercussions for domestic production. Summarizing the various studies on German FDI and its impact on employment, the German Council of Economic Experts (*Sachverständigenrat* 2004: 369) came to the conclusion that from a macro-economic point of view there is no clear picture, and that if there are any negative employment effects they are not very dramatic.

Globalization as a political instrument

There is a growing disproportion between the overall positive effects of globalization for the German economy and the negative effects assumed in the public debate. According to a representative survey carried out by the Ipsos polling institute in spring 2006, more than two-thirds of German people believe that globalization has a negative impact on their own lives, and about 40 per cent think that globalization makes it more difficult for them to find a job (Ipsos, 2006). This negative perception reflects the fact that the neoliberal restructuring of German capitalism, with its deteriorating consequences for the living and working conditions of many people, has often been justified as an alleged necessity resulting from globalization. As the policies of neoliberalism have created a growing division between winners and losers, the losers have become widely regarded as the 'victims' of globalization.

Against the background of persistent mass unemployment it usually does not matter whether a company is really willing and able to shift its production abroad. The threat of relocation is often sufficient to pressure workers into accepting changes in wages or working conditions. When in 2004 two prominent German companies (Siemens and Daimler-Chrysler) succeeded in gaining far-reaching concessions from their workforces following the announcement of possible relocations, a representative survey (Ipsos, 2004) found that more than a third of German workers were afraid of losing their jobs because companies might shift activities to low-wage countries. Moreover, three out of four workers would have been prepared to accept a wage freeze for two years in order to keep their jobs.

CHALLENGES FOR TRADE UNIONS

Changing employment structure

Like other western European economies, Germany has witnessed a major shift in employment towards the service sector. In 1990 the share of employment in this sector reached the 60 per cent margin, and in 2006 almost three-quarters of all employees worked in some kind of public or private service job. This does not mean that manufacturing has lost its weight within the German export-oriented economy, but only a minority of workers are still employed in the classic industries which have been one of the traditional pillars of organized labour in Germany. The other has been the public sector, which underwent fundamental changes as a result of restructurings and privatization (Dribbusch and Schulten, 2007). About 2 million jobs were either cut or moved outside the public service between 1991 and 2005. In the same period its employment structure changed significantly. Whereas white-collar employees continued to represent almost half of the public sector workforce, the share of civil servants (who are excluded from collective bargaining and have no right to strike) grew from 28 per cent to 38 per cent, whereas the share of manual workers who traditionally formed the backbone of public-sector unionism fell from 25 per cent to 12 per cent.

Casualization of the workforce

Since the early 1990s Germany has seen a growing tendency towards the development of 'non-standard' forms of employment. Between 1991 and 2005 the number of full-time jobs declined by more than six million or about 21 per cent whereas the number of part-time employees more than doubled (BMAS, 2006). In December 2005 about 4.4 million part-time employees were liable to social security contributions (*sozialversicherungspflichtige Beschäftigte*), and an additional 4.9 million employees had a type of mostly marginal part-time employment referred to as a 'mini-job' in Germany (Bundesagentur für Arbeit 2006b). 'Mini-jobs' are jobs paid a maximum of €400 a month, which, since April 2003, is the threshold above which jobs are liable to social security contributions. They are widespread in private households and in the private service industries. In some sectors such as industrial cleaning almost half of employees are 'mini-jobbers' (Kalina and Voss-Dahm, 2005).

Temporary agency work has been growing since it became almost completely deregulated in 2002. By 2005 this form of employment had risen by almost 40 per cent to 444,000 workers. However, agency workers represented at that time only 1.5 per cent of the workforce – a small group in comparison to some other European countries (Promberger, 2006). Other forms of casual employment are hidden within self-employment. Between 1991 and 2004 the number of self-employed people, including unpaid family workers, increased by 20 per cent to 4.2 million (Deutsche Bundesbank, 2005).

Seasonal and informal employment

Although labour migration is a widely discussed issue in Germany, reliable data on how many people migrate to Germany and take up a job is lacking. In 1973 recruitment of workers from outside the European Union was stopped. Since then it has been relatively difficult for workers from non-EU countries to get a work permit. At the end of the 1980s bilateral agreements with some central and eastern European states were concluded which regulated seasonal employment, in particular in the hotel and restaurant sector and in agriculture. Between 1991 and 2005 the number of officially registered seasonal employees grew from 129,000 to 330,000.

Posted workers – workers who are sent to Germany by employers from outside Germany – are found particularly in the building industry. In 2005 some 90,000 posted workers, for whom employers from outside Germany paid contributions to the building industry's leave-scheme, were registered in Germany (SOKA-Bau, 2006).

The extent of informal employment and so-called undeclared work – that is, work not declared to the authorities – is by its very nature difficult to assess as there are no reliable figures available. Some kind of undeclared work is performed by employees working on the side. Undocumented workers have hardly any other chance to get a job than to work in the informal sector. Informal employment is estimated to exist in particular in private households, the building industry, the hotel and catering sector, and agriculture.

Low pay

The proportion of employees in low-paid employment has increased continuously since the mid-1990s as a result of declining collective bargaining coverage and decreasing union bargaining power (Schulten, 2006a). According to the Organisation for Economic Co-operation and Development (OECD), which defines the threshold for low pay as being two-thirds of the median wage, there are nearly 7 million low-paid workers in Germany, of which about 3 million are full-time employees. The proportion of low-paid workers in east Germany is more than twice as high as in the west. More than two-thirds of the low-paid workers are women.

Acknowledging that organization is too weak to be able to tackle low pay by means of collective agreements, two unions in the service sector the large United Services Union (*Vereinte Dienstleistungsgewerkschaft*, ver.di) and the comparatively small Trade Union of Food, Beverages, Tobacco, Hotel and Catering and Allied Trades (*Gewerkschaft Nahrung-Genuss-Gaststätten*, NGG) have started a campaign for a national statutory minimum wage of €7.50 per hour. This would positively affect about 4.9 million employees or 15 per cent of all employees (Kalina and Weinkopf, 2006). Despite opposition from the Mining, Chemicals and Energy Industrial Union (*Industriegewerkschaft Bergbau, Chemie, Energie*, IG BCE) this demand was adopted at the 2006 congress of the DGB (Schulten, 2006a).

Unemployment

The most important factor that affects the power relationship between labour and capital is the persistently high level of mass unemployment. In 2005 Germany faced a post-war peak with nearly 5 million people officially registered as unemployed. Although unemployment declined somewhat in 2006 as a result of a cyclical upswing, the official unemployment rate for Germany was still 10.8 per cent (9.1 per cent in western and 17.3 per cent in eastern Germany). Almost 40 per cent of those registered as unemployed had been out of work for more than a year. Immigrant workers are strongly affected by unemployment. The unemployment rate for non-German nationals stood at 23.6 per cent in 2006 (Bundesagentur für Arbeit, 2006a).

The bargaining strength of unions and the effectiveness of collective bargaining are certainly not exclusively tied to the labour market situation, but the observation that the rise of unemployment in Germany since the 1970s corresponds with a decline in average wage increases tells a story about the general development of employees' bargaining power (see Figure 10.2).

Declining trade union membership

Mass unemployment undermines the collective organization of workers, especially if unions cannot compensate for job losses in their classical strongholds in mining, shipyards, steel and manufacturing by organizing employees in other sectors of the economy. German unions still find it very difficult to organize employees where the bulk of employment is – in private services (Dribbusch, 2003). A general problem is their weak presence amongst young employees. The union density of all German union confederations, that is total membership excluding pensioners and the unemployed as a proportion of all civilian employment of wage and salary earners, was 32 per cent in 1970. It rose to 35 per cent in 1980 but declined in the 1990s and stood just under 23 per cent in 2003 (Visser, 2006: 45).

The decline in membership has in particular affected the Confederation of German Trade Unions (*Deutscher Gewerkschaftsbund*, DGB). Membership in the DGB rose from 5.5 million in 1950 to 7.9 million in 1990. With the enrolment of most members of the former east German unions, membership numbers peaked at almost 12 million

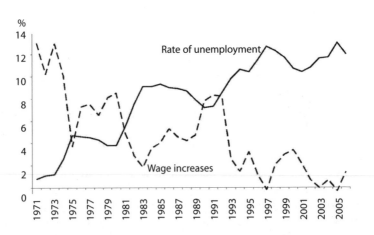

Figure 10.2 Wage increases and unemployment in Germany

Based on annual increases of wages and rate of unemployment ((until 1990, for West Germany).
Sources: Statistisches Bundesamt, Fachserie 18; Bundesagentur für Arbeit, Arbeits-marktstatistik.

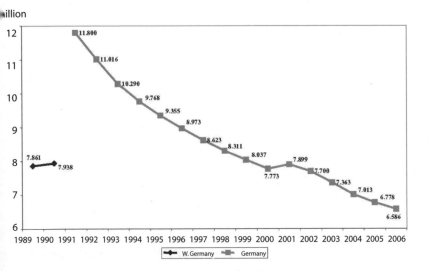

Figure 10.3 DGB membership 1989–2006

Source: DGB.

in 1991, only to collapse during deindustrialization and restructuring in eastern Germany (Dribbusch, 2004b). Membership also declined in western Germany, albeit more slowly. By 2006 overall membership of the DGB had fallen well below the 7 million mark (Figure 10.3).

Whereas union membership is still relatively strong in (western) German metal manufacturing and amongst the remaining blue-collar workforce in the public sector, DGB affiliates experience difficulties in establishing a substantial presence in many parts of the private service sector, including the private transport business, and in public administration. The organizational weakness in private services corresponds with a low effectiveness in collective bargaining, which in turn does not raise the attractiveness of unions. Exceptions are found in the airline industry and the health service, where strong professional unions for pilots and medical doctors emerged which rely on their particular workplace bargaining power and challenge the principle of industrial unionism.

Changes in collective bargaining

Since the early 1990s employers and government have demanded a turnaround in collective bargaining. In the 1993/94 bargaining round employers' associations first tried a roll-back, demanded the renegotiation of collective agreements and tabled catalogues of their own demands. The traditional role allocation in German post-war collective bargaining whereby the unions took the initiative and employers only reacted had ended. Increased international competition led to new management policies with a sharper focus on continuous cost-cutting programmes. Growing unemployment, the opening of the eastern European labour market and better opportunities for companies to relocate production made employees sensitive to employers' pressure. Employers' demands were focused on an increase of working time and cuts in benefits, but also included the renunciation or delay of wage increases and even outright pay cuts.

Bargaining coverage declined in the 1990s but remained at a comparatively high level, particularly in western Germany. In 2005 about 41 per cent of western German establishments representing 67 per cent of employees were covered by a collective agreement, whereas in eastern Germany only 23 per cent of establishments with 53 per cent of all employees were covered (Kohaut and Schnabel, 2006).

Furthermore, there is a strong tendency towards a more decentralized bargaining system (Bispinck, 2006). Traditionally, the German collective bargaining system has been dominated by negotiations at sectoral level. The pressure of employers on existing standards of terms and conditions led to the introduction of so-called opening clauses in many sectoral collective agreements. These clauses allow for deviations from agreed terms and conditions at company or plant level if the employer claims economic difficulties. This resulted in a great number of agreements at company level, sometimes labelled 'Pacts for Employment and Competitiveness' (Seifert and Massa-Wirth, 2005), which established a new form of 'concession bargaining' whereby employees had to make concessions on wages and working conditions in exchange for limited job guarantees for the core workforce.

Decentralization of collective bargaining is also evident in the public sector (Dribbusch and Schulten, 2007). Until the mid-1990s a more or less uniform package of national collective agreements covered all public employees at federal, regional and municipal level. This system has been eroded since then. Privatization moved considerable numbers of workers outside the scope of the national collective agreements. A neoliberal tax policy reduced public income and put increasing pressure on public authorities to reduce labour costs in order to tackle their budget problems.

Western German metal workers still have a comparatively strong bargaining position at sectoral level, especially when the economic situation is temporarily improving as it was in 2005 and 2006, but the overall picture is that of unions on the defensive. The proactive approach of reducing weekly working time with wage compensation to tackle unemployment, which was prominent among German unions during the 1980s, ended in the early 1990s, and since the mid-1990s employers have succeeded in turning the tide towards longer working hours – despite union resistance and some long strike disputes in the public sector in 2006. The 'grand coalition' of conservatives and social democrats which succeeded the Red-Green government in 2005 disregarded union protests and extended the legal retirement age from 65 to 67.

TRADE UNIONS' RESPONSES AND STRATEGIES

German unions' policies are largely focused on the national arena. This is not surprising as it is here that their core business of collective bargaining takes place. However, there is an increasing awareness that collective bargaining within national borders is often at odds with the volatility of capital and the growing possibilities of employers to circumvent or opt out of the national framework. Both of these factors undermine the underlying goal of collective bargaining, which is designed to effectively limit and regulate concurrence between workers. Some German unions, as in particular IG Metall, have been very active in developing a strategy for a coordination of collective bargaining at European level, which however has not been very effective so far (Schulten, 2004; Chapter 13, in this volume).

As Riexinger and Sauerborn (2004) have pointed out, globalization would require a recovery of control over the labour market at an international level. Given the slow progress of transnational union cooperation even at the level of the European Union, it is hard to imagine that the unions will be able to establish such a control in the near future. German unions do not ignore the process of globalization. They have developed a range of political positions and some practical initiatives which, however, often remain restricted to a small number of full-time officials in the international departments or to some groups of lay activists. Because of their size, German unions play an important role in shaping the positions of international union bodies towards globalization, in particular at the European level.

Political responses to globalization

With regard to neoliberal globalization, the current leading social-democratic position within the German union movement follows what Streeck (1998: 172) labels a 'social-liberal' position. This position, while accepting the paradigm of national competitiveness, stresses that competitive advantage could best be won through investments in education and training to improve productivity and via the pacifying effects of the welfare state with its integration of the unions. In this view unions and works councils improve competitiveness because they mediate potential conflicts at industry and company level. In the field of international economics the demands focus on a re-regulation of the financial markets and the implementation of international social standards.

In Germany this 'social liberal' position is most explicitly represented by the IG BCE, the third biggest of the German unions. At its third congress in 2005 it adopted a motion in which it stated that:

> through access to new markets, globalization offers additional opportunity, particularly to the export-driven German industry .... This also benefits and strengthens industrial locations in Germany. However, it is also true that these locations have to face global benchmarking by companies. To make sure this does not lead to a ruinous competition for ever lower standards and wages, global minimum social and ecological standards are required.
>
> (IG BCE, 2005a)

The two other major German unions, IG Metall and ver.di, are less enthusiastic in their official declarations about the prospects of globalization, but they share the overall view that a reconciliation of employers' and employees' interests is also possible at global level (IG Metall, 2005; ver.di, 2006). Ver.di and the IG BCE (2005b) both underline the beneficial effects of 'social responsibility' for the competitiveness of enterprises because 'employees who are treated in a fair manner are more productive and stay longer with the employer' (ver.di, 2006: 27).

IG Metall and DGB stress the responsibility of the state for adding a 'social dimension' to globalization (IG Metall, 2005: 3). Points of reference are the International Labour Organization (ILO) *Declaration on Fundamental Principles and Rights at Work*, the Global Compact initiative of the United Nations and the *OECD Guidelines for Multinational Enterprises*. IG Metall and DGB

demand that the ILO standards shall be embedded in the World
Trade Organization (WTO) framework as a binding obligation, but
as long as this is not achieved IG Metall pursues the way of consen-
sual talks. The signing of the Global Compact by companies is
regarded as a starting point to enter into talks (ver.di, 2006: 25). The
aim is to negotiate so-called international framework agreements by
which companies agree to implement the ILO standards at all sites
round the globe.

If there is some common ground between the three major unions
in the general position towards globalization, there are political
differences between them with regard to the international opposition towards neoliberal globalization. In an article published in
2000, setting out basic principles towards globalization and called
'Free trade and social responsibility', Manfred Warda, the head of
international relations Europe of IG BCE, criticizes the resistance of
employers to international social dialogue and the 'aggressive behaviour of local management', which 'fuels militancy at the grass roots
level of trade unions, ... complicating the necessary task of overcoming traditional modes of thinking which still stand in the way of
effective trade union cooperation' (Warda, 2000). He worries that
some unions 'increasingly listen to the simplistic reasoning put
forward by self-appointed leaders of civil society, not noticing that
they offer no new alternatives, but, at best, re-packaged old solutions which have already proved to be unworkable'. Warda deplores
the fact that representatives of international union organizations
'seem to want to hail the debacle of ... [the] World Trade Conference in Seattle and the OECD's inconclusive discussions on a
Multilateral Agreement on Investment (MAI) as a successful result
of trade union mobilization'.

In contrast to this position both ver.di and IG Metall are aware
that there is a need to develop union power as a prerequisite to any
substantial class compromise with international companies. Both
organizations are not only more open for a debate with critics of
neoliberal globalization, they seek at least partial cooperation. This is
also partly the case with the DGB, which published in 2002 a joint
paper with Attac and other non-governmental organizations (NGOs)
on a 'fair re-regulation of globalization' (DGB, Attac and VENRO,
2002). Under the impact of the growing alienation between the Social
Democratic Party and unions, in particular IG Metall and ver.di
became interested in broadening the spectrum of their potential coalition partners. This includes not only the newly established Left Party
(Die.Linke) but also the cooperation with other social movements,

such as the participation in national, European and World Social Forums. In May 2004 IG Metall and ver.di were amongst the main organizers of a joint conference of unions and various NGOs, including the globalization critics of Attac, on alternatives to neoliberal policies and the perspectives of cooperation between unions and social movements. Although this conference exposed substantial differences between the various participants it was a strong sign that the mobilizations following Seattle and the emergence of a movement against neoliberal globalization had left a positive impression within the ranks of German unions.

Labour protectionism and boundary drawing

Labour internationalism was always much more difficult to put into practice than the slogan 'workers of all countries unite' suggested. 'Precisely because the ongoing unmaking and remaking of working classes creates dislocations and competitive pressure on workers, there is also an endemic tendency for workers to draw non-class borders and boundaries as a basis for claims for protection from the maelstrom' (Silver, 2003: 22). Under transitional arrangements agreed by the European Union and the new Member States in Central and Eastern Europe which joined in 2004, the existing Member States are allowed to limit the free movement of workers from the new Member States for a period of up to seven years (that is until 2011 at the latest). The German government has received full support from the DGB for making full use of these restrictions on labour migration. German unions feared that unregulated labour migration, combined with the possibility of employers paying workers according to the conditions agreed in their country of origin and not according to German collectively agreed standards, would lead to social dumping on pay and conditions.

A similar pattern of argumentation can be found in the opposition of unions to the European Services Directive (so-called Bolkestein Directive), presented by the European Commission in 2004 and aimed at liberalizing the provision of private services within the European Union. The DGB rejected this directive in line with the European Trade Union Confederation (ETUC). The union opposition in Germany was particularly directed at the so-called 'country of origin principle' which would have allowed companies or individuals to provide services to consumers in another Member State on the basis of the laws of their country of origin without having to honour specific regulations or collective agreements in the host country. Although the opposition to the Services Directive was much less explicitly directed towards the exclusion of foreign workers from the labour market, it was also about drawing a boundary against the 'unfair' competition of the low-waged 'Polish tiler'. It reflected the fact that the working class is no uniform entity, but segmented at national or international level, and that the interests of individual workers may collide.

Activities and initiatives

The main international activities of German unions are embedded in policies of international – but in particular European – union organizations. Within this framework German unions are engaged in political lobbying of international bodies such as the IMF, WTO and the European Union. The day-to-day activities are usually delegated to officials who work with or within the international union organizations. They are only occasionally highlighted in union publications and remain largely unnoticed by the rank and file. The regional bodies of the DGB and its affiliates are also engaged in cross-border cooperation with unions of neighbouring countries.

The second pillar of international activity has become the work within the European Works Councils (EWCs). Since 1994 there is a legal basis for the establishment of EWCs at EU level. The EWCs give unions a platform to establish transnational cooperation networks within TNCs. Moreover, EWCs have some information and consultation rights which in practice, however, are rather limited (Waddington, 2006). In some larger TNCs – for example General Motors and Volkswagen – the EWCs have tried to influence the companies' location policy and to limit the competition between individual plants through 'European action days' and other forms of transnational action. Very few TNCs have even accepted the establishment of worldwide works councils on a voluntary basis.

Outside these formal structures there are some union-supported exchange programmes and cooperative undertakings. One example is a network of union representatives of the chemicals transnational BASF in Latin America. This network emerged from a rank and file initiative of German unionists within BASF, and was officially set up in 1999 with the support of IG BCE and the Global Union Federation in chemicals, ICEM. Union representatives of the BASF sites in Argentina, Brazil and Chile meet and elect committees at regional and national level which then meet twice a year with management.

The participation in European mobilizations called by the ETUC varies according to the issue and the priorities set by the DGB affiliates. Sometimes only a number of officials or groups of active pensioners form the German delegation; on other occasions the mobilization is more substantial. The latter was the case in 2005 and 2006 when some thousands of DGB members took part in international rallies against the Bolkestein Directive in Brussels and Strasbourg.

There is some cooperation with NGOs. Ver.di, IG Metall and the DGB support the international Clean Clothes Campaign. Ver.di also cooperates with WEED (World Economy, Ecology and Development) and seeks from time to time the cooperation with other NGOs. IG BAU, the construction workers' union, cooperates with the Flower Label Program initiated 1999 by the human rights organization FIAN (FoodFirst Information- und Aktions-Netzwerk). Whereas the NGOs often contribute committed activists and creative ideas which sometimes transcend the conventional union repertoire, unions can provide infrastructure and have the potential to mobilize large numbers of people. Cooperation is not always easy, especially as unions sometimes regard such cooperation as a temporary coalition in which they are the natural and undisputed leaders.

Some examples of cooperation that are directly linked to union activities can be found in the retail sector, which is organized by ver.di (Bormann, Deckwirth and Teepe, 2005). One such example is the rank and file initiative 'exChains' in which ver.di activists working in the retail trades have organized a collaboration with union activists from Bangladesh and Sri Lanka. The initiative was supported by the international network TIE (Transnationals Information Exchange), which is an independent organization to promote transnational union contacts at rank-and-file level.

In September 2004 IG BAU established a new union called European Migrant Workers Union (Dribbusch, 2004a). The aim is to organize itinerant workers of all nationalities who work for a limited period of time in a EU Member States (other than their own), especially in industries such as construction or agriculture. So far the union has offices in Germany and Poland. Given its limited resources it has made good progress without becoming a huge mass organization – something that realistically could not be expected given the difficult nature of organizing amongst itinerant workers. Its day-to-day work consists to a large degree of claiming unpaid wages from employers who blatantly cheat employees whom they consider to be unprotected. The initiative is very remarkable not only because it addresses itinerant workers regardless of their legal status, but because it has a cross-border focus and recognizes itinerant workers as colleagues and not as opponents on the labour market.

International cooperation

A very effective way of tackling internationally operating companies is direct international union cooperation. A prominent example has been the successful mobilization of dockworkers in Europe against two European Union directives on the deregulation of dock work called 'Port Package 1 and 2'. Dockworkers, although smaller in numbers since the introduction of the modern container transport, are well organized and aware of their power – based on their crucial position in the international transport chain. This helped to develop a successful international campaign supported by the European Transport Federation (ETF), to which ver.di is affiliated, and the International Dockworkers Council (IDC), which unites unions outside the ETF. It culminated in two days of action and a rally in front of the European Parliament in Strasbourg in January 2006. The activities resulted in the directive being rejected by the European Parliament.

This kind of direct international action is, however, the exception from the rule. In other sectors this kind of international cooperation has less tradition and seems to be more difficult to organize. An interesting kind of cooperation took place in 2006 in the security industry in the city of Hamburg, where the American-based Service Employees International Union (SEIU) actively supported ver.di in training a team of organizers to build the union in this sector (Bremme, Fürniss and Meinecke, 2007). The rationale behind this cooperation was that the global players in property services are transnational companies, and that it is in the interest of both unions that they be unionized. Ver.di is also seeking international cooperation to tackle German discount chains such as Lidl which are widely considered to be anti-union not only in their domestic market but also in other countries.

Other activities

It is not possible to feature all union activities in the field of international cooperation and solidarity. The DGB has its own structure called Nord-Süd-Netz (North-South network) for supporting development projects and union solidarity groups in Germany. The network which is funded by the DGB, public subsidies and donations had four staff in 2006 and supported international projects in Latin America, Africa and Asia. The traditional focus had been on Brazil and South Africa. In Brazil it cooperates with Observatório Social – a research and training institute of the Brazilian union centre CUT – which is promoting the compliance with social and labour standards in national and multinational companies in Brazil. In South Africa the DGB supported in 2006 the South African Domestic Workers Union (SADSAWU) in campaigns to help domestic workers to become recognized and fairly treated at work.

At the fringes of the unions

There are a number of initiatives outside or at the fringes of the union movement. The German branch of TIE was in the past instrumental in organizing some international conferences where rank and file unionists of Germany met with colleagues from other countries. In the car and the chemicals industry a few rank and file networks were established by activists outside the official union channels. Where they exist they often result from a situation where the official union structures had hindered rather than supported direct international contacts between activist and activist. These structures often struggle with a lack of resources, and the sustainability relies heavily on the commitment and skills of active individuals. Language skills are crucial, and sometimes established links between workers of different countries within an international company simply run into problems when an activist retires because no one is trained to answer Spanish or English emails.

Founded in December 1999 by union and social movement activists as a means to use the Internet to strengthen and build organized labour, the German website Labournet (http://www.labournet.de) has become the number one German website for news on workers' activities around the globe. The website is in the style of similar websites in the United Kingdom and United States, and puts an emphasis on rank and file activities and on organizing international solidarity. In 2006 there were on average about 300,000 visitors to the site a month.

OUTLOOK: WHAT FUTURE FOR GERMAN TRADE UNIONS?

During the past decade German unions have entered a structural crisis which has various dimensions. First, there is a *crisis of legitimation and representation*, as the unions have been faced by a considerable decline in membership and a significant weakness in organizing workers outside of their traditional core groups in manufacturing and the public sector. Second, there is a *crisis of political influence* since the neoliberal restructuring of German capitalism has significantly diminished the corporatist channels of influence and political lobbying, and the close alliance between unions and the SPD has been disrupted.

Third, *union reactions* towards the attempts at neoliberal restructuring have often been *rather ambiguous*. There has been a fundamental contradiction between progressive political concepts and a pragmatic subordination under the paradigms of competitiveness (Riexinger and Sauerborn, 2004). On the one hand most unions have defended a Keynesian-oriented approach to macro-economic policy, stressing the demand side of the economy and demanding public investment and a more expansive wage policy. On the other hand they have often followed a bargaining policy which contradicted the macro-economic policy approach by agreeing to cost-cutting programmes at company level. While they have opposed the idea that wage moderation would have positive employment effects at national level, they accept pay restraint in exchange for jobs at company level.

Decades of social partnership have deeply shaped the thinking of German union officials and the rank and file alike, not least because they went along with the achievement of comparatively high wages, six weeks of paid leave and partly a 35-hour week. Many German unionists hoped in the 1990s for a re-establishment of a class compromise similar to the one of the post-war period. They advocated new forms of alliances at local, regional and national level, typically labelled 'alliances for jobs and competitiveness'. The aim was to manage the 'necessary modernization process' in a 'socially acceptable' manner. This often translated into safeguarding jobs for existing staff in exchange for temporary or permanent concessions, and the introduction of two-tier arrangements for new recruits. Leading to similar demands by competitors, this strategy encouraged the erosion of once-agreed standards. Its limits became obvious when some companies relocated despite substantial offers by works councils and unions to accept wage cuts or extended working times.

Against the background of declining membership and diminishing political and bargaining power, German unions have started to discuss and develop new political strategies which aim at a revitalization of the union movement. Two strategic approaches in particular are discussed among union circles (Urban, 2005).

The first has a kind of 'back-to-the-roots' attitude and wants to concentrate the union activities to the 'core businesses': that is, collective bargaining and workers' interest representation at company level. Its basic assumption is that unions will only over-come their crisis if they regain strength at company level. Therefore, all organizational efforts should be concentrated in this area. In contrast to that, the second approach wants to strengthen the union voice in the overall political arena by promoting social movement unionism and seeking new alliances with other social movements.

Both approaches do not necessarily compete with each other, but could form complementary parts of a comprehensive strategy which aims at a re-strengthening of both bargaining and political power. Core elements of both approaches are a renewed focus on strengthening the union at the workplace (Wetzel, 2005) and new approaches to organizing which draw on international union expe-rience (Bremme et al., 2007). This debate on strategies of union renewal is linked to a discussion on how to organize transnational union action successfully, and how to develop an internationalist answer beyond the neoliberal concepts of globalization and compet-itiveness. There are many in the German union movement who sympathize with the slogan 'another world is possible', but the discussion about alternatives is still very much open.

Chapter 11

Swedish unions and globalization: labour strategies in a changing global order

Andreas Bieler and Ingemar Lindberg

INTRODUCTION

As a result of the processes of global restructuring, labour has increasingly come under pressure over the last 30 years. This chapter will analyse Swedish trade unions' perceptions of globalization and their possibilities of defending the interests of their members in times of global restructuring. Swedish unions, together with those of Denmark and Finland, have the highest unionization rate in the world, with between 75 and 80 per cent of all employees including the unemployed (Kjellberg, 2003: 346). There are three main trade union confederations in Sweden. The Swedish Trade Union Confederation (LO) organizes blue-collar workers and lower non-manuals. The Swedish Confederation of Professional Employees (TCO) organizes white-collar employees, while the Swedish Confederation of Professional Associations (SACO) mainly represents university-trained professionals. All three peak associations consist of a range of affiliated unions, which have gained in independence since the 1980s. Historically, LO was the dominant trade union. Its membership has fallen over recent years, but it remains the largest trade union with 1,892,000 members. The TCO with 1,275,975 white-collar workers as members, and SACO, which organizes 556,000 professionals, enjoy a strong and independent position.[1]

During the 1960s and 1970s, Sweden was considered to be one of the most progressive models of capitalism in the Western World thanks to its solidaristic wage policy, gender equality in the work place, expansive welfare state and a strong commitment to full employment. Trade unions enjoyed strong impact on policy making during this time, especially due to the close relationship between the blue-collar union LO and the Swedish Social Democratic Party (SAP) as well as multi-sector collective bargaining, initially dominated by the LO and the employers' association SAF, later complemented by additional bargaining between the white-collar unions and SAF.

At the beginning of the 1990s, however, the Swedish model seemed to fall apart. Multi-sector collective bargaining broke down in 1990, and one year later the SAF left the tripartite institutions. Parallel to these developments, the SAP replaced its traditional full employment policy with a new emphasis on low inflation and price stability, and initiated Sweden's move towards EU membership, at a time when the European Union itself had moved towards a neoliberal Anglo-American model of capitalism. Nevertheless, partly due to the continuing strength of Swedish trade unions, collective bargaining was re-established at the sectoral level from 1997 onwards (Bieler, 2005a; Ryner, 2002: 123–87). Today Sweden is classified by the Organisation for Economic Co-operation and Development (OECD) as the fastest growing economy in Europe, and there is an increasing interest again in discussing a 'Nordic model' (OECD, 2005).

It is for this reason – the trade unions' continuing strength – that Sweden is a good case study for an assessment of Western European trade unions' strategies and possibilities within a changing global order. Only from a position of strength can trade unions expect to mount a successful response to current challenges. Nevertheless, comparative strength also implies the danger of overlooking the losses in relation to their own past and the risk of becoming complacent in the face of ongoing structural change. For this reason too, Swedish unions are an important object of investigation.

The challenges faced by trade unions as a result of globalization are here understood to be fourfold:

- the increasing transnationalization of production – expressed in the increasing importance of transnational corporations (TNCs) and measured in rising foreign direct investment (FDI) levels and the resulting pressures on jobs, wages and working conditions
- the growth of the marginalized sector of an increasingly larger peripheral segment of the labour market, and the related pressure on those in stable employment at the core of production
- transnational finance and the related free flow of capital, making long-term productive strategies increasingly difficult
- the neoliberal ideology driving these restructuring processes and challenging directly notions of an expansive welfare state and established trade union participation in policy-making (Bieler, 2006: 47–54).

All four challenges can be identified in Sweden. Production has always been characterized by TNCs in Sweden. The degree of transnationalization, however, increased dramatically in the second half of the 1980s, when there was a drastic upturn in outward FDI. While inward FDI had only risen from US$396 million in 1985 to US$2,328 million in 1990, outward FDI increased from US$1,783 million to US$14,136 million during the same period (Luif, 1996: 208). The transnationalization of Swedish production further intensified during the 1990s. Outward FDI investment increased to US$39,481 million in 2000 (UN, 2001: 296) and inward FDI also increased drastically, reaching US$21,449 million in 2000, after an exceptional year of US$60,801 million in 1999 (UN, 2001: 191).

Second, the Swedish rate of marginalization is certainly lower than elsewhere, but it has increased from 6–9 per cent of the labour force in the 1960s to 15–30 per cent in the 1990s (Lindberg, 1999). Third, the deregulation of the national financial market and abolition of exchange rate controls during the 1980s ensured that Swedish finance became tightly integrated into the global financial market. Finally, the policy shift towards neoliberalism can be most clearly identified with the Social Democratic government's decisions to deregulate capital markets in 1985 and to replace full employment with price stability as main policy goal, as well as applying to the European Union for membership in 1990.

This chapter analyses how trade unions see these challenges, and what strategies they perceive to be possible in this situation to represent the interests of their members as well the wider public effectively. This will include an analysis of the contents of union policies as well as their levels of activities, ranging from the company, sectoral and national via the European to the international level. The empirical analysis will draw directly on the conceptual considerations, outlined in the introduction of this volume.

When selecting interviewees for this project, we made sure that in addition to interviewees from the three confederations we interviewed representatives of transnational and national sector unions to investigate whether a split between the two has developed in practice. Thus, in addition to interviews with three leading LO representatives (Interview no. 6, Interview no. 7 and Interview no. 8), we also interviewed representatives of Handels (the Commercial Workers' Union), and the Transport Workers' Union, which both mainly organize workers in small domestic companies and shops, indicating a predominantly domestic production structure (Interview no. 3 and Interview no. 9), and of the Swedish Metal Workers' Federation, which organizes workers in the highly transnationalized manufacturing sector (Interview no. 1). Moreover, an interview with a core TCO representative (Interview no. 5) was complemented with interviews with representatives of the Union of Local Government Officers (SKTF), organizing employees in the domestic local government sector (Interview no. 4), as well as of the Swedish Union of Clerical and Technical Employees in Industry (SIF), the members of which are white-collar workers mainly in transnational manufacturing (Interview no. 2).

Second, we queried trade unions about their positions in the marginalized sector in relation to the second potential division between established and non-established labour. Here, the interview with a leading representative of SACO was especially important, since this union organizes highly educated employees, who are often employed in core managerial positions (Interview no. 10). Third, it was asked whether trade unions are prepared to cooperate with other social movements, linking this discussion to the extended notion of class struggle. Finally, we attempted to find out whether trade unions continue to reject neoliberal restructuring or whether they have accepted neoliberalism.

LABOUR MARKET STRATIFICATION

The Swedish economy has been quite healthy for some years after a deep crisis during the first half of the 1990s. The growth rate has been among the highest in Europe, almost at the same level as that of the United States, even if employment growth has been slow. A report commissioned by the European finance ministers council Ecofin identifies a comparatively successful Nordic model within the European Union – including not only Denmark, Finland and Sweden but also Austria and the Netherlands – a model which according to the rapporteur, Professor André Sapir (2005) seems able to combine an efficient labour market with income security and universal welfare systems.

However, after the economic crisis and the shift towards neoliberal economics of the early 1990s, an increasing gap and growing polarization emerged in Swedish society. During the crisis years 1991–93 overall unemployment jumped from 2 to 12 per cent. Among the young (20–24 years) unemployment rose from 3 to 22 per cent. The employment rate for the young fell from 81 to 55 per cent, and half of those employed got only temporary contracts. Recovery since then is only half-way. Income differentials are still comparatively low in Sweden, but they have been on the rise for more than 20 years now. Out of a total labour force of 3.7 million, 525,000 workers were employed on temporary contracts as of the first quarter of 2005. This represents an increase of 190,000 over 1990.

The most rapidly rising form of temporary employment is 'employment when needed', which has increased from 40,000 workers in 1990 to 145,000 in 2005. During the same period the core sector of unlimited-term contracts has shrunk from 3.6 million to 3.2 million workers. Involuntary part-time work and part-time unemployment are much more common among women: seven out of ten part-time unemployed are women. Temporary employment is also more frequent among women, but this gap has been closing during the last few years. Temporary employment in particular hits young workers, both men and women (LO, 2005). The wage gap between men and women continued to decrease until the 1980s, but has more or less been at a standstill since then. Unemployment among migrants from Eastern and Southern Europe is double, and among migrants from the Middle East and North Africa four times as high as that among those born in Sweden (Socialstyrelsen, 2006). Only about 40 per cent of migrants to Sweden from Eastern and Southern Europe could make their living from work during the year 2002, compared with 70 per cent of those born in Sweden (in the age group 16–64 years).

Ethnic segregation has increased substantially during the period from 1990 to 2002. In urban areas with low economic resources in or around Stockholm, Gothenburg and Malmo, poverty has increased, and in 2002 only one-third of the population in these areas of working age could make a living from work. It is hard to assess the number of 'paperless' migrants (without permit and not seeking asylum), but it has been estimated at around 20,000 persons in 2003–04. They are mainly hidden refugees (who have been denied asylum), black-market workers and victims of trafficking. They are outside social security, and often deprived of health care (except for emergencies) and schools. They mainly depend on relatives, friends or non-governmental organizations (NGOs) for their living.

SWEDISH TRADE UNIONS AND THE TRANSNATIONAL RESTRUCTURING OF SOCIAL RELATIONS

In general, the Swedish trade unionists interviewed for this project agreed with the picture of a weakening between 1983 and 1997 followed by a stabilization of labour's fortunes from 1997 onwards. The four globalization challenges were also recognized by trade unions. They identified the transfer of production units abroad combined with an increasing foreign ownership of companies in Sweden as signs of the transnationalization of production (Interview no. 5; Interview no. 9).

Increasing foreign ownership would make it difficult to find employer representatives who actually had a mandate to negotiate with Swedish unions (Interview no. 2). The transnationalization of production as such implied destructive changes to Swedish production. Sweden's traditional policy of supporting the shift from declining to expanding sectors had become increasingly difficult in the global economy, it was argued (Interview no. 8). Others referred to the deregulation of the financial markets in the 1980s as the core problem, as well as Sweden's fixed exchange rate policy in the early 1990s, characteristics of the transnationalization of finance (Interview no. 3; Interview no. 5). Neoliberal globalization itself was also understood in its ideological dimension, since it was pointed out that it had often been used as a discourse to justify and demand restructuring and deregulation (Interview no. 6).

Nevertheless, while there was agreement on the nature of globalization, two different camps could be identified in relation to the question of how to respond to these structural changes. On the one hand, there was the 'defend and restore' camp, believing that it was still possible to maintain the traditional achievements at the Swedish national level through national strategies. To ensure that foreign companies operating in Sweden pay according to Swedish collective agreements was identified as the core challenge. Some smaller transport and construction sector companies had already attempted to employ foreign workers in Sweden at lower wage levels. Unionists should react to the liberalization drive through:

- arguing that there was still space for full employment policies
- fighting against exemptions from labour law
- working towards the regulation of the global economy and financial flows in order to reduce risks of serious financial instabilities
- defending the public sector and the welfare state at the national level (Interview no. 7).

Another interviewee argued that LO-internal coordination of bargaining was the best way of fighting off demands by employers for decentralization of collective bargaining (Interview no. 6). In short, it should be ensured that Swedish policies are adhered to.

On the other hand, we identified a 'modernize and adapt' camp.

Globalization was accepted as a fact requiring new strategies in response, to restore the balance with capital. These new strategies may include issues such as European tax harmonization (Interview no. 2). Others argued that in order to make the best of the new situation and to avoid marginalization in the decision-making process, unions had to accept companies' need for increasing flexibility (Interview no. 1). It was argued that the changes related to globalization should be supported, but transformed into a win-win situation through an emphasis on a high rate of unemployment benefit combined with life-long learning, assistance with changing jobs and rising working conditions in those service sectors where the future expansion of employment will take place (Interview no. 8).

To sum up, while the 'defend and restore' camp tended to rely on past strategies in their resistance to neoliberal restructuring, the 'modernize and adapt' group argued that the new realities demand strategic change, implying the acceptance of some neoliberal concepts. Indeed, two interviewees from white-collar unions first, did not regard globalization as a particular problem, and second, suggested the negotiation of frameworks for individual bargaining as the right way forward under new conditions (Interview no. 4; Interview no. 10). What both camps have in common, however, is an emphasis on the national level. With the exception of Interviewee no. 2, nobody considered the European or international level as the right arena for future activities. Moreover, in relation to the hypotheses about a split between national and transnational labour and secure labour and precarious labour, unions organizing domestic production workers (Handels, Interview no. 3) and blue-collar workers more generally (LO, Interview no. 6; Interview no. 7) are in the 'defend and restore' camp, while unions organizing workers in the transnational sector (Metall, Interview no. 1, and SIF, Interview no. 2) and/or white-collar employees in more secure positions with more responsibilities (SKTF, Interview no. 4, and SACO, Interview no. 10) tended to be a part of the 'modernize and adapt' camp.

Possibility of full employment?

At the time of our interviews Sweden had 6 per cent unemployment (plus close to 3 per cent in labour market programmes) and a labour market participation rate of 77 per cent. The then ruling Social Democratic government set a goal to bring down unemployment to 4 per cent as a step towards full employment, as well as to increase the rate of participation in the labour market by the adult population to 80 per cent. We asked our interviewees whether it was still possible today to bring unemployment down to 2 per cent as before, and, if so, how? The answers show an interesting set of divergent positions and are not homogeneous within the two camps.

Within the 'defend and restore' camp, two interviewees argued that there is still a trade-off – at least from a short and medium-term perspective – between low inflation and high unemployment, and that a higher inflation target is still a possible option for Sweden. One of them (Interview no. 3) argued that a higher inflation rate of 3 to 5 per cent would be helpful. The other (Interview no. 5) argued slightly more cautiously for raising the inflation target to 2.5 to 3 per cent, combined with a strong emphasis on public sector investment. Equally, both still assumed that there is a possibility for demand-side policies at the national level. But in line with this camp's main focus on the defence of traditional achievements at the national level, they did not argue for European employment policies.

By contrast, other interviewees accepted the harsh neoliberal policy restrictions imposed on Sweden. One interviewee, while leaving the question of full employment open, assumed that there is still some room for manoeuvre. Hence, he advocated a combination of more active fiscal policies within the 2 per cent inflation framework, selective labour market policies, gradual expansion of the public sector and improvements in the field of education and training (Interview no. 7). Another interviewee straightforwardly denied the possibility of regaining full employment: 5 per cent unemployment plus 2 per cent of workers in labour market initiatives was the best one could currently hope for. In their policies, unions should therefore focus on obtaining as high wage increases as possible without threatening the 2 per cent inflation norm, as well as control the distribution of wage increases in order to obtain increases for the low paid and close the pay gap between male and female sectors. The low inflation policy itself, however, decided by capital and anchored in a transnational framework, could currently not be challenged (Interview no. 6).

The 'modernize and adapt' camp is characterized by a similar division. One interviewee argued that Sweden could do better than at present through industrial policies. In particular, Swedish small and medium-sized companies, who used to rely on Swedish TNCs, needed active state support to cope with international competition. This should include an active R&D policy, good education policies, venture capital provision as well as the use of pension funds. Nevertheless, in general unions would have to accept that full employment is no longer possible. The free flow of capital and the competition between production sites, challenges resulting from globalization, would make the low-inflation regime necessary (Interview no. 1).

By contrast, another interviewee of the 'modernize and adapt' camp insisted that full employment is still possible. The way this is to be achieved, however, is clearly different from that suggested by the 'defend and restore' camp. A higher inflation level should be ruled out and the public sector could not be expanded further, at least not by Sweden alone. Tax levels would already be too high. Instead, the focus is on neoliberal supply-side policies of a better education and training system. Moreover, Sweden would need to tackle structural problems in relation to its education system and labour market. In general, interviewees in this camp denied that demand-side policies are still possible at the national level (Interviews no. 2 and 10). There was some agreement across the camps on the need for risk capital, and the possible role of pension funds was discussed.

One interviewee, however, argued that capital accumulation is developing too fast. Demands for returns on investments have become higher and higher. Hence, employers relocate production to low-cost countries. This is only possible, first, because transport has become too cheap. Second, we need to think about how to reclaim more of the profits made by capital. So far, workers and the welfare state have been the clear losers of these super-profits. We do not have the necessary tools today to get these profits back to the workers. The core aim has to be to reclaim as much money as possible from these super-profits, it was argued (Interview no. 9). Another interviewee, while accepting that unions could currently not challenge the low inflation policy, pointed out that this situation could change rapidly, as it did in the late 1960s (Interview no. 6).

Marginalization

We asked our respondents whether they were concerned about increasing marginalization and the related gap between core workers and those in the periphery of the labour market. A majority of them confirmed that marginalization is an increasing problem. Important differences appeared, however, when they described the kind of marginalization they see and its consequences.

The difference between the two camps came out most clearly in Interviews no. 3 and no. 1. Marginalization is one of the big issues in our area, said the former, and has mainly resulted from changing opening hours in the retail sector. Thirty per cent of part-time workers would like to work longer hours and 20 per cent of all jobs are temporary and insecure. In order to win this fight, he continued, workers would have to rely on the legislative support by the state (Interview no. 3). The other respondent too acknowledged that the marginalized sector is growing. Yet increasing marginalization, he said, is the result of flexibility, and in order to make the best out of the new situation and to avoid marginalization, trade unions have to accept companies' need for increasing flexibility. What unions can do is to outline to companies the disadvantages of a strategy often leading to low-skilled workers working for a temporary period for a company, before they are replaced by equally low-skilled workers. Overall, it would be the union's task in cooperation with the employers to find ways to combine flexibility with a permanent workforce (Interview no. 1). Thus, domestic sector workers seem to find solutions in stronger national protective legislation, while transnational-sector workers emphasize the need to find other and better types of flexibility, and to convince employers about the advantages of such an approach.

A similar split can be identified between educated workers in core positions, generally part of the 'modernize and adapt' camp, and workers in manual jobs often on the periphery of the labour market. Respondents from unions for white-collar workers and professionals do not themselves experience part-time/marginalized workers as a problem (Interview no. 4). Marginalization has had on the whole only an indirect impact on their members, who usually have a fairly strong position in the core of the labour market (Interview no. 10). Overall, however, with one exception (Interview no. 9), marginalization is not yet regarded as a general concern for Swedish unions (Interview no. 6). This clearly illustrates that the marginalized sector of the labour market in Sweden, while growing, is still comparatively small.

Swedish unions' levels of activity

As outlined so far, the two core groups, 'defend and restore' as well as 'modernize and adapt', despite all their differences have continued to concentrate on the domestic level. In relation to the European level, unions engage in an analysis of the benefits and problems of operating within the EU institutional set-up in more detail. The 'defend and restore' camp, dominated by domestic production-sector unions, is rather sceptical of European cooperation. Too much emphasis would be placed on political lobbying in Brussels, rather than collective bargaining and the labour market

(Interview no. 6). In any case, the final decisions should be taken at the national level with a specific focus on the workplace (Interview no. 3). It was, however, acknowledged that common EU minimum standards are helpful in that they make it easier for unions in Sweden to defend their higher standards. To support this strategy, the right to solidarity actions across borders was demanded (Interview no. 8).

The 'modernize and adapt' camp, dominated by transnational production sector unions as well as SACO, representing privileged workers at the core of the labour market, were more positive about the European level. Both the Metal Workers' Union and SIF, representing workers in the transnational manufacturing sector, demanded a strengthening of European Works Councils (EWCs), including the right to discuss and negotiate wages. The right to information alone would not be enough. The multi-sector bargaining between the European Trade Union Confederation (ETUC) and the Union of Industrial and Employers' Confederations of Europe (UNICE) should be strengthened (Interview no. 1; Interview no. 2). At least one of the interviewees acknowledged that the European-level coordination of national collective bargaining by the European Metalworkers' Federation (EMF) would play a more important role now for the union's national bargaining than five years ago (Interview no. 2). Overall, however, the concrete actions of the 'modernize and adapt' camp also concentrate on the possibilities within the national institutional set-up, and here especially the cooperation with employers' associations.

Expanding the basis for resistance: trade union–social movement cooperation

As outlined in the introduction to this volume, capitalist exploitation has increasingly been extended into the sphere of social reproduction. This offers the possibility of cooperation between trade unions and social movements in order to expand the social basis for resistance against neoliberal restructuring (Bieler and Morton, 2004b). We asked our interviewees whether their union pursued this strategy.

Many in the 'defend and restore' camp demonstrated reluctance over closer ties with social movements. Unions could not risk their internal unity over potential cooperation with social movements (Interview no. 6). Unions should focus on their own organization as well as their influence on employers and the government (Interview no. 7). The emphasis has to be on one's own strengths and union internal organization and coherence

(Interview no. 8). Only one interviewee acknowledged that this continuing reliance on one's own strengths could be a dead end. More and more union activities, such as boycotts of companies in Sweden as well as pressure on Swedish employers to sign collective agreements abroad, would rely on support by the wider public. Cooperation with social movements was deemed necessary to ensure this wider support (Interview no. 3).

The 'modernize and adapt' camp showed even less inclination to cooperate with other social movements, which partly at least reflects these unions' acceptance of some neoliberal principles. One interviewee argued that in contrast to many social movements, his union understands globalization as a positive development, which could not be stopped anyway. He also questioned social movements' different internal structure as well as their legitimacy (Interview no. 1).

Two exceptions are, however, noticeable. One interviewee pointed out that some movements are potentially good partners for joint activities in the future (Interview no. 2). Another argued that in the long run, cooperation with other social movements is necessary. There would still be a lack of understanding of each others' intentions, but both sides could learn from each other and perhaps even cooperate on specific issues in the short term. His union actually sent for the first time a delegation, consisting of the president and international officer, to the World Social Forum in Porto Alegre in 2005 (Interview no. 9).

CONCLUSIONS: FUTURE STRATEGIES FOR THE SWEDISH LABOUR MOVEMENT

As conceptualized in the introduction to this volume, there is a division between domestic and transnational sector labour, as well as workers at the core of the labour market and those in the periphery, in Sweden. One of the two main strategies today of the Swedish union movement facing the four globalization challenges seems to be *'defend and restore'*. This strategy is mainly supported by domestic production-sector unions and blue-collar worker unions more generally, which are more likely to represent workers in the marginalized part of the labour market. It stresses the domestic role of unions to uphold national agreements and responsible levels of wage increases so as not to undermine competitiveness and create inflationary pressures. It emphasizes the need to maintain Swedish collective agreements on all jobs that are carried out in Sweden. It supports the existing welfare state arrangements. Some members of this tendency advocate higher inflation nationally as a way to combat unemployment. As a variant of this main strategy we can see a kind of national inwardness and longing for the good old days, resistance to European collaboration and tendencies to overstate the degree of remaining national sovereignty in relation to globalized capitalism.

The alternative strategy, *'modernize and adapt'*, is predominantly put forward by transnational sector unions and those unions that represent workers in the core of the labour market. It agrees with the first strategy concerning the national role of unions to uphold national agreements and responsible levels of wage increases so as not to undermine competitiveness and create inflationary pressures. But this national role is seen as different from before. In the eyes of the second strategy, if unions are to survive they must accept new production patterns, including new types of flexibility in employment conditions. Blue-collar unions must collaborate with salaried employees and professionals, and they must all collaborate with managers and employers to develop the long-term competitiveness of Swedish production of goods and services. The acceptance of higher levels of flexibility by this camp indicates that these unions have accepted some neoliberal concepts.

Both these strategies are, as we see it, inadequate; the first one because it fails to address the shift of power resulting from the global restructuring of production, the second one since it accepts as unavoidable a weakening of the position of workers and growing gaps in society. A possible third strategy could perhaps be called *'defend, modernize and strike back'*. It would agree with the first strategy concerning the national role of unions to uphold national agreements and responsible levels of wage increases so as not to undermine competitiveness and create inflationary pressures. In using the word 'defend' it would emphasize that unions are always basically defensive by nature in a society where ownership of production constitutes decision-making power over the economy. On the other hand, the third strategy would agree with the second tendency in saying that unions need to modernize because new production patterns have meant deep changes in the conditions of production; indeed, a new phase in the development of capitalism.

But the third strategy would then go on to say that such modernization does not need to be mainly adaptive. It could maintain the conflict-of-interest perspective and aim at building new strength on the side of workers. The third strategy would aim at a transformation of present institutions, which are based on neoliberal ideologies and give strong power to TNCs. It would also aim at a basic transformation of current power relations between workers and owners of capital. Therefore, it would not only define the type of policies needed, but also be concerned with the power relations that are necessary for these policies to be implemented. And it would emphasize the new possibilities for a deepening of (economic) democracy inherent in the new patterns of the social relations of production, indeed the possibility of a transformation of the present capitalist order of production.

Considering the responses of our interviewees, the Swedish labour movement, it seems, is at a loss on the fundamental issue that once was the main pillar of the Swedish model – full employment. Still, to us it seems quite possible from some of the answers we obtained to form one element of a policy for full employment – *the national part*. The inflation target of the Swedish National Bank could be raised to 2.5–3 per cent. Expansion of the public sector could be part of the answer: better schools and day care, investment in children, housing policies to make it easier for people to move to the places where there are jobs.

In the longer-term perspective practically everyone would agree on the importance of good macro-economic management, education and training, as well as selective labour market measures. Better wage subsidies for groups with a weak position on the labour market like the disabled would also be required. Industrial policies are an important cornerstone of successful employment policies. Small and medium-sized companies, which used to rely on Swedish TNCs, need active state support to cope with international competition. This should include an active R&D policy, good education policies and venture capital provision. Additionally, codetermination should not be under-valued as a competitive advantage. Swedish unions have a role in making workplaces function properly. Additional tools could be used, such as life-long learning and the use of pension funds for the development of small companies.

It is remarkable, however, that with one exception not one of our interviewees considered *the European or international level* as the right arena for future activities. A European policy for full employment was not discussed. The prevailing opinion in the Swedish union movement seems to be that the European level is less important because Swedish unions will never have a strong influence there anyway. However, the third strategy, as we conceive it, should aim at a strategy for full employment in Europe. Such a strategy could be based on a new macro-economic policy mix with a primary focus on growth and employment. Similarly to the national level, the inflation target could be raised to

2.5 or 3 per cent. Additionally, slightly higher levels of inflation should be accepted temporarily to allow for growth leading to the creation of new employment. As for fiscal policy, the Stability and Growth Pact needs to be revised so that it makes possible national and joint European-level public investment in infrastructure projects as well as human capital. A distinction needs to be made between borrowing for investment in social and economic infrastructure, and borrowing for funding short-term spending, where the former is not part of a deficit calculation. Finally, wage formation needs to be coordinated at the European level to ensure that wages increase along the lines of inflation plus productivity. This ensures that demand levels are maintained (Bieler, 2006: 209–11; see also Chapter 13).

A strategy for full employment must also challenge dominant power relations and the hegemonic neoliberal discourse. It is obvious to us that the present concentration on the national level, with European collaboration seen more as a restriction or a threat than as a possibility, is counterproductive for the Swedish union movement. Persistent high unemployment and the lack of visions for changing this, together with growing gaps in society, create an extremely dangerous situation. The present confusion after the double-no to the proposed European constitution is further evidence of the problematic situation also for the dominant circles in Europe. This may have created a situation where the possibilities for a new offensive for a different, leftist Europe could get broad support and even have a chance to form the basis for a new historic compromise – like the one behind the so-called Swedish model in the past. This offensive to push back neoliberalism and the employers´ attacks could and should be combined with a new fight for economic democracy.

During the era of welfare capitalism, companies were regarded as having a number of things they had to give consideration to – employees, suppliers, customers, the community and shareholders. Now there is one single express goal, the satisfaction of shareholders. The power of ownership has shifted from major private owners to institutional ownership (pension funds, insurance companies, foundations and so on). The financier takes power from the factory owner, and the vacuum after the factory owner is filled by an increasingly powerful director bureaucracy – steered by proprietary interest that sees only stock market values and short-term maximization of profits. The company executives devote themselves more to financial transactions, buyouts and mergers than to long-term development of production. Remuneration of directors is increasing, and the gap between them and the employees is growing.

At the same time, organizing production in large, integrated companies has been replaced by a system of long value chains where many production units are involved. The owner is more distant and difficult to identify for workers. The latter are continuously played off against each other in a fight to protect their own jobs. Nevertheless, as the assets of a company consist more and more of the knowledge and experience of the employees, unions can, based on knowledge and long-term strategies, fill the vacuum that exists today between macro-ownership and day-to-day production decisions. This is a transformation that has already started in many knowledge and technology-intensive workplaces.

This trend calls up two basic questions (Lindberg, 2005). The first is, how do we want the money that belongs to the Swedish people, but which is deposited in banks, insurance companies and pension funds, to be used? As part of an offensive strategy, workers should demand that the money be used in a way that benefits our interests in the long term as employees, consumers and citizens. Workers should form a strategy for the ownership of the funds, and establish representatives in the fund leadership who are able to distinguish between the interests of the elite and those of the people.

The second basic question is, who is best suited to decide the organization of labour and production – the shareholders or the employees? In an increasingly knowledge-rich production there is a large and growing percentage of the business assets lodged in the knowledge and experience of employees. When production becomes more decentralized and customized, the knowledge, responsibility and initiative of those who directly carry out the work become increasingly important. At the same time people's knowledge, independence and participation demands grow, which is one of our society's deepest and most hopeful characteristics of change. And the demands for influence and independent responsibility are well in line with what modern goods and services production requires. We have perhaps arrived at the point when employees can start to hire capital instead of the other way round. To really give employees the right to determine the organization of work would threaten the power and privileges of employers and management. In fact, employers are in a dilemma. Their goal is not only maximization of profit but also to keep power at the top, which a hierarchically organized production process does. The development of production may today hold the potential for liberation, which these power structures are suppressing. The social possibilities of technology are on a collision course with the prevailing ownership and power structures.

In order to construct the necessary alliance, powerful enough to put this programme into practice, trade unions first must improve their mutual cooperation within Europe. These patterns need to include strengthened trade union institutions in Brussels, but they also need to go beyond hierarchic structures of representative democracy and develop a network of horizontal links. New trust and new structures will certainly not be all-European across all branches from the start. Rather, they should link workers in the same company, the same network of producers and subcontractors, the same branch, the same region. The links should be open and transparent rather than closed and hierarchic. This horizontal collaboration should develop the understanding and trust between workers necessary for joint industrial action. It should also develop, from below, the necessary vertical decision-making structures for making such industrial action strong enough. This collaboration between unionists should go beyond a lobbying role in the political game within the European Union, and focus more intensively on the confrontation with employers at the national and European levels. The need for a reorientation of the Swedish union movement as a result of globalization should not, however, stop at a European level. Capitalism today can only be transformed in a transnational operation that connects local, national, regional and global processes.

Second, trade unions need to cooperate more extensively with other social movements involved in resistance to neoliberal restructuring. The Swedish and European trade union movements find themselves at a crossroads. Should workers in the North join with workers, the unemployed and landless in the South? Or should workers in the North join with the 'western' powers against the poor and 'dangerous' people of the South? The challenge is that of a major reorientation, a giant future trade union task. It concerns broadening local and national trade union work to build up new forms of cooperation for a global working class. It is time for the labour movement once more, though in a different form and with partly new goals, to lay emphasis on broad mobilization. And today the struggle must be internationally directed against a capitalist world order and a global class society.

It is not at all certain that the search for alternatives will be transnational and progressive. Instead, there are today strong tendencies in a nationalistic, protectionist and xenophobic direction. Such developments are a threat not only to workers but also to the dominant capitalist interests in Europe and in the world. The annual meetings of those in power behind barbed wire fences in Davos are the symbol of a counter-market, the inaccessible power centre of capitalism. The global justice movement's annual meetings in Porto Alegre have become the opposite pole to Davos; a symbol of the open diversity of social and anti-imperial movements. What we today call popular movements constitute a phenomenon that is only just over 100 years old. Social movements have emerged against the power of capital, with the trade union movement as a core part. Should capitalism be preserved or transformed? The question is being asked by a growing opposition movement in the South and by a new peace movement in the North. It should also be asked by the labour movement in the North. Today it is possible for social and anti-imperialist movements to form a joint offensive against globalized, unregulated capitalism. Trade unions have the potential to play a crucial role in this offensive.

INTERVIEWS

Interview no. 1: Metall (LO), Stockholm, Monday, 13 December 2004.
Interview no. 2: SIF (TCO), Stockholm, Monday, 13 December 2004.
Interview no. 3: Handels (Commercial Workers' Union, LO), Stockholm, Monday, 13 December 2004.
Interview no. 4: SKTF (TCO), Stockholm, Tuesday, 14 December 2004.
Interview no. 5: Confederation of Salaried Employees (TCO), Tuesday 14 December 2004.
Interview no. 6: Swedish Trade Union Confederation (LO), Tuesday 14 December 2004.
Interview no. 7: Swedish Trade Union Confederation (LO), Stockholm, Tuesday 14 December 2004.
Interview no. 8: Swedish Trade Union Confederation (LO), Stockholm, Wednesday, 15 December.
Interview no. 9: Transport Workers' Union (LO), Stockholm, Wednesday, 15 December 2004.
Interview no. 10: SACO, Stockholm, Wednesday, 15 December 2004.

Our interviewees included two first vice presidents, three chief economists, one senior economist, one European officer, one deputy negotiations officer, one head of policy department as well as one chief negotiations officer. These high-level interviewees ensured that unions' official positions were obtained rather than simply personal views.

NOTE

1   See Eironline 2004, http://www.eurofound.europa.eu/eiro/2004/05/inbrief/se0405102n.html; accessed 15 July 2007.

Chapter 12

Building alliances between formal and informal workers: experiences from Africa

Ilda Lindell

GLOBALIZING INFORMALITY AND CHALLENGES FOR COLLECTIVE ORGANIZING

The latest decades have seen the rise of the informal economy as a global phenomenon. Informal forms of work were long considered to be a particular feature of developing countries. They were interpreted as a remnant of traditional relations or the manifestation of an incomplete transition from a pre-capitalist to a capitalist mode of production. Such 'atypical' forms of labour were expected to disappear in pace with modernization and the deepening incorporation of developing societies into the international economy. Today, informal forms of work are evident where they were least expected. Major cities in post-industrial societies have become sites of informalization, as manifested in the casualization of labour and an increase in self-employment (Castells and Portes, 1989; Sassen-Koob, 1989; Sassen, 1998, 2000; Castells, 1996; Burbach et al., 1997). In world cities in core regions, the nerve centres of global capitalism, informality reportedly exists side by side with corporate culture, functioning as an 'infrastructure' for the growth sectors of the new urban economy (Sassen, 2000). Informality thus can be interpreted as a facet of late capitalist accumulation.

Such informalization has been interpreted as part of the shift towards 'flexible production', as one of the strategies used by capital to reduce costs, increase flexibility and protect its profits in the face of changing international conditions and of formerly attained high levels of state regulation and organized labour in industrialized countries. Large firms increasingly use and benefit from a large pool of precarious labour in the unregulated economy. This shift has often been reported to have resulted in a disenfranchisement of the working class and a 'downgrading of labour' (Castells and Portes, 1989; Sassen-Koob, 1989; Sassen, 2000).

Informalization of work has become a global trend, on the increase in both developed and developing countries (Portes and Schauffler, 1993; Potter and Lloyd-Evans, 1998; Meagher, 1995; Bryceson and Potts, 2006). In many countries of the South, however, informality has a longer history. In Africa and beyond, colonialism marginalized a segment of the indigenous population from employment opportunities in the 'modern' economy, and in many cases relied extensively on unregulated work as a means for appropriating wealth. In the last decades, informality has become a major way by which large numbers of people in Africa handle the current economic crisis. As a good part of Sub-Saharan Africa has been sidelined from the growth sectors of the global economy, wage work opportunities have rather decreased in many places. Neoliberal policies of economic liberalization and further deregulation of labour conditions, accompanied by large-scale retrenchments of wage workers and falling real wages, have contributed to the rapid expansion of the informal economy, where new groups now try to make a living. The situation in most African cities today could be described as a shrinking and 'aborted' formal economy and an extensive informal economy where the majority of people make a living (Rakodi, 1997a; Rogerson, 1997). Arguably then, Africa and its cities are experiencing a new wave of informalization, in the context of neoliberal restructuring of domestic and international economies and global deregulation (Lourenço-Lindell, 2002).

This rampant informalization in Africa and beyond poses major challenges for the collective organization of workers. How to organize 'workers' in extensively informalized economies, such as those of most countries in Africa? This is the general concern of this chapter. These deep transformations require a reconsideration of taken for granted notions and strategies. To begin with, the far-reaching changes are disturbing the conventional understanding of 'worker', not only because so-called 'standard labour' to which it used to apply is becoming a minority in many places, but also because a new generation of people involved in informal kinds of work are increasingly asserting themselves as 'workers' – with the right to a decent work, free from harassment and so on.

Second, the deregulation of markets and the informalization of work are posing a direct challenge to traditional labour organizations. The loss of wage jobs, the casualization and informalization of labour are often referred to as undermining the conditions of organized labour and the organizational power of unions. While trade union membership declines, the numbers of informal workers continue to grow. Trade unions are often both disturbed by and ill-equipped to deal with these challenges.

In the face of these new realities, there is a growing debate about strategies for 'trade union renewal' that will help trade unions deal with the effects of neoliberal globalization. New concepts have emerged that try to capture new trends in union action as well as suggest alternative models of organization. The related terms 'social movement unionism' and 'new social unionism' (Moody, 1997a, 1997b; Waterman, 1999, 2001c; Lier and Stokke, 2006) have gained prominence in this debate. Among other things, these terms point to the necessity of trade unions broadening their agendas to include a greater range of concerns that stretch beyond the sphere of production. They emphasize the importance of trade unions creating alliances with other social movements and popular social forces, by engaging in horizontal and flexible coalitions which encourage pluralism and innovation (Waterman, 2006c). Of particular relevance here, trade unions are expected to reach out to wider communities of the poor and to the 'unorganized' segments of the working class – such as casual workers and the self-employed.

Indeed, trade unions are increasingly attempting to reach out into the informal economy and to bring into their ranks the vast numbers of informal workers (Sitas, 2001; Vlok, 1999; Gallin, 2001, 2002). At the same time, informal workers in a variety of contexts are increasingly organizing themselves to pursue their interests as workers. These parallel developments raise the question of how these two different kinds of organizing initiatives relate to each other. This is the central question in this chapter.

This chapter discusses the evolving relations between trade unions and organizations of informal workers in Africa. First, it illustrates the varied nature of these relations on the continent. Second, it discusses some of the benefits and challenges involved in creating alliances across the formal–informal divide. Third, it briefly presents some developments in international organizing of informal workers where trade unions are also involved. The analysis draws on examples from a number of countries in Africa as well as on a deeper analysis of the Mozambican case.

The analysis is based on different sets of empirical data, collected between 2003 and 2007. Interviews have been conducted with leaders of organizations of informal workers operating in eight countries in Sub-Saharan Africa. Naturally, their views are not necessarily representative of those of their constituencies, but provide a sense of the nature of the relations between their organizations and trade unions.

The Mozambican case and the sections on Uganda and Ghana rely on more extensive fieldwork data, including interviews with leaders and members of associations of informal workers as well as with trade union officials. Finally, the international coordinator of an international network of informal workers' organizations, StreetNet International, has also been interviewed on several occasions (in 2004, 2006 and 2007). The organizations studied often work with informal vendors – though not exclusively – as this is a central group in my research.

OVERVIEW OF RELATIONS BETWEEN TRADE UNIONS AND ORGANIZATIONS OF INFORMAL WORKERS: AFRICAN EXPERIENCES

This section briefly illustrates the variety of relations and institutional arrangements that are emerging between trade unions and organizations of informal workers in a number of African countries, in the context of an extensive informalization of work. These relations range from distanced or even antagonistic relations to various forms of collaborative relations. I should begin by saying that, more often than not, organizations of informal workers have no collaboration with or support from trade unions.

Perhaps the best documented country case is South Africa, where academic debate about the consequences of casualization for collective organizing has been going on for some years. Trade union responses to the growing number of informal workers have however been slower than in some other African countries – although South Africa is often used as a showcase of 'social movement unionism'. A formerly existing Self-Employed Women's Union (SEWU) organized independently and had no collaboration with the South African trade unions (Interview no. 1). This was not simply a result of the reluctance of the federations to embrace these informal workers, but also a strategy of SEWU to ensure that the organization was led by women and gave the highest priority to the concerns of women members – although gender equality issues were not the only divisive ones. There are indications that the Congress of South African Trade Unions (COSATU) is becoming more open to the concerns of informal workers.

In Malawi, the relationship between the Malawi Union for the Informal Economy (MUFIS) and the trade union movement has been particularly difficult. In 2006, when vendors came under attack by the authorities and many were arrested, the organization was able to mobilize considerable international support from sister organizations. 'But at home', the leaders expressed, 'we were alone!', referring to the lack of allies on the national scene, including the trade unions (Interview no. 2).

A similar national organization in Zambia, the Alliance of Zambian Informal Economy Associations (AZIEA), however has a different kind of relationship with the trade unions. The Alliance is an associate member of a trade union federation, although it took four years to attain that status (Interview no. 3). Associate membership means that the Alliance is autonomous from the trade union federation and can decide its own priorities, but cannot vote or be voted for positions of leadership in the trade union federation. The leaders of the Alliance see its constituencies as 'part and parcel of the labour movement' and have chosen a strategy of 'belonging to the labour movement' because this 'provides access to the government'. While the Alliance and the trade union federation have a cordial relationship, in the opinion of the interviewed representative of the Alliance, there is a need for the federation to engage genuinely with the concerns of informal workers and to consult with the Alliance about trade union activities and policies oriented towards informal workers.

In a few cases, organizations of informal workers enjoy full affiliated membership in trade unions. Two examples of this are Uganda and Mozambique – the latter is described at greater length in the next section. In Uganda, the Central Organization of Free Trade Unions (COFTU) created the National Alliance of Informal Economy Workers Organizations in Uganda in 2004, in order to congregate the existing dispersed associations of informal workers (Interviews nos 4 and 5). The intent of both parties is that the Alliance can register as a union and become affiliated to COFTU. The process of registration as a union, however, has been a lengthy one and was not yet finalized at the time of writing. The National Alliance is free to organize elections and to run its own affairs, but having emerged from within COFTU, it participates in most activities organized by the federation. The close link with COFTU is expected to provide considerable support in terms of advocacy in favour of informal workers. Although this relationship is still in its beginning, there seems to exist a genuine engagement of trade union leaders in the concerns of informal workers.

In Ghana, relationships between trade unions and informal workers have a longer history (Adu-Amankwah, 1999), and have evolved into a variety of arrangements. The General Agricultural Workers' Union, for example, has been organizing informal workers in the rural sector for decades. According to leaders of the union interviewed, the union has a number of associations of informal workers as fully affiliated members. At the time of writing, the union is revising its constitution with the intent of improving the representation of informal workers in the union structures. The Ghana Private Road Transport Union, a pioneer member of the Ghana Trades Union Congress (GTUC), is a fully fledged informal economy union, whose membership consists of self-employed commercial drivers and vehicle owners (Adu-Amankwah, 1999; Owusu, 2007).

There are also more recent initiatives linking the Ghanaian trade union movement to informal economy workers. In 1996 GTUC adopted a policy on organizing in the informal economy (Owusu, 2007), which was further revised in 2004 (GTUC, 2004). One stated objective was to 'extend union coverage to the informal economy' (GTUC, 2004: 44). GTUC created an informal economy desk, as well as an umbrella organization, StreetNet Ghana Alliance, for informal economy associations. GTUC also changed its constitution to allow informal economy associations to affiliate directly to the federation as associate members. At the time of writing, three associations had become members. GTUC also encouraged affiliated national unions to develop their activities in the informal economy, as reported by interviewed heads of the relevant departments of the federation. Thus, the Local Government Workers Union, for example, as reported by its general secretary, since it initiated such activities around 2002, has recruited into its fold three informal economy associations as associate members of the union. Another national union, the Industrial and Commercial Workers Union (now independent from the GTUC), has also established close relationships with several informal economy associations, particularly in the hairdressing and the tie and dye sectors. These associations enjoy full affiliation in the union, as reported by several union officials and interviewed leaders of two of the affiliated associations. Finally, the Ghana Federation of Labour, a new federation whose leaders were interviewed, has also initiated its activities of organizing in the informal economy, by either bringing into its fold existing associations or creating new associations for informal workers.

In sum, the deep informalization of work in Africa and the emerging organizing initiatives have resulted in a highly diverse situation in terms of the relations between trade unions and organizations of informal workers, ranging from antagonism to full integration. While we cannot predict that relations between the two kinds of constituencies will follow a particular direction, there seems to exist a novel trend whereby trade unions and organizations of informal workers increasingly engage into some form of collaborative relationship. This justifies taking a closer look at one example of such a close relationship. The next section presents a more detailed description of such a relationship between an organization of informal workers and trade unions in Mozambique. It is based on a large number of interviews with both leaders and members of an association of informal workers, as well as with top officials in the two trade union federations in Mozambique.

MOZAMBIQUE: AN ALLIANCE ACROSS THE FORMAL–INFORMAL DIVIDE

Maputo, similarly to many cities in Africa, is experiencing an accelerated informalization, manifested in the proliferation of unplanned marketplaces and street vending in the city. The local government has a negative attitude towards the growing number of people making a living in the city streets and markets. Government agents frequently harass and use physical violence towards vendors. Unplanned markets are considered illegal and are frequently threatened with eviction.

Against this background, a national trade union federation, Organisação dos Trabalhadores Moçambicanos Central Sindical (OTM-CS), considered that there was a need to organize people in the informal economy. As an interviewed high official in the federation described, due to changes in economic policies, many of the former trade union members were now spread in the street corners and city markets, being chased by the municipal police on a daily basis. Thus in 1998 the federation invited a number of these informal workers to a seminar to encourage them to organize and create their own association. The following year, the Associação dos Operadores e Trabalhadores do Sector Informal (ASSOTSI, Association of Informal Sector Operators and Workers) was formed. It drew up its own statutes and was registered, thus acquiring a legal status.

The association grew rapidly and established committees in many market places in Maputo, and more recently branches in other urban centres in the country. With a constituency of around 36,000 vendors, the association is led by elected representatives, all of whom must be informal economy workers in order to be eligible. The work of the association is of two kinds. On the one hand, its market committees provide infrastructure and services in their respective markets, which they finance through fees regularly collected from the vendors. On the other hand, the association is the only institution in the city that defends the rights of informal vendors (although with varying success). Relations between the association and Maputo city council are generally tense and frequently degenerate into conflict situations. Conflicts often revolve around, among other things, vendors' rights to use urban space for earning a living. Although the association is registered, and thus legal, the city council is reluctant to recognize it as a legitimate organization. Thus, the association is still struggling for its constitutional right to exist.

ASSOTSI is an affiliated member of the national trade union federation and is fully integrated in its structure. Therefore, as stated by representatives of ASSOTSI and of the federation, the association has the rights and duties of an affiliated trade union. As a fully affiliated member of OTM-CS, the association has a seat in the executive committee of the federation, and its representatives are also eligible for positions of leadership in the federation. In return, according to the executive secretary of OTM-CS, the federation expects the association to respect the law, the statutes of the federation, and to submit regular activity and financial reports to the federation. The federation was not insisting on the payment of affiliation fees, because of the poor resources of the association.

The association maintains its autonomy in important respects. Besides having its own statutes and its own bodies to approve activity plans and budgets, the association has the autonomy to call by its own initiative for meetings with officials in the local government, in the party and even with the president. But the federation seems also to be entitled to some extent to interfere in the internal affairs of the association. For example, as explained by representatives of both organizations, if the association wants to carry out a demonstration or a strike, it is expected to first turn to the federation for advice.

According to the executive secretary of OTM-CS, the association can expect as much assistance from the federation as any affiliated union, including support, training of the leadership and facilitating contacts with the government. OTM-CS has provided courses on collective bargaining for the leaders of the association and for the market committees, which have been useful for negotiating with local government institutions. The leaders of the association place great value on this close relationship with the federation. They consider it to be an important way of gaining public visibility and recognition. In their view, the federation has been pivotal in creating political space for the creation and existence of the association and for the association to publicly voice its concerns. Association leaders also consider the close link to the trade unions to be a major source of strength when the association comes under pressure by the state. In the words of its president, 'the strategy that the association chose in order to confront the local government was to become affiliated to OTM-CS'. 'When we have problems with the government, the government has to face not only the association but also the trade union movement.'

By being an integral part of the structure of OTM-CS, the association has also become part of the wider trade union movement in Mozambique. As an affiliated member of OTM-CS the leadership of the association has a seat in the national forum of trade unions (Forum de Concertação Sindical), where the two national federations, OTM-CS and CONSILMO, participate. While the forum deals primarily with the concerns of formal labour, according to interviewed high officials of both federations, the forum was at the time of fieldwork developing a common position in support of informal workers. It could be said that the association enjoys broad support from the Mozambican trade union movement.

THE BENEFITS AND CHALLENGES OF ORGANIZING ACROSS THE FORMAL–INFORMAL DIVIDE

The Mozambican case illustrates well the benefits of a close relationship between an organization of informal workers and trade unions. On the one hand, the relationship increases the leverage of the federation, which is now in a position to claim to represent a large number of informal workers. On the other hand, the association benefits from the organizing experience of the trade unions, and acquires bargaining and leadership skills. More importantly, it enjoys the support of the federation during situations of crisis with the authorities. This support is of critical importance for the association in its struggle for recognition. In fact, legal organizations of informal workers in Africa often experience lack of recognition and are treated as illegal. Trade unions, with their well-established position in the public sphere, can potentially play a major role in this respect: that is, in supporting informal workers' rights to organize.

As a fully affiliated member of the trade union federation, the Mozambican association can participate in the highest organ of the trade union and directly represent the concerns of informal workers there. In this way, its members are potentially well positioned to influence the agenda of the trade union federation. Through membership in the federation, the association is also in a position to represent the interests of its constituency in the wider trade union movement (i.e. the national forum of trade unions) and to claim that the federation represents those interests in negotiations with the government. Indeed, access to a platform for negotiation with national governments is a major benefit mentioned by the interviewed representatives of other organizations of informal workers engaged in a collaborative relation with trade unions.

Membership in trade unions may entail a certain loss of autonomy in decision making for organizations of informal workers. In the Mozambican case, whether to conduct a strike or a demonstration appears to be subjected to the approval of the federation. And indeed, membership has been found to sometimes slow down processes of decision making in such organizations (War on Want, AZIEA and WEAZ, 2006).

The Mozambican case of full integration of an organization of informal workers into the structures of a trade union federation is not the most common situation in African countries. Establishing a close collaboration between the trade unions and informal workers presents considerable challenges, which need to be considered in any strategy aimed at building such alliances. First, informal workers have interests, concerns and needs that are different from those of formal wage workers, and trade unions are often ill-equipped to address those needs. Within particular economic sectors, the interests of the two constituencies may be outright antagonistic, and trade unions might find it very difficult to reconcile those interests – for example, the interests of vendors of second-hand clothing and those of garment industry workers. Trade unions in some sectors appear less open than others to collaboration with informal workers (Interviews nos 6 and 7), and this may create divisions among trade unions about whether to allow informal workers to become part of the trade union movement.

Second, the enormous heterogeneity and differentiation (along income, gender, generational, ethnic and racial lines) found within contemporary informal economies poses a major challenge to both organizing and collaboration across the formal–informal divide. It raises the basic question, who are these 'informals' that trade unions are supposed to organize or enter alliances with? The informal economy encompasses a great variety of labour relations – including self-employment, unregulated apprentice work and casual work – and informal workers in these different categories will have very different needs and concerns. Most trade unions are yet to develop the knowledge and skills to meet these various demands from different types of informal workers. Furthermore, there are collisions of interests among different groups of informal workers, and the consequences of a selective alliance between trade unions and some of these groups must be considered.

Third, there are certain mutual suspicions that are often referred to by actors as standing in the way of collaboration between trade unions and organizations of informal workers. Trade unionists often fear that if they allow informal workers to be part of their trade union, these will 'take over' the leadership of the union. Leaders of organizations of informal workers sometimes wonder about the real motives behind the interest that some trade unions display in informal workers. Some complain about a lack of genuine interest on the part of trade unions in the concerns of informal workers and about lack of reciprocity. They refer to the danger of being 'utilized' for the ends of trade unions without getting much in return.

Finally, and related to the last point, is it possible to have an equal relationship between trade unions and informal workers or their organizations, as advocated by proponents of 'new social unionism'? Such a relationship is potentially a highly unbalanced one. While trade unions have a greater experience and a platform for negotiation with the state, organizations of informal workers are still struggling for recognition, have no established channels of dialogue with the government and have a large share of illiterate members. The sheer numbers of informal workers however may be a source of leverage for their organizations, and the basis for claiming equal terms of exchange in their relations with trade unions.

GLOBAL INFORMALITY, INTERNATIONAL ORGANIZING AND SCALING UP ALLIANCES

This chapter opened by stating that the informalization of work is becoming global in scope. Some would argue that a globalizing informality begs for an organizing of informal workers that transcends national borders. Trade unions have long since established international links, but what are the prospects for informal income earners to organize across borders? One sector of informal workers is casual workers linked to transnational production networks, which may provide the grounds for transnational solidarity. However the self-employed, who are a larger category in Africa, may also find it advantageous to organize internationally. This is well illustrated by the emergence of StreetNet International, an international federation of organizations that defend the rights of vendors.

Founded in 2002, StreetNet had at the time of writing 26 affiliated organizations in some 22 countries in Africa, Asia and Latin America (Interview no. 8). Its ambition is to become global in scope but to retain a 'Southern bias', ensuring that its leadership is recruited among its constituencies in the South (Horn, 2007). The affiliates include self-organized groups of street vendors, market vendors and hawkers as well as trade unions that are active in organizing informal vendors. The international federation benefits its member groups in several ways, as reported by both its international coordinator and leaders of member organizations interviewed. First, StreetNet organizes international conferences and exchange visits between affiliates, both of which facilitate the sharing of experiences and strategies between organizations from different countries. Second, it represents the interests of informal workers in certain international fora. This includes meetings at the International Labour Organization (ILO) as well as participation at the World Social Forum in Nairobi in 2007. Last but not least, StreetNet has a policy of supporting affiliated organizations in their local struggles (Horn, 2007). This latter kind of support is of particular importance, since vendors are a category of informal workers frequently subjected to harassment and hostilities by their governments. In fact, on the basis of interviews with the leaders of the various organizations of informal workers (which are StreetNet affiliates), it appears that this is a major motivation for organizing internationally (Lindell, 2007).

One of the strategies of StreetNet is to engage in alliances with the labour movement (Horn, 2007). As mentioned, StreetNet welcomes trade unions as member organizations, and it has developed relationships with national trade union centres in a number of countries across the developing regions. In other countries, its relations with national trade union centres have developed through collaboration between its affiliated organizations of informal vendors and trade unions in their respective countries. Indeed, StreetNet encourages collaboration between local self-organized groups of informal workers and trade unions (interviews with the international coordinator). At the international level, StreetNet collaborates with some global union federations as well as with some international worker education organizations (Horn, 2007). Another key global actor in this context is the ILO, which in recent years has been advocating a role for trade unions in creating 'decent' work' conditions in the informal economy (ILO, 2002b).

CONCLUSION

This chapter addresses the potential and perils of organizing across the formal–informal divide. It provides an overview of how relations between trade unions and organizations of informal workers are evolving in Africa, as well as a closer look at such relations in Mozambique. The overview uncovers the highly varied nature of these relations on the continent. On the basis of the Mozambican case, it can be argued that considerable benefits can be derived from collaboration between the two kinds of organization. The challenges involved in developing such collaboration are also considerable. The complex composition of informal economies, the variety of interests involved and various reasons for mutual suspicion may stand in the way of a close collaboration, but some examples in this chapter indicate that building such alliances is not impossible. When discussing the possibilities of organizing across the formal–informal divide, however, the debate should not be reduced to the imperatives of 'trade union renewal'. Trade unions that reach out to the informal economy out of instrumental motives will probably sooner or later meet with resistance from informal workers. Rather, long-lasting collaboration probably requires that trade unions develop a genuine interest in the needs and concerns of informal workers.

Ultimately, a globalizing informality begs for an organizing of informal workers that transcends national borders. Such international initiatives have already emerged, as exemplified by the case of StreetNet International, in collaboration with a section of the labour movement. There are challenges at this level too. Among international trade union organizations, while some are active in supporting the organizing of informal workers in the South, others are yet to acknowledge the importance of these issues in their agendas. In addition, there is always the risk that their support might impose certain conditionalities that constrain the choices of local organizations. More generally, supporting organizations of informal workers in the South without reproducing unequal North–South relations is a major challenge.

INTERVIEWS WITH LEADERS OF INFORMAL WORKERS' ORGANIZATIONS IN AFRICA

Interview no. 1: Self-employed Women's Union (South Africa), March 2004.
Interview no. 2: Malawi Union for the Informal Economy, May 2006.
Interview no. 3: Alliance of Zambian Informal Economy Associations, May 2006.

Interview no. 4: Central Organization of Free Trade Unions, Uganda, October 2004.

Interview no. 5: National Alliance of Informal Economy Workers Organizations in Uganda, and the Uganda Workers Education Association, May 2006.

Interview no. 6: StreetNet International, March 2004.

Interview no. 7: StreetNet International, May/July 2006.

Interview no. 8: StreetNet International, April 2007.

ACKNOWLEDGEMENTS

The author wishes to acknowledge the assistance of IFWEA, Streetnet International and its coordinator in facilitating interviews with leaders of some of the organizations mentioned in this paper. Thank you also to the many respondents who have shared their experiences and views. The research was carried out with the financial support from the Department for Research Cooperation (SAREC) of the Swedish Agency for International Development Cooperation (SIDA).

Chapter 13

European integration: a strategic level for trade union resistance to neoliberal restructuring and for the promotion of political alternatives?

Andreas Bieler and Thorsten Schulten

INTRODUCTION

Within current discussions about restructuring of the European political economies, the so-called European social model of capitalism is frequently mentioned by trade unions and social democratic parties as an institutional arrangement, which must be preserved and further developed. While its concrete features differ from country to country, in general we can identify as its core characteristics an engagement of trade unions and employers as social partners in collective bargaining, their participation together with the state in the implementation of a generous welfare state, providing social security in the workplace and beyond, as well as a macro-economic emphasis on full employment (Hyman, 2006: 1; Marginson and Sisson, 2004: 1; Waddington, 2005: 518).

As the country case studies on Germany and Sweden in this volume indicate, however, it has become increasingly difficult to maintain the European social model at the national level. Hence, the European Union is frequently looked upon as the new, more appropriate level for this model in times of global restructuring. Supporters point here especially to the Social Chapter of the Treaty of Maastricht in 1991 and its provision for direct negotiations between so-called 'social partners' at the European level, as well as the partial introduction of qualified majority voting (QMV) for Council decisions on social issues. They further mention the Employment Chapter, initiated by the Treaty of Amsterdam in 1997, as well as the EU Charter of Fundamental Rights adopted at the EU summit in Nice in 2000, which includes some basic social rights such as the right for fair and just working conditions, the right for protection in the event of unjustified dismissal, the right for collective bargaining, and workers' right to information and consultation within the company. Finally, advocates of the European social model refer to the Lisbon strategy of 2000 and its goal to develop the European Union into 'the most competitive and dynamic knowledge-based economy in the world capable of sustainable economic growth with more and better jobs and greater social cohesion' (European Council, 2000).

In the next section, this chapter will first assess European integration with a particular emphasis on the post-1985 developments, then investigate to what extent the European Union actually offers trade unions a better way forward in the struggle for a European social model of capitalism. In the third section, a comparative overview of European trade unions is provided, before their possibilities as well as concrete activities at the European level are evaluated. The conclusion will outline core principles of an alternative way forward for trade unions.

EUROPEAN INTEGRATION AND THE MYTH OF SOCIAL EUROPE

The European social model of capitalism is not only put forward as a desirable goal by trade unions, but references to it can also be found in a whole range of official EU documents. Moreover, it can be seen 'as rhetorical resources intended to legitimize the political constructed and identity-building project of the EU institutions' (Jespen and Pascual, 2005: 231). While there is a lot of talk about social Europe and the so-called social dimension, European integration has been dominated by a neoliberal agenda aiming at a fundamental restructuring of European capitalism. 'Though rhetorical commitment to the European social model persists, there is increasing pressure to redefine this in terms of its opposite: the mantra of competitiveness which allows minimal legitimate space for employment protection and public welfare' (Hyman, 2006: 4). The Internal Market programme of 1985, Economic and Monetary Union (EMU) as part of the Treaty of Maastricht in 1991 and the Lisbon strategy of 2000 are key steps in this process (Bieler, 2006: 9–14).

In 1985, the Commission published its famous White Paper *Completing the Internal Market*, which proposed 300 measures designed to facilitate progress towards the completion of the Internal Market by 1992 through the abolition of non-tariff barriers. The Single European Act (SEA) of 1987, which institutionalized the Internal Market programme, spelled out the goals of the four freedoms: of goods, services, capital and people. While tariff barriers had been abolished by the end of the 1960s in the European Union, there had been many non-tariff barriers which had impeded free trade. This was now to be remedied.

The rationale underlying the Internal Market programme was clearly of a neoliberal nature (Grahl and Teague, 1989). A bigger market was supposed to lead to tougher competition resulting in higher efficiency, greater profits and eventually through a trickle-down effect in more general wealth and more jobs. National markets should be deregulated and liberalized; national companies were to be privatized. An emerging common competition policy was to secure that the market was no longer disturbed through state intervention or ownership even in areas such as telecommunications, public procurement and energy.

The Treaty of Maastricht was signed in 1991. Amongst other changes, it laid out the plan for EMU, including a single currency to be administered by a supranational and independent European Central Bank (ECB). In January 1999, eleven member states carried out this step, when they irrevocably fixed their exchange rates. The underlying rationale of EMU is embodied in the statutory role of the ECB and the convergence criteria. As for the former, the primary target of the ECB and its interest rate policy is the maintenance of price stability and low inflation. Economic growth and employment are only secondary objectives, subordinated to price stability. As for the convergence criteria, most importantly, the criteria obliged member states to have a government budget deficit of no more than 3 per cent of gross domestic product (GDP) and government debt of no more than 60 per cent of GDP. They do not include a criterion on unemployment. This is of secondary importance and thought to be solved through the trickle-down effect.

The EMU member countries, in order to meet the criteria, had to implement tough austerity budgets in the run-up to EMU. Within EMU, continuation of neoliberal budget policies is ensured through the Stability and Growth Pact, adopted at the Amsterdam European Council summit in June 1997. It commits members to stay within the neoliberal convergence criteria even after the start of EMU on 1 January 1999, and through the requirement to adhere to the Broad Economic Policy Guidelines including a general commitment to a balanced budget, further emphasizes the overriding focus on low inflation (Jones, 2002: 37–40). In sum, both the Internal Market and EMU firmly put the European Union on the road towards a neoliberal model of capitalism.

Finally, with the adoption of the Lisbon agenda in 2000 the

European Union claims to follow a strategy, which aims at more economic efficiency as well as full employment and social cohesion. Indeed, new political initiatives have been developed in the area of labour market and social policy which so far have been very much neglected at the European level. However, these new initiatives went along with a political redefinition of its fundamental goals and its subordination under the principles of neoliberal economic policy. For example, the so-called 'European Employment Policy', which focuses mainly on the deregulation of labour markets, 'was made to fit the existing integration project and thus became one of the pillars of supply-side-oriented neo-liberal restructuring' (Tidow, 2003: 78). In the area of social policy the European Union promotes a fundamental reorientation of European welfare state systems into the direction of less collective and more private social security, in order to open them for private capital markets (Urban, 2003). To sum up, the larger importance of the 'social dimension' of European integration 'appears to have proceeded largely as part of the market-building process, and was sucked into a free mobility and competition-enhancing process' (Leibfried, 2005: 257, 262).

Considering all major political projects of the European Union since the mid-1980s, none of them fulfilled its widespread promises to create new economic growth with 'more and better' jobs. On the contrary, the dominant feature of the European Union today is the picture of an 'unsocial Europe' (Gray, 2004): in the mid of 2006 nearly 18 million people, or 8 per cent of all employees in the European Union, were officially registered as unemployed (Eurostat, 2006). This does not include the further millions of 'hidden unemployed' which are not covered by any statistics.

As far as new jobs have been created, they often contain rather precarious employment conditions. In recent years Europe saw a steady increase in the number of part-time work, work with limited contracts, temporary agency work and so on, as well as an overall extension of the low-wage sector. More than 16 per cent of the EU population, or 72 million EU citizens, are currently considered at the risk of poverty: that is, living in households with a disposal income below 60 per cent of the median income (Guio, 2005). The growing discrepancy between the idea of a European social model and the reality of rather unsocial consequences of neoliberal policies in Europe led the European Union into a growing crisis of legitimacy. This was reflected in the rejection of the European Constitution, which would have given neoliberal policies a constitutional status, by the French and Dutch populations in 2005 (Wehr, 2006). In almost all European countries there is a growing division between rather pro-European elites and a more or less Euro-sceptical mass of people for whom EU policies are often associated with a threat to the existing social standards (Schulten, 2006b).

TRADE UNIONS IN EUROPE: A COMPARATIVE OVERVIEW

The notion of the European social model has always been associated with a relatively strong labour movement capable of guaranteeing a more socially regulated form of capitalism. In comparison with many other world regions European trade unions have always had a relatively strong political position. However, as a result of specific national historical developments trade unions in Europe have also always shown major differences regarding their organizational structure and union density, their political strategies and ideological orientations, as well as their political involvement in the national economic and political system.

The differences between European unions correspond to a certain extent with the different forms of welfare capitalism existing in Europe. According to Ebbinghaus (1999), there are not one but at least four different European social models. The Nordic model covering the Scandinavian countries has been characterized traditionally by a strong corporatist system with powerful social democratic parties, strong centralized trade unions with a high union density, and rather centralized bargaining structures. By contrast, the Anglo-Saxon model covering the United Kingdom and to a lesser extent Ireland has traditionally been described as a system of voluntarism, with rather fragmented trade union organizations and decentralized bargaining structures. The Centre model covering states like Germany, Austria and the Netherlands also has strong corporatist traditions which compared with the 'Nordic' model, however, were much more influenced by Christian democratic rather than social democratic ideas and policies. Although union density in these countries has never reached Scandinavian standards, the political influence of the unions has been relatively strong through various forms of involvement into the economic and political system. Moreover, the Southern model covering countries like France, Spain, Portugal, and to a lesser extent Italy, has been characterized by a more fragmented trade union landscape, with union organizations divided along different political orientations, including historically a relatively strong communist wing of the labour movement. With the exception of Italy union density rates have always been comparatively weak. Considering, finally, the breakdown of the former socialist regimes in Eastern Europe after 1990, one might add an 'Eastern model' where unions had to either transform themselves from a former socialist state agency or create completely new organizations. The transformation process of the former socialist countries in Eastern Europe has led in most cases to relatively weak and fragmented union organizations and rather decentralized bargaining structures, which are most similar to the Anglo-Saxon model (Kohl and Platzer, 2004).

Against the background of the emerging neoliberal hegemony in the 1980s, trade unions in almost all European countries were pushed onto the political defensive. Most European unions have suffered massive membership losses, with the most dramatic falls in the larger countries (see Table 13.1).

The reasons for the union membership decline in most European countries are of course manifold. The most significant structural

Table 13.1 Union density in the European Union, as a percentage of all employees

	1970	1980	1990	2003
Sweden	67.7	78.0	80.8	78.0
Finland	51.3	69.4	72.5	74.1
Denmark	60.3	78.6	75.3	70.4
Belgium	42.1	54.1	53.9	55.4[1]
Austria	62.8	56.7	46.9	35.4[1]
Ireland	53.2	57.1	51.1	35.3
Italy	37.0	49.6	38.8	33.7
United Kingdom	44.8	50.7	39.3	29.3
Germany	32.0	34.9	31.2	22.6
Netherlands	36.5	34.8	24.3	22.3
Spain	–	12.9	12.5	16.3
France	21.7	18.3	10.1	8.3
Slovak Republic			78.7	36.1[2]
Czech Republic			78.8	27.0[2]
Hungary			63.4[3]	19.9[2]
Poland			53.1[4]	14.7[2]
European Union	37.8	39.7	33.1	26.3[1]

1: 2002; 2: 2001; 3: 1995; 4: 1989.
Source: Visser (2006: 45).

causes lie in the composition of the active labour force and the nature of employment relationships. Traditionally, the organizational core of the trade union movement consisted of male industrial workers, employed in relatively secure employment relationships. Gains in membership in the 1970s were also largely due to an increase in public-sector employment. Both groups – male industrial workers and public-sector employees – have continued to constitute the organizational core of most unions. The decline in membership since the 1980s has not only been the result of high unemployment, but was also caused by to unions' failure to gain new members in the expanding private services sector. Moreover, women are markedly under-represented in most European trade unions, although their participation in paid employment has grown virtually everywhere in recent decades. Finally, most trade unions have extreme difficulties in organizing the growing numbers of workers with non-standard and often precarious forms of employment.

A further sign of the weakening in trade union power is the dramatic decline in industrial action. In the 1990s, the number of working days lost as a result of industrial conflict was only about 20 per cent of the corresponding number in the 1970s (Scheuer, 2006). The weakened position of most European trade unions has also had a negative impact on their bargaining power. In the field of wage policy, for example, unions have no longer been able to keep real wage developments in line with productivity growth since the 1980s. As a result the wage share (the proportion of workers' income in relation to the overall national income) has shown a decline in almost all European countries, leading to a significant income redistribution from workers to capital (Schulten, 2004: 179–99; 2005: 270; see Figure 13.1).

The political reactions of European trade unions to the neoliberal offensive have differed from country to country, and were sometimes even contradictory. On the one hand, some unions have more or less accepted the neoliberal perception of globalization and competition, and called for new social compromises with capital at the national level in order to achieve more socially acceptable ways in increasing competitiveness. During the 1990s many European countries have seen the emergence of both a new form of 'competitive corporatism' as well as new competitive alliances at company level (Bieling and Schulten, 2003; Schulten, 2004: 245–75). On the other hand, many unions in Europe started to become outspoken critics of neoliberal Europe.

Following the large strike against a reorganization of the social security system in France in winter 1995 there have been several

Figure 13.1 Development of the adjusted wage share in the EU15 (1960–2005)

Note: wage share = compensation per employee as a percentage of GDP at factor costs per person employed.
Source: European Commission (2006).

waves of protests or even 'general strikes' in many European countries (Taylor and Mathers, 2002; Deppe, 2003; Waddington, 2005). Within these struggles trade unions not only searched for new alliances with other social movements, but changed themselves at least partly in the direction of a new social movement unionism. Especially the French *Solidaires, Unitaires et Démocratiques* (SUD) unions are a good example in this respect (Damesin and Denis, 2005). French unions have shown on this occasion that their organizational weakness as far as members are concerned is not necessarily preventing them from successfully organizing large-scale actions of resistance. Taking into account both the degree of economic integration in Europe and the crucial role of the EU institutions in promoting neoliberal restructuring, however, it has become clear that resistance as well as the fight for alternatives could no longer be limited to the national level.

TRADE UNIONS AT THE EUROPEAN LEVEL: BETWEEN SOCIAL PARTNER AND SOCIAL MOVEMENT

At European level most national union organizations are members of the European Trade Union Confederation (ETUC), which claims to represent about 60 million workers in 36 countries. Furthermore, there are eleven European Industry Federations (EIFs) representing national unions from certain industries, such as the European Metalworkers Federation (EMF) and the European Federation of Public Service Unions (EPSU) (http://www.etuc.org/r/13). Traditionally, the European trade union organizations have mainly acted as a workers' lobby organization with the EU institutions in order to influence EU legislation and policy. In the last two decades, they have also tried to develop a European system of labour relations with employer organizations through the establishment of a European 'social dialogue'. Finally, at company level they have attempted to establish so-called European Works Councils (EWCs), which should bring together workers' representatives from various national subsidiaries within transnational corporations (TNCs).

The European trade union organizations were frequently accused of having become co-opted into neoliberal restructuring at the European level as a result of their social partnership approach towards European employers' associations and EU institutions (e.g. Gobin, 1997). Their general attitude of 'yes, but' (Dolvik, 1999) according to which they have always supported every project of economic integration but demanded its 'social dimension', has resulted in some gains such as the introduction of a legal basis for European Works Councils, but it did not change the general neoliberal direction of integration. In fact, the employment and social policy gains at the European level were used by the European Union to justify neoliberal restructuring (Schulten, 2006b).

The result is, it is alleged, some kind of 'symbolic Euro-corporatism', where unions can participate in discussions without having the chance of making a more significant impact on the fundamental direction of European integration (e.g. Bieling and Schulten, 2003; Schulten, 2004: 262–7). As Taylor and Mathers (2002: 54) have put it, '"the social partnership" approach that dominates the thinking of leading members of the European labour movement amounts to a strategy that not only further abandons the autonomy of the labour movement but confirms the logic of neo-liberalism through "supply side corporatism" or "progressive competitiveness".' Instead what is needed, so the argument goes, is a shift towards social movement unionism, which potentially provides the avenue for a more radical challenge to the current order.

The multi-level nature of governance in the European Union provides trade unions as well as other interest groups with easy access to supranational decision makers, but with a related much lower chance of making an impact on the outcome of policy making (Greenwood, 2003: 29, 73). 'The Commission's role in drafting legislation, together with its interdependencies with outside interests, make it the foremost venue for outside interests' (Greenwood, 2003: 30). This is also the case in relation to trade unions, which have particularly close contact with the Directorate General (DG) for Employment and Social Affairs, formerly DG V. Overall, however, the Commission has 23 DGs, and not all DGs are equally important. The DG for Competition and the DG for Economic and Financial Affairs are more decisive within the European Union. Together with the DG Internal Market and DG Trade they are the hard core of the Commission, driving the neoliberal project through the discourse of competitiveness (Rosamond, 2002). Trade unions' focus on the DG for Employment and Social Affairs has often marginalized them within the Commission internal decision-making process. The European Parliament (EP) has become a focus of interest groups, since it can amend and co-decide legislation. The overall position of the EP within the EU decision-making process remains weak, however (Hyman, 2006: 5).

Multi-sector social dialogue has been one of the core avenues for the ETUC to influence policy making in the European Union since the Treaty of Maastricht in 1991. Should the ETUC and their employers' counterpart, the Union of Industrial and Employers' Confederations of Europe (UNICE), agree on a particular issue, this agreement is then passed to the Council of Ministers, which transfers it into a directive without further discussion. First successes include the Parental Leave Directive in 1996 (Falkner, 1998). Overall, however, the significance of the social dialogue should not be exaggerated. To date, it has concluded only few agreements establishing minimum standards (Greenwood, 2003: 68). The agreement on teleworking in 2002 is merely voluntary, the implementation of which is not via an EU directive, but remains the task of the social partners themselves (Broughton, 2002). The same is the case in relation to the latest agreement on work-related stress (Broughton, 2004; see also Keller, 2003: 415–17).

Moreover, the areas covered by the social dialogue are compartmentalized and do not include issues of the general macro-economic direction of the European Union. More fundamental issues such as the right to strike, the right to association and wage bargaining have been excluded from European competencies (Greenwood, 2003: 150). Sectoral social dialogue is hardly developed – for an overview see Keller (2003: 418–23) – and EWCs could prove divisive for trade unions (Martin and Ross, 1999: 343–4). In short, trade unions are structurally disadvantaged in the EU institutional set-up, which confirms those who are sceptical of the benefits of a social partnership strategy at EU level. Nevertheless, there are also some examples where trade unions have successfully managed to develop strategies that have the potential to overcome this situation.

One example is the attempt of European trade unions to coordinate their national collective bargaining policy at European level. It has been the EMF, in particular, that realized in the early 1990s that plans for EMU implied the danger of social dumping through the undercutting of wage and working conditions between several national collective bargaining rounds (EMF, 1998: 1–2). In response, the EMF started restructuring itself and began amongst other things to work towards the European coordination of national collective wage bargaining. The coordination of national wage bargaining was approved in 1998, and the EMF tries to ensure that national unions pursue a common strategy of asking for wage increases along the formula of productivity increase plus inflation rate (EMF, 1998: 3; see also Schulten, 2005: 274–89).

The main goals of the coordination of collective bargaining are to avoid the downward competition between different national bargaining rounds, and to protect workers against the related reduction in wages and working conditions. Thus, it is expected that 'a coordinated European collective bargaining policy will play a major role in intensifying and reinforcing the social dimension of European unity' (EMF, 1998: 1). The coordination of bargaining provides a good, alternative way forward in a situation of structural disadvantage and is characterized by the following three advantages:

- It does not rely on an employers' counterpart, which has not been willing to engage in meaningful social dialogue.
- The disadvantaged position within the EU institutional framework is of no consequence, since inter-union coordination does not rely on the compliance of EU or national institutions.
- This strategy makes it possible to take national differences into account, something that is often cited as the core reason that European-wide union cooperation is impossible.

In the meantime almost all EIFs as well as the ETUC have adopted this coordination approach, although its practical impact on national bargaining policy has so far been rather limited (Schulten, 2004: 307–11).

Another more innovative approach can be found in the recent

attempt by some European trade union organizations to strengthen their links with other social movements in order to fight against specific neoliberal EU projects. A pioneer of such a strategy has been the EPSU, the affiliated national unions of which organize workers in the civil service from local to European government, as well as in the health sector and general utilities such as energy and water, that is the traditional public sector (Bieler, 2005b: 475–7). Confronted with intensified neoliberal restructuring resulting from the Services Directive, initiated by the Commission to deregulate and liberalize national public sectors, as well as the negotiation of a General Agreement on Trade in Services (GATS), EPSU has struggled to preserve a system of integrated public services within EU member states. The union has engaged in lobbying EU institutions as well as in discussions with employers' associations.

The most innovative strategy is, however, EPSU's increasing cooperation with other social movements. In relation to GATS, EPSU participated in demonstrations organized by Belgian unions and the *Association pour la Taxation des Transactions Financiers pour l'Aide aux Citoyens* (ATTAC) in February 2003 to keep public services out of GATS. Furthermore, it took part in the European day of national action on GATS and public services organized by the European Social Forum (ESF), as well as the ETUC European day of national action for a Social Europe in March 2003 (EPSU, 2003). The link with other social movements is also visible in relation to public procurement. EPSU and several other EIFs cooperated with a range of environmental and other social movements such as Greenpeace Europe and the Social Platform, itself a network of European non-governmental organizations (NGOs) promoting the Social Dimension of the European Union, in lobbying the EU Council of Ministers to amend the Draft Directive on Public Procurement towards the inclusion of social, ecological and fair trade criteria in the award of public procurement contracts (Coalition for Green and Social Procurement, 2002). In short, EPSU has formed close alliances with not only other trade unions, but also wider social movements. These alliances present 'an agreement between trade unions, NGOs and employers, that social Europe is the bridge that connects Europe to the citizen' (EPSU, 2002). Hence, a separate 'social discourse' has emerged in the European Union, and trade unions have successfully used it to broaden their social basis of the struggle against neoliberal restructuring of the public sector, thereby increasing their impact on EU policy making (Greenwood, 2003: 150, 155–8).

More generally, there are growing indications that other European trade union organizations are also 'undergoing a shift in strategic orientation from an exclusive focus on institutional "social partnership" within the European Union towards a more campaigning "social movement" model' (Taylor and Mathers, 2004: 267) The biggest success of such a strategy to date is the campaign against the European Services Directive, which aimed at a far-reaching liberalization of European services and would have led to a fundamental undermining of national labour standards. The campaign culminated in two large European demonstrations in Brussels and Strasburg in 2005 and early 2006, attracting trade unions and other social movements from all over Europe. In the end it was at least successful in preventing the adoption of the initial draft of the directive (Waddington, 2005: 533–4).

CONCLUSION: AN ALTERNATIVE STRATEGY FOR EUROPEAN LABOUR

Today, most national trade unions in Europe are in favour of a further expansion and deepening of European integration, although there are still some significant variations in emphasis and commitment (Bieler, 2006). After neoliberal policies had placed them on the defensive for about two decades, Europe has become a strategic level to enforce political alternatives. The concept of 'social Europe', therefore, represents the vision of a re-establishment of social regulation and protection at a higher level, which can no longer be exclusively provided at the national level due to the tight integration of European markets. However, there is 'an emerging contradiction between the support of trade unions for European integration and the increasingly neoliberal character of policies intended to "modernise" the European economy' (Waddington, 2005: 518). Although leading political actors within the European Union are officially referring to the European social model as a basic concept for the political design of European capitalism, they more and more try to redefine it in order to justify their neoliberal policies. The latter has become very obvious, in particular, with the adoption of the EU Lisbon strategy, which demands the 'modernization' or the creation of a 'new' European social model (European Council, 2000).

Since the concept of the European social model has become increasingly contested, European labour has to give its own answers to which concrete political projects should constitute 'social Europe' in order to counter neoliberal restructuring. In the process it can draw on a broad range of proposals, coming from the trade unions themselves (e.g. ETUC, 2005, 2006), from the various social movements such as ATTAC (e.g. ATTAC France, 2005) or from various groups of critical academics (e.g. Fondation Copernic, 2003; EuroMemorandum Group, 2005).

Despite all the differences in detail there seems to be an agreement on some core principles for an alternative political agenda for Europe. First, there is the demand for a new economic policy which overcomes the currently dominating neoliberal regime through a modern form of 'Euro-Keynesianism'. The latter aims at a close coordination of macro-economic policy (i.e. monetary, fiscal and wage policy) at European level in order to create 'more and better jobs' (e.g. Bieler, 2006: 209–10; Hein et al., 2005; Monks, 2006). This implies – among others – a fundamental revision of the Stability and Growth Pact and a redefinition of the role and policy of the ECB, including the democratic control of its decisions. Furthermore, Europe would have to determine a certain minimum level for corporate taxes in order to prevent downward tax competition. Finally, an alternative economic policy would have to re-establish the role of the public sector against neoliberal deregulation and privatization policies. It should develop a new investment strategy at European level financed by a significantly increased EU budget.

Second, there is a demand for a stop to all EU policies that promote a further deregulation of labour markets and the privatization of social security. Instead, 'social Europe' should include the definition of European-wide minimum standards, and criteria for a process of social convergence covering issues like minimum wages, maximum working hours, holiday payments, dismissal protection as well as social welfare payments, health care, pensions, housing, education (e.g. ATTAC France, 2005). Depending on the concrete issue, the European Union could determine certain minimum requirements which are related to the national economic performance and should become gradually harmonized. One example for such a social convergence process could be a European minimum wage policy, according to which every worker in the European Union should have the right for a minimum wage, which is at least equivalent to 50 per cent of the average national wage level and which later on should be increased to 60 per cent (Schulten, Bispinck and Schäfer, 2006: 369–75; Schulten and Watt, 2007).

A third element of 'social Europe' would have to be the

strengthening of workers and union rights. At company level the debate has focused so far very much on EWCs. Nevertheless, it has become obvious that the existing EWC directive is in many respects insufficient and needs a fundamental revision in order to intensify the contacts between workers' representatives in TNCs and to give them a real influence on transnational relocation and company investment strategies. In general, what is needed is a much more developed discussion of what kind of economic and industrial democracy should be associated with 'social Europe'.

Fourth, in the area of collective bargaining unions have started to coordinate their bargaining policies at the European level in order to prevent mutual dumping of wages and other labour costs. However, these approaches are still at a very initial stage and so far not very efficient. Moreover, they are lacking an overall vision of a 'European solidaristic wage policy' as a counter-model to the neoliberal concept of wages subordinated to the battle for competitiveness (Schulten, 2004, 2005). This also includes the need to defend or even re-establish a nationally coordinated bargaining policy based on multi-employer agreements. This is an important institutional precondition for a solidaristic wage policy, which does not depend on the economic performance of the individual company.

Nevertheless, it is not enough to develop core characteristics of an alternative model. The possible strategies and alliances of forces, able to put such a model into practice, also need to be reflected upon (Bieler, 2006: 210–19). In its struggle for a 'social Europe', European labour clearly has to advance further its political strategies. European integration is indeed a strategic level for resistance against neoliberal restructuring and the promotion of alternatives. However, this has at least four important implications.

First, the European labour movement should give up their 'yes, but' attitude towards the European Union and make it clear that they will support further economic integration only when there are new substantial regulations into the direction of a 'social Europe'. Second, trade unions should further intensify their cooperation and coordination at the European level, and work towards overcoming national differences and priorities. Importantly, a strengthening of political action at European level does not mean that other levels (national, regional etc.) become less important. On the contrary, without strong political movements at all these levels, there would be little room to manoeuvre at the European level. However, what will be the biggest task for the European trade union organizations in future is to link the national struggles and make clear that they are all part of a European struggle against neoliberal restructuring, which can mutually reinforce each other. Third, the European trade union organizations should change their strategic policy from being primarily an EU lobby organization working within EU institutions, towards becoming a more European social campaigning and movement organization. This would also mean that they should not only react defensively to the political agenda set by the European Union but operate more proactively with their own social topics and issues. Fourth – and closely related to a transformation towards a social movement organization – European unions should further develop their cooperation with other social movements, as they have started to do so in recent years, for example, in the fight against the European Services Directive (see above).

This cooperation has most prominently been developed within the ESFs, the meetings of anti-neoliberal globalization movements in Europe. From 6 to 10 November 2002, European 'anti-globalization' movements including trade unions, NGOs and other social movements, gathered in Florence, Italy for the first ESF. During 400 meetings around 32,000 to 40,000 delegates from all over Europe, plus 80 further countries, debated issues related to the three main themes of the Forum: 'Globalization and [neo-] liberalism', 'War and Peace', as well as 'Rights–Citizenship–Democracy'. The ESF culminated in one of the largest anti-war demonstrations ever on the afternoon of 9 November, when 500,000 protestors according to police estimates – almost 1 million according to the organizers – marched peacefully through the streets of Florence against the impending war on Iraq.

Clearly, there were differences between the various social movements, established trade unions and new, radical unions as far as strategies and contents of opposition to neoliberal globalization are concerned. These differences, however, should not make us overlook the commonalities and resulting possible joint activities. Despite different structures and strategies, all movements present at the ESF identified neoliberal globalization, in its economic, deregulatory form as well as its militaristic version (as embodied in the war on Iraq) as the main target for resistance. Hence a convergence of opinions emerged around several areas for joint activities, including the call to hold worldwide demonstrations against the impending war on Iraq on 15 February 2003, as well as joint activities in defence of the public sector against neoliberal restructuring (Bieler and Morton, 2004b: 312–19).

Importantly, the ESFs have also provided a framework for cooperation between established and non-established, informal labour.

While trade unions represent the former, Euromarches, for example, organizing the European unemployed (Mathers, 1999), was also a prominent participant in, and co-organizer of, the various ESFs. In short, the ESFs offer significant potential to overcome the divide between formal and informal labour, and thereby to enlarge the social basis for change.

Chapter 14

A trade union internationalism for the 21st century: meeting the challenges from above, below and beyond

Peter Waterman

> [D]ecent work is a worthy slogan, but it is a sign of how far we
> have regressed that international trade unionism has needed to
> make this its strategic centrepiece. To build an effective counter-
> force in the battle of ideas, to inspire and attract the idealistic,
> unions need a more ambitious programme: regaining a role in
> fighting for a decent life, a decent society, a decent Europe and
> a decent world.
>
> (Hyman, 2007)

INTRODUCTION

This chapter considers, first, the structure of the traditional international unions; next, the responses of the broader labour movement to
globalization, then the new 'global justice and solidarity movement',
followed by a comparison between the two types, and then some questions remaining or arising. The chapter ends with a brief 2007 update.
A draft of this paper was criticized online by Paul Garver (2006), an
officer of the International Union of Foodworkers (IUF), who clearly
felt I had not done justice to bodies such as his. This response is
welcome in so far as there is so little dialogue here. In cutting the paper
to editorial requirements, however, I fear it has become even more
impressionistic. But truth (on international labour issues, as on others)
is not something possessed by one person, position, ideology or institution. Rather does it come precisely out of a public dialogue and
dialectic, to which this paper should be considered a contribution.
Readers should know where this provocation 'comes from', which is a
lifetime engagement with labour and internationalism (as necessary
for global social emancipation), experience of the Communist union

internationalism of the 1960s, of the 'new internationalisms' of the 1970s, the 'shopfloor internationalism' of the 1980s, of the 'new international labour studies' of the 1970s–80s, and of the 'global justice and solidarity movement' of the new century. For better or for worse, it also comes from an academic (retired), promoting and reflecting on all of these.

THE STRUCTURES OF INTERNATIONAL UNIONISM

During the later 20th century the international trade union movement was dominated by a small number of organizations, not all of them international (Waterman, 2001a: ch. 5). The best-known are or were:

- the Communist-controlled World Federation of Trade Unions (WFTU) in Prague, largely denuded of members and influence by the collapse of the Communist world in 1989 (Waterman, 2001b)
- the social-reformist International Confederation of Free Trade Unions (ICFTU) in Brussels, which grew as a result of the same process
- the (ex-) Social Christian World Confederation of Labour (WCL), also in Brussels, which had a certain membership in Latin America, if a marginal one elsewhere.

Throughout the 20th century and beyond, the American Federation of Labour-Congress of Industrial Organizations (AFL-CIO) has played a major international role. It has been inspired more by the American variant of social reformism, known as 'business unionism', than by social democracy. The AFL-CIO has been a major influence within the ICFTU and also a major independent operator. It has acted through corporate and/or state-funded agencies for Asia, Africa and South America, and also engaged in activities in Europe and the Third World in a clandestine or at least low-profile manner (Carew, 1996; Clarke, 1994; Ruiz, 2004). Its work is now carried forward by its Solidarity Centre.

Then there are the oldest international union organizations, those originally related to specific trades or industries. These were once called international trade secretariats (ITSs), now reduced in number by mergers (as a consequence of industrial transformation and/or falling union membership) and renamed global union federations (GUFs) or simply global unions (GUs). ITSs/GUs have long considered themselves more 'unionist' and less 'political' than the ICFTU. They have, however, been similarly associated with social reformism and the ICFTU, and were then literally linked to it through the GU website. Their industrial specificity requires them to address themselves more directly to the workers – or at least the unions – they represent. Also allied to GU has been the Trade Union Advisory Committee of the OECD.

Formal structures of regional organizations are dependent on the international confederations and their related industry-specific federations. But within Europe there is the independent, but also social-reformist, European Trade Union Confederation (ETUC), simultaneously addressed to and dependent on the European Union. Something similar may be emerging in the Common Market of the Southern Cone of Latin America (MERCOSUR). But the challenge to neoliberal regionalism by the left-populist regimes in the region may affect this. Significant regional union structures have existed in Asia, particularly those of the ICFTU (Greenfield, 1999). And then there are the 'autonomous' regional internationals, dependent on inter-governmental structures, in the Arab world and Africa. Efforts have been made to coordinate the policies and activities of European/international federations and those of Latin America. But this process has been somewhat overtaken by the recent unification (see Update below).

Formally speaking, most of the world's trade unions are representative-democratic organizations, are controlled by their members, and advance the interests of the working class generally. They act either defensively for particular categories of workers, or more assertively, often by becoming partners or leaders in movements for national liberation, for political and social democracy or for general movements of the poor. However, as critical observers have repeatedly noted, they are also subject to the 'iron law of oligarchy' (Michels, 1915), have themselves become 'managers of discontent' (Mills, 1948/2001; Catalano, 1999), and become involved forms of 'neo-corporatism' at the risk of making themselves irrelevant (Gorz, 1999a). Throughout the 20th century, at the regional and global levels these threats to the unions' social presence and impact increased.

The distance of the union internationals from their worker base increases such dangers. Despite their considerable differences – involving ideology, industry/occupation, worker constituency, or geographical reach – the international organizations share a number of common characteristics. They are remote from workers on the shop floor, in the office or in the community, who, with exceptions, are unaware of their existence. They were and are marked by their past participation in the cold war. They tend to reproduce or at least reflect the structure and behaviour of inter-state agencies. They were and are largely Northern-based, led and staffed. They have tended to reduce the complex reality of working people worldwide to a western model of the unionized (or unionizable) male worker in life-time employment in large-scale capitalist or state enterprise. Where they have adapted western unionism and International Labour Organization (ILO) tripartism in response to the problematic third world, they have often adopted the developmentalist ideologies dominant in the North. The 'free' western internationals have become increasingly dependent on state funding for their 'regional' or 'development' activities, thus taking on the role of state or inter-state development agencies. While they are critical of developmental non-governmental organizations (NGOs), the unions commonly reproduce their top-down, North-South, patron-client relations (Waterman, 2004b). To the best of my knowledge no international union or international labour researcher has ever tried to find out whether union members or shopfloor activists even know the name of 'their' international, or what it does, or whether they feel they in any way own it.

Where independent Southern regional organizations have been set up, such as the International Confederation of Arab Trade Unions (ICATU) or the Organization of African Trade Union Unity (OATUU), they have, as suggested above, often been dependent on the initiative of such states or groups. And such organizations have, like the Southern states and inter-state agencies themselves, tended to reproduce rather than challenge the traditional model and rela-tionships. Various projects of South–South collaboration between unions or workers have so far shown limited results. Such may be better developed amongst the specialized new international networks for fishing communities, small farmers, banana workers, street and home workers, or slum dwellers. These lack, perhaps, the state-national assumptions of the national unions, their dependence on the state locally and the Northern unions internationally.

LABOUR INTERNATIONALISM UNDER GLOBALIZATION: WITHIN AND BEYOND UNIONS

At the end of the 20th century international trade unionism was confronted by a tragic paradox. There were more wage earners than ever before, around 3 billion (Freeman, 2006). The ICFTU/GU, with 150 or more million members, covered more countries, unions and workers than ever before. This was due, as suggested, to the incorporation of most of the formerly Communist or national-populist unions. But neoliberal globalization implied the simultaneous weakening of traditional unionism's century-old national-industrial base, the shift of that base to countries of the South (particularly China), the undermining of traditional job security and union rights, and the decline or disappearance of support from social-democratic parties, socially reformist governments and the most powerful inter-state agencies. Moreover, the unions were being confronted with a fact that – in their industrial, national or industrial-relations cocoons – they had never previously felt necessary to face: in this globalizing world of labour, maybe only one worker in 18 was unionized. Finally, with the disappearance of their competitors in Communist or national-populist unions, the ICFTU/GU found itself not only in an alien and hostile world but ideologically disoriented. Previously it had been able to see itself not only as representing the most advanced union model but as part of the 'free west', opposed to both Communist and national-populist unionism. Now it found itself left behind by the globalization of capital and by the decreasing political interest of the international hegemons.

THE INTERNATIONAL UNIONS RESPOND

If the union internationals initially responded in equal measure with disorientation and retreat, they are now increasingly raising the old notion of 'social partnership' with capital and state from the national to the global level (Waterman, 2006a). This has implied a series of specific campaigns, addressed sometimes directly to multinational corporations, sometimes to the international financial institutions and other promoters of globalization (the World Trade Organization (WTO), the World Economic Forum (WEF) and so forth). 'Over the years, the global union federations have established an ongoing social dialogue with a number of multinational enterprises in their sectors or industries' (Justice, 2002: 96).

Three major areas of this union work are international labour standards, codes of conduct and corporate social responsibility policies (Jenkins, Pearson and Seyfang, 2002). The five 'core labour rights' set out below are currently represented by a set already issued by the ILO, of which only one is actually less than 30 years old (it should be noted that none of the ILO's approximately 175 member states has endorsed all of them):

- the right to form trade unions ('freedom of association')
- the right to effective collective bargaining between workers and management
- freedom from forced or compulsory labour
- an end to child labour
- freedom from discrimination in the workplace.

This list does not, notably, include an explicit right to the international solidarity strike, as called for by the International Centre for Trade Union Rights (Ewing and Sibley, 2000). Directly or indirectly related to this declaration was the 15-year-plus campaign for a 'social clause' under which the WTO (initially the General Agreement of Tariffs and Trade, GATT) would discriminate against states that did not respect international labour rights. This attempt to get labour rights institutionalized by the very organization that was promoting 'free trade' at the cost of labour not only failed, but provoked much disagreement as well as forceful criticism within the union movement in the South and among labour specialists (John and Chenoy, 1996; *Working USA*, 2001).

'Global Framework Agreements' between particular GUFs and multinational corporations are described as:

> agreement[s] negotiated between a multinational company and a global union federation concerning the international activities of that company. The main purpose of a framework agreement is to establish a formal ongoing relationship ... which can solve problems and work in the interests of both parties.
>
> (ICFTU, 2004)

Such agreements do not require internationally enforceable legislation – a problem with voluntary 'codes of conduct', which can be difficult to monitor and are often left to under-funded and unaccountable NGOs (Oliviero and Simmons, 2002; Jenkins et al., 2002).

Such voluntary global social contracts have been presented on a more public stage by union endorsement of the UN's Global Compact. This is another voluntary initiative, aiming to 'mainstream' socially responsible business activities through policy dialogues, learning and local projects. Union support for the Global Compact, even though the initiative lacked the power of enforcement or monitoring, was revealed in a joint UN-ICFTU/GU declaration:

> It was agreed that global markets required global rules. The aim should be to enable the benefits of globalization increasingly to spread to all people by building an effective framework of multi-lateral rules for a world economy that is being transformed by the globalization of markets . . . the Global Compact should contribute to this process by helping to build social partnerships of business and labour.
>
> (ICFTU, 2000)

More recently we have seen union co-sponsorship of the ILO's World Commission on the Social Dimension of Globalization (also dominated by statespeople, corporate figures and academics (ILO, 2004).

Together these activities suggest the international union movement is shifting focus from states and inter-state bodies, previously seen as the major locus of regulation, toward the multinational corporations, seen as the major powers in the global economy. While the social-democratic international unions broadly welcome such projects (Justice, 2002), others see in these accords an embrace by UN institutions of the multinationals at the expense of civil society (Judge, 2001).

While such efforts suggest a reorientation in reaction to globalization, international trade unions are continuing their traditional efforts at union building, in defence of labour rights and in support of workers and unions internationally. This seems to involve new and more assertive language. An example might be the International Transport Workers' Federation, the 2002 Congress of which was devoted to the theme of 'Globalizing Solidarity' (ITWF, 2002). A turning point in its practical solidarity activity is indicated by, on the one hand, its failure to effectively support the Liverpool dock workers during a major lockout in 1995–8 (Waterman, 1997), and on the other, its more effective support for the Australian dock workers during a related dispute later.

True, much national and international union solidarity activity is carried out under the rubric of 'development cooperation' and financed by the state or inter-state organizations. At other times such activity is combined with union-to-union or worker-to-worker solidarity, as possibly with the Irish Congress of Trade Unions (ICFTU Global Solidarity). It is, however, notable that most of this solidarity activity appears to be on a North-South axis and in a North-South direction. A more holistic, multifaceted and multidirectional notion of labour solidarity is yet to emerge; and the ICFTU website reveals only an implicit recognition of the broader global solidarity movement.

While the ICFTU moved toward a top-level merger with the (ex-) Social-Christian WCL, this did not necessarily signify a surpassing of turf wars between established union bureaucracies, which could be expected to continue at various levels within the unified structure. Nor did it mean that the ICFTU was opening up rather than hunkering down. Its regional organization in the Americas, known by its Spanish initials as ORIT (in English, the Inter-American Regional Organization of Workers), was heavily involved in drawing up, with many of the inter/national union centres in the region, *Labour's Platform for the Americas* (Global Policy Network, 2006a), supplemented by an attractive comic-strip version (Global Policy Network, 2006b). While this is entirely oriented toward government policy changes and in no way breaks with the discourse of social partnership, it certainly struck a more assertive and popular note than the ICFTU in Brussels. The ICFTU/GU websites gave this document no place and referred to it, if at all, only in passing. The ICFTU has become increasingly involved with such 'single issues' as human rights and the environment. But its new initiative with respect to the latter shows all the signs of having been initiated (and being generously funded by?) state or inter-state 'partners' (SustainLabour, 2006; WILL, 2006).

THE GLOBAL JUSTICE AND SOLIDARITY MOVEMENT AND A GLOBAL CIVIL SOCIETY IN CONSTRUCTION

If the unions were thus responding to the challenge 'from above', they were also responding to that 'from below' or at least 'from the side'. For labour's asserted place as 'by far and away the most democratic institution in every society and certainly the only major democratic international movement' (Spooner, 2005: 27) is increasingly being challenged by the 'new global justice and solidarity movement' fighting on a broader social and ideological terrain, that of 'global civil society'. The 'new global social movements' (ecological, women's, anti-war, human rights, indigenous peoples and so on) have been gathering strength since the 1970s and 1980s, as have international labour networks, concerned with 'atypical' workers, with publications or audio-visuals, information and communication technology. Moreover, since the close of the 20th century and the beginning of the 21st, there has been an explosion of global civil society events, actions and organizations, such as the World Social Forums (WSF) (Glasius, Kaldor and Anheier, 2005). Significantly, the international women's movement seems to have produced the most challenging new international/ist manifesto (World March of Women, 2004).

The new international/ist labour NGOs, although customarily linked to trade union organizations, differ from them in their origins, membership (if any), constituencies, financing, 'relational form' (networks rather than institutions), and their typical forms of action and expression. They commonly concentrate on a single campaign, aspect of worker life, type of previously unrepresented labour, world area, and form of international labour solidarity activity (education, research, communication). Sometimes they overlap with community movements. Sometimes they are not even identifiable as 'labour-oriented', but rather take up labour issues as part of a more general set of popular or democratic complaints and demands. An example is international networking between peasants and small farmers (Edelman, 2003). Another is the International Collective in Defence of Fishworkers (Dietrich and Nayak, 2001). A significant 'national/international solidarity movement' is that developing around immigrant rights in the United States (Lovato, 2006). Better-known internationally are those western-based projects that have addressed themselves energetically and publicly to issues like child labour and sweated labour more generally (Silvey, 2004) and to high-profile attacks on corporations or brands such as McDonald's (Ghigliani, 2005; McSpotlight, 2007). Another widespread type of NGO is those that concentrate on labour rights, often linking unions, academics and legal professionals, such as the International Centre for Trade Union Rights (ICTUR) in the United Kingdom.

CONTRASTING THE RESPONSES

It would be easy to set up a whole series of binary or Manichean oppositions between the old international union organizations and the new labour and social justice movements, and between their responses to globalization. But perhaps the most significant differences here are those between the moments of capitalist development at which they took shape (beginning or the end of the 20th century); between organizations (representative-democratic membership) and networks (often initiated by non-worker, activists); between the customarily national and frequently cross-national or global constituencies; between 'political-institutional' and 'social-communicational' internationalism; and between references to a traditional 'representative-democracy frame' and those to a growing 'civil society frame'. However, it is not, in practice, possible to simply identify such characteristics with the union organization on the one hand and the labour NGO or social movement network on the other (Eade and Leather, 2005).

Some of the earlier-mentioned international labour NGOs or networks directly challenged the union internationals from, as it were, 'below', 'the Left' and 'the South' (Waterman, 2001a, ch. 5). They certainly opened up new issues and perspectives for the unions, thus having had at very least the impact of pressure groups or of raisers of consciousness for a new kind of labour internationalism. But neoliberal globalization in the 1990s had an impact on networks as well as institutions, and many of the NGOs today limit themselves to roles of support or extension, having abandoned any notion of publicly challenging the international unions or even of initiating public dialogue with them. On the other hand, many unions have been taking up activities (on women, 'atypical' workers) or attitudes (solidarity discourse, openness to other movements) previously highlighted by the networks. Given, further, the increasing presence of unions on major national or international demonstrations against neoliberal globalization, the relationship between the unions and the social movements is becoming not only intertwined but interdependent.

Possibly the most dramatic and visible evidence of what does happen is provided by the WSF. The WSF process has been taken to symbolize the new 'movement of movements' against and beyond neoliberal globalization. It is significant that two Brazilian labour organizations were involved in the Organizing Committee (later Secretariat) of the Forums held in Porto Alegre, Brazil, from 2001. The first was a 'new' union, the Central Trade Union Confederation (CUT), itself critical of the ICFTU (Jakobsen, 2001). The second was the Movement of Landless Rural Workers (MST), an even newer movement, which has its own tensions with CUT and its political arm, the Brazilian Workers' Party (PT). Exceptionally, this new internationalist initiative is as much Southern as it is Northern.

QUESTIONS REMAINING: A GLOBAL WORKING CLASS? GLOBALIZED UNIONISM? A REINVENTED LABOUR INTERNATIONALISM?

The globalization of the working-class condition has clearly not worked out in the way that Marxists (and other socialists) assumed or hoped for. Instead of generalizing and homogenizing the condition of the industrial proletariat (of mid-19th century Britain), we see proletarianization occurring without the Marxists' internationalist and revolutionary proletariat. Differentiation rather than homogenization seems to be the rule. The appeals, 'Workers of the world unite!', 'You have nothing to lose but your chains!', 'You have a world to win!', 'One solution, revolution!', or 'Black and white, unite and fight!' fail to appeal to workers who experience international competition, who may also have a job, or television or pension to lose, and whose religious, ethnic or local identity may be as significant to them as their class. It is the internationalists who still have a class to win, and this task is as much a matter of winning hearts and minds as is the internationalism of women, of indigenous peoples, of Africans or of slum dwellers. Given, indeed, that the differentiated and dispersed working classes also have these other identities, a new working-class internationalism would seem to be dependent on an intimate articulation of this with the internationalism of those. The question remains of whether trade union internationalism will further, rather than obstruct, such a reinvented internationalism!

We could imagine various scenarios for the future of union internationalism. Indeed, we could project most, if not all, of these from the five possible identities suggested for unionism in Europe (Hyman, 1999: 128–30). They are those of the guild (of an occupational elite), the friendly society (of individualized workers), the company union (a productivity deal between workers and owners), the social partner (a political trade-off between union and state) and the social movement (a campaigning unionism seeking mass support). Each of these could have, and often has had, its own internationals and internationalisms. In so far as these are ideal types, we are likely to find, in reality, ambiguous union types and ambiguous internationalisms. It might have been suggested above that international unionism is today hegemonized by social partnership unionism. Yet, in practice, we find varying syntheses of at least social partnership and social movement unionism.

The growing presence of international unions within the global justice and solidarity movement in general, or the WSF in particular, might suggest a development in the direction of some kind of 'international social movement unionism' (Waterman, 2004a, app. 1). However, unlike the Communist International, neither the WSF in particular nor the global justice and solidarity movement (GJ&SM) in general has 21 conditions of membership. So the unions enter this new movement without necessarily abandoning or even qualifying their long-standing traditions of social partnership and/or company unionism. Moreover, neither the WSF nor the GJ&SM represents some utopia of global solidarity. What the latter do provide is a new form of international articulation (with 'articulation' referring to both joining together and expression). The new joining together is represented by the centrality of both networking and the agora – a meeting place of diverse movements and a marketplace of ideas. The new expression is largely shaped by such guiding ideas as 'Another world is possible!', 'Alternative globalization', 'Anti-capitalism', 'Global civil society', and the notion that, given opposition to neoliberal globalization, such ideas must find shape through a dialogue and dialectic between class, ideological, social-geographical, gender/sexual, ethnic and other differences.

The presence of the trade unions within this new movement of movements implies the hypothetical possibility of not only adding maybe 150 to 200 million organized workers to the somewhat inchoate and changing constituency of the GJ&SM, but also of making 'work' as central to the WSF as trade and peace have been in the past. So far, however, work has appeared within the WSF largely in the guise of 'decent work' (ICFTU et al., 2005), as sponsored originally by that inter-state Vatican of social partnership, the ILO. The ILO has incorporated social partnership since 1919. And whereas there has been a considerable presence within the WSF of labour's 'others' (female, rural, indigenous, the precariat, unemployed, migrant labour), and of 'other' ideas about work (cooperatives, the solidarity economy, alternative trade), it cannot be said that there is represented here any such holistic alternative to capitalist work as that at least implied by Gorz (1999b).

What the new movement does make hypothetically possible is the emancipation of the unions from two historical, and now archaic, notions of labour internationalism: one that suggested that labour was the privileged bearer of social emancipation and international solidarity, and one that conceived unions in junior partnership with (sections of) national and international capital and (certain) inter-state institutions. If, as Hyman (2004) says, playing safe is the riskiest strategy for international labour, the new agora provides the possibility of working out, together with others, a more adventurous – and effective – one.

Promising signs might be in the number of 'single-issue' (actually life issue) campaigns, many originating with the new social movements (previously dismissed as 'unrepresentative NGOs'), to be found on inter/national union websites: environment, gender, forced labour, indigenous peoples, children, migrants, trafficking, human rights, democracy, HIV/AIDS, corporate accountability, racism, education for all, public services, peace, information and communication technology – even minority sexual rights.

There are, however, no guarantees here. The dialogue or dialectic between the old trade union movement and the new global justice one might just as well witness the 'infection' of the latter by the former as vice versa. The problematic outcome of such engagements is revealed by the impact of 'second wave' feminism on the trade union movement. After an initial and emancipatory moment, there was, according to Warskett (2001: 230), a loss of energy and direction on both sides. All the activity of the feminists has 'not changed in any fundamental way labour unions' vision of what the workplace, community and society could be'. For this she holds both parties responsible. Another feminist records the substantial progress made internationally by the unions but nonetheless notes this more general obstacle to labour movement revival:

> Separate or self organisation presents ideological and practical difficulties to traditional trade unionism, which sees such practices as divisive, as detracting from espoused main aims and methods, as setting up alternative centres of power, and of entrism. Critical tensions, resistance and backlash arise when traditional power holders see their position and status threatened, usurped by the new democratic order.
>
> (Ledwith, 2005: 108)

What, therefore, seems least likely to occur is some kind of dramatic change of heart – or model – within the international trade union movement. It is difficult to imagine an explicit abandonment of the old social partnership with capital and state for a new one with a global civil society that is still – as all serious supporters agree – in the making. Left to its century-old devices, the international trade union organizations are more likely to continue with their present contradictory partnerships – one with capital-and-state, the other with the GJ&SM.

If, however, we address ourselves to the more dynamic party in the relationship, then there is something more to be said. It is this: the new movement might begin to question its own marginalization of the labour question, and its simultaneous fear of serious dialogue with the traditional trade unions. The movement already provides space for some expression of that majority of the world's labour force that is beyond either the unions' concerns or their present reach, such as migrants (WSFM, 2006). It also has means of communication, including the kind of presence in the mass and alternative media that labour once enjoyed. These resources allow it to approach the base of the international trade union movement – people with little knowledge and less control over those who currently speak or act for them. An energetic address to the increasingly globalized workers of the world – with the unions, through the unions, around the unions, even despite the unions – might actually help to reinvent the international labour movement for the century ahead (Waterman, 2006b). Those within the unions – from bottom to top – who prefer risk to safety (Hyman, 2004) are likely to welcome the challenge.

UPDATE 2007

The merger that brought about the creation of the International Trade Union Confederation (ITUC) in November 2006 was inspired by the much-repeated notion that unity is strength. It did not, however, imply any change in the base, structure, relationships or ideology of the merging bodies. The base remains western Europe, the structure pyramidal, the relationships (with member unions, workers, capital, (inter-)state bodies, the global justice movement) untransformed, the ideology that of a global neo-Keynesianism via social partnership. Given, indeed, the continuing attack of capital and state on workers and unions worldwide, this unification has to be considered more a defensive than an assertive act. The event caused no noticeable alarm on the part of the global hegemons, and indeed was hardly noted in the international media, dominant or alternative. Moreover, and more significantly, it was preceded and followed by little discussion amongst either the unions concerned or their allies (Waterman, 2007a).

The new ITUC appeared at the World Social Forum, Nairobi, January 2007, with the umbrella slogan 'Decent work for a decent life'. This campaign (originated actually by the Director-General of the ILO) had both appeal and impact, even on labour networks independent of the ITUC. However, there was friction with the WSF when union spokespeople tried to make the umbrella slogan that of the Forum itself and to appoint themselves to control of a planned labour dialogue. Although the ITUC urged member unions to use the opportunity to develop relations with friendly NGOs, there was little visible evidence of such.

The Nairobi WSF did see the marginal appearance of a political/communicational initiative to create a space and process by which the labour movement, in its broadest terms, could hold a dialogue about its role in the struggle against globalization in general and within the WSF more specifically (Waterman, 2007b). This produced a proposal which might possibly advance the principle of networking within the global labour movement:

PROPOSAL FOR A LABOUR NETWORK ON AND IN THE WORLD SOCIAL FORUM PROCESS

Neoliberal globalization implies the most vicious attack on labour in living memory.

Yet labour has so far had neither the necessary centrality, nor even visibility, within the WSF process.

We propose for this purpose to build a labour network on and in the WSF process. This network will link different experiences, understandings of and skills engaged in every place and every aspect of work.

We believe that such a network can help us to:

- Give more centrality and visibility, in this crucial historical phase, to labour issues and workers' rights in the WSF process.
- Develop a permanent exchange of experiences, information and knowledge.
- Discuss a new and enlarged understanding of labour, considering not only productive but also reproductive work; not only formal, but also informal work.
- Strengthen the alliances between unions, movements, intellectual forces and citizens.
- Go beyond defensive, isolated and – for that matter – failing struggles and find a new transnational capacity for action.
- Find common global objectives for such action.
- Confront the question of the meaning of production (what to produce, how, for whom).
- Map all the different labour actors so as to enlarge the network.

This initiative came from Italy, although it was endorsed at the Nairobi WSF by a geographically wide, socially broad and ideologically varied range of unions and networks. Within Italy it came from a particular set of union activists or tendencies, themselves allied with people who seem to prioritize the WSF as the privileged space for the solution to labour's international crisis.

Although I myself consider the WSF as providing a privileged space, I feel that we should not be making an emancipatory global labour project a hostage to the fortunes of the WSF. While sympathetic to this initiative, my feeling is that we need some space(s), autonomous from both the old institutionalized unions and the new

WSF, in which international(ist) labour networking can occur. Examples of such are appearing in cyberspace (Union Ideas Network, New Unionism), even if they may themselves be hostages to the fortunes of 20th-century social reformism. But we need to also identify and promote local and physical (as distinguished from electronic) places and spaces where this is occurring, independent of the old institutions and the new moments of labour internationalism. We need, too, to create coordinations (networks of networks, movements of movements) to produce some 21st-century equivalent to the *Communist Manifesto*, but this time seen as something open to continual re-evaluation and reinvention. And, while considering that document, we really need to remember the working-class, labour and socialist culture which it both expressed and shaped. Contemporary labour internationalisms – left, right and centre – are largely expressed in terms of interest (be this long-term and general), rather than value, emotion and cultural expression. This is not a matter of nostalgia for, or a reproduction of, 19th-century internationalism, based as it was on communities and experiences that may no longer exist. It is a matter of both inventing relevant new cultural forms (of which I consider the New Unionism site a provocative example), and certainly, yes, seeking relevant historical inspiration for current struggles (for which see the path-breaking book of Paul Mason (2007), *Live Working or Die Fighting*, and its related website).

ACKNOWLEDGEMENT

This is a much abbreviated but also updated version of Waterman and Timms (2004). Appreciation is expressed to Jill Timms, the editors and publishers for their permission to adapt that original.

Chapter 15

What future strategy for the global working class? The need for a new historical subject

Andreas Bieler, Ingemar Lindberg and Devan Pillay

Throughout this volume, two core, interrelated challenges for labour movements have been identified. First, as a result of the spatial fix by capital and the related increasing transnationalization of production, there has been a danger of workers in different countries competing against each other for jobs, and of different national labour movements underbidding each other for the sake of national competitiveness. Second, due to technological, product and financial fixes (see Silver, 2003) and the increasing neoliberal restructuring of the social relations of production – expressed in the privatization and liberalization of the traditional public sector and a general deregulation of labour markets, as well as movements off the land as a result of amongst other things the commercialization of agriculture – there has been increasing unemployment and an expanding informalization of work, within both the informal and the formal sector. As a result of these two challenges there has been a clear change in the balance of forces between capital and labour in favour of the former. National labour movements are under considerable pressure in general as a result of the onslaught by capital, particularly transnational capital.

Nevertheless, we also see new or renewed labour responses. Workers in transnational companies and transnational chains of production or distribution are beginning to link up with each other to protect their common interests. See for instance Chapter 10 on Germany for interesting examples, including a network of union representatives of the transnational chemicals company BASF in Latin America. Moreover, new types of union organization are emerging, as shown in Chapters 6 on Argentina, 4 on India and 2 on South Korea. Even among the most exploited groups of informal-sector workers, organizations for self-help and joint action are being formed in relation to counterparts such as local government or large wholesalers. Here, Chapters 7 on Brazil, 4 on India, 2 on South Korea and 12 on Africa provide examples.

The purpose of this volume has been to provide an overview of the situation of various national labour movements around the world in order to identify the specific challenges they face, but also to discuss the possibilities for a new global working-class strategy based on transnational solidarity. It is to the latter task we return to in these concluding remarks. Can regular workers organized in unions, mainly based in the North, and the hundreds of millions of non-regular or informal workers, mainly in the South, understand each other and begin to define common goals? Can the global working class be a new collective actor? Who are the global working class? We see signs of new patterns being developed. Nevertheless, the obstacles are there, in organization, conflicting interests and differences in experience and analysis of the present world system.

The so-called 'Fordist' organization of production that marked a large part of the last century created the conditions for collective negotiations between trade unions and employers' associations within national welfare states. As Samir Amin argues in the Foreword, the then dominant forms of organization of the working class, political parties and trade unions, as well as the institutions concerning the organization of struggles, such as strikes, negotiations, demonstrations and elections, were produced within this framework. These turned out to be efficient and therefore credible and legitimate. Almost 'full' employment, social security and a stable income distribution were secured in developed countries as a result. In the peripheries of the global system, however, the same model could at best be partially implemented in 'modernized-industrialized' enclaves. The limitations of the system – such as patriarchal or even male chauvinist ideologies and practices, waste of natural resources and disregard for the environment – were criticized by women and environmental movements, who progressively raised popular awareness in this regard.

The present phase of globalized capitalism, which is characterized by the increasing transnationalization as well as informalization of the social relations of production, has led to the recurrence of mass unemployment, the informalization of labour and the resurgence of 'poverty' in the relatively privileged centres. In the peripheries of the system, the integration of peasant reserves into neoliberal capitalist social relations of production, and the rise of low-paid informalized labour in the modernized enclaves, resulted in a gigantic growth of the 'informal' sector and with it growing slums around big cities. These developments have undermined the forms of organization and struggles of the previous phase. Social democratic parties and trade unions are equally in crisis as a result. The new social movements that have emerged in recent decades have been too fragmented and in some cases too ephemeral to form the basis of an alternative. Today, it is necessary to develop responses that address the situation of both the more privileged segments of the working class and the impoverished ones. It is also necessary to link responses by urban workers with the strategies of rural proletariats, within the spheres of both production and consumption.

The proportion of the precarious and pauperized working class (broadly defined) has risen from less than one-quarter to more than one-half of the global urban population, including the developed centres themselves. According to Samir Amin's calculations, the destabilized urban population increased in half a century from less than a quarter of a billion to more than a billion and a half individuals. This is a growth rate that surpasses previous periods of economic expansion, population growth, or the process of urbanization itself. Mass unemployment and the increasing informalization of work make the reconsideration of existing organizations of the working class imperative. A transnational strategy for labour must not reflect only on the situation of workers who are in secure employment. In the majority of the countries of the South, informalized workers – temporary labour, informal labour, the self-employed, the unemployed, street salespeople, those who sell their own services – constitute the majority of the working class. These groups of informal workers are growing because of high unemployment, the decreasing availability of guaranteed employment and increased informal employment; and the continuous migration from the rural areas to the towns and cities. Pauperization in the urban working class is therefore closely linked to developments that victimize third-world peasant societies. The submission of these societies to the demands of capitalist market expansion supports new forms of social polarization which exclude a growing proportion of farmers from access to the land. These peasants, who have been impoverished or become landless, feed the migration to the slums – even more than population growth. Yet all these phenomena are destined to get worse as long as liberal dogmas are not challenged and their spread not halted.

SHORTCOMINGS OF PRESENT STRATEGIES

For the existing organizations of labour the present phase of globalized capitalism presents three major challenges, as we can see from the country reports. First, the basic union task to prevent underbidding between workers can no longer be met successfully at the national level alone. This aspect concerns perhaps core workers more than non-core, and workers in the North more than workers in the South, because it is more among core workers rather than informal sector workers that it has been possible – to some extent – to regulate wages through nation-wide collective agreements. Second, the increasing informalization of work creates a threat to basic living standards and the dignity of hundreds of millions of workers and their families. This threat assumes enormous proportions in the South but informalization also poses an increasing challenge in the North. Finally, the hegemonic neoliberal ideology, underlying the current restructuring of the social relations of production, and a system of related institutions including the World Trade Organization (WTO), are a threat to workers in both the South and the North. These three interrelated challenges together pose a menace to workers, both core and non-core, both in the North and in the South. While there is an enormous disparity in the situation of workers in different positions in the global production and distribution system, it will be decisive to understand the similarity of these challenges for the working class as a whole. This insight must form the basis for discussions about common strategies.

Union responses so far have been mainly defensive. In the North, trade unions have frequently attempted to cooperate with employers' associations in the restructuring process through the formation of so-called social pacts at the national level (Fajertag and Pochet, 2000). The results have been less than positive. These pacts generally included wage restraint and a flexibilization of labour markets. Their goal has not been the smooth interaction of macro-economic policy, with a focus on full employment, but the strengthening of 'national competitiveness' (Bieling and Schulten, 2003: 239). Instead of receiving compensation by the government in exchange for wage moderation, unions could hope for a negotiated adjustment for voluntary wage restraint. At best, job guarantees were obtained in exchange for lower wages and/or longer working hours. This is complemented by a symbolic Euro-corporatism at the European level, which allows trade unions to participate in discussions about the future direction of European integration, without being able to challenge the more general direction of neoliberal restructuring (see Chapter 13). The very focus on social pacts, social dialogue and corporatism is a reference to the past and based on the experience of welfare state capitalism.

This is also reflected in the current initiative by the International Trade Union Confederation (ITUC) and its alliance for 'Decent Work'. The goal of this campaign is to achieve decent work for all, consisting of 'equal access to employment, living wages, social protection, freedom from exploitation and union rights' (ITUC, 2007). Judging from their presentations to the World Social Forum (WSF) in Nairobi (Bieler, 2007), there is a clear sense of hierarchy, with union members being encouraged to listen and follow their leaders. Emphasis is placed on core workers as the main or only important agents for change, and traditional tripartite institutions such as the International Labour Organization (ILO) are regarded as the best organizational way forward. As Waterman outlines in this volume, many international organizations of labour are still driven by a notion of 'social reformism', based on experiences of social pacts in a previous era of 'embedded capitalism', aiming at improvements within the current capitalist system. This includes cooperation with transnational corporations (TNCs), states and international organizations such as the WTO in the traditional form of 'social partnership', with initiatives including global framework agreements and support for the UN's Global Compact initiative. In the South, trade unions have increasingly concentrated on organizing and representing the dwindling core labour force (see Chapter 3). As a result, the concerns of the large informalized sections of the working class, rural and urban, have often remained unheard. Unions are increasingly at risk of developing into a 'labour aristocracy'.

To sum up, the present organizational set-up of the global working class is deficient in two main respects. One is that TNCs and production networks are increasingly able to play workers in different countries against each other, through practices such as benchmarking between production sites and threats to move production units altogether. The potential of workers to negotiate and to take industrial action today is still contained at the national level, while capital is able to move freely across national borders. The other deficiency is that existing unions mainly organize core workers, whereas those with insecure jobs, those working in the informal sector, the self-employed and the unemployed – that is, the majority of the global working class in both urban and rural areas – are outside. There is a clear danger that if unions continue to be dominated by male, formal-sector urban workers, they will become isolated, focusing exclusively on their particular interests.

DIVISIONS WITHIN THE GLOBAL WORKING CLASS: THE NEED FOR TRANSNATIONAL SOLIDARITY?

Globalization affects different groups of workers in different ways, depending on their market power, bargaining power and their position in the present economic and political world order. We seem to see a strong and dangerous tendency of polarization, rather than a general race to the bottom. Two major gaps must be bridged if the global working force shall be able to develop as a global actor: first, the North–South divide, and second, the division between (mainly urban) established and non-established workers (urban and rural).

One important aspect in overcoming the divide between workers in the North and the South is to find a common understanding of their respective positions in the current system of production and within the existing world order. Such a common understanding of the structures of neo-imperialist subordination of workers and production sites in the South, including the role of capitalist interests in the Southern countries themselves and of workers in the North, is a necessary basis for common action. Workers need to exchange glasses across the North–South divide and look at the situation from each others' perspectives. But workers also need to face squarely existing conflicts of interest and discuss how they can be solved or at least handled in a way that can bridge the gap.[1] It will be essential to find new ways of action, effective across borders, and ways of building broad alliances against increasingly faceless, transnational capitalism. The aim of this book, and the discussions we hope that it will lead to, is to contribute to this undertaking and attempt to assess and sketch out possible strategies, which could allow the successful establishment of solidarity within and across borders despite these pressures.

The second gap that has to be bridged is that between established and non-established workers related to 'North–South divisions' *within* countries. Here too, solidarity between the two groups is anything but automatic. Those in secure employment emphasize the maintenance of their particular position and often fear that solidarity with workers in the periphery may undermine their own working contracts. Employers frequently use the reference to unemployment and cheaper labour costs elsewhere to pressure workers and unions into making concessions. Workers in the periphery of the labour market are often very difficult to organize because of their constantly changing employment situation. Moreover, the interests of the unemployed are not fully taken into account by trade unions, which tend to concentrate on protecting the interests of their (more established) members.

This discussion about two gaps however needs strong qualifications. Workers in Sweden are competing much more with workers in Germany than with those in China. Workers in Poland are competing with low wages in relation to workers in Sweden or Germany, but they are themselves exposed to the same type of low-wage competition from Russian or Ukrainian workers, and so on. Likewise, the gap between established and non-established workers at a closer look presents itself in the form of a range of different relationships to various chains of production and distribution, and these relationships are under continuous change. Street traders in Lusaka selling domestic products are suddenly affected by low-cost products from young women workers in China, sold in Lusaka by Chinese traders, and so on.

Further studies of these complex relationships will improve our understanding, and help clarify that North/South or established/non-established must not be interpreted as two blocs standing in opposition to each other. It is the room between dichotomies such as North/South and established/non-established that provides space, where new ideas and identities can be formed and new forms of organization developed. Furthermore, there are other important divisions within the global working class. Class identities are complicated by race, ethnicity, gender, sexuality and nationality, interwoven with the structures of production and consumption of today's global capitalism. And workers are not only exposed to these divisions. Through their ideologies and actions they are part of the upholding or the reversal, the accommodation to or the transformation of these divisions. The gender dimension is particularly evident in several of the chapters of this book. See for instance Chapter 2 on South Korea.

Do we see today a new transnational working class in the making? When the embryo of a working class emerged more than 100 years ago in the then-industrialized parts of the world, a coherent class did not exist in advance: it was formed in a gradual process. In his famous work *One Hundred Years of Socialism*, Donald Sassoon states that 'the great intuition of the socialist activists was that they had identified a new political subject with definite political aspirations, able to produce a coherent set of political demands for both the short and the long term. If politics is an art, then this was one of its masterpieces' (Sassoon, 1997: 7).

The working class was created in action, step by step, and no advance blueprint could be followed. If workers are to conclude that they need to establish links of transnational collaboration, they must be able to see a kind of mutual advantage in doing so. Why would auto workers or teachers or bus drivers in different countries feel solidarity with each other? Why would they build up structures for mutual action together? On an abstract or theoretical level it may be easy to motivate transnational worker coherence against transnational owners and managers. But from a bottom-up perspective, what are the concrete gains for workers?

A study of the Driving Up Standards (DUS) campaign among bus drivers in Britain and the United States, employed by the same British-based company, shows different reasons on both sides of the Atlantic. Bus drivers in the United States, exposed to union-busting, wanted support from their better organized and share-owning British colleagues. They were also surprised and taken aback when they discovered that the bus company was not a US local firm, as they had thought, and that the company could offer better working conditions in another country. British bus drivers on the other hand expressed their own interest in saying that 'if they get away with it over there, they will soon try the same here'.

Among leading British activists their support also had an important ideological element, going back to ideals of international worker solidarity, which had been more predominant in the 1970s and 1980s (Anderson, 2007). Solidarity between workers has historically always been based on two components. Benevolence and empathy are good, but not enough; there has to be an element of mutual benefit. But mutual advantage is not sufficient; there also has to be a sense of common situation or identity. In the example of the British and US bus drivers their identity was that they were doing the same kind of job for the same company. In the 'Bolivia war on water', mentioned below, the 'new working class' that won the war were held together by their common need for affordable water, and the threat against this basic human right coming from a monopolizing transnational company. Bus drivers in Britain and the United States do not compete with each other for the same jobs. School buses have to go where the children live and the schools are situated, and the same is the case with a large part of all service jobs. Here the risk of underbidding between workers, and the need to counteract this through organizing and collective agreements, is still taking place locally and perhaps regionally or nationally. And yet, as the study of the DUS campaign shows, in so far as service workers are linked by TNCs, they can have good reasons to develop joint action across national borders.

The increased risk for underbidding between workers resulting from globalization is however much more obvious when it comes to production that can easily be transferred from one country to another. Often-cited examples are the transfer of the production of mass consumer goods to China and the outsourcing of call centres and IT services to India, but such competition between workers very often takes place between countries more close to each other both geographically and in terms of wage levels. All over the globe these increased possibilities of relocation, and the threat to relocate, are creating widespread risks of underbidding, where workers are forced to press down each others' wages and working conditions in face of risking losing their jobs. Here the stakes are higher than in locally based service production. On the one hand, it is more difficult for workers in different countries to agree and take action together, because at first sight they are actually competing with each other over the same jobs. On the other hand, the mutual benefit, if they can join forces, is much more direct. How can such conflicts be handled in order to build up mutual benefit and a sense of identity – the basis for solidarity?

POSSIBILITIES FOR MORE OFFENSIVE STRATEGIES TOWARDS TRANSNATIONAL SOLIDARITY

Possible future strategies should in our view take into account the following two principles. First, these strategies need to include short-term goals as well as medium to long-term targets. The former is important, because unless there are some immediate, tangible results, it will be difficult to hold together large alliances for change. The latter is, however, equally important, because unless the short-term goals are linked to more fundamental aspirations, it will not be possible to challenge neoliberal capitalism more broadly. Second, discussions about future strategies should not only focus on their contents, but also reflect on the possible alliances of forces able to promote and support these strategies.

The problems to be tackled are, therefore, clearly of a programmatic as well as organizational nature. Conflicts of interest and differences in world view within the global working class must not be swept under the carpet. How far can workers in low-income countries use low wages as a competitive advantage without being accused of 'social dumping' by workers from high-income countries? Is a trade system without customs and subsidies within the framework of the present world order 'fair', or is it imperialist? Is it possible to establish new transnational collective agreements, making it possible for workers in the North and the South to struggle together for a fair share of the result of production, instead of underbidding each other in competing for jobs? Only if workers in the North and the South can gradually through mutual dialogue develop common answers to these questions, only if they can develop some kind of common ground on what is fair and what is unfair, can they become a joint collective actor.

The programmatic challenges

In relation to short-term goals of future strategies, we may assume in principle that there are two roads to choose from: social dumping or fair and regulated competition, based on competitive advantages. Social dumping means unregulated underbidding between workers. When jobs are transferred to low-income countries, particularly where workers are not even allowed to organize, wages in high-income countries are depressed and unemployment grows. This has a negative effect on the world economy at large, affecting negatively workers in the North and South. Clearly, this scenario has to be avoided from a working-class point of view. The other road to go is fair and regulated competition. This road, however, is not analogous with the 'free-trade agenda' promoted by the WTO. Its basis would be strong national regulations of the labour market through law and collective agreements. It would include the right of national governments to regulate and impose conditions on foreign investors – in sharp contrast to the investment rules pressed for in WTO negotiations by dominant forces in the centres of capitalism.

The road defined as 'fair and regulated competition, based on competitive advantages' raises two related questions. What kind of regulation? And, what is fair competition? In relation to the first question an initial step should be rather uncontroversial. All workers should have the right to form genuine and independent organizations of their own. Basic requirements concerning prohibition of child labour and other forms of obvious abuse might also be fairly easy to agree upon. Indeed such rules already exist, and the problem is rather how to enforce these provisions effectively so that they are not just benevolent exclamations from enterprise leaders like the Global Compact. Global contracts concluded between TNCs and their union counterparts ('global unions') are a more promising way here.

This leads us to the second question: what is fair competition and what is social dumping? Where do you draw the line between socially progressive protection against underbidding, on the one hand, and protectionist practices on behalf of the privileged, on the other? And how do you discuss this among workers with conflicting interests? The challenge is to convince workers with a strong position (established workers, workers with special skills, workers in the North) to use their strength in the interests also of workers with a weak position when it comes to market and negotiation power. Only then can groups of workers in a more privileged position maintain the legitimacy of their own fight for improved working conditions and avoid the risk of being classified as a 'labour aristocracy'. To achieve this, a new vision, a new ideological project is necessary, able to bring together privileged and disadvantaged workers.

A distinction between accommodatory and transformatory solidarity, made by Rebecca Johns, seems particularly relevant to our discussion here (Johns, 1998). Accommodatory solidarity seeks to level out social conditions by supporting union organization and improved wages and working conditions in countries to which capital seeks to relocate production. This kind of solidarity is meant to improve the situation of exploited workers in low-income countries, while simultaneously reducing the stimuli of capital to relocate from high-income countries, thereby protecting the interest of workers in the centres of capitalism in retaining their jobs and wages. It does not, however, address the structure of capital investments and power, underlying uneven development between the centres and the peripheries of the global economy. It fails to address or take into account the situation of the unemployed masses and the vast groups of informal workers, devoid of any kind of contract.

Transformatory solidarity on the other hand seeks to go beyond worker rights and corporate responsibility, to address job creation in a wide sense as well as the roots of uneven development. It recognizes that the material basis for conflict between workers across space lies in capital's constant production of uneven development. In a short-term perspective one job more here means one job less there, and as long as there are not enough jobs to go round, workers in different locales will be forced to compete for these jobs. A transformatory solidarity must therefore, in our understanding, aim at a fundamental transformation of existing power structures, ideologies and trade regimes, in particular the dominant 'free trade' ideology which in practice functions to uphold and strengthen such uneven development.

In this transformatory perspective, therefore, trade issues are not a side-issue for economists to discuss, with unions being just one of many lobby organizations, perhaps asking for some kind of corporate responsibility. Instead a transformation of the dominant trade regime is a necessary condition for transnational worker solidarity. One of the potential weapons on the side of workers in such a transformatory perspective is the ownership and management of wage-earner pension funds, a weapon that might at least partially challenge the private ownership of the dominant means of production. Workers should establish that their retirement funds are not placed in companies that prevent workers from forming their own independent organizations. In view of the North–South divide, an international trade union machinery should be established so that decisions to that effect should be taken not only by workers having large sums in their own pension funds (core workers, often in the North) but jointly with more exploited groups of workers without possibilities of their own to pose such threats. Moreover, the discussion of economic democracy needs to be raised again. The knowledge-intensive style of modern production makes it increasingly feasible, if not necessary, that workers themselves take charge of the organization of production. Control over the production process, however, could then be regarded as a necessary first step towards the common ownership of the dominant means of production.

There is not a sharp line to be drawn between accommodatory and transformatory strategies for transnational solidarity. But it is obvious that it is mainly the former that has dominated mainstream international unionism so far, including the campaigns for global contracts and decent work. This is not surprising. Concentrating on such issues means avoiding the more controversial issues about trade regimes and the prevailing power structure in the world of today. Furthermore, a strategy which mainly aims at improving working conditions for those in regular employment is understandable as a reflection of the relatively weak status within the union movement of those outside employment or in non-established employment. As such, there is nothing wrong with accommodatory strategies and the possible gains they yield for some sections of the working class. Nevertheless, they must not be an endpoint in themselves, but a transitional step towards transformatory strategies, which will not only focus on the non-established, the informalized and the unemployed, but will also transcend fair competition among workers and improve the preconditions for real transnational solidarity by reverting uneven development and reversing the present trend towards increasing gaps between different parts of the global working class.

However, to achieve this requires a radically transformed global governance architecture. The key global institutions governing globalization, namely the United Nations, the World Bank, the International Monetary Fund and the WTO, need to be democratized and radically reoriented to meet the challenges of a global cosmopolitanism based on global social justice. Various proposals have emerged in recent years (see Bond, 2001; Cavanagh and Mander, 2004; Held, 2004; Stiglitz, 2006), which could form the basis of joint campaigns that unite the working class across North–South and core–periphery boundaries. It would also involve, in particular instances, forging alliances with democratic governments against the interests of TNCs, the chief beneficiaries of the current neo-imperialist system protected in particular by the United States.

Three organizational tasks

Who are the possible forces able to push these strategies forward? As we see it, there are three organizational tasks:

- establishing transnational links between existing trade unions
- strengthening organizations in the informal sector
- intensified cooperation between unions and other social movements.

First, existing unions, representing mainly core workers in their respective countries, must develop organizational arrangements to be able to negotiate and take industrial action with regard to a transnational counterpart and a production system that can easily move across national frontiers. National regulations and strong national unions should be the basis. States continue to play a significant role in the organization of the global economy, and the national level is where labour movements have established themselves most as significant political actors. Nevertheless, this will not suffice when it comes to preventing underbidding across national borders.

Transnational strategies are only at the beginning, but there are some early positive examples, which may be an indication of future things to come. To establish transnational regulations of wages, such as stipulating minimum wages for certain jobs, would be a much more controversial step than to regulate the right to organize. The most important and interesting example is probably the attempts of the seafarers and dockers to regulate wages and working conditions on ships bearing flags of convenience, the so-called FoC campaign by the International Transport Workers' Federation (ITF). Experience shows that the campaign has been to some extent successful and at the same time controversial. Effective blockades against FoC ships have improved working conditions for the crew, but tensions have also been obvious between the interests of Northern (such as Swedish) seafarers, trying to impose a fairly high minimum wage level, and those of Southern (for instance Philippine) workers, competing for the jobs, and coming from a nation and a region where unemployment is widespread and general wage levels are very much below those required in the FoC campaign (Segerdahl, 2004).

Other work-related issues, such as health and safety at the workplace and training, may be easier to agree upon than wages. In this respect, there are widely diverging conditions in different branches. But in general the working classes in low-income countries must have a right to compete with the comparative advantage they have: low wage costs. Maybe it is more fruitful in this situation to consider the coordination of wage increases rather than coordination of wage levels. Bieler and Schulten in Chapter 13 discuss the example of the European Metalworkers' Federation (EMF) and its attempt to coordinate national collective bargaining at the European level. This strategy acknowledges that there are different productivity as well as inflation levels in the various EU Member States. Hence, it would make little sense to argue for similar specific wage increases in all countries. Instead, the push is for national negotiators to ask for wage increases according to the same formula: inflation plus a productivity increase. This approach is, therefore, able to take into account national differences, while at the same time avoiding the underbidding of each other by different national labour movements. A similar argument could be developed concerning the global working class. Workers everywhere should demand wage increases corresponding to the increase in productivity and inflation, and they should then also develop effective ways of supporting each other in fighting for a fair share of productivity gains.

Another progressive example is the signing of a European Solidarity Pledge (GM Europe-EEF and EMF, 2005) by six European unions, the British union Amicus, the Belgian union ABVV, the German union IG Metall, the Polish union Solidarnosc and the Swedish unions Metall and SIF, in the face of the intention by General Motors Europe to organize a competition between five production sites over which three sites will be chosen to produce the new Astra, with the danger that one of the two other sites will be closed down.

The solidarity pledge will guarantee a number of minimum standards, agreed by the trade unions, which no plant will go below. In addition, they agree to adopt a joint negotiating strategy and a common code of conduct vis-à-vis the management of the GM group, which will stop General Motors from selecting sites on the basis of who would take the biggest pay cut, who would increase their hours and who would give up much of their holiday entitlements.

(Amicus, 2005)

Nevertheless, while this is a significant achievement, it is still easier to achieve such an agreement within Europe, where production cost differences are comparatively small, than in companies with production sites in both the North and South. Here, the initiative by the works council of Volkswagen (VW) may indicate possible ways forward. Cooperation between workers across the various production sites of VW in Germany, Brazil, Mexico, China and South Africa, as well as Central and Eastern Europe, is difficult because of the different national labour standards, the works council representative Thilo Reusch of VW in Wolfsburg/Germany outlined at the World Social Forum in Nairobi in January 2007.[2] Nevertheless, the VW works council attempts to overcome these differences through the objective of improving the conditions of the workers in all production sites. In 1980, VW agreed to recognize trade unions in their Brazilian and South African production sites. In 1982 the working group InterSoli was established, which became the driving force behind further international cooperation. The most important success of this strategy of transnational solidarity was the signing of a social charter with VW in June 2002, which confirms social minimum standards across all production sites around the world. These standards include the right of workers to establish works councils, basic rules about wages and working time, as well as a commitment to equal opportunities regardless of gender, religion and social background of individual workers (IG Metall Wolfsburg, n.d.: 9).

The second organizational line of action is that organizations in the informal sector must grow in strength and capacity to take coordinated action. They could be like unions in their structure and task, as for instance the Korean movements of irregular workers (see Chapter 2). But they will also sometimes be quite different, because they may have the local government as their main counterpart rather than a group of employers, and they may have to resort to other types of weapons than those of traditional industrial action.

StreetNet International is a good example of a first step in this area. It is an international organization consisting of 25 affiliated groups which organize street vendors, market vendors and/or hawkers. Affiliates include the Self-Employed Women's Association (SEWA) in Ahmedabad, India; the Self-Employed Women's Union (SEWU) in Durban, South Africa; Women's World Banking in New York, and the International Coalition of Women and Credit in New York. In other words it is a truly international network. The goal is to exchange information on how to best organize people in the peripheries of the labour market so that they can represent their interests in the most effective way through local, national and international campaigns.[3] To push this agenda forward, StreetNet International organized, for example, a meeting on Collective Bargaining in the Informal Economy as well as Laws and Litigation Strategies in the street vending sector in Dakar/Senegal from 26 to 30 March 2007. As Pat Horn, the coordinator of StreetNet International, pointed out at the World Social Forum in Nairobi/Kenya in 2007, the organization of street vendors is a response to globalization itself in that it confronts the increasing casualization of labour markets. Importantly, different circumstances would require different forms of organizing in the informal sector, and these attempts should be mapped to illustrate opportunities but also difficulties.[4]

As has become clear throughout the book, trade unions are not necessarily the actors most suited to organize informal workers and the unemployed: that is, non-established labour. As a result, they either need to transform themselves internally, as for example the Argentine Workers' Confederation (CTA) (see Chapter 6) or they have to open themselves up to cooperation with other social movements active, for example, within the informal labour market. These alliances need to be based on respect for each other and without subordination of one to the other. Pat Horn from StreetNet International (see above) stressed the potential of cooperation with trade unions, provided they are prepared to adjust their internal structure towards being more open to organizing the informal sector.

Importantly, the need to build up organizational strength on the part of irregular or informal-sector workers is not only a question pertaining to the South. Who represents the 70 million poor in the European Union? Where are the uncounted millions of paperless immigrants in Europe or Japan organized? What about the homeless and those outside the labour market? An interesting example at the European level is Euromarches,[5] which organizes the unemployed across the European Union. It came into existence at the EU summit in Amsterdam in 1997 as a rallying point for a series of European marches against unemployment, and has continued since then to demonstrate at EU summits as well as hold counter-summits against unemployment, job insecurity and social exclusion. Among its demands is the call for a European minimum income, which is not related to the work an individual carries out (Mathers, 1999, 2007).

Third, as was indicated in the introduction, exploitation has now also increasingly reached into the sphere of social reproduction, leading to a whole range of new struggles around the protection of the environment, for example. These struggles can also be understood as class struggles, and in order to broaden the social basis of their resistance to neoliberal restructuring, trade unions must also start cooperating more intensively with this kind of social movement.

Clearly, if organized labour wishes to enjoy the solidarity of other social movements in their own struggles at the point of production, they need to offer active solidarity to struggles in other spheres of contestation. The 'water war' in Cochabamba, Bolivia is a striking example of the strength that unified action can bring. The groundwork was laid by the factory unions (Fabrilles) reaching out to the informal-sector workers. The activist group, which defeated the monopolistic privatization project carried out by a transnational water company supported by the government and the World Bank, was composed of tens of thousands of people from a broad spectrum of peasants, environmentalists, workers and other social movements. From a union perspective this type of struggle involves new alliances and new forms of leadership. 'We learned the importance of ... a transparent leadership and ... the mass mobilization of workers from both the city and the countryside .... with these conditions it is possible to defeat neoliberal policies and twist the arm of an indolent state', concludes union leader Oscar Olivera (2004: 126).

Apart from struggles against privatization of basic needs (such as water, health, education and transport), organized labour needs to actively support global campaigns that strike at the heart of the logic of neoliberal globalization, putting on the agenda a new form of globalization governed by the logic of people's needs. Such campaigns include the demand for a global social wage, such as a global basic income grant, which implies global taxation of various kinds as well as other mechanisms to divert the social surplus towards meeting people's needs (such as reforming the global reserve system based on the dollar, the cost of which to developing countries is in the region of $300 billion a year, according to Stiglitz (2006)).

This will ensure that the fruits of globalized production and ever-improving technology are redistributed throughout the global economy, and do not only go to particular enclaves of privilege.

Other important campaigns against the increased power of TNCs challenge the commodification of public goods and the destruction of the natural environment, which have an impact on the working class as producers, consumers and citizens. This affects particularly workers in developing countries, although ultimately the entire working class suffers from the global instability, suffering and insecurity caused by these developments. These campaigns deal with intellectual property rights and bio-piracy; global warming; debt forgiveness, particularly the odious debt incurred by authoritarian governments; global monopolies; banking secrecy; corporate governance and corruption; regulating global financial flows; and fair trade. The latter includes the enhanced 'special and differential treatment' of least-developed and middle-income countries, and thus reinstates the ladder to development that was kicked away by the WTO-imposed liberalization. Within Europe it is the European Social Forum, with its various meetings since November 2002, that has provided the basis of several joint initiatives between social movements and trade unions, including calling for anti-war demonstrations in 2003 and demonstrations to protect the public sector (Bieler and Morton, 2004b; see also Chapter 13). There can hopefully be many different patterns of such collaboration in different countries and regions as well as the global level.

In Chapter 14 Peter Waterman provides an assessment of the possibilities for union–social movement cooperation at the global level, pointing to developments around what he calls a 'new global justice and solidarity movement'. First signs of a new international initiative of this kind were also visible at the World Social Forum in Nairobi/Kenya in January 2007. In addition to the Decent Work initiative by the ITUC (see above), there was a group of more radical trade unionists and social movement activists, who focused on establishing a 'Labour Network on and in the World Social Forum process' (*Proposal for a Labour Network*, quoted in Waterman, 2007b: 4). Here, it is argued that in order to respond to the vicious attack on labour by neoliberal globalization, new alliances of forces are necessary, including unions, social movements and intellectuals. At the session Assembly on 'Labour and Globalization' on 24 January, a representative of the Italian CGIL public-sector union argued that while a common platform was not necessary, cooperation with social movements through the development of common aims and objectives had to be the way forward despite the differences between trade unions and social movements. A speaker of the New Trade Union Initiative, India pointed out that the working class had much to learn from social movements. The divisions within society, for example along gender lines, had to be addressed more effectively, and cooperation with movements that address these issues of discrimination was the way forward.[6]

In sum, these organizational tasks imply clear tensions for trade unions' strategies. Should they concentrate on the social partnership approach with employers, should they pursue a strategy of political unionism based on close cooperation with political parties and the attempt to gain power at the ballot box, or should they pursue more a line of social movement unionism, which may facilitate cooperation with other social movements? Are these strategies mutually exclusive or can they be combined in a productive way? Are there perhaps different struggles in different industries or different geographical locations, which may require a different combination of these possible organizational ways forward? These are issues that need to be discussed in different concrete situations, and it is unlikely that the answer will always be the same. However, one thing is clear. An intensified cooperation between trade unions and social movements is even more important when thinking about medium to long-term goals and strategies in relation to neoliberal globalization, which have the ambition to challenge the capitalist social relations of production more fundamentally.

CONCLUDING REMARKS

As we have argued above, in response to the challenges of transnationalization and informalization of production, the working classes and their organizations need to handle their internal divisions, including both the North–South divide and the division between established and non-established workers. The enormous tasks of forming organizations among the informal workers, and building effective organizational structures across national borders that can take industrial action against transnational companies, have not been accomplished yet. At the World Social Forum in Nairobi/Kenya in January 2007, there were two – in many respects contrary – strategies put forward as far as the future shape of transnational solidarity is concerned. One has a clear organizational basis, but looks back at the strategies of the post-war decades; the other is still in the process of establishing transnational links, but has acknowledged the wider, new implications of neoliberal globalization, and as a result, the requirements of a new strategy in response. In many respects these two strategies represent the wider, more general tensions of labour movements in the North as well as the South. What are the implications of these two strategies for labour internationalism and resistance to neoliberal restructuring?

Our argument is that while contradictory at first sight, they can be combined in a more unified way forward. First, while the Decent Work initiative can be said to be based on the social partnership ideology of a previous phase of capitalism, there are potential short-term gains to be obtained through it. The alliance itself is comparatively powerful, considering that the ITUC represents over 168 million workers in 304 affiliated unions in 153 countries and territories.[7] This cannot be overlooked when thinking about resistance to neoliberal globalization. Moreover, this initiative speaks to the concerns of workers around the world and provides the opportunity to garner support. If short-term gains are obtained in some industrial sectors in some parts of the world, then this offers the possibility to recruit new members and involve the rank and file more actively in struggles. However, while potentially significant in the short term, the Decent Work initiative must not be the endpoint of the strategy. It may not be able to reach even its own more social reformist goals without a strong ability to take on fights and engage in industrial action. Only if the Decent Work campaign is regarded as a first step towards a more drastic challenge to neoliberal restructuring can it actually mobilize, together with others, the broad popular forces that can transform global capitalism more fundamentally.

There are positive signs. As outlined above, established labour rejects the neoliberal rationale that currently drives globalization. It is this rejection that can provide a common basis for cooperation with the second group, consisting of radical trade unions and social movements. Established trade unions clearly need to restructure themselves internally, and this process has already started. Not only do they need to give a stronger voice to the rank and file, they also need to open themselves up to cooperation with other social movements. They increasingly recognize the need to accept that workers in formal, secure employment are not the only agents of resistance and mobilization for change. The very fact that the Decent Work initiative was launched at the World Social Forum indicates that established trade unions are at least in principal open to this form of cooperation. Provided they do this, however, a unified strategy with the second group may emerge over time. This would allow the broadening of the social basis for resistance against neoliberal globalization, and in favour of an economy where production is no longer organized around private ownership of the dominant means of production.

Importantly, this struggle requires a new historical subject, which includes traditional workers, but goes beyond them at the same time. The Labour Network initiative (see above) contains potential core principles of such a new definition. First, cooperation between unions and social movements is based on an understanding of the new dynamics of globalization, with exploitation being extended beyond the sphere of production into the realm of reproduction. The goal has to be the fight-back against TNCs and neoliberal restructuring, as a representative of the Norwegian Municipal Workers' Union declared,[8] but this struggle goes beyond demands for rights at the workplace, as demanded by the Decent Work Alliance. It also involves struggles related to amongst other things informal work, gender discrimination, the commodification of basic needs, land rights, environmental degradation and indeed the democratization of the national and global spheres of governance. It is this expansion of the agenda that makes possible cooperation with social movements operating in these areas beyond the workplace.

Second, this is then linked to a wider understanding of labour, which does not only include workers and the production of physical goods, but also extends to labour in the sphere of social reproduction (including amongst others the household and education), the latter being as much part of the global working class as the former. Moreover, as we have seen in the various contributions to this volume, the new historical subject of progressive, transformatory change is not limited to workers on established contracts, but also includes all those workers with unstable, temporary contracts at the periphery of the labour market, as well as those eking out a living within the informal sector, such as self-employed street traders and home-based workers. It also includes the dependants of those who work, including the unemployed and students. It is this new historical subject, based on a much broader understanding of the global working class, that may be in a position to challenge global capitalism successfully.

Is it naïve to call for a new historical subject capable of undertaking the necessary historical transformation and putting an end to the hugely destructive dimensions of senescent capitalism? Samir Amin reminds us that active subjects of this kind appear only at particular stages and for relatively brief periods in history, when a favourable combination of economic, political and geostrategic circumstances converge. Such moments, when potential subjects may or may not crystallize into decisive agents of change, have never been predictable in advance; who could have foretold that the nascent bourgeoisie of the Italian and Dutch towns marked the beginnings of a system of production and a ruling class that would be dominant for centuries (Amin, 2006: 240)? Today capitalism has built a world system producing growing inequalities within and between nations, a world system that can really be transformed only at the level of the planet. But such a transformation must inevitably start locally, nationally and regionally, in an open process that leads beyond the logic of capital accumulation. If a sufficient number of breakthroughs occur in a number of places over a concentrated period of time, they may snowball and radically overhaul today's dominant world order.

NOTES

1   'North' and 'South' do not strictly follow the geographical location of countries in the Northern and Southern hemispheres. By North we mean countries that have reached an advanced level of economic development, where unemployment is relatively low, and formal established employment predominates or is 'typical'. The South, by contrast, refers to developing or under-developed countries that are dominated by informalized, non-established employment and unemployment, such that formal, established labour is 'atypical'. Many countries formally classified as Southern, such as the East Asian economies, would now be regarded as Northern. Nevertheless, the predominant picture remains that of the developed countries being mainly located in the Northern hemisphere (Western Europe, North America, Japan and South Korea), although the 'South' is represented in both hemispheres.

2   Thilo Reusch at the workshop on 'Trade union responsibility in transnational companies', at the World Social Forum in Nairobi/Kenya on 21 January 2007. Participant observation by the authors.

3   See http://www.streetnet.org.za/index.htm, accessed 30 March 2007.

4   Pat Horn at the workshop on 'Towards transnational solidarity? Global Working Class Project, Part III' at the World Social Forum in Nairobi/Kenya on 22 January 2007. Participant observation by the authors.

5   http://www.euromarches.org/, accessed 02 April 2007.

6   Participant observation by the authors at the Assembly on 'Labour and globalization' at the World Social Forum in Nairobi/Kenya on 24 January 2007.

7   http://www.ituc-csi.org/IMG/pdf/ITUC_List_Affiliates_Nov._2006.pdf, accessed 24 February 2007.

8   Participant observation by the authors at the Assembly on 'Labour and globalization' at the World Social Forum in Nairobi/Kenya on 24 January 2007.

Bibliography

Adams, R. (2006) *Labour Left Out* (Ottawa: Canadian Centre of Policy Alternatives).

Adler, G. and E. Webster (1995) 'Challenging transition theory: the labor movement, radical reform, and the transition to democracy in SA', *Politics and Society*, Vol. 23, No. 1: 75–106.

Adu-Amankwah, K. (1999) 'Ghana: organizing informal sector workers', *Labour Education*, Vol. 3, No. 116: 1–14.

Akyeampong, E.B. (2006) 'Unionization', *Perspectives on Labour and Income, Statistics Canada*, August: 18–42.

Altman, M. (2005) 'The state of employment', pp. 423–54 in J. Daniel, R Southall and J. Lutchman (eds), *State of the Nation: South Africa 2004–2005* (Pretoria: HSRC Press).

Amicus (2005) 'European unions pledge solidarity against General Motors Europe's 'race to the bottom' (14 December) (online) http://www.amicustheunion.org/development/default.aspx?page=3253 (accessed 30 March 2007).

Amin, S. (2006) *A Life Looking Forward: Memoirs of an independent Marxist* (London and New York: Zed).

ANC (1994) *The Reconstruction and Development Programme: A policy framework* (Johannesburg: Umanyano).

Anderson, J. (2007) 'Stationary bodies, mobile imaginaries: transnational labour organising and the spatiality of class loyalties'; paper presented at the Department of Human Geography, Stockholm University, Stockholm, Sweden, 13 March.

Apeldoorn, B. van (2002) *Transnational Capitalism and the Struggle over European Integration* (London: Routledge).

— (2004) 'Theorizing the transnational: a historical materialist approach', *Journal of International Relations and Development*, Vol. 7, No. 2: 142–76.

ATTAC France (2005) 'Quel modèle social européen? Propositions d'Attac-France' (What European social model? Attac France's proposals), 26 October (online) www.france.attac.org/article.php3?id_article=6035 (accessed 20 August 2006).

Bagchi, A.K. (2004) 'Nanny state for capital and social Darwinism for the workers', *Indian Journal of Labour Economics*, Vol. 47, No. 1: 69–80.

Ballard, R., Habib, A. and Valodia, I. (eds) (2006) *Voices of Protest: Social movements in post-Apartheid SA* (Scottsville: University of KwaZulu-Natal Press).

Barbosa, A. F. (2004) 'O Mercado de Trabalho Brasileiro pós-1990: Mudanças Estruturais e o Desafio da Inclusão Social' (Brazilian labour market after the 1990s: strucutural changes and the challenge of social inclusion), paper presented at the Seminário Internacional Empleo, Desempleo y Politicas de Empleo en el Mercosur y la Union Europea, Buenos Aires Argentina (18–20 August).

Barchiesi, F. and Bramble, T. (eds) (2003) *Rethinking the Labour Movement in the 'New South Africa'* (Aldershot: Ashgate).

Basualdo, E. and Lozano, C. (2000) 'A 25 años del golpe. La economía argentina luego de la dictadura' (25 years after the hit: the Argentine economy after the dictatorship) (online) http://www.cta.org.ar (accessed 9 July 2007).

Bedard, E. (2005) 'Union membership in Canada, 2005', Human Resources and Social Development Canada (online) http://www.hrsdc.gc.ca/en/lp/wid/union_membership.shtml (accessed 9 July 2007).

Belluzzo, L. G. M. and Almeida, J.G. (2002) *Depois da Queda: A Economia Brasileira da Crise da Dívida aos Impasses do Real* (After the Fall: The Brazilian economy from the debt crisis to the real plan) (Rio de Janeiro: Editora Civilização Brasileira).

Bezuidenhout, A. and B. Kenny (2002) 'The social cost of subcontracting in the South African gold mining industry', in Third World Network (ed.), *Mining, Development and Social Conflicts in Africa* (Accra: Third World Network).

Bhattacherjee, D. (1999) 'Organised labour and economic liberalisation in India: past, present and future', Labour and Society Programme, Discussion Paper No. DP/105/1999 (Geneva: ILO).

Bhorat, H. and Kanbur, R. (eds) (2006) *Poverty and Policy in Post-Apartheid South Africa* (Pretoria: HSRC Press).

Bieler, A. (2000) *Globalisation and Enlargement of the European Union: Austrian and Swedish social forces in the struggle over membership* (London: Routledge).

— (2005a) 'The "demise" of the Swedish model: globalisation, neoliberalism and class struggle', pp. 266–80 in B. Moss (ed.), *Monetary Union in Crisis: The European Union as a neo-liberal construction* (London: Palgrave).

— (2005b) 'European integration and the transnational restructuring of social relations: the emergence of labour as a regional actor?', *Journal of Common Market Studies*, Vol. 43, No. 3: 461–84.

— (2006) *The Struggle For a Social Europe: Trade unions and EMU in times of global restructuring* (Manchester: Manchester University Press).

— (2007) 'Labour at the World Social Forum 2007 in Nairobi/Kenya' (online) http://www.choike.org/nuevo_eng/informes/5380.html (accessed 30 March 2007).

Bieler, A. and Morton, A.D. (2003) 'Globalization, the state and class struggle: a "critical economy" engagement with open Marxism',

British Journal of Politics and International Relations, Vol. 5, No. 4: 467–99.

— (2004a) 'A critical theory route to hegemony, world order and historical change: neo-Gramscian perspectives in international relations', *Capital & Class*, No. 82: 85–113.

— (2004b) '"Another Europe is Possible"? Labour and social movements at the European Social Forum', *Globalizations*, Vol. 1, No. 2: 303–25.

Bieling, H.-J. and Schulten, T. (2003) '"Competitive restructuring" and industrial relations within the European Union: corporatist involvement and beyond', pp. 231–59 in A.W. Cafruny and M. Ryner (eds), *A Ruined Fortress? Neoliberal hegemony and transformation in Europe* (Lanham, Md: Rowman & Littlefield).

Bienkowski, W. (1981) *Theory and Reality: The development of social systems* (London/New York: Allison & Busby).

Bispinck, R. (2006) 'Abschied vom Flächentarifvertrag? Der Umbruch in der deutschen Tariflandschaft', pp. 39–66 in *WSI Tarifhandbuch* (Farewell to the Sectoral Collective Agreement? German collective bargaining in transition) (Frankfurt am Main: Bund-Verlag).

BMAS (Bundesministerium für Arbeit und Soziales) (ed.) (2006) *Statistisches Taschenbuch: Arbeits- und Sozialstatistik* (Statistical Pocket Book: work and social statistics) (Bonn: BMAS).

Bobrow, D. and Na, J. (1999) 'Korea's affair with globalization: deconstructing Segyehwa', in I.C. Moon and J.R. Mo (eds), *Democratization and Globalization in Korea: Assessments and prospects* (Seoul:Yonsei University Press).

Bond, P. (2001) *Against Global Apartheid: South Africa meets the World Bank, IMF and international finance* (Cape Town: UCT Press).

— (2005) *Elite Transition: From apartheid to neo-liberalism in SA* (Scottsville: UKZN Press).

Bormann, S., Deckwirth, C. and Teepe, S. (2005) *Grenzenlos billig? Globalisierung und Discountierung im Einzelhandel* (Low Prizes Without Limits? Globalization and hard discounting in retail) (Berlin: WEED).

Bremme, P., Fürniss, U. and Meinecke, U. (eds) (2007) *Never Work Alone. Organizing – ein Zukunftsmodell für Gewerkschaften* (Organizing: A model for trade union renewal) (Hamburg: VSA).

Broughton, A. (2002) 'Social partners sign teleworking accord' (online) www.eiro.eurofound.eu.int/2002/07/feature/eu0207204f.html (accessed 14 February 2003).

— (2004) 'Social partners sign work-related stress agreement' (online) www.eiro.eurofound.eu.int/2004/10/feature/eu0410206f.html (accessed 27 October 2004).

Bryceson, D. and Potts, D. (eds) (2006) *African Urban Economies: Viability, vitality or vitiation* (Hampshire: Palgrave Macmillan).

Buhlungu, S. (ed.) (2006) *Trade Unions and Democracy: COSATU workers' political attitudes in South Africa* (Pretoria: HSRC Press).

Bundesagentur für Arbeit (2006a) 'Der Arbeits- und Ausbildungsmarkt in Deutschland Monatsbericht Dezember und Jahresbericht' (Labour and

Training Market in Germany, Monthly Report for December and Annual Report) (online) http://www.pub.arbeitsamt.de/hst/services/ statistik/000100/html/monat/200612.pdf (accessed 25 April 2007).

— (2006b) 'Statistik: Ausschließlich geringfügig entlohnte Beschäftigte nach Ländern' (Statistics: marginal part-time (geringfügig Beschäftigte) as sole employment by federal states (Länder)) (online) http://www.pub. arbeitsamt.de/hst/services/statistik/aktuell/iiia6/sozbe/zr_geb_bld.xls (accessed 20 December 2006).

Burbach, R.; Nuñez, O. and Kagarlitsky, B. (1997) Globalization and its Discontents: The rise of postmodern socialisms (London/Chicago: Pluto Press).

Canadian Labour Congress (CLC) (2002) Aboriginal People's Representation in the Canadian Labour Movement (Ottawa: CLC).

Cardoso Jr, J.C. (1999) 'Estrutura Setorial-Ocupacional do Brasil e Evolução do Perfil Distributivo nos Anos 90', Discussion Paper, Brasília.

Carew, A. (1996) 'The American labour movement in fizzland: the free trade union movement and the CIA', Labor History, Vol. 39, No. 1: 25–42.

Castel, R. (1999) As Metamorfoses da Questão Social: uma Crônica do Salário (Petrópolis: Vozes).

Castells, M. (1996) The Information Age: Economy, society and culture, Vol. III: End of Millennium (Malden, Mass.: Blackwell).

Castells, M. and Portes, A. (1989) 'World underneath: the origins, dynamics and effects of the informal economy', pp. 11–37 in A. Portes, M. Castells and L. Benton (eds), The Informal Economy: Studies in advanced and less developed countries (London: Johns Hopkins Press).

Catalano, A.M. (1999) 'The crisis of trade union representation: new forms of social integration and autonomy-construction', pp. 27–40 in R. Munck and P. Waterman (eds), Labour Worldwide in the Era of Globalisation: Alternative union strategies in the New World Order (Houndmills: Macmillan).

Cavanagh, J. and Mander, J. (eds) (2004) Alternatives to Economic Globalization (San Francisco: Berret Koehler).

Chandrasekhar, C.P. and Ghosh, J. (2002) The Market that Failed: A decade of neo-liberal economic reforms in India (Delhi: Leftword).

Chen, M. (2004) 'Rethinking the informal economy: linkages with the formal economy and the formal regulatory environment', paper presented to the EGDI and UNU-WIDER Conference, Helsinki, 17–18 September.

Chinese Academy of Social Sciences (2007) Report on the Study of Chinese Peasant Workers (in Chinese) (Beijing: Chinese Academy of Social Sciences).

Chinese State Statistics Bureau (2006) China Statistics Yearbook 2004 (in Chinese) (Beijing: Chinese State Statistics Bureau).

Chinese State Statistics Bureau (2006) Summary of Chinese Statistics 2006 (in Chinese) (Beijing: Chinese State Statistics Bureau).

Choi, S.-R. (2000) 'The reality of Korean women workers and the activities of the Korean Women's Trade Union. The strategies of organizing women workers in the 21C: the experiences of the women's trade union and its future tasks,' International Conference Proceedings, 28 August–1 September 2000, organized by Korean Women's Trade Union and Korean Women Workers Associations United.

Chun, J.J. (2005) 'Public dramas and the politics of justice: comparison of janitors' union struggles in South Korea and the United States', *Work and Occupations*, No. 32: 486–503.

— (2006) *The Symbolic Politics of Labor: Transforming employment relations in South Korea and the United States,* PhD dissertation, University of California.

Clarke, R. (1994) 'US labour "missionaries"' – no blessing for Russian workers' (online) http://www.nathannewman.org/EDIN/.labor/.files/.internat/.russia.html (accessed 9 July 2007).

Coalition for Green and Social Procurement (2002) 'Proposal for a directive on the coordination of procedures for the award of public supply contracts, public service contracts and public works contracts' (online) http://www.eeb.org/activities/product_policy/Coalition-PP-April-2002-v3.pdf (accessed 10 July 2007).

Coates, D. (2000) *Models of Capitalism: Growth and stagnation in the modern era* (Cambridge: Polity).

Cohen, R. and Rai, S.M. (2000) *Global Social Movements* (London/New Brunswick: Athlone Press).

COSATU (2000) *Accelerating Transformation: COSATU's engagement with policy and legislative processes during SA's first term of democratic governance* (Johannesburg: COSATU).

— (2005) Declaration of the Third COSATU Central Committee, August 2005, Johannesburg.

— (2006a) *Secretariat Report* (Book 1) COSATU 9th National Congress 2006.

— (2006b) *State of Affiliates Report* (Book 7), COSATU 9th National Congress 2006.

— (2006c) *Possibilities for Social Change*, Discussion Document , COSATU 9th National Congress 2006.

— (2006d) *Naledi Survey on Workers* (Book 5), COSATU 9th National Congress 2006.

Cox, R.W. (1981) 'Social forces, states and world orders: beyond international relations theory', *Millennium,* Vol. 10, No. 2: 126–55.

— (1983) 'Gramsci, hegemony and international relations: an essay on method', *Millennium,* Vol. 12, No. 2: 162–75.

— (1989) 'Production, the state, and change in world order', pp. 37–50 in E.-O. Czempiel and J.N. Rosenau (eds), *Global Changes and Theoretical Challenges: Approaches to world politics for the 1990s* (Lexington, Mass./Toronto: Lexington Books).

Cranford, C. and Vosko, L. (n.d.) *Conceptual Guide to the Precarious Employment Module,* Gender and Work Database, York University (online) http://www.genderwork.ca/cms/displayarticle.php?sid=15&aid=26partid=958 (accessed 12 August 2006).

Cranford, C., Vosko, L. and Zukewich, N. (2003) 'Precarious employment in the Canadian labour market: a statistical portrait', *Just Labour*, Vol. 3: 6–22.

CRIAW (n.d.) *Women's Experience of Racism: How race and gender interact* (Ottawa: Canadian Research Institute for the Advancement of Women).

Cross, P. (2006) 'Emerging patterns in the labour market: a reversal from the 1990s', *Canadian Economic Observer*, February 3.1–3.13, 11-010-XIB (Ottawa: Statistics Canada) (online) http://www.statcan.ca/english/freeup/11-010-XIB/00206/feature.htm (accessed 12 July 2006).

Crotty, J. and Lee, K.K. (2005) 'The effects of neoliberal "reforms" on the post-crisis Korean economy', Political Economy Research Institute Working Paper Series No. 111 (Amherst: University of Massachusetts Amherst).

CUPE (2007) *Canadian Union of Public Employees: Economic Climate for Bargaining*, Vol. 4, No. 2 (online) http://www.cupe.ca/updir/Economic_Climate_Vol.4_No.2.pdf (accessed 17 July 2007).

Curto, J. and Rothwell, N. (2002) 'Part-time employment in rural Canada', *Rural and Small Town Canada Analysis Bulletin, Statistics Canada*, Vol. 4, No. 1: 1–13.

Damesin, R. and Denis, J.-M. (2005) 'SUD trade unions: the new organisations trying to conquer the French trade union scene', *Capital & Class*, No. 86: 17–37.

De Gennaro, V. (2001) 'Transiciones políticas y procesos de recomposición sindical en Argentina' (Political transitions and trade union recomposition in Argentina), in Enrique de la Garza Toledo (ed.), *Los sindicatos frente a los procesos de transición política* (Trade unions at the forefront of political transition processes) (Buenos Aires: CLACSO) (online) http://www.clacso.org (accessed 9 July 2007).

Deppe, F. (2003) 'Die Gewerkschaften und der "Euro-Kapitalismus"' (Trade unions and 'EURO-Capitalism'), pp. 169–95 in M. Beckmann, H.-J. Bieling and F. Deppe (eds), *'Euro-Kapitalismus' und globale politische Ökonomie* (Euro-Capitalism and Global Political Economy) (Hamburg: VSA).

Deutsche Bundesbank (2005) 'Rascher Wandel der Erwerbsarbeit' (Rapid change in employment), *Deutsche Bundesbank Monatsbericht* (Deutsche Bank Monthly Report), July, 15–27.

— (2006) 'Die deutschen Direktinvestitionsbeziehungen mit dem Ausland: neuere Entwicklungstendenzen und makroökonomische Auswirkungen' (German FDI: recent trends and macroeconomic consequences), *Deutsche Bundesbank Monatsbericht* (Deutsche Bank Monthly Report), September, 45–61.

Devenish, A. and Skinner, C. (2006) 'Collective action in the informal economy: the case of the Self-Employed Women's Union, 1994–2004', in R. Ballard, A. Habib and I. Valodia (eds), *Voices of Protest: Social movements in post-Apartheid SA* (Scottsville: University of KwaZulu-Natal Press).

DGB, Attac and VENRO (2002) 'Globalisierung gerecht gestalten' (Make globalization fair), joint paper, 5 December.

Dietrich, G. and Nayak, N. (2001) 'Exploring possibilities of counter-hegemonic globalisation of fishworkers' movement in India and its global interactions', (Portugal: Center of Social Studies, University of Coimbra) (online) http://www.ces.fe.uc.pt/emancipa/research/en/ft/fishworkers.html (accessed 9 July 2007).

DIHK (2006) 'Investitionen im Ausland. Ergebnisse einer DIHK-Umfrage bei den Industrie- und Handelskammern' (Investments Abroad. results from a DIHK-survey amongst the chambers of commerce), Deutscher Industrie- und Handelskammertag, Spring.

Dolvik, J.-E. (1999) An Emerging Island? ETUC, social dialogue and the Europeanisation of trade unions in the 1990s (Brussels: ETUI).

Dribbusch, H. (2003) Gewerkschaftliche Mitgliedergewinnung im Dienstleistungssektor. Ein Drei-Länder-Vergleich im Einzelhandel (Trade Union Organizing in Private Services: A comparative study in the retail industry of three countries) (Berlin: Edition Sigma).

— (2004a) 'European Migrant Workers Union founded', EIROnline (online) http://www.eiro.eurofound.ie/2004/09/feature/de0409206f.html (accessed 9 July 2007).

— (2004b) 'From boom to bust: trade union membership in eastern Germany in the 1990s. The case of retail', paper presented at the 5th European Social Science History Conference, Berlin, 24–27 March.

_____ (2004c) 'Laws on protection against dismissal and unemployment benefit amended', EIROnline (online) http://www.eiro.eurofound.eu.int/2004/01/feature/de0401205f.html (accessed 9 July 2007).

Dribbusch, H. and Schulten, T. (2007) 'The end of an era: structural changes in German public sector collective bargaining', pp. 155–76 in P. Leisink, B. Steijn and U. Veersma (eds), Industrial Relations in the New Europe: Enlargement, integration and reform (Cheltenham: Edward Elgar).

Eade, D. and Leather, A. (eds) (2005) Trade Unions and NGO Relations in Development (Bloomfield, Conn.: Kumarian).

Ebbinghaus, B. (1999) 'Does a European social model exist and can it survive?', pp. 1–26 in G. Huemer, M. Mesch and F. Traxler (eds), The Role of Employer Associations and Labour Unions in the EMU (Aldershot: Ashgate).

Edelman, M. (2003) 'Transnational peasant and farmer movements and networks', in M. Kaldor, H. Anheier and M. Glasius (eds), Global Civil Society (Oxford: Oxford University Press).

Edwards, P., Hall, M., Hyman, R., Marginson, P., Sisson, K., Waddington, J. and Winchester, D. (1998) 'Great Britain: from partial collectivism to neo-liberalism to where?', pp. 1–54 in A. Ferner and R. Hyman (eds), Changing Industrial Relations in Europe, 2nd edn (Oxford: Blackwell).

EMF (1998) 'Collective bargaining with the euro', 3rd EMF Collective Bargaining Conference, Frankfurt Germany (9–10 December) (online) http://www.emf-fem.org/index.cfm?target=/default.cfm (accessed 26 October 2004).

EPSU (2002) 'Services of general interest and the Convention on the future of Europe – you can shape the future of Europe!' EPSU General Circular No. 13 (1712/2002) (online) http://www.epsu.org/ Campaigns/sgi/gen13.cfm (accessed 17 June 2003).

— (2003) '2003: a crucial year for public services in Europe', letter by the EPSU General Secretary Carola Fischbach-Pyttel to all affiliated unions (online) http://www.epsu.org/gen1.cfm (accessed 30 January 2003).

ETUC (2005) 'The case for Europe: shaping a strong and social Europe, November 2005' (online) www.etuc.org/IMG/doc/04-EN-Hampton Court-Booklet.doc (accessed 20 August 2006).

— (2006) 'Move Social Europe up a gear! Resolution adopted by the ETUC Executive Committee in their meeting held in Brussels on 14–15 March 2006' (online) http://www.etuc.org/a/2209 (accessed 20 August 2006).

EuroMemorandum Group (2005) 'Democratic policy against the dominance of markets: proposals for an integrated development strategy in Europe', Euromemorandum 2005, November (online) http://www.memoeurope.unibremen.de/downloads/2005_English_Eur omemorandum5.12.05.pdf (accessed 20 August 2006).

European Commission (1985) Completing the Internal Market, White Paper, European Commission, Brussels.

European Commission (2006) European Economy, Statistical Annex, Spring (online) http://ec.europa.economy_finance/publications/ european_economy/statisticalannex0206_en.htm (accessed 22 November 2007).

European Conference on Sex Work, Human Rights, Labour and Migration (2005) (online) http://www.sexworkeurope.org/website/index.htm (accessed 9 July 2007).

European Council (2000) Lisbon European Council – Presidency conclusions (online) http://www.consilium.europa.eu/ueDocs/cms_ Data/docs/pressData/en/ec/00100-r1.en0.htm (accessed 19 February 2003).

Eurostat (2006) 'June 2006 – Euro area unemployment down to 7.8%. EU down to 8.1%', Eurostat press release No. 103, 1 August.

Ewing, K. and Sibley, T. (2000) International Trade Union Rights for the New Millennium (London: International Centre for Trade Unions Rights and Institute for Employment Rights).

Fajertag, G. and Pochet, P. (eds) (2000) Social Pacts in Europe: New dynamics (Brussels: ETUI).

Falkner, G. (1998) EU Social Policy in the 1990s: Towards a corporatist policy community (London: Routledge).

Fernandes, F. (1987) A Revolução Burguesa no Brasil (The Bourgeois Revolution in Brazil) (3rd edn) (Rio de Janeiro: Editora Guanabara).

Fondation Copernic (2003) Europe: Une Alternative (Europe: An alternative) (Paris: Editions Syllepse et Fondation Copernic).

Franco, G. (1999) O Desafio Brasileiro: Ensaios sobre Desenvolvimento, Globalização e Moeda (The Brazilian Challenge: Essays on development, globalization and currency) (São Paulo: Editora 34).

Freeman, R. (2006) 'China, India and the doubling of the global labor force:

who pays the price of globalization?' (online) http://www.zmag. org/content/showarticle.cfm?ItemID=8617 (accessed 11 September 2007).

Friedman, S. (1992) 'Bonaparte at the barricades: the colonization of civil society', *Theoria*, No. 79: 83–95.

— (2005) 'Embedding the "developmental" state in South Africa', pp. 18–21 in O. Edigheji (ed.), *Trajectories for South Africa: Reflections on the ANC's 2nd National General Council's discussion documents* (Special edition of *Policy*, Vol. 18, No. 2) (Johannesburg: Centre for Policy Studies).

Fudge, D. and Brewin, J. (2005) *Collective Bargaining in Canada: Human right or Canadian illusion?* (Ottawa: NUPGE and UFCW).

Furtado, C. (1998) *O Capitalismo Global* (Rio de Janeiro: Editora Paz e Terra).

Gallin, D. (2001) 'Propositions on trade unions and informal employment in times of globalisation' *Antipode*, Vol. 33, No .3: 531–49.

— (2002) 'Organizing in the informal economy', *Labour Education*, Vol. 2, No. 127: 23–7.

Gamble, A. (2001) 'Neo-liberalism', *Capital & Class*, No. 75: 127–34.

Garver, P. (2006) 'Comments on Waterman' (online) http://www. nottingham.ac.uk/shared/shared_scpolitics/documents/gwcprojectPape rs/Comments_on_Waterman.pdf (accessed 17 July 2007).

Garza Toledo, E. (2001) *Los sindicatos frente a los procesos de transición política* (Buenos Aires: CLACSO) (online) http://www.clacso.org (accessed 9 July 2007).

General Motors Europe-European Employee Forum and European Metalworkers Federation (GM Europe-EEF and EMF) (2005) 'European solidarity pledge' (online) http://www.amicustheunion. org/development/PDF/solidarity%20pledge%20delta%20group-uk.pdf (accessed 30 March 2007).

Ghigliani, P. (2005) 'International trade unionism in a globalising world: a case study on new labour internationalism', *Economic and Industrial Democracy*, Vol. 26, No. 2: 359–82.

Ghosh, J. and Chandrasekhar, C.P. (2007) 'Economic growth and employment generation in India: old problems and new paradoxes', paper presented at the IDEAs International Conference on Sustainable Employment Generation in Developing Countries, University of Nairobi, Kenya, 25–27 January.

Gill, S. (1995) 'Globalisation, market civilisation, and disciplinary neoliberalism', *Millennium*, Vol. 24, No. 3: 399–423.

Gills, B.K. and Gills, D.S. (2000) 'Globalization and strategic choice in South Korea: economic reform and labor', in S.S. Kim (ed.), *Korea's Globalization* (Cambridge UK: Cambridge University Press).

Ginsberg, D., Webster, E., Southall, R., Wood, G., Buhlungu, S., Maree, J., Cherry, J., Haines, R. and Klerck, G (1995) *Taking Democracy Seriously: Worker expectations of parliamentary democracy in South Africa* (Durban: Indicator Press).

Glasius, M., Kaldor, M. and Anheier, H. (eds) (2005) *Global Civil Society 2005–6* (London: Sage).

Global Policy Network (2006a) 'Labour's Platform for the Americas' (online) http://www.gpn.org/research/orit2005/index.html (accessed 9 July 2007).

— (2006b) 'Labour's platform for the Americas' (online) http://www.gpn.org/research/orit2005/popular/platform-eng-low-res.pdf (accessed 9 July 2007).

Gobin, C. (1997) *L'Europe Syndicale. Entre Désir et Réalité* (Bruxelles: Éditions Labor).

Gorz, A. (1999a) 'A new task for the unions: the liberation of time from work', in R. Munck and P. Waterman (eds), *Labour Worldwide in the Era of Globalisation: Alternative union strategies in the New World Order* (Houndmills: Macmillan).

— (1999b) *Reclaiming Work: Beyond the wage-based society* (Cambridge: Polity).

Government of India (various years) *Labour Statistics in India*, Labour Bureau, Ministry of Labour.

— (2002) *Report of the National Commission on Labour.*

Grahl, J. and Teague, P. (1989) 'The cost of neo-liberal Europe', *New Left Review*, No. 174: 33–50.

Gray, A. (2004) *Unsocial Europe: Social protection or flexploitation?* (London: Pluto).

Gramsci, A (1919/1980) 'Workers' democracy', in B. Turok (ed.) *Revolutionary Thought in the 20th Century* (London: Zed).

Greenfield, G. (1999) 'Democratic trade union responses to globalisation: a critique of the ICFTU-APRO's "Asian Monteray Fund" Proposal', paper presented to the Hong Kong Confederation of Trade Unions, September (online) http://www.labournet.de/diskussion/gewerkschaft/greenf.html (accessed 9 July 2007).

Greenwood, J. (2003) *Interest Representation in the European Union* (London: Palgrave).

Grest, J. (2002) *Urban Management, Urban Citizenship and the Informal Economy in the 'New' South Africa: A case study from Central Durban* (Durban: Political Science Programme, University of Natal).

GTUC (Ghana Trades Union Congress) (2004) *Policies of the Ghana Trades Union Congress* (Accra: GTUC).

Guimarães, N. (2006) 'Trabalho em Transiçãp' (Labour in transition), *Novos Estudos Cebrap*, No. 76, São Paulo.

Guio, A.-C. (2005) 'Income poverty and social exclusion in EU 25,' in Eurostat (ed.), *Population and Social Conditions No. 13*, Statistic in Focus Series (Brussels: Eurostat).

Habib, A., Pillay, D. and Desai, A. (1998) 'South Africa and the global order: the structural conditioning of a transition to democracy', *Journal of Contemporary African Studies*, Vol. 16, No. 1: 95–115.

Hall, P.A. and Soskice, D. (2001) 'An introduction to varieties of capitalism', pp. 1–68 in P.A. Hall and D. Soskice (eds), *Varieties of Capitalism* (Oxford: Oxford University Press).

Hargrove, B. (2000) 'Open letter to progressive labour activists', 11 October (online) http://groups.yahoo.com/group/workersdemocracy/message/1403 (accessed 9 July 2007).

Hein, E., Niechoj, T., Schulten, T. and Truger, A. (eds) (2005) *Macroeconomic Policy Coordination in Europe and the Role of the Trade Unions* (Brussels: ETUI).

Held, D. (2004) *Global Covenant: The social democratic alternative to the Washington Consensus* (Cambridge UK: Polity).

Heller, P. (1999) *The Labor of Development: Workers and the transformation of capitalism in Kerala, India* (Ithaca, NY: Cornell University Press).

Higgott, R., Underhill, G. R. D. and Bieler, A. (eds) (2000) *Non-State Actors and Authority in the Global System* (London: Routledge).

Hirsch, A. (2005) *Season of Hope: Economic reform under Mbeki and Mandela* (Scottsville: University of Kwazulu-Natal Press).

Holdt, K.C. von and Webster, E. (2005) *Organising the Periphery: South African trade unions and a fragmenting world of work* (Durban: International Sociological Association).

Honda, K. (2005) 'Part timer no Sosikika no Igi' (The effectiveness of the labour unions organizing activities for part-time workers), *Japanese Journal of Labour Studies*, No. 544: 60–73.

Horn, P. (2003) 'Organising in the informal economy' *SA Labour Bulletin*, Vol. 27, No. 2: 43–5.

— (2007) 'Experiences of international organising', paper presented at the conference Informalizing Economies and New Organising Strategies in Africa', Uppsala, Sweden (20–22 April).

Hyman, R. (1999) 'An emerging agenda for trade unions?', paper delivered to an online conference on Organised Labour in the 21st Century (Geneva: International Institute of Labour Studies, International Labour Organisation) (online) www.ilo.org/public/english/bureau/inst/project/network/hyman.htm (accessed 9 July 2007).

— (2004) 'Agitation, organisation, diplomacy, bureaucracy: trends and dilemmas in international trade unionism', *Labor History*, Vol. 45, No. 3.

— (2006) 'Structuring the transnational space: can Europe resist multinational capital?' (online) http://www.uin.org.uk (accessed 29 March 2006).

— (2007) 'Labour markets and the future of "decommodification"', mimeo, Employment Relations and Organisational Behaviour Department, London School of Economics.

ICFTU (International Confederation of Free Trade Unions) (2000) 'Joint UN-ICFTU Statement on the Global Compact' (online) http://www.icftu.org/displaydocument.asp?Index=991209381&Language=EN (accessed 9 July 2007).

— (2004) 'Framework agreements with multinational companies' (online) http://www.icftu.org/displaydocument.asp?Index=991216332&Language=EN (accessed 9 July 2007).

ICFTU, WCL, ETUC, Social Alert, Solidar and GPF (2005) 'Decent work:

the heart of a fair globalisation' (online) http://www.solidar.org/
English/pdf/english%20WSF%2005%2017%20March.pdf (accessed 9
July 2007).

IEDI (Research Institute for Industrial Development) (2005) *Ocorreu uma
Desindustrialização no Brasil?* (São Paulo: IEDI).

IG BCE (2005a) 'Extension of the European Union and
globalisation/challenges to trade union co-operation', Motion adopted
by the Third Statutory Congress of IG BCE [English version]
(Hannover: IG BCE).

— (2005b) *Globalisierung sozialer Verantwortung. Soziale
Mindeststandards, internationale Rahmenvereinbarungen und
Netzwerke* (Globalizing Social Responsibility: minimum standards,
international framework agreements and networks) (Hannover: IG
BCE, together with DGB Bildungswerk, Düsseldorf and Observatório
Social Europa, Amsterdam).

IG Metall (2005) *Soziale Verantwortung konkret. Regeln für multinationale
Konzerne* (Social Responsibility in Practice: Rules for transnational
corporations) (Frankfurt a. M.: IG Metall, together with DGB
Bildungswerk, Düsseldorf and Observatório Social Europa,
Amsterdam).

IG Metall Wolfsburg (n.d.) '20 Jahre "Internationale Solidarität" in
Wolfsburg' (20 years of international solidarity in Wolfsburg) (online)
http://www.igmetall-wob.de/arbeitskreise/interSoli/
Geschichte_InterSoli_WOB.pdf (accessed 30 March 2007).

ILO (2002a) *Women and Men in the Informal Economy: A statistical
picture* (Geneva: ILO).

— (2002b) *Unprotected Labour: What role for unions in the informal
economy?* (Geneva: ILO).

— (2004) 'A fair globalisation: creating opportunities for all' (online)
http://www.ilo.org/public/english/wcsdg/docs/report.pdf (accessed 9
July 2007).

— (2005) *World Employment Report 2004–05* (Geneva: ILO).

— (2007a) *African Employment Trends* (Geneva: ILO).

— (2007b) *Global Employment Trends Brief* (Geneva: ILO).

Ipsos (2004) 'Globalisierung der Arbeitswelt' (Globalization of the working
world), Summary of a survey carried out in July 2004 (online)
http://www.ipsos.de/downloads/news/FinancialTimes/Ipsos-
Globalisierung-der-Arbeitswelt-Juli04.pdf, (acccessed 9 July 2007).

— (2006) 'Trend Monitor Globalisierung – Deutsche pessimistisch' (Trend-
Monitor Globalization – Germans pessimistic), press release, 2 June
(online) http://www.ipsos.de/default.asp?c=234 (accessed 9 July 2007).

ITF (2005) 'Competition gone mad', *Transport International*, No. 20: 23–4.

ITUC (2007) 'Decent Work Campaign Launched in Nairobi' (online)
http://www.ituc-csi.org/spip.php?article583 (accessed 13 February
2007).

ITWF (International Transport Workers Federation) (2002) *Globalising
Solidarity Manual* (online) http://www.itfglobal.org/files/seealsodocs/
ENG/974/globalisingsolidarity.pdf (accessed 9 July 2007).

Jackson, A. (2002) *Is Work Working for Workers of Colour?* Research Paper No. 1 (Ottawa: Canadian Labour Congress).

— (2004) *Gender Inequality and Precarious Work: Exploring the impact of unions through the Gender and Work Database*, Research Paper No. 31 (Ottawa: Canadian Labour Congress).

— (2006) 'Rowing against the tide: the struggle to raise union density in a hostile environment', Canadian Labour Congress (online) http://canadianlabour.ca/index.php/Role_of_Unions/899 (accessed 9 July 2007).

Jackson, A. and Schetagne, S. (2003) *Solidarity Forever? An analysis of changes in union density*, Research Paper No. 25 (Ottawa: Canadian Labour Congress) (online) http://canadianlabour.ca/index.php/confernce_res/493 (accessed 9 July 2007).

Jacobi, O. , Keller, B. and Müller-Jentsch, W. (1998) 'Germany: facing new challenges', pp. 190–238 in A. Ferner and R. Hyman (eds), *Changing Industrial Relations in Europe*, 2nd edn (Oxford: Blackwell).

Jakobsen, K. (2001) 'Rethinking the International Confederation of Free Trade Unions and its Inter-American regional organisation', in P. Waterman and J. Wills (eds), *Place, Space and the New Labour Internationalisms* (Oxford: Blackwell).

Japan SB-MIAC (Statistics Bureau, Ministry of Internal Affairs and Communications) *Labour Force Survey*.

Jenkins, R., Pearson, R. and Seyfang, G. (eds) (2002) *Corporate Responsibility and Labour Rights* (London: Earthscan).

Jeong, J. (2005) 'Diversity in union security among enterprise unions: cases of Korean metal firms from a micro-socioeconomic perspective', *Journal of Industrial Relations*, No. 47: 43–61.

Jespen, M. and Pascual, A.S. (2005) 'The European Social Model: an exercise in deconstruction', *Journal of European Social Policy*, Vol. 15, No. 3: 231–45.

John, J. and Chenoy, A. (eds) (1996) *Labour, Environment and Globalisation: Social clause in multilateral trade agreements – a Southern response* (New Delhi: Centre for Education and Communication).

Johns, R. (1998) 'Bridging the gap between class and space: U.S. worker solidarity with Guatemala', *Economic Geography*, Vol. 74, No. 3: 252–71.

Jones, E. (2002) *The Politics of Economic and Monetary Union* (Lanham/Md: Rowman & Littlefield).

Judge, A. (2001) '"Globalisation": the UN's "safe haven" for the world's marginalised – the global compact with multinational corporations as the UN's "final solution"' (online) http://laetusinpraesens.org/docs/globcomp.php (accessed 9 July 2007).

Justice, D. (2002) 'The international trade union movement and the new codes of conduct', in R. Jenkins, R. Pearson and G. Seyfang (eds), *Corporate Responsibility and Labour Rights* (London: Earthscan).

Kalina, T. and Voss-Dahm, D. (2005) *Mehr Mini-Jobs = mehr Bewegung auf dem Arbeitsmarkt? Fluktuation der Arbeitskräfte und Beschäftigungsstruktur in vier Dienstleistungsbranchen* (More Mini-

Jobs = More Fluctuation on the Labour Market? Turnover amongst the workforce and employment structure in four service industries), Institut für Arbeitswissenschaft und Technologiemanagement (IAT) Report No. 7.

Kalina, T. and Weinkopf, C. (2006) 'Ein gesetzlicher Mindestlohn auch für Deutschland?!' (A Statutory Minimum Wage in Germany?) IAT Report No. 6.

Kaplinsky, R. (2005) *Globalization, Poverty and Inequality* (Cambridge: Polity).

Kautsky, K. [1899] (1988) *The Agrarian Question*. Winchester, Mass.: Zwan Publications.

KCTU (2005) *KCTU Report on Recent Situation of Labour Laws and Industrial Relations* (Seoul: Korean Confederation of Trade Unions).

Keller, B. (2003) 'Social dialogues – the state of the art a decade after Maastricht', *Industrial Relations Journal,* Vol. 34, No. 5: 411–29.

Kenny, B. (2003) 'Labour market flexibility in the retail sector: possibilities for resistance' in F. Barchiesi and T. Bramble (eds), *Rethinking the Labour Movement in the New South Africa* (Aldershot: Ashgate).

Kim, A.E. and Park, I. (2006) 'Changing trends of work in South Korea', *Asian Survey,* No. 46: 437–56.

Kim, H.-M. (1997) 'Gender/sexuality system as a labor control mechanism: gender identity of Korean female workers in a U.S. multinational corporation', *Korea Journal,* No. 37: 56–70.

— (1998) 'Power and representation: the case of South Korean women workers', *Asian Journal of Women's Studies,* No. 4: 61–108.

Kim, S.-K. (1996) 'Big companies don't hire us married women: exploitation and empowerment among women workers in south Korea', *Feminist Studies,* No. 22: 555–71.

— (1997) *Class Struggle or Family Struggle? The lives of women factory workers in South Korea* (Cambridge UK: Cambridge University Press).

Kitschelt, H., Lange, P., Marks, G. and Stephens, J.D. (1999) 'Convergence and divergence in advanced capitalist democracies', pp. 427–60 in H. Kitschelt, P. Lange, G. Marks and J.D. Stephens (eds), *Continuity and Change in Contemporary Capitalism* (Cambridge UK: Cambridge University Press).

Kjellberg, A. (2003) 'Arbetsgivarorganisationer och fackföreningar i ett föränderligt arbetsliv' (Employer organisations and unions in a continuously changing working life), in von Otter (ed.) *Ute och inne i svenskt arbetsliv* (Outside and inside Swedish working life) (Stockholm: Arbetslivsinstitutet Arbetsliv i omvandling (Swedish National Institute of Working Life; Changing Working Life)).

Kohaut, S. and Schnabel, C. (2006): Tarifliche Öffnungsklauseln. Verbreitung, Inanspruchnahme und Bedeutung (Collectively Agreed Opening-Clauses: Diffusion, usage and relevance). University of Erlangen, Nürnberg, Lehrstuhl für Arbeitsmarkt- und Regionalpolitik. Discussion paper no. 41 (online) http://www.arbeitsmarkt.wiso.uni-erlangen.de/pdf/Diskussionspapiere/dp41.pdf (accessed 29 August 2007).

Kohl, H. and Platzer, H.-W. (2004) *Industrial Relations in Central and Eastern Europe. Transformation and integration. A comparison of the eight new EU Member States* (Brussels: ETUI).

Koo, H. (2000) 'The dilemmas of empowered labor in Korea: Korean workers in the face of global capitalism', *Asian Survey*, No. 40: 227–50.

— (2002) 'Engendering civil society: the role of the labor movement', in C.K. Armstrong (ed.), *Korean Society: Civil society, democracy, and the state* (London/New York: Routledge).

Kosugi, R. (2004) *Furita toiu Ikikata* (What is Freeter?) (Tokyo: Keiso Shobo).

— (2004) '"Furita" toha Darenanoka' (Who is the 'Freeter'?), *Japanese Journal of Labour Studies*, No. 525: 46–9.

Koun Rokyo (2006) *Kiseikanwa go no roudou jittai tenken ankeito chousa houkokusho* (Report of the safety survey on the consequences of deregulation and its effect on working conditions) (Tokyo: Koun Rokyo).

Ledwith, S. (2005) 'The future as female? Gender, diversity and global labour solidarity', pp. 91–134 in C. Phelan (ed.), *The Future of Organised Labour: Global perspectives* (Oxford: Peter Lang).

Lee, B.H. (2004) 'Solidarity crisis of Korea's labor union movement', *Journal of Asiatic Studies*, No. 47.

Lee, B.H. and Frenkel, S.J. (2004) 'Divided workers: social relations between contract and regular workers in a Korean auto company', *Work, Employment and Society*, No. 18: 507–30.

Lee, E. (2005) *How Internet Radio Can Change the World: An activist's handbook* (Lincoln: Universe). (online) http://www.iuniverse.com (accessed 9 July 2007).

Lee, W. and Choi, K.S. (1998) *Labor Market and Industrial Relations in Korea: Retrospect on the past decade and policy directions for the 21st century* (Seoul: Korea Labour Institute (KLI)).

Lee, W. and Lee, J. (2002) *Will the Model of Uncoordinated Decentralization Persist? Changes in Korean industrial relations after the financial crisis. The changing nature of the structure of collective bargaining: is 'coordinated decentralization' the answer?* (Ithaca: ILR/Cornell University).

Leibfried, S. (2005) 'Social policy', pp. 243–78 in H. Wallace and W. Wallace (eds), *Policy-Making in the European Union*, 5th edn (Oxford: Oxford University Press).

Lenin, V.I. (1902/1970) 'What is to be done?' in *On Trade Unions* (Moscow: Progress).

Le Roux, P. (1996) 'The state and social transformation' in J. Coetzee and J. Graaf (eds), *SA in Reconstruction, Development and People* (Johannesburg: ITP).

Lessa, C. (2005) 'A Civilização Brasileira como Sonho' (Brazilian civilization as a dream) in *Economia Brasileira: Perspectivas do Desenvolvimento* (Brazilian Economy: Development Outlook) (São

Paulo: Centro Acadêmico Visconde de Cairu, FEA-USP (Faculdade de Economia e Administração, Universidade de São Paulo)).

Lier, D. and Stokke, K. (2006) 'Maximum working class unity? Challenges to local social movement unionism in Cape Town', *Antipode*, Vol. 38, No. 4: 802–24.

Lindberg, I. (1999) *Välfärdens idéer – globaliseringen, elitismen och välfärdsstatens framtid* (Welfare and Ideas: Globalisation, elitism and the future of the welfare state) (Stockholm: Atlas).

—— (2005) *Den globala kapitalismen – och det nya motståndet* (Global Capitalism – And the new resistance) (Stockholm: Atlas).

Lindell, I. (2007) '"Glocal movements": the multi-scalar agency of organised vendors in Maputo', paper presented at the conference Informalising Economies and New Organising Strategies in Africa, 20–22 April 2007, Uppsala, Sweden.

LO (Landsorganisationen i Sverige) (2005) *Anställningsformer och arbetstider* (Forms of Employment and Working Hours) (Stockholm: LO).

Lourenço-Lindell, I. (2002) *Walking the Tight Rope: Informal livelihoods and social networks in a West African city*, Stockholm Studies in Human Geography 9 (Stockholm: Acta Universitatis Stockholmiensis).

Lovato, R. (2006) 'Voices of a New Movimiento', *Nation*, 19 June (online) http://www.thenation.com/doc/20060619/lovato (accessed 9 July 2007).

Lozano, C. (1999) *El trabajo y la política en la Argentina de fin de siglo* (Work and politics in Argentina at the end of the century) (Buenos Aires: Eudeba-CTA).

— (2000) *Escenario político, económico y social de la Argentina* (Political, economic and social scenarios of Argentina) (Instituto de Estudios y Formación de la CTA, Instituto de Estudios sobre Estado y Participación y ATE).

— (2000) *Fundamentos del Movimiento por la Consulta Popular* (Basic principles of the Movement by Popular Referendum) (Instituto de Estudios sobre Estado y Participación y ATE).

Luif, P. (1996) *On the Road to Brussels: The political dimension of Austria's, Finland's and Sweden's accession to the European Union* (Vienna: Braumüller).

Lund, F. and Skinner, C. (1999) 'Promoting the interests of women in the informal economy: an analysis of street trader organisations in South Africa', Research Report No. 19 (Durban: School of Development Studies, University of Natal).

Luxemburg, R (1906/1925) *The Mass Strike, the Political Party and the Trade Unions* (London: Merlin).

Macpherson, C.B. (1977) *The Life and Times of Liberal Democracy* (Oxford: Oxford University Press).

Mainichi Shinbun (2006) Bus untenshu no kakoku (Bus driver's hardship), letter from a reader, 27 February.

Malentacchi, M. (2005) 'Time for a change in Japan', *Metal World*, No. 3: 2.

Marais, H. (2001) *South Africa: Limits to change*, 2nd edn (Cape Town: UCT Press).

Marginson, P. and Sisson, K. (1998) 'European collective bargaining: a virtual prospect?', *Journal of Common Market Studies*, Vol. 36, No. 4: 505–28.

— (2004) *European Integration and Industrial Relations: Multi-level governance in the making* (Basingstoke: Palgrave).

Martin, A. and Ross, G. (1999) 'In the line of fire: the Europeanization of labor representation', pp. 312–67 in A. Martin and G. Ross (eds), *The Brave New World of European Labor: European trade unions at the millennium* (New York/Oxford: Berghahn).

Mason, P. (2007) *Live Working or Die Fighting* (London: Harvill Secker).

Mathers, A. (1999) 'Euromarch – the struggle for a social Europe', *Capital and Class*, No. 68: 15–20.

— (2007) *Struggling for a Social Europe: Neoliberal globalization and the birth of a European social movement* (Aldershot: Ashgate).

Mayekiso, M. (1992) 'Working class civil society', *African Communist*, No. 129: 33–40.

McSpotlight (2007) 'The issues, employment' (online) http://www.mcspotlight.org/issues/employment/index.html (accessed 9 July 2007).

Meagher, K. (1995) 'Crisis, informalisation and the urban informal sector in Sub-Saharan Africa', *Development and Change*, Vol. 26, No. 2: 259–84.

MHLW (Japanese Ministry of Health, Labour and Welfare) (1970–2004), Basic Survey on Labour Unions (Tokyo: Ministry of Health, Labour and Welfare).

— (1995–2005) *Monthly Labour Survey* (Tokyo: MHLW).

— (1999–2003) *Basic Survey on Labour Unions* (Tokyo: MHLW).

— (2002a) *Pâto rôdô no kadai to taiô no hôkôsei* (Status and Issues of Part-time Workers) (Tokyo: MHLW).

— (2002b) *Income Redistribution Report* (Tokyo: MHLW).

— (2002c) *Basic Survey on Wage Structure* (Tokyo: MHLW).

— (2003a) *Foreigner Employment Situation Report* (Tokyo: MHLW).

— (2003b) *General Survey on Diversified Types of Employment* (Tokyo: MHLW).

— (2005) *Labour Force Survey* (Tokyo: MHLW)

Micheli, P. (2004) 'Carlos Marx y los desafíos del Siglo XXI' (Karl Marx and the challenges of the 21st century), paper at 2nd International Conference, Havana, Cuba, May.

Michels, R. (1915) *Political Parties* (London: Jarrold).

Mills, C.W. (1948/2001) *The New Men of Power: America's labour leaders* (Champaign, Ill.: University of Illinois Press).

Monks, J. (2006) 'Plus d'emplois et de meilleur emplois. L'Europe a besoin de politiques macroéconomiques plus souples' (Lack of jobs and of good jobs. Europe needs more developed macroeconomic policies), *L'Economie politique*, No. 29 (January): 65–79.

Moody, K. (1997a) *Workers in a Lean World* (London: Verso).

— (1997b) 'Towards an international social-movement unionism', *The New Left*, No. 225: 52–72.

Morissette, R., Schellenberg, G. and Johnson, A. (2005) 'Diverging trends in unionization', *Perspectives,* Statistics Canada, Summer: 1– 8.

Morton, A.D. (2007) *Unravelling Gramsci: Hegemony and passive revolution in the global political economy* (London: Pluto Press/Ann Arbor: University of Michigan Press).

Mosoeta, S. (2001) 'The Manchester Road: women and the informalisation of work in South Africa's footwear industry', *Labour, Capital and Society*, Vol. 34, No. 2: 184–206.

Müller-Jentsch, W. and Weitbrecht, H. (eds.) (2003) *The Changing Contours of German Industrial Relations* (München and Mering: Rainer Hampp).

Naidoo, R. (2003) 'The union movement and South Africa's transition, 1994–2003', paper presented to a Centre for Policy Studies Seminar, Johannesburg, South Africa, 23 June.

Nakamura, K. (ed.) (2005) *Suitai ka Saisei ka* (Decline or Revival? Japanese labour unions) (Tokyo: Keiso shobo).

Nam, J.L. (2000) 'Gender politics in the Korean transition to democracy', *Korean Studies*, Vol. 24: 94–112.

Nambiar, R.G., Mungher, B.L. and Tades, G.A. (1999) 'Is import liberalisation hurting domestic industry and employment?' *Economic and Political Weekly*, Vol. 34, No. 7: 417–24.

Nippon Keidanren (1995) *Shin Jidai no 'Nihonteki Keiei* (The New Japanese Management of Time) (Tokyo: Nippon Keidanren).

OECD (2005) *Economic Outlook*, No. 78 (Paris: Organization for Economic Cooperation and Development).

Okubo, T. (2005) *Nikkeijin no Rodosijo to Esunisithi* (Labor Market and Ethnicity of Nikkeijin: Employment of Japanese-Brazilians in local industrial cities) (Tokyo: Ochanomizu shobo).

Olivera, O. (2004) *Cochabamba – Water war in Bolivia* (Cambridge, Mass.: South End Press).

Oliviero, M.B. and Simmons, A. (2002) 'Global civil society and corporate responsibility', pp. 77–107 in M. Glasius, M. Kaldor and H. Anheier (eds), *Global Civil Society Yearbook 2000* (Oxford: Oxford University Press).

Ong, Aihwa (2006) Neoliberalism as Exception: Mutations in citizenship and sovereignty (Durham, NC: Duke University Press).

Osawa, M. and Houseman, S. (eds) (2003) *Hatarakikata no Mirai* (Nonstandard Work in Developed Economies: Causes and consequences) (Tokyo: Japan Institute for Labour Policy and Training).

Owusu, F. (2007) 'Diverse strategies of Ghana Trades Union Congress to reach out to the informal economy', paper presented at the conference 'Organising in the informal economy and new organising strategies in Africa', Uppsala, Sweden, 20–22 April.

Park, W., Nho, Y. and Kim, D. (2004) 'Unions and the contingent workers: the Korean evidence' paper for IIRA 5th Asian Regional Congress, Seoul Korea, 24–26 June.

Patnaik, P. (2003) *The Retreat to Unfreedom* (Delhi: Tulika).

— (2005a)'The crisis in India's countryside', paper presented at the seminar India: Implementing Pluralism and Democracy, University of Chicago USE, NW, 13 November.

— (2005b) 'The judiciary and the empowerment of the people', Braja Mohan Sharma Memorial Lecture, mimeo.

Patnaik, P. and Chandrasekhar, C.P. (1995) 'Indian economy under structural adjustment', *Economic and Political Weekly*, Vol. 30, No. 47: 3001–13.

Patnaik, U. (2003) 'Foodstocks and hunger: the causes of agrarian distress', *Social Scientist*, Vol. 31, No. 7/8: 15–41.

Pereira, L.V. (2005) *Brazil Trade Liberalization Program*, mimeo.

PICIS (2001) *The Organizing of Women Workers and Their Struggles, Part 3* (Korea: Policy and Information Center of Internal Solidarity).

Pijl, K. van der (1998) *Transnational Classes and International Relations* (London: Routledge).

Pillay, D. (1989) *Trade Unions and Alliance Politics in Cape Town, 1979–1985*, unpublished PhD thesis, University of Essex.

— (1996) 'Social movements, development and democracy in Post-Apartheid SA' , pp. 324–52 in J. Coetzee and J. Graaf (eds), *Reconstruction, Development and People* (Johannesburg: ITP).

— (2006) 'COSATU, alliances and working class politics' in S. Buhlungu (ed.), *Trade Unions and Democracy: COSATU workers' political attitudes in South Africa* (Pretoria: HSRC Press).

Pochmann, M. (1998) *O Trabalho sob Fogo Cruzado* (Labour in the Crossfire) (São Paulo: Editora Contexto).

Pochmann, M., Guerra, A., Amorim, R. and Aldrin, R. (2006) *Atlas da Estratificação Social no Brasil: Classe Média, Desenvolvimento e Crise* (Atlas of Social Stratification in Brazil: Middle classes, development and crisis) (São Paulo: Editora Cortez).

Portes, A., Castells, M. and Benton, L. (eds) (1989). *The Informal Economy: Studies in advanced and less developed countries* (London: Johns Hopkins Press).

Portes, A. and Schauffler, R. (1993) 'Competing perspectives on the Latin American informal sector', *Population and Development Review*, Vol. 19, No. 1: 33–60.

Potter, R. and Lloyd-Evans, S. (1998) *The City in the Developing World* (Essex: Addison Wesley Longman).

Promberger, M. (2006) 'Leiharbeit – Flexibilität und Prekarität in der betrieblichen Praxis' (Temporary agency work – flexibility and precariousness at operational level), *WSI-Mitteilungen*, Vol. 59, No. 5: 263–9.

Przeworski, A. (1991) *Democracy and the Market: Political and economic reforms in Eastern Europe and Latin America* (Cambridge UK: Cambridge University Press).

Rakodi, C. (ed.) (1997) The *Urban Challenge in Africa* (Tokyo/New York/Paris: United Nations University Press).

— (1997a) 'Global forces, urban change and urban management in Africa', pp. 17–73 in C. Rakodi (ed.), *The Urban Challenge in Africa* (Tokyo/New York/Paris: United Nations University Press).

Ramos, L. (2002) 'A Evolução da Informalidade no Brasil Metropolitano: 1991–2001' (Evolution of informality in Brazilian metropolitan areas: 1991–2001), Discussion Paper No. 914, November (Rio de Janeiro: Instituto de Pesquisa Econômica Aplicada (IPEA)).

Rauber, I. (1997) *Actores sociales, luchas reivindicativas y política popular* (Social Actors, Protests and Popular (Mass) Politics) (Buenos Aires: UMA).

— (1998) *Una historia silenciada* (A Silenced History) (Buenos Aires: Pensamiento Jurídico Editora).

— (1999) 'Tiempo de Herejías' (Time of Heresies), *Pasado y Presente* (Past and Present) 21, 2nd edn (Buenos Aires: Instituto de Estudios y Formación de la CTA).

— (2000) *Claves para una nueva estrategia, construcción de poder desde abajo* (Keys for a New Strategy, the Construction of Power from the Bottom Up) (Santo Domingo: Pasado y Presente XXI).

— (2003) *Movimientos sociales y representación política* (Social Movements and Political Representation), 3rd edn (Bogotá: Ediciones Desde Abajo).

— (2005) 'Sujetos Políticos' (Political subjects), *Pasado y Presente (Past and Present)* 21 (Buenos Aires: CTA).

Reddy, S. (2005) 'Counting the poor: the truth about world poverty statistics', pp. 169–78 in L. Panitch and C. Leys (eds), *Telling the Truth: Socialist Register 2006* (London: Merlin).

RENGO (2004) *Rengo White Paper2005* (Tokyo: RENGO).

Riexinger, B. and Sauerborn, W. (2004) 'Gewerkschaften in der Globalisierungsfalle' (Trade unions in the globalization trap), *Supplement der Zeitschrift Sozialismus* 10 (Hamburg: VSA).

Rigane, J. (2000) 'Rigane, a fondo' (Rigane, in depth), interview. Revista *Nos/otros de ATE*, Buenos Aires.

Robinson, W.I. (2001) 'Social theory and globalization: the rise of a transnational state', *Theory and Society*, Vol. 30, No. 2: 157–200.

— (2004) *A Theory of Global Capitalism: Production, class, and state in a transnational world* (Baltimore/London: Johns Hopkins University Press).

Robinson, W.I. and Harris, J. (2000) 'Towards a global ruling class? Globalization and the transnational capitalist class', *Science and Society*, Vol. 64, No. 1: 11–54.

Rocha, S. (2004) *Pobreza no Brasil: Afinal do Que se Trata?* (Poverty in Brazil: How to explain it?) (Rio de Janeiro: Editora FGV).

Rogerson, C. (1997) 'Globalization or informalization? African urban economies in the 1990s', pp. 337–70 in C. Rakodi (ed.), *The Urban Challenge in Africa* (Tokyo/New York/Paris: United Nations University Press).

Rosamond, B. (2002) 'Imagining the European economy: "competitiveness" and the social construction of "Europe" as an economic space', *New Political Economy*, Vol. 7, No. 2: 157–77.

Roychowdhury, S. (2004) 'Globalisation and labour', *Economic and Political Weekly*, Vol. 39, No. 1: 105–8.

Ruiz, A. (2004) 'The question remains: what is the AFL-CIO doing in Venezuela?' (online) http://www.zmag.org/content/print_article.cfm? itemID=5074&sectionID=45 (accessed 9 July 2007).

Rupert, M. (2000) *Ideologies of Globalization: Contending visions of a new world order* (London: Routledge).

Ryner, M. (2002) *Capitalist Restructuring, Globalisation and the Third Way: Lessons from the Swedish model* (London/New York: Routledge).

Sachverständigenrat (2004) *Jahresgutachten 2004/2005* (Annual Report 2004/2005) (Wiesbaden).

Saka, Y. (2001) 'Gaikokujin Tanjunginou Roudosha no Roudosijo to Jigyoshonai Roudoryoku Haichi no Tenkai' (Labour market and labour management of unskilled foreign workers), *Journal of Ohara Institute for Social Research,* No. 515: 18–31.

Sakamoto, S. (2006) 'Kiseikanwa ga anzen unkou wo sogai' (Deregulation is hampering safe operation), *Gekkan Rodo Kumiai*: 58–61.

Santos, J.A.F. (2002) *Estrutura de Posições de Classe no Brasil* (Strucuture of Class Positions in Brazil) (Rio de Janeiro: Iuperj).

Sapir, A. (2005) 'Globalisation and the reform of European social models' (online) http://www.bruegel.org/Files/media/PDF/Publications/Papers/ EN_SapirPaper080905.pdf (accessed 27 March 2007).

Sassen, S. (1998) *Globalization and Its Discontents: Essays on the new mobility of people and money* (New York: New Press).

— (2000) *Cities in a World Economy* (Thousand Oaks and London: Pine Forge Press).

Sassen-Koob, S. (1989) 'New York City's informal economy', pp. 66–77 in A. Portes, M. Castells and L. Benton (eds), *The Informal Economy: Studies in advanced and less developed countries* (London: Johns Hopkins Press).

Sassoon, D. (1997) *One Hundred Years of Socialism: The West European left in the twentieth century* (New York: New Press).

SB-MIAC(1970–2005) *Labour Force Survey* (Tokyo: Statistics Bureau, Ministry of Internal Affairs and Communications (SB-MIAC)).

Scheuer, S. (2006) 'A novel calculus? Institutional change, globalization and industrial conflict in Europe', *European Journal of Industrial Relations,* Vol. 12, No. 2: 143–64.

Schmidt, V.A. (2002) *The Futures of European Capitalism* (Oxford: Oxford University Press).

Schulten, T. (2004) *Solidarische Lohnpolitik in Europa. Zur Politischen Ökonomie der Gewerkschaften* (Solidaristic Wage Policy in Europe: On the political economy of trade unions) (Hamburg: VSA).

— (2005) 'Foundations and perspectives of trade union wage policy', pp.263–92 in E. Hein, T. Niechoj, T. Schulten and A. Truger (eds), *Macroeconomic Policy Coordination in Europe and the Role of the Trade Unions* (Brussels: ETUI).

— (2006a) 'Einkommen ohne Auskommen – Zur aktuellen Debatte über den Niedriglohnsektor und die Einführung von Mindestlöhnen in Deutschland' (Income but no living – the current debate about a low-wage sector and the introduction of minimum wages in Germany), pp.41–50 in Wissenschaftliche Arbeitsstelle des Nell-Breuning-Hauses (ed.), *Voll prekär – total normal? Die Arbeitsrealitäten wahrnehmen, Jahrbuch für Arbeit und Menschenwürde* (Precariousness as Standard? Perceiving work realities) No. 7 (Aachen: Lit-Verlag).

— (2006b) 'Problemi e Prospettive della Politica Sindacale Europea' (Problems and perspectives of European trade union policies), pp.99–123 in Associazione per il Rinnovamento della Sinistra (ed.), *Quale Futuro per il Sindacato* (What Future for Trade Unions?) (Bologna: Futura Press).

Schulten, T., Bispinck, R. and Schäfer, C. (eds) (2006) *Minimum Wages in Europe* (Brussels: ETUI).

Schulten, T. and Watt, A. (2007) 'European minimum wage policy – a concrete project for a social Europe', ETUI-REHS European Economic and Employment Policy Brief, No. 2.

Segerdahl, M. (2004) *FoC-kampanjen som kom ur kurs* (The FOC campaign that lost its track) (Oslo: Nordiska transportarbetarefederationen, NTF (Nordic Transport Workers Federation)).

Seifert, H. and Massa-Wirth, H. (2005) 'Pacts for employment and competitiveness in Germany', *Industrial Relations Journal*, Vol. 36, No. 3: 217–40.

Seo, Y. (2004) *Industrialization, Globalization and Women Workers in South Korea, 1960–2003* (Lowell, Mass.: University of Massachusetts).

Silver, B.J. (2003) *Forces of Labor: Workers' movements and globalization since 1870* (Cambridge UK: Cambridge University Press).

Silvey, R. (2004) 'Intervention symposium: geographies of anti-sweatshop activism', *Antipode*, Vol. 36, No. 2: 191–7.

Sitas, A. (2001) 'The livelihoods sector: opportunities for unions', *South African Labour Bulletin*, Vol. 25, No. 3.

Sklair, L. (2001) *The Transnational Capitalist Class* (Oxford: Blackwell).

Socialstyrelsen (Swedish National Board of Social Welfare) (2006) '*Social rapport 2006*' (Social report 2006) (online) http://www.socialstyrelsen. se/NR/rdonlyres/6BA28164-0E48-4F40951B181A84A2E74A/0/ 20061111.pdf (accessed 8 November 2006).

SOKA-Bau (2006) 'Statistiken zum Urlaubskassenverfahren für Entsendebetriebe' (Statistics on the Leave and Wage Equalisation Fund of the German building industry) (online) http://www.soka-bau.de/switchbox.php?page=585 (accessed 20 December 2006).

South African Communist Party (SACP) (1962) *The Road to South African Freedom* (London: Inkululeko).

— (1989) *The Path to Power* (London: Inkululeko).

— (2006) *Bua Komanisi! Information bulletin of the Central Committee Of The SACP*, May (Special Edition).

South African Institute of Race Relations (SAIRR) (2005) *2004/05 South Africa Survey* (Johannesburg: SAIRR).

Southall, R. (2006) 'Introduction: can South Africa be a developmental state?' pp. 3–18 in S. Buhlungu, J. Daniel, R. Southall and J. Lutchman (eds), *State of the Nation: South Africa 2005–2006* (Pretoria: HRSC Press).

Spooner, D. (2005) 'Trade unions and NGOs: the need for cooperation', pp. 11–32 in D. Eade and A. Leather (eds), *Trade Unions and NGO Relations in Development* (Bloomfied, Conn.: Kumarian).

Statistics Canada (2006a) *Employment by Industry* (online) http://www 40.statcan.ca/l01/cst01/econ40.htm (accessed 9 July 2007).

— (2006b) *Women in Canada: A gender-based statistical report* (5th edn) (Ottawa: Statistics Canada).

Stats SA (Statistics South Africa) (2003) *Labour Force Survey, September 2003* (Pretoria: Stats SA).

— (2005) *Labour Force Survey, September 2000 to March 2005* (Pretoria: Stats SA).

— (2006) *Labour Force Survey, September 2005* (Pretoria: Stats SA).

Stiglitz, J. (2002) *Globalization and its Discontents* (London: Penguin).

— (2006) *Making Globalization Work: The next steps to global justice* (London: Allen Lane).

Stiglitz, J. and Charlton, A. (2005) *Fair Trade for All: How trade can promote development* (New York: Oxford University Press).

Streeck, W. (1997) 'German capitalism: does it exist? Can it survive?', pp. 33–54 in C. Crouch and W. Streeck (eds), *Political Economy of Modern Capitalism* (London: Sage).

— (1998) 'Industrielle Beziehungen in einer internationalisierten Wirtschaft' (Industrial relations in an internationalized economy), pp. 169–202 in U. Beck (ed.), *Politik der Globalisierung* (Politics of Globalization) (Frankfurt am Main: Suhrkamp).

Suh, D. (2003) 'Korean white-collar unions' journey to labor solidarity: the historic path from enterprise to industrial unionism', pp. 153–82 in H.J. McCammon and D.B. Cornfield (eds), *Labor Revitalization: Global perspectives and new initiatives* (Oxford: Elsevier JAI).

Sundaram, K. and Tendulkar, S.D. (2002) 'The working poor in India: employment – poverty linkages and employment policy options', Discussion Paper 4 (Geneva: ILO).

SustainLabour (2006) 'International Labour Foundation for Sustainable Development' (online) http://www.sustainlabour.org/ (accessed 17 July 2007).

Swilling, M. (1992) 'Socialism, democracy and civil society: the case for associational socialism', *Theoria*, No. 79 (and *Work In Progress*, No. 76, 1991).

Taylor, G. and Mathers, A. (2002) 'The politics of European integration: a European labour movement in the making?', *Capital & Class*, No. 78: 39–60.

— (2004) 'The European Trade Union Confederation at the crossroads of change? Traversing the variable geometry of European trade unionism', *European Journal of Industrial Relations*, Vol. 10, No. 3: 267–85.

Teelucksingh, C. and Galabuzi, G.-E. (2005) *Working Precariously: The impact of race and immigrants status on employment opportunities and outcomes in Canada* (Canadian Race Relations Foundation).

Thakur, C.P. (2007) 'Review of Indian labour policy and related legal framework', mimeo, Institute for the Studies in Industrial Development, New Delhi.

Theron, J. and Godfrey, S. (2000) *Protecting Workers on the Periphery,* Development and Labour Monographs 1 (Capetown: Institute of Development and Labour Law, University of Cape Town).

Tidow, S. (2003) 'The emergence of European employment policy as a transnational political arena', pp. 77–98 in H. Overbeek (ed.), *The Political Economy of European Employment* (London: Routledge).

Tsuru, T. (2002) *Roushi Kankei no Nonyunionka: Mikuroteki Seidoteki Bunseki* (The Nonunionization of Labor Relations: Micro and institutional analysis) (Tokyo: Toyo Keizai Shinposha).

Turner, R. (1972) *The Eye of the Needle: An essay on participatory democracy* (Johannesburg: Special. Programme for Christian Action in Society).

UN (2001) *World Investment Report 2001: Promoting linkages* (New York/Geneva: United Nations).

UNDP (2005) *Human Development Report 2005 – International cooperation at a crossroads: aid, trade and security in an unequal world* (New York: UN Development Programme).

Urban, H.-J. (2003) 'Perspektiven der Gesundheitspolitik im neuen Europäischen Sozialmodell' (Perspectives of health care policy in the new European social model), *Prokla – Zeitschrift für kritische Sozialwissenschaft*, Vol. 33, No. 132: 433–53.

— (2005) 'Wege aus der Defensive. Schlüsselprobleme und -strategien gewerkschaftlicher Revitalisierung' (Ways out of the defensive: key problems and strategies of trade union revitalization), pp. 187–212 in R. Detje, K. Pickshaus and H.-J. Urban (eds), *Arbeitspolitik kontrovers* (Work Policy in Discussion) (Hamburg: VSA).

Van Zyl Slabbert, F. (1992) *The Quest for Democracy: SA in transition* (Oxford: Penguin).

Vavi, Z. (2005) Address to the COSATU Conference celebrating Ten Years of Democracy and Freedom, Johannesburg, South Africa, 5 March.

Ver.di (2006) *Soziale Verantwortung in transnationalen Unternehmen?. Neue Wege zur Internationalisierung gewerkschaftlichen Handelns* (Social Responsibility in Transnational Corporations? New ways towards an internationalization of union action) (Berlin: ver.di).

Visser, J. (2006) 'Union membership statistics in 24 countries', *Monthly Labor Review,* Vol. 129, No. 4: 38–49.

Vlok, E. (1999) 'Being casual', *South African Labour Bulletin,* Vol. 23, No. 3.

Waddington, J. (2005) 'Trade unions and the defence of the European social model', *Industrial Relations Journal,* Vol. 36, No. 6: 518–40.

— (2006) 'The performance of European Works Councils in engineering: perspectives of the employee representatives', *Industrial Relations,* Vol. 45, No. 4: 681–708.

Wahl, A. (2002) 'European labor: social dialogue, social pacts, or a social Europe?', *Monthly Review*, Vol. 54, No. 2: 45–55.

Warda, M. (2000) 'Free trade and social responsibility', *Umschau*, No.10/11 (online) http://www.igbce.de/portal/site/igbce/menuitem. 22f2499a6b7e60f33b791789c5bf21ca/ (accessed 1 November 2006).

War on Want, Alliance for Zambia Informal Economy Associations and Workers Education Association of Zambia (2006) *Forces for Change: Informal economy organisations in Africa* (London: War on Want).

Warskett, R. (2001) 'Feminism's challenge to unions in the north: possibilities and contradictions', in L. Panitch and C. Leys (eds), *Socialist Register 2001: Working classes: global realities* (London: Merlin).

— (2004) 'Thinking through labour's organizing strategies: what the data reveal and what the data conceal', paper presented at the Gender & Work: Knowledge Production in Practice Conference, 1–2 October 2004, York University, Toronto.

Waterman, P. (1997) 'New interest in dockers and transport workers: locally, nationally, comparatively, globally – some real and virtual resources' (online) www.labournet.net/docks2/9712/itf1212.htm (accessed 11 September 2007).

— (1999) 'The new social unionism: a new union model for a new world order', in R. Munck and P. Waterman (eds), *Labour Worldwide in the Era of Globalization: Alternative union models in the new world order* (London and New York: Palgrave).

— (2001a) *Globalisation, Social Movements and the New Internationalisms* (London: Continuum).

— (2001b) 'A spectre is haunting labour internationalism, the spectre of the ghost of communism' (online) http://www.globallabour.org/prague_1968_the_last_late_short_spring of_the_wftu.htm (accessed 9 July 2007).

— (2001c) 'Trade union internationalism in the age of Seattle', *Antipode*, Vol. 33, No. 3: 312–36.

— (2004a) 'Adventures of emancipatory labour strategy as the new movement challenges international unionism', *Journal of World-System Research*, Vol. 10, No. 1: 217–54 (online) http://jwsr.ucr.edu/archive/vol10/number1/pdf/jwsr-v10n1-waterman.pdf (accessed 9 July 2007).

— (2004b) 'Trade unions, NGOs and global social justice: another tale to tell', pp. 161–75 in Craig Phelan (ed.), *The Future of Organised Labour: Global perspectives* (Oxford: Peter Lang).

— (2006a) 'Social movements and the Augean stables of global governance' (online) http://www.nu.ac.za/ccs/default.asp?3,28,11,2493 (accessed 9 July 2007).

— (2006b) 'Toward a Global Labour Charter Movement for the 21st century (GLCM21)' (online) http://www.nu.ac.za/ccs/files/GLCM21%20Mayday06.pdf (accessed 9 July 2007).

— (2006c) 'A new social unionism, internationalism, communication and culture: a sketch', Open Space Forum: The Bamako Appeal – a Post-

Modern Janus? (online) http://www.openspaceforum.net/twiki (accessed 15 September 2006).

— (2007a) 'The international union merger of November 2006: top-down, eurocentric and ... invisible?' pp. 450–8 in J. Sen and M. Kumar (with P. Bond and P. Waterman) (eds), *A Political Programme for the World Social Forum? Democracy, substance and debate in the Bamako Appeal and the global justice movements* (New Delhi and Durban: CACIM and Centre for Civil Society).

— (2007b) 'Labour at the World Social Forum, Nairobi, January 20–25, 2007: reviving and reinventing the labour movement as a sword of justice' (online) http://www.openspaceforum.net/twiki/tiki-read_article.php?articleId=334&page =1 (accessed 24 February 2007).

Waterman, P. and Timms, J. (2004) 'Trade union internationalism and a global civil society in the making', pp. 178–202 in M. Kaldor, H. Anheier and M. Glasius (eds), *Global Civil Society 2004/5* (London: Sage) (online) http://www.choike.org/documentos/waterman_unions.pdf (accessed 9 July 2007).

Webster, E. (2003) 'New forms of work and worker organisation: a Durban case study', paper presented to the Crisis States Programme Annual Workshop, Johannesburg South Africa, 14–18 July.

Webster, E. and Adler. G. (1999) 'Towards a class compromise in SA's "double transition": bargained liberalisation and the consolidation of democracy', *Politics and Society*, Vol. 27, No. 3: 347–85.

Wehr, A. (2006) *Das Publikum verlässt den Saal. Nach dem Verfassungsvertrag: Die EU in der Krise* (The Public Leaves the Hall. After the constitutional treaty: the EU in crisis) (Cologne: PayRossa Verlag).

Wetzel, D. (2005): '"Tarif aktiv" – "besser statt billiger" Leitprojekte für eine veränderte Praxis' (Active collective bargaining' – 'Better instead of only cheaper' lead-projects for an alternative practice), pp. 161–71 in R. Detje, K. Pickshaus and H.-J. Urban (eds), *Arbeitspolitik kontrovers* (Work Policies in Discussion) (Hamburg: VSA).

WILL (Workers Initiatives for a Lasting Legacy) (2006) *Workers Initiatives for a Lasting Legacy* (online) http://www.will2006.org/index_noflash.php (accessed 17 July 2007).

Williams, M. (2002) 'Building democratic socialism in Kerala', *African Communist,* First Quarter: 20–2.

Working USA (2001) 'Labour rights in the global economy' (Special Focus), *WorkingUSA*, Vol. 5, No. 1: 3–86.

World March of Women (2004) 'Women's Global Charter for Humanity' (online) http://www.worldmarchofwomen.org/qui_nous_sommes/charte/en (accessed 17 July 2007).

World Social Forum on Migration (WSFM) (2006) Website (online) http://www.fsmm2006.org/en/index.php (accessed 11 September 2007).

World Trade Organization (2004) *Trade Policy Review – Brazil* (Geneva: WTO).

Yorimitsu, M. (2005) *Nihon no Imin Seisaku wo Kangaeru* (Considerations on Immigration Policy in Japan) (Tokyo: Akashi Shoten).

Zeltzer, S. (2006) 'First Working-Class Film and Video Festival in Turkey a "resounding success"' (online) http://mrzine.monthlyreview.org/zeltzer 230506.html (accessed 9 July 2007).

Zenjiko (2006) http://www.zenjiko.or.jp (accessed 24 November 2006).

Zhou, D. (2005) *Will for Survival: An anthropological study of migrant rural labour* (in Chinese) (Zhongshan: Zhongshan University Press).

Contributors

Samir Amin is head of the World Forum for Alternatives (WFA), which was one of the initiators of the World Social Forum. He has been a professor of economics at the Universities of Poitiers, Dakar and Paris, and he was head of the Institut Africain de Développement Économique et de Planification (IDEP) from 1970 to 1980 and a Director of the Third World Forum in Dakar from 1980 onwards. He has written more than 30 books including *Imperialism & Unequal Development, Specters of Capitalism: A critique of current intellectual fashions, Obsolescent Capitalism: Contemporary politics and global disorder* and *The Liberal Virus*. His autobiography was published in October 2006 by Zed Books.

Alexandre de Freitas Barbosa is a senior researcher with the Instituto Observatorio Social (IOS) – an NGO dealing with labour issues, based in Brazil. He also holds a master's degree in economic history from the Department of History of USP (State University of São Paulo) and a doctorate in labour economics from the Institute of Economics of UNICAMP (State University of Campinas).

Geoff Bickerton is director of research for the Canadian Union of Postal Workers. He is also labour columnist for *Canadian Dimension* magazine.

Andreas Bieler is professor of political economy and fellow of the Centre for the Study of Social and Global Justice (CSSGJ) in the School of Politics and International Relations, University of Nottingham/UK. His research is predominantly focused on understanding the current struggle over the future economic-political model of the European Union and the possibilities for resisting neo-liberal restructuring. He is author of *Globalisation and Enlargement of the European Union* (Routledge, 2000) as well as *The Struggle for a Social Europe: Trade unions and EMU in times of global restructuring* (Manchester University Press, 2006).

Jennifer Jihye Chun is assistant professor in the Department of Sociology at the University of British Columbia, Canada. Her major areas of research include comparative labour movements, global political economy, and the interlinkages among race, gender and migration. She has authored journal articles in *Work and Occupations* (2005) and *Economy and Society* (2003). Her PhD thesis investigates new forms of labour organizing for immigrant and women workers in the United States and South Korea in the context of neoliberal globalization.

Heiner Dribbusch is senior researcher with the Institute of Economic and Social Research (WSI) within the Hans-Böckler-Foundation in Düsseldorf, Germany. His major research areas are national and international industrial relations and trade unionism, with a special focus on the developments of structural and associational power of employees. His most recent publication is 'The end of an era: structural changes in German public sector collective bargaining' in *Industrial Relations in the New Europe: Enlargement, Integration and Reform*, (ed. P. Leisink et al., Cheltenham: Edgar Elgar 2007) (together with Thorsten Schulten). He is co-editor of *Strikes Around the World 1968–2005: Case studies of 15 countries* (Aksant, forthcoming).

Praveen Jha is a faculty member at the Centre for Economic Studies and Planning, Jawaharlal Nehru University, New Delhi, India. He is also a visiting faculty at the University of Bremen, Germany. His major areas of interest include labour and agriculture with special focus on the developing countries. He has authored/edited five books and has published several articles in different journals. He has been the honorary economic advisor to the Centre for Budget and Governance Accountability, New Delhi since its inception.

Kjeld Jakobsen is a consultant on international relations and former international secretary of the Central Trade Union Confederation (Brazil) as well as of São Paulo's Municipality. He was Chair of the Instituto Observatorio Social (IOS) in Brazil until June 2007.

Ingemar Lindberg is a former researcher and social policy adviser to the Confederation of Swedish Trade Unions (LO) where he was responsible for the Social Justice Project 1991–95 and the main report to the 1996 LO Convention. He has written many books and articles, the latest being *Den globala kapiutalismen och det nya motståndet* (Global capitalism and the new resistance, Atlas, 2005).

317

Ilda Lindell is a researcher at the Nordic Africa Institute, Uppsala, Sweden. Her current research focuses on collective organizing in the informal economy in Africa, including links to international movements and relations with trade unions. She is the author of *Walking the Tight Rope: Informal livelihoods and social networks in a west African city* (Almqvist & Wiksell International, 2002), which deals with processes of informalization and how vulnerable groups are dealing with the changes.

Devan Pillay is associate professor in sociology, University of the Witwatersrand. A former political prisoner in the 1980s, he was a writer with the *SA Labour Bulletin*, editor of the journal *Work In Progress*, director of the Social Policy Program at the University of Durban-Westville, research director at the National Union of Mineworkers and a director of Policy in the Government Communication and Information System. He has published extensively in journals, books and newspapers on issues related to globalization, labour, politics, the media and social movements.

Isabel Rauber has a PhD from the University of Havana and is a scholar of Latin American social movements. She is director of Past and Present XXI, a member of the Scientific Advisory Council to the Cuban Workers Federation as well as a member of the Third World Forum and the World Forum for Alternatives.

Thorsten Schulten is a senior researcher at the Institute of Economic and Social Research (WSI) within the Hans Böckler Foundation in Düsseldorf, Germany. His research is predominately focused on European labour relations. He is the author of *Solidaristic Wages Policy in Europe* (Routledge, 2008).

Wakana Shutô is a lecturer in industrial relations at Japan Women's University. She worked for Yamagata University as an associate professor from 2000 to 2007 and was affiliated with the London School of Economics and Political Sciences as an academic visitor in 2003–04. She is the author of *Togosareru Danjo no Shokuba* (Keiso Shobo, 2003, in Japanese) which examines changes in industrial relations caused by the increasing numbers of women workers entering occupations customarily considered the domain of men.

Jane Stinson is senior officer in union development for the Canadian Union of Public Employees.

Mac Urata is a section secretary of the International Transport Workers' Federation (ITF). He heads the Inland Transport Sections, representing road transport and railway workers' unions worldwide. Prior to his arrival in the London headquarters of the ITF in 1997, he worked in its regional office in Tokyo for nearly four years. Before his involvement in the international trade union movement, he was a member of staff for international affairs in Shitetsu Soren, a Japanese public transport unions' federation, for eight years. Recently, he served as the workers' group secretary at an ILO tripartite conference on cross-border issues for international drivers.

Peter Waterman (London 1936) worked twice for the world Communist movement in Prague (mid-1950s, late-1960s) before becoming an academic specialist on third world and international labour and unionism. He edited the *Newsletter of International Labour Studies* in the 1980s. Since retiring from the Institute of Social Studies, The Hague, 1998, he has specialized in international labour and social movements, in both organizational and communicational terms. He has travelled, researched and published widely, most recently with *The New Nervous System of Internationalism and Solidarity* (in Spanish), Lima 2006. Much of his recent work relates to labour and the World Social Forum.

Wen Tiejun is professor at the Renmin University of China in Beijing. He is the founder of Common People's Education as well as Speaking for Marginalized Populations. He received the State Awarded Specialists award in 1998 and was deputy secretary-general of the China Society for Restructuring the Economic System in 2000. He was recognized by China Central TV with the Top 10 Economic Talents award in 2003 and became a member of the State Committee for Environment Protection in 2006.

Abbreviations

ACHIB	African Council of Hawkers and Informal Business
AFL-CIO	American Federation of Labour-Congress of Industrial Organizations
AITUC	All India Trade Union Congress
ANC	African National Congress (South Africa)
APF	Anti-Privatization Forum (South Africa)
Asgisa	Accelerated Shared Growth Initiative (South Africa)
ASSOTSI	Associação dos Operadores e Trabalhadores do Sector Informal (Association of Informal Sector Operators and Workers, Mozambique)
ATE	Asociación de Trabajadores del Estado (Association of State Employees Argentina)
ATTAC	Association pour la Taxation des Transactions Financiers pour l'Aide aux Citoyens (Association for the Taxation of Financial Transactions to Help Citizens)
AZIEA	Alliance of Zambian Informal Economy Associations
BEE	black economic empowerment (South Africa)
BIG	basic income grant (South Africa)
BMAS	Bundesministerium für Arbeit und Soziales (Ministry for Work and Social Security, Germany)
BMS	Bharatiya Mazdoor Sangh (Bharatiya Janata Party, India)
BNDES	Banco Nacional de Desenvolvimento Econômico e Social (National Development Bank, Brazil)
CAW	Canadian Autoworkers' Union
CCC	Class and Combative Current (Argentina)
CEC	Central Executive Committee
CGT	General Labour Confederation (Argentina)
CIS	Commonwealth of Independent States
CITU	Centre of Indian Trade Unions

CLC	Canadian Labour Congress
COFTU	Central Organization of Free Trade Unions (Uganda)
Consawu	Confederation of South African Workers' Unions
CONTAG	National Confederation of Agriculture Workers (Brazil)
COSATU	Congress of South African Trade Unions
CPI	consumer price index/Communist Party of India
CPI(M)	Communist Party of India (Marxist)
CRIAW	Canadian Research Institute for the Advancement of Women
CSN	Companhia Siderúrgica Nacional (steel producer, Brazil)
CTA	Central de Trabajadores Argentinos (Argentine Workers' Federation)
CTERA	Confederación de Trabajadores de la Educación de la República, (Confederation of Argentine Education Employees)
CTUO	central trade union organizations
CUFTA	Canada-USA Free Trade Agreement
CUPE	Canadian Union of Public Employees
CUT	Central Única dos Trabalhadores (Central Trade Union Confederation, Brazil)
DG	Directorate General
DGB	Deutscher Gewerkschaftsbund (Confederation of German Trade Unions)
DIEESE	Departamento Inter-Sindical de Estatística e Estudos Sócio-Econômicos (Brazil)
DIHK	Deutscher Industrie- und Handelskammertag (Germany)
DUS	Driving Up Standards
EAP	economically active population
ECB	European Central Bank
EIF	European Industry Federation
EMF	European Metalworkers' Federation
EMU	Economic and Monetary Union
EP	European Parliament
EPSU	European Federation of Public Service Unions
ESF	European Social Forum
ETUC	European Trade Union Confederation
ETF	European Transport Federation
EU	European Union
EWC	European Works Council

FDI	foreign direct investment
Fedusa	Federation of Unions of South Africa
FHC	Fernando Henrique Cardoso
FIAN	FoodFirst Information- und Aktions-Netzwerk (Food First Information and Action Network, Germany)
FKTU	Federation of Korean Trade Unions
FTAA	Free Trade Agreement of the Americas
FTV	Federación de Tierra y Vivienda (Federation for Land, Housing and Habitat, Argentina)
GATS	General Agreement on Trade in Services
GDP	gross domestic product
Gear	Growth, Employment and Redistribution (South Africa)
GJ&SM	global justice and solidarity movement
GTUC	Ghana Trade Unions Congress
GUs	global unions
GUFs	global union federations
HMS	Hind Mazdoor Sabha (Indian Labour Association)
IAT	Institut für Arbeitswissenschaft und Technologiemanagement (Institute for Work Knowledge and Techology Management) (Germany)
IBGE	Instituto Brasileiro de Geografia e Estatística (Brazilian Institute of Geography and Statistics)
ICATU	International Confederation of Arab Trade Unions
ICFTU	International Confederation of Free Trade Unions
ICTU	Irish Congress of Trade Unions
ICTUR	International Centre for Trade Union Rights
IDC	International Dockworkers Council
IDEP	Institut Africain de Développement Économique et de Planification (African Institute for Economic Development and Planning)
IEDI	Research Institute for Industrial Development (Brazil)
IG BAU	Construction workers union (Germany)
IG BCE	Industriegewerkschaft Bergbau, Chemie, Energie (Mining, Chemicals and Energy Industry Union, Germany)
ILO	International Labour Organization
IMF	International Monetary Fund
IMWF	International Metal Workers Federation
INGOs	international non-governmental organizations

INTUC	Indian National Trade Union Congress
IPE	international political economy
IR	industrial relations
ITF	International Transport Workers' Federation
ITS	International Trade Secretariat
ITUC	International Trade Union Confederation
IUF	International Union of Foodworkers
IWA	International Woodworkers of America
JAW	Japan Automobile Workers' Union
JNU	Jawaharlal Nehru University
KCTU	Korean Confederation of Trade Unions
KLI	Korea Labour Institute
KSCW	Korean Solidarity for Contingent Workers
KT	Korea Telecom
KWTU	National Women's Trade Union (South Korea)
KWWA	Korean Women Workers Association
KWWAU	Korean Women Workers Associations United
LO	Landsorganisationen i Sverige (Swedish Trade Union Confederation)
LPM	Landless People's Movement (South Africa)
MAI	Multilateral Agreement on Investment
MERCOSUR	Common Market of the Southern Cone of Latin America
MNC	multinational corporation
MST	Movement of Landless Rural Workers (Brazil)
MTA	Movimiento de Trabajadores Argentinos (Argentine Workers' Movement)
MTD	Movimientos de Trabajadores Desocupados (Movement of Unemployed Workers, Argentina)
MTL	Movimiento Territorial Liberación (Territorial Liberation Movement, Argentina)
MUFIS	Malawi Union for the Informal Economy
Nactu	National Council of Trade Unions (South Africa)
NAFTA	North American Free Trade Agreement
Naledi	National Labour and Economic Development Institute (South Africa)
NDP	New Democratic Party (Canada)
NEDLAC	National Economic Development and Labour Council (South Africa)
Nehawu	National Education, Health and Allied Union (South Africa)
NFITU	National Front of Indian Trade Unions

NGG	Gewerkschaft Nahrung-Genuss-Gaststätten (Trade Union of the Food, Beverages, Tobacco, Hotel and Catering and Allied Trades, Germany)
NGO	non-governmental organization
NLO	National Labour Organisation (India)
NSS	National Sample Survey Organisation (India)
NTUI	New Trade Union Initiative (India)
NUM	National Union of Mineworkers (South Africa)
Numsa	National Union of Metalworkers of South Africa
NUPGE	National Union of Public and General Employees (Canada)
OATUU	Organization of African Trade Union Unity
OECD	Organisation for Economic Co-operation and Development
OPSEU	Ontario Public Service Employees Union (Canada)
ORIT	Inter-American Regional Organization of Workers
OTM-CS	Organisação dos Trabalhadores Moçambicanos Central Sindical (Central Syndicate of Mozambican Workers Organizations)
PNAD	Pesquisa Nacional por Amostra de Domicílios (Brazilian national household survey)
PSB	Brazilian Socialist Party
PT	Brazilian Workers' Party
QMV	qualified majority voting
SACO	Swedish Confederation of Professional Associations
SACP	South African Communist Party
Sactwu	South African Clothing and Textile Workers' Union
SADSAWU	South African Domestic Serviced and Alllied Workers' Union
SAF	Swedish Employers' Confederation
SAIRR	South African Institute of Race Relations
Samwu	South African Municipal Workers Union
SAP	Swedish Social Democratic Party
SAREC	Department for Research Cooperation (Sweden)
Sasbo	South African Society of Bank Officials
SB-MIAC	Statistics Bureau, Ministry of Internal Affairs and Communications (Japan)
SEA	Single European Act
SEADE	Fundação Sistema Estadual de Análise de Dados (Brazil)
SECC	Soweto Electricity Crisis Committee (South Africa)

SEIU	Service Employees International Union (USA and Canada)
SEWA	Self Employed Women's Association (India)
SEWU	Self-Employed Women's Union (South Africa)
SIDA	Swedish Agency for International Development Cooperation
SIF	Swedish Union of Clerical and Technical Employees in Industry
SKTF	Union of Local Government Officers (Sweden)
SNCL	Second National Labour Commission (India)
SPD	German Social Democratic Party
SUCI	Socialist Unity Centre in India
SUD	Solidaires, Unitaires et Démocratiques (Solidarity, Unity, Democracy, France)
TAC	Treatment Action Campaign (South Africa)
TCO	Swedish Confederation of Professional Employees
TIE	Transnationals Information Exchange
TNCs	transnational corporations
TUCC	Trade Unions Coordination Centre (India)
TVE	township and village enterprise
UFCW	United Food and Commercial Workers (Canada)
UNDP	United Nations Development Programme
UNICE	Union of Industrial and Employers' Confederations of Europe
USWA	United Steelworkers of America (Canada)
UTUC	United Trade Union Congress (Revolutionary Socialist Party, India)
UTUC (LS)	United Trade Union Congress –Lenin Sarani (India)
VENRO	Verband Entwicklungspolitik deutscher Nichtregierungsorganisationen (Germany)
VRS	voluntary retirement schemes
VW	Volkswagen
WCL	Social Christian World Confederation of Labour
WEAZ	Workers Education Association of Zambia
WEED	World Economy, Ecology and Development
WEF	World Economic Forum
WFTU	World Federation of Trade Unions
WIEGO	Women in the Informal Economy: Globalizing and Organizing
WSF	World Social Forum
WSI	Institute of Economic and Social Research
WTO	World Trade Organization

Index